Arthur Raistrick was born in Yorkshire and educated at Bradford Grammar School and at Leeds University, where he gained an MSc degree in Civil Engineering and MSc and PhD degrees in Geology. Actively involved in industrial archaeology since 1922, when he first began lecturing for the WEA, he was until his retirement in 1970 Reader in Applied Geology at Newcastle University and Extra-Mural Tutor at the Universities of Leeds and Durham. Dr Raistrick is currently President of the Industrial Archaeology Unit of Bradford University, as well as Honorary Curator of Coalbrookdale Museum, Vice-President of the Ironbridge Gorge Museum Trust, and an Honorary Life Member of the Newcomen Society.

Arthur Raistrick

Industrial Archaeology

An Historical Survey

Paladin

Granada Publishing Limited
Published in 1973 by Paladin
Frogmore, St Albans, Herts AL2 2NF

First published in Great Britain by Eyre Methuen Ltd 1972
Copyright © Arthur Raistrick 1972
Made and printed in Great Britain by
Richard Clay (The Chaucer Press) Ltd
Bungay, Suffolk
Set in Monotype Ehrhardt

Contents

PREFACE

1 Introduction: What is Industrial Archaeology?   1

PART ONE *The Materials and Field Evidence of Industrial Archaeology*   15
2 The Metallic Raw Materials   17
3 Metal-based Industries   35
4 Non-metallic Raw Materials   51
5 Manufactures Based Upon Non-metallic Raw Materials   67
6 Organic Raw Materials and Industries Based Upon Them   86
7 Power and Fuel   110
8 Transport   127
9 Accommodation – Buildings and Structures   144

PART TWO *A View of Industrial Archaeology in Britain*   159

10 Prehistoric and Roman Industries   161
11 Dark Age and Medieval Industries   179
12 Prelude to the Industrial Revolution – the Sixteenth and
Seventeenth Centuries   200
13 The Industrial Revolution – the Eighteenth Century   221
14 The Industrial Revolution – the Nineteenth Century   245

PART THREE *The Place of Museums in Industrial Archaeology*   265

15 Museums and Industrial Archaeology   267
16 Preservation, Restoration, and Recording   282
Bibliography   303
Index   307

Illustrations

1   Horse whim on a coal pit
2a Modern blast furnaces
2b I.C.I.'s chemical plant, Billingham
3a Trip hammers, Abbeydale Industrial Hamlet
3b Helve hammer, Kirkstall Forge, Leeds
4   Iron Forge at Tintern, Monmouthshire
5a Architect's drawing for a steel works
5b Cementation furnaces
6a Stone Ridge quarry, Embsey Moor
6b Pulping rollers at Kenton quarry, Gosforth
7a A stone saw
7b Wheelwrights constructing a mill
8a Lime kiln, Toft Gate, Pateley Bridge
8b Scotch tile kiln, Rilston
9a Old alum quarries at Ravenscar
9b Remains of wharf, Sandsend, 1948
10a Brick works at Wrose, Airedale, 1930
10b The glass cone at Catcliffe, Yorkshire
11 Oast houses, Kent
12a Oxen ploughing
12b Horse mill with edge runners
13 Bourn post-mill, Cambridgeshire
14a Overshot water wheel, Foster Beck flax-mill
14b Small-diameter wheel at Linton cotton-mill
15 Atmospheric engine made at Coalbrookdale, 1776
16 Heslop engine made at Coalbrookdale
17a Levant Mine, Cornwall, 1895

17b Thackthwaite Mine, Wensleydale, 1910
18a Charcoal burning, Wyre Forest, 1934
18b Stourport harbour
19a Sunk road and bridge over the Ribble at Stainforth
19b Pack-horse bridge at Oardale, near Harrogate
20a Scribbling mill, Upper Clough House, Merrydale
20b Weaver's cottage near Huddersfield
21a Grassington Low Mill, Wharfedale, c. 1790
21b Abraham-Darby Furnace, Coalbrookdale
22a Canal warehouse, Leeds and Liverpool Canal, Skipton, 1780
22b Dent Head viaduct, Settle to Carlisle Railway, 1875
23a Pattern and moulding shop cranes, Coalbrookdale, c. 1800
23b Pit wheel at Newby Bridge
24 Roman smelted lead pigs from Charterhouse, Somerset
25 Morwellham Harbour on the river Tamar, Devon, c. 1870
26 Engine house, Botallack Mine, Cornwall
27 Five Rise Locks, Leeds and Liverpool Canal, Bingley
28 Abbeydale Industrial Hamlet
29 Grassington Moor smelt-mill chimney being repaired, 1971
30a Octagon smelt-mill, Arkengarthdale, 1923
30b Water wheel at Octagon Mill
31a Ore crusher and wheel at the Providence mine, Kettlewell,
    1924
31b Providence crushers, 1960
32 Fourteenth- or fifteenth-century frame house being rebuilt,
    Weald Museum

DRAWINGS

1 Tanyard with pits   101
2 Ironstone bell pits near Bentley, Yorkshire   181
3 Colliers waiting in the Tyne at Shields   217

DIAGRAMS

1 Rosedale glass kiln, Yorkshire   81
2 Distribution of furnaces etc. associated with the Spencer
   Group, 1725   123

3   Marrick smelt-mills, Swaledale   125
4   Pattern of principal drove roads down the Pennines   131
5   Tramways between ironstone and coal pits, *c.* 1750   139
6   Low Moor ironworks, *c.* 1860   140
7   Skipton Castle quarry roads   190
8   Mid-Pennine salt roads   198
9   Blast Furnace   205
10   Water corn-mill, Bainbridge, Yorkshire   237
11   Detail from Boston Mill, Yorkshire   239
12   Water mills in upper Wharfedale, *c.* 1830   241
13   Buddle, *c.* 1790, Grassington Moor, Yorkshire   250
14   Priest Tarn Water Course   252
15   Duke's Water Course   254
16   Roman Pottery Kiln, Cantley, Doncaster   296

Acknowledgements and thanks for permission to reproduce the photographs are due to the National Museum of Wales, Cardiff, for plate 1; to Appleby-Frodingham Steel Co. for plate 2a; to Imperial Chemical Industries for plate 2b; to Sheffield City Museums for plates 3a and 28; to Kirkstall Forge Co. for plate 3b; to the British Museum for plate 4; to Firth Brown Ltd, Sheffield, for plates 5a and 5b; to G. Clemetson for plate 11; to the Radio Times Hulton Picture Library for plate 13; to C. Crosthwaite for plates 14a and 22b; to the Science Museum for plate 15; to Colliers (Dover Street) Ltd for plate 16; to D. B. Barton Ltd for plate 17a; to M. Wright for plate 18a; to Studio Two, Stourport, for plate 18b; to Bertram Unne for plates 19a, 19b, and 27; to the Tolsen Museum, Huddersfield, for plates 20a and 20b; to W. G. Hoskins for plate 25; to R. Vine for plate 26; and to the Weald and Downland Open Air Museum for plate 32. Plate 9a is Crown Copyright.

Drawing 1 is from *Useful Arts and Manufacture* and drawing 2 is Crown Copyright. All the diagrams were re-drawn by Neil Hyslop from originals supplied by the author.

Preface

Industrial archaeology as a named subject is not yet twenty years old, but it has attracted remarkable interest among diverse groups of people. In the field of adult education, courses given in the university extra-mural departments, in the Workers Educational Association and in other bodies under this title are increasing in number year by year. In technical institutions departments of 'general studies' are finding this new subject a useful part of their teaching of the history of their technologies. Outside the academic walls, bodies of enthusiasts with special interests – such as railways, mines, canals, early steam engines, and many other aspects of nineteenth-century life – and others more akin to local history societies are forming the nuclei of groups which join the regional Industrial Archaeology and History sections of the Council for British Archaeology. The pace at which the subject is progressing has produced a wonderful diversity of activities, and of ideas of what should be the definitions and content of industrial archaeology.

This book is an attempt to set out a possible scheme of industrial archaeology which reduces the over-concentration on the Industrial Revolution and the present, and tries to improve the status of the term 'archaeology' in the hybrid title. Instead of the recording and preservation of monuments of the Industrial Revolution having the over-emphasis given in most current definitions, the author suggests a more evenly balanced investigation of industry from pre-Roman times to the present, by the application of many of the techniques of archaeology. These will dominate the earlier periods and will gradually give place to visual recording as the principal method used in studying the recent two centuries of the Industrial Revolution and the twentieth century.

Like many other members of the Newcomen Society and of the various professional institutes concerned with engineering, mining, and other technologies, the author, during the last forty and more years, has taken an active interest in much that is now being gathered into the new subject. Trained as I am as an engineer and with a long experience as a university teacher in geology applied to engineering and mining and as a tutor for fifty years in the Workers Educational movement, industrial history and archaeology being my hobbies, it is natural that individual ideas on what has now been christened industrial archaeology should have developed. Those ideas are the subject of this book.

Since I live and work in the North of England it is inevitable that a strong northern bias will be evident in many parts of the book. It is always easier to discuss examples and to provide illustration from an area one knows in intimate detail than to make one's points from quoted material from less well-known areas. Nonetheless, the strength of the Workers Educational Association and the extra-mural teaching from its universities are making the North one of the busiest areas for the practice of the new subject. Coal and lead mining, textiles, early colliery wagonways and railways, canals, iron and steel, and chemicals, these are naturally associated with the North, which provides an unrivalled field for the exploration of heavy industries. The earliest periods of iron and glassmaking, early textiles, agriculture, brewing, and many other trades offer a similar richness in the South.

The book would not have been possible without the generous help of a large number of workers in all parts of the country who have allowed the quotation of their own researches. It would be difficult to list them individually, but some formal acknowledgements are made in the text, though these cannot express the admiration I have for much of the work that is being done. Nor can I speak highly enough of the genuine friendliness that is permeating the many industrial archaeology groups with which I have contact.

As a widespread activity the subject is only in its second decade, and it is essential that these years of abundant and increasing enthusiasm shall be used to guide it into a sound and systematized course. Industry in many of its branches is becoming far too technical and its plant and processes too complex for even the best of non-technicians to understand and record it. Some pruning of the twentieth-century material is needed and it might even be questioned how far into the post-war decades the subject can extend, except as a very useful, and in fact essential, recording organization for buildings and activities which are being abandoned and which disappear at an alarming rate. Much depends upon the significance afforded to the term 'archaeology' in the chosen title of the subject as to how far this recording shall go in depth.

No kind of authority is claimed for this book beyond its being a survey of a subject which has been practised quietly by a large number of people during most of this century, and now has achieved a sudden and amazing popularity under a rather questionable title. It is the very personal view of the author, arrived at during several decades of work in what is now accepted as part of industrial archaeology, which is displayed in this book as the result of a real concern for the subject, and a feeling that over-emphasis on the Industrial Revolution will reduce the scope and import-ance of work which could properly be sponsored under a wider definition.

Linton,   ARTHUR RAISTRICK
Skipton, Yorkshire.
1971

CHAPTER I

Introduction:
What is Industrial Archaeology?

The fifteen years from 1955 to the beginning of this decade witnessed the remarkable growth of a 'new' subject, to which a hybrid name, 'industrial archaeology', was given. In spite of some criticisms, the appearance of an extensive literature and the involvement of large numbers of interested workers in the suggested new subject prevented any serious attempt being made to find a more logical or rational name. Thus, 'industrial archaeology' has been accepted and has passed into the everyday language of the country. Before a new subject can progress very far, however, its scope, content, and techniques must receive some kind of definition, and, if it is to become academically acceptable, it must exhibit a coherent and comprehensive discipline.

On 5 December 1965, Kenneth Hudson, as the last contributor to a B.B.C. series of programmes on industrial archaeology, mentioned an aspect of the subject that in some degree explains the difficulty of its definition: that, according to the temperament of the individual, it could be regarded either as an academic subject, or as an agreeable hobby.[1] In these first fifteen years there is no doubt that a great proportion, possibly the majority, of those who would now call themselves industrial archaeologists, are pursuing not a whole subject but that small portion of it which provides an expansion of, and gives a new purpose to, their own already existing hobby. The recording work these people are doing is essential and much of it is of high quality. The diversity and high degree of selective specialization of many of these contributions, however, increase the difficulty of formulating a general descriptive discipline which will include them all within a single simple and workable definition.

[1] *Industrial Archaeology*, B.B.C. Publications No. 6292, 1965, p. 28. See also, K. Hudson, *Industrial Archaeology*, 1963, p. 34.

The progress of the subject has been too rapid for such a discipline to have been studied in depth, and the many definitions which have been attempted lack those elements which would distinguish it clearly and with precision from many subjects already well established, fully accepted, and long practised. In a view or review of the subject we must therefore look critically and constructively at the chief definitions which have been given, and at the general body of the literature that is pouring from the presses. We must seek out the areas of common agreement but at the same time study what might be lacking and in what respect the definitions appear to be inadequate or weak. The volume of published work is already large enough to afford some recognition of trends and to offer the expectation of results to be achieved from an impartial critical study, however difficult this may be.

The term 'industrial archaeology', which had appeared in spoken context, was used in print for the first time when Michael Rix, of Birmingham University Extra-Mural Department, introduced it in an article written for the *Amateur Historian*.[1] Sufficient interest had been aroused and a large enough body of people was drawn to take part in the subject for a Conference to be arranged by the Council for British Archaeology, which was held in 1959. This conference launched the subject with an official blessing. Before this Conference, the Council had decided to prepare a *Handbook of Industrial Archaeology*, which might help towards an answer to the question 'What is an industrial monument?' This question was being asked with increasing urgency by the Inspectorate of Ancient Monuments at the Ministry of Works and they accepted as a definition, 'An industrial monument is any building or other fixed structure, especially of the period of the Industrial Revolution, which either alone or associated with primary plant or equipment, illustrates the beginning and development of industrial and technical processes, including means of communication.' This definition has been generally accepted, with only slight verbal alterations, but retaining without change the phrase 'especially of the period of the Industrial Revolution'.

This authoritative definition, which had been evolved only to assist in the scheduling of an industrial class of Ancient Monument, was given prominence in the definition of industrial archaeology which Rix finally gave in his handbook on the subject in 1967, 'as recording, preserving in selected cases and interpreting the sites and structures of early industrial

[1] M. Rix, *Amateur Historian*, 1955.

activity, particularly the monuments of the Industrial Revolution'.[1] He notes that the name has been criticized as a contradiction in terms, then says, 'But its use can be justified on the following grounds. Within living memory the motor car, radio and aeroplane have been invented. Yet the "tin lizzy", the crystal set and the biplane are already so out of date as to be museum exhibits . . . . whatever name may be attached to it, the message of industrial archaeology is both valid and urgent. After all, the Industrial Revolution which is still changing the face of the globe was largely pioneered in this country and in consequence its prime monuments are more thickly sown in Britain than anywhere else in the world. In fact they are so commonplace here that we tend to underestimate their value and belittle their importance. The movement for their study and preservation has appeared none too soon.'

This can hardly be improved upon so far as it goes. He then gives examples of industrial archaeology in several fields. In that of ironmaking he uses Coalbrookdale and the work of the Darbys, starting in 1709. In the next field, that of building structures, the starting-point is the metal-framed mills and structures of 1792. Civil engineering and transport begin with the eighteenth-century turnpike roads and bridges, and the agrarian revolution with Jethro Tull's seed drill of 1701. Railways, industrial housing, chapels' entertainments, and the like bring the story forward to the mid twentieth century.

All this is good and necessary, but it gives a menacing and exclusive weight to the phrase in the original definition 'particularly the monuments of the Industrial Revolution', and it ignores all previous time and concentrates activity on recording. This approach probably explains some of the sudden popularity of the subject. Any town will provide structures, houses, mills, older roads, bridges, all easy to appreciate and fairly easy to study after a little training in recording techniques. They can be drawn, measured, photographed, and in many cases read about in the local histories or among archives still existing; they can be neatly docketed and a satisfactory index card can be filed for them. This work, when properly coordinated, is valuable, but how much of this is anything more than added illustration to industrial, social, or architectural history, and what essential part of it merits the distinction of a new name and gives it such significance that industrial archaeology can claim it as its very own distinctive subject matter ?

[1] M. Rix, *Industrial Archaeology*, 1967, Historical Association.

The most perceptive statement of some of these doubts and difficulties is that by Kenneth Hudson, when he makes a brief survey of some of the early conferences and courses which were held under an industrial archaeology title.[1] At Liverpool University in 1962, an extra-mural course was held to study 'the early days of industrialism in terms of its machinery, buildings, the housing of workers, and so on'. If the single word 'processes' is added, this is almost a paraphrase of courses held by the author in the extra-mural department of King's College, Newcastle-upon-Tyne, in the late 1930s and between 1946 and 1949, under a general title, 'Industrial development of Tyneside'. It would also serve to describe an increasing number of courses being given in the Workers' Educational Association, and in extra-mural classes in many parts of the country under the general title of 'Industrial History', which, however, is now frequently changed to industrial archaeology.

Weekend or summer school courses at Manchester and Shrewsbury in 1961 and 1962 had included accounts of Coalbrookdale and the Darby family (by the author), studies of factory structures, canals, steam engines, a turnpike road, and other similar subjects, which it would be impossible to distinguish from industrial, economic or technological history. Hudson, after reviewing these and other similar studies in the new subject, arrives at a brief but very significant definition of industrial archaeology as 'the organised, disciplined study of the physical remains of yesterday's industries'. He continues, 'it would be a great pity and a great handicap if its boundaries were to become too rigid'. A liberal interpretation of 'yesterday's industries' offers the way of escape from the incubus of the Industrial Revolution and would allow us to explore many centuries prior to the eighteenth.

Again, Hudson identifies another characteristic of industrial archaeology as it has tended to develop, when he says, 'the architects, the engineers, the social historians, the economic historians, the planners, the members of preservation societies, all have valuable contributions to make towards a better understanding of our industrial past, and the existence of a co-ordinating subject, even if it bears as explosive and paradoxical a name as industrial archaeology, makes it easier for them to become conscious of their common interests. . . .' I would like him to have stopped there, but he continues, 'and to function in a better informed, more discriminating and more effective way when attempting to influence official decisions or to tap public funds.' This, of course, swings the emphasis back to the

[1] K. Hudson, *Industrial Archaeology*, 1963, pp. 17–21.

preservation aspect and the essential task of preparing lists of monuments for the consideration of the Ministry of Public Buildings and Works,[1] and other grant-giving bodies for the purposes of scheduling and preservation.

Dr E. R. R. Green has given us another definition of industrial archaeology which takes us a step further.[2] 'Briefly, the industrial archaeologist,' he writes, 'is concerned with recording and studying early industrial remains, especially those of the eighteenth and nineteenth centuries, which have not hitherto been the subject of field study. The methods of field study and record and even of excavation on appropriate sites make the subject properly a branch of archaeology, even though the results obtained are likely to prove of most value to the historian of technology and to the economic historian.'

Here we are taken right into the world of the increasingly popular 'field studies', and even promised the occasional active physical effort of excavation. Field studies under many names is now a well-established subject with a good deal of experience behind some of its techniques. It has already taught us the value of the study of distributions and of environments over a wider area than that of a particular site. The idea of occasional excavation suggests the search for, and discovery and exposure of, sites of former activity on which imaginative interpretation and reconstruction will be necessary. The student no longer requires a mill to be still standing and architecturally complete, but can deal with half-buried foundations, water courses, water-wheel pits, and other incomplete remains. The methods of archaeology can be applied to sort out the structural history of a complex, and the archaeologist is no longer tied to the centuries of the Industrial Revolution, but by his training is equipped to deal with the long periods which have only very slight or (in most cases) no documentation. In this approach the time scale for 'yesterday's industries' need no longer have a starting date in the seventeenth or eighteenth centuries, but can leap back even beyond the Romans. The archaeologist has already shown us that organized activities are to be found in the periods of prehistory, as far back as the neolithic. If we apply to some of these activities the criteria which define an industry, we shall find industrial archaeology taking some of its earliest material not from the Industrial Revolution, but from what Gordon Childe has so rightly called the neolithic revolution.[3]

If this extension of Hudson's 'yesterday's industries' were to be

[1] Now incorporated in the Department of the Environment.
[2] E. R. R. Green, *The Industrial Archaeology of County Down*, 1963, p. iii.
[3] V. Gordon Childe, *What Happened in History*, 1942.

adopted, we could enter on an expansive phase of industrial archaeology that would reduce the preoccupation with the Industrial Revolution to tolerable proportions. It would not so much curb this later work as bring it into balance with the much broader foundations from which it has evolved. In the literature there is some slight perception of this pre-Industrial Revolution territory, but it is usually approached timidly. The abundance and clarity of the eighteenth- and nineteenth-century material is sufficient to occupy all the time and effort of most individuals.

A recent account of the industrial archaeology of an area– a scholarly, most illuminating, and very valuable text–[1] displays this hesitance to venture outside the safe limits set by the eighteenth century. The account of the iron industries, however, opens in this way. 'Like coal mining, the iron industry has a long history. . . . Unfortunately, little is known about the history and location of the early iron industry. The industrial archaeologist is therefore faced with the initial problem of finding out where to look before there is any chance of discovering remains of charcoal furnaces, and much documentary and field research remains to be done.' Some technical knowledge of the early mining and metallurgical methods and requirements would help in the recognition of sites. The author continues by drawing attention to Farey's list of sites, where slags, bloomeries, or old furnaces were to be seen in Derbyshire about 1800,[2] but then adds, 'but excavation would be required to reveal anything today, even if the exact site could be discovered.' After this introduction the account jumps directly to a furnace operating between 1725 and 1780, and the only other remains of which a description is given are those of a furnace built between 1800 and 1804.

Although this account of the iron industry only starts in the mid eighteenth century, these introductory paragraphs could act as an inspiring call to a wide and rewarding earlier field for the enthusiastic worker.

As the definitions of the subject have varied, though all of them stress the importance of recording the Industrial Revolution, so the books already published treat the material in varied order. In one regional study, the story starts with the development of a port and its associated industries and then progresses through coalmining, metal, and miscellaneous industries, then by public services to transport.[3] Another starts with the chang-

[1] D. M. Smith, *Industrial Archaeology of the East Midlands*, 1965, p. 123.
[2] J. Farey, *General View of the Agriculture and Minerals of Derbyshire, 1811–17*, Vol. 1, p. 396.
[3] A. Q . Buchannan, N. Cossons, *Industrial Archaeology of the Bristol Region*, 1969.

ing economy since 1707 and approaches transport by way of agriculture and food industries, rural crafts, textiles, mining, metallurgy, and chemicals.[1] Others could be quoted, all taking a different starting-point and progressing through comparable subjects in different order towards the same end-point, transport. This different treatment has much to recommend it – it allows the personality and interest of the writer to assert itself, and it usually brings to the forefront the dominant industry of the area in the eighteenth and nineteenth centuries.

A series of volumes written to an identical plan would make a dull and somewhat boring series. Nonetheless, for the person seeking a basic pattern – a logical relationship between the many aspects of the subject – this diversity of statement and exposition tends to obscure any overall unity and system it may have.

In the periodical literature the diversity is of course far greater, and this is right, the journals being the repository in which brief records of specialist and very localized material is stored and into which the worker can dip at any time to extract the particular piece of research which fits into place in his own work.

Most of what has been published so far emphasizes the preoccupation with the remains of the Industrial Revolution and the still existing material of the very recent past, Rix's 'tin lizzy' and 'crystal set'. It is this dominance which has made the problem of acceptable definitions more acute. In the studies of these eighteenth- and nineteenth-century industries, and their ancillaries, a host of workers, to be found under many designations, increase the difficulty of any attempt to separate the industrial archaeologist as a different worker in his own right. Where does the industrial archaeologist, busy measuring, photographing, recording the rows of small industrial houses in a textile town, differ from the social historian or architectural student of town and housing development? Studying and recording machinery, processes, mill engines and so on merges imperceptibly into the work of the historian of technology and engineering. This is not wrong, but it has obscured the 'separateness' of industrial archaeology. In many cases we may be tempted to ask whether or not the industrial archaeologist is only doing in an amateur way what a technologist working in the history of his subject would do in greater detail and with more perceptive accuracy.

This dilemma is not special only to the later centuries. Our knowledge

[1] J. Butt, *Industrial Archaeology of Scotland*, 1967.

of, say, the Roman industries of Britain derives from the careful and skilled work carried out by true archaeological techniques. If we look through the archaeologists' detailed reports of excavations we can find abundant evidence of industries and of industrial organization in all parts of Romanized Britain. The archaeologist will see them as an activity illustrating the daily life of the people or culture whose history he is elucidating. The industrial archaeologist would look upon them as evidences contributing to our knowledge of the history and evolution of particular industries and processes, and of the development of industry in general. It would be proper for the industrial archaeologist to undertake some of his own excavations on purely industrial sites, but this would need to be done with the care, precision, and training of the true archaeologist. He would to that extent have to be an archaeologist with a special knowledge of, and interest in, industries. W. G. Hoskins, writing on field work, explains that he has not the technical knowledge necessary to enable him to include industrial archaeology among his field studies, and then makes a very valid criticism of much of the current publication in the subject. 'A number of books have appeared in the last two or three years on this subject, and it now has its own *Journal*, started in 1964. I do not always find the treatment of the subject in books and articles completely satisfactory for it seems to me to contain too much economic and business history and not enough about the visible remains, the pure archaeology, of our industrial and commercial past. Indeed I am coming to the conclusion that the best people to write industrial archaeology are engineers and others with a special technological knowledge, provided they are prepared to acquire an adequate knowledge of economic and business history. ... Some of the best 'industrial archaeology' – though it was not called that then – has appeared in the *Transactions of the Newcomen Society*, and other technical journals. Nevertheless there are great advances to be made in this new branch of archaeology.'[1]

Industrial archaeology clearly impinges upon and claims assistance from a large number of already well-established subjects. It might be said that its function is merely that of coordinating the results of work being done in many established disciplines. If it is no more than this, there might still be a place for it, and a reason for its continuance, but the question must be asked whether or not there is some more specific purpose and reason for its pursuit. Is it more than a very useful and urgently needed recording

[1] W. G. Hoskins, *Fieldwork in Local History*, 1967, pp. 11–12.

organization? Can it supply some central idea or purpose which will link its great diversity of subjects into a coherent whole? Can it discover lines of thought and action peculiar to itself? Is the prime function of industrial archaeology, so-called, only to share in part in the interests and work of this great diversity of skills, and from them, by integration and synthesis, add a small but new dimension to our knowledge and understanding of man's progress.

Much depends upon the significance we attach to the name, 'industrial archaeology'. Are we to take this, as much of the work done so far would suggest, as the archaeology (description and recording) of the Industrial Revolution, or do we take it as the archaeology (exploration and recording) of industry as a whole belonging to all periods from the prehistoric to the present? A recent study of Roman ironworks suggests that Britain might have been a major producer of iron for Gaul, Germany, and Spain,[1] and the newest British Museum Guide to Roman Britain (1951) says, 'The great development of centralized industries during the Roman occupation was associated with the improved facilities for transport and trade, provided by the Roman system of communications. . . . Ports were developed to deal with import and export trade.'

So far, therefore, as the iron industry, particularly the furnace and foundry remains, is concerned, there is now a considerable body of skilled metallurgists and practical foundrymen excavating sites all over the country. They are creating a new picture of the extent, the techniques and the remains of a widespread and advanced Roman industry, capable of supporting an important export trade. Should not these investigations have a place in industrial archaeology as important as that of Abraham Darby's furnace and the Industrial Revolution? Sites of Saxon and medieval iron-working lead on to charcoal iron furnaces of the sixteenth and seventeeth century which are proving to be far more numerous than was hitherto thought. The exploration and excavation involved in this work is surely industrial archaeology in the purest sense of the term. If we push back the starting-point of industrial archaeology to the appearance of organized industry with special techniques, on a scale larger than what would be called a craft, then we can accept the name without qualm.[2]

[1] H. F. Clure, 'Roman ironworks in Britain', *British Steel* (1969), March, pp. 6–9.
[2] Much of this work on the early sites is being inspired and carried out by the Historical Metallurgy Group in the Iron and Steel Institute. Some of their work is published in the *Bulletin of the Historical Metallurgy Group*.

Professor Minchinton has recently stated in a single sentence a definition of industrial archaeology which is freed from the dominance of the
eighteenth and nineteenth centuries and which can be applied with equal
force to the prehistoric iron worker and to one of our Sheffield forges: 'the
industrial archaeologist is concerned to locate, record and, when appropriate, preserve the physical survivals of past industrial processes together
with the ancillary buildings associated with such activity.'[1] Here the
emphasis is rightly on locating the site of *past* industry, which will call for
every kind of field work and library research on the physical evidences of
past industry, and a return to the field to complete the study and recording
of the site.

When the phrase 'with special reference to the Industrial Revolution' is
dropped, as in this definition, it becomes much easier to see industrial
archaeology as the investigation of the whole history of industry through
the ages. If the clause 'with special reference to' is still to be included it
will not be to a particular period of history, say the eighteenth to twentieth
centuries as now, but to a particular aspect, that of material structures as
the evidence of industrial conditions and processes.

Most workers are likely at present to be attracted to the monuments of
the eighteenth and nineteenth centuries because of their abundance and
familiarity and their accessibility. The remains of earlier industries call for
special circumstances for their discovery and for special skills in their
recognition and interpretation. If we can now regard the subject of industrial archaeology as extending from prehistoric into recent time, we may
perceive a clearer pattern running throughout. We might be able to make
a logical scheme for studying and arranging our material. Workers with
different skills and background would probably make different schemes,
but through them all we ought to escape some of the dilemma and complexity of the dominating Industrial and post-Industrial Revolution which
so overshadows the earlier periods.

If we agree that the basic fact on which industry is built is the exploitation of some natural raw material, mineral, plant, animal, or even (in some
parts of the chemical industry) the atmosphere, followed by the processing
and shaping of this material for man's use, then a logical starting-point for
a scheme of industrial archaeology will be found in the discovery and
exploitation of raw materials. The preparation of materials for use will
include all manufacturing processes; then the products so made will have

[1] In the course of a book review in *Industrial Archaeology*, 7 (1970), 99.

to be distributed to the potential users. This will demand the supply of power and the making and use of transport and communication. How far the organization, finance, and control of industries and transport should come within the essential studies of industrial archaeology is a very debatable question. It would seem logical to leave these in their present context of economic history.

All manufactures require work to be done on raw material of some kind, and the power expended in this work can be supplied in a great variety of ways. It is not easy, for instance, to devise a completely satisfactory classification of power, but for the purpose of this present discussion a five-fold division could be used. (a) The power of living muscle, either of man or beast. This is expended in lifting, pushing, and pulling, and its conversion into useful and special movements through levers, wheels, or other mechanical devices; (b) power derived from the movements of the atmosphere – sailing ships, windmills, etc. – and water – water wheels and turbines, tidemills, etc.; (c) the action of gravity, for example, some water wheels hydraulic engines, some clocks, and other weight-operated mechanisms; (d) power released by the consumption of fuels, wood, coal, oil, and chemical reactions which are exothermic; (e) during the last few decades a new source of power, still mainly in the form of the translation of energy into heat, has been exploited in the breakdown of heavy atoms.[1]

The means of changing the power from any of these sources into useful work involves mechanisms which become progressively more complex, particularly in the case of the conversion of heat and chemical energies. Here the whole range of prime movers belong to the science of engineering and can best be studied and recorded there. The provision of power is bound to be at least a fringe interest of the industrial archaeologist, particularly in its more primitive forms, but the delineation of what is industrial archaeology and what is pure engineering is very difficult.

Somewhat similar arguments could be applied to machines. At what point does a machine become the proper subject for the historian of technology or mechanics and at what point should he, rather than the industrial archaeologist, record it? In a study of an operative mill with its engine, machinery, and the equipment for the processes carried on there, can the industrial archaeologist retain his identity and contribute something more than, or at least different from, what the engineer or technician

An excellent discussion of this subject of power, on a very wide basis, is to be found in H. P. Vowles, *The Quest for Power from Prehistoric times to the Present Day*, 1931.

could give? This is part of the basic dilemma which becomes more and more insistent as the period of the Industrial Revolution and the passage into our present technological age dominate our studies. The engines, the machines, the processes of nineteenth- and twentieth-century industry are becoming so complex and involve so many different skills and professions that it is very difficult to define the legitimate place of the industrial archaeologist other than as that of the recorder of their existence and their overall appearance.

Neither the technician, the engineer, nor the industrialist has yet isolated the aspect of his plant or organization which should be the special study of the industrial archaeologist. Can we reasonably expect them to do this? It is for the newcomer, the industrial archaeologist, to demonstrate that he has a different approach which can detect a new element to be added to all that the engineer and technologist are doing. He must offer something that will extend and enrich what is already being done in other disciplines. This new aspect must be such that it will obviate any suspicion of 'poaching', of picking up in an amateur way odds and ends to make a new subject. In the area of recording there is an obviously useful place for a body of people who can cope with the rapidly changing scene, and who will have time and interest to measure, photograph, and describe the minutiae and the ancillary, as well as the broader non-technical background for which the technologist can hardly spare time. If he can fill in detail which the technologist, the social historian, or other specialist would not normally record, he may go a long way towards presenting a more integrated picture of industry and all its human implications than might otherwise be available. Is this to be the function of industrial archaeology—not merely to record the remains of industry, but to place industry in its proper environment and perspective as a continuing and developing theme in human endeavour? Industry has been, from the earlier periods, man's attempt to enrich his environment by the provision of tools, shelter, and protection. Until the profit motive and salesmanship began to dominate, industry was primarily concerned to produce articles of use and beauty. Industrial archaeology must also be a human study, and industry will appear as a means by which man has achieved his material civilization and modified or created the environment in which he lives. The subject must be one of the humanities and it must achieve a view of man at work in varying tasks and surroundings, in which view the recording of a factory is as much a recording of the place in which lives have been spent as one which sheltered archaic machines. Again, the old dilemma persists – can we, with this approach, find something to do which the social historian has not already done for us? We are forced back into the view that industrial archaeology must be an integration of man at work, with the tools, structures, and materials with which he works, and the immediate environment in which his work is done. By investigation, recording, and preservation we are trying to demonstrate and display the progress through the centuries of the material environment of man's working life and the increasing skills in manipulating the raw materials of that environment.

Might it not be reasonable to accept what is at present implied but not stated by the Council for British Archaeology, that as its main subject archaeology has, as recognized popular subdivisions, 'prehistoric', 'classical', and 'medieval' and, as it has sponsored its research committee on industrial archaeology, this latter subject should be placed alongside the other sections as one more 'subdivision of convenience' of the master subject, archaeology? We now have societies and journals for medieval and for post-medieval archaeology. These are major time divisions and an Industrial Revolution archaeology would have followed on logically to take care of the special concern for that period expressed by the creators of 'industrial archaeology'. On the other hand, industrial archaeology is not properly a time division but one by subject and emphasis extending through all the sub-divisions of archaeology. It would be convenient to sort out the present rather mongrel subject into at least two sections, retaining the name industrial archaeology for all that research of whatever age to which strict archaeological method and techniques will apply, and allow much that now shares the name to become 'industrial recording'.

No rigid date-line could separate these two sections, but there would be a distinct difference in their methods. The second would concern itself with photographing, measuring, describing, and so far as possible documenting buildings, engines, machinery, lines of communication, still or recently in use, providing a satisfactory record for the future before the object may become obsolete or be demolished. The sections would not be mutually exclusive but would be recognizably distinct. Whether or not these two sections could remain under a single title, such as 'industrial archaeology', is a matter for discussion. Would the industrial recording be a kind of appendix to the earlier section, should they share a common title, or could a new compound title, such as 'industrial archaeology and recording', be found?

In this book an attempt is made to formulate a logical order of the subject matter of industrial archaeology as just stated, and this can be treated in two ways. First we can follow the raw materials of industry from their collection or extraction through preparation for manufacture. The processes of manufacture and the diversity into the vast complex of present-day industry provides material for a variety of specialist skills in their recording. The distribution of both intermediate and end products involves the whole world of transport. Finally, but running through the whole, there are the structures required for the activities of industry and for the maintenance of workpeople and their dependants without whom industry would not exist. In dealing with this scheme of subjects, the main emphasis will be placed on the physical evidence left by each activity. This will become, in fact, an outline account of the origins of the field material by which industrial processes can be recognized and interpreted. This was the principal idea behind the proposed 'handbooks' which were replaced by Hudson's admirable summary and expansion.[1]

The whole story of civilization has been that of man's progressive use of his environment and the increasing exploitation of the raw materials provided by the earth around him. In this story industry is a major factor and a continuing thread in the means and method of this exploitation. Man has been defined as a tool-making animal, and in the shaping of even the most primitive tools lies the form of all future industry. Industry has an evolutionary history which progresses step by step with the evolution of societies and civilizations. The commencing date for industrial archaeology will be taken not at the beginning of the Industrial Revolution or even with the one or two centuries immediately preceding it, but far back in prehistory. Starting from this early period, the second part of the outline proposed will be based on the chronological succession. In this part, a few of the clearest examples of the work of the industrial archaeologist (under this expanded definition) will be described from various industries at successive dates from the neolithic to the mid nineteenth century. The remains of the last two centuries are already the subject of an abundant literature, so only one or two examples will be taken from these, which can illustrate special points or trends.

[1] K. Hudson, *Industrial Archaeology*, 1963.

PART ONE

The Materials and Field Evidence of Industrial Archaeology

CHAPTER 2

The Metallic Raw Materials

Assuming the basic pattern of industrial archaeology to be somewhat as suggested in the first chapter, then the following scheme adheres closely to it and will be used as the outline of the subject as this book is intended to expound it. It will always be a help when investigating industrial remains of any age to know something of the processes of that industry and of the structures and evidence that is likely to persist from them. It is for that reason that these early chapters will give a very brief outline of the industries listed in the general scheme, and of their operation. The later chapters are used to describe a few of the excavations and investigations which appear to illustrate methods of practical industrial archaeology and to be excellent examples of the results to be obtained by such work. They are also chosen to show something of the standard of work that ought to be aimed at.

A SUGGESTED SCHEME OF INDUSTRIAL ARCHAEOLOGY

Metallic mineral raw materials

Mines and mining sites of various ores.
Methods of ore dressing and preparation.
Smelting to extract and refine metals.
    lead ores; bolehill, blast furnace, reverberatory furnace.
    copper ores; roasting and reverberatory furnace.
    tin ores; Jew's houses, blowing houses, reverberatory furnace.
    iron ores; bloomery and bowl furnace, blast furnace.
    zinc ores; roasting, distillation.
    gold; melting and refining.

Metal-based manufactures

    lead; red and white lead, pipe, sheet, shot.
    copper; battery, wire, and bronzes.

tin; pewter, tin plate.
iron; wrought iron, wire, foundry work, steel.
zinc; brass, Muntz's metal, bell metal, galvanizing.
alloy steels and rare metals.

Non-metallic raw materials, inorganic

Coal and coalmining; bellpits, shafts and drifts, whims,
    fireclay; shale, ginister.
Stone; building stones, grindstones, millstones, limestone and marble,
    clay, sand and gravel, gypsum, alabaster.
Chemicals; salt, alum, arsenic, and sulphur.

Manufactures based on the above materials

Coal gas, coke, coal tar products, oil and oil shales.
Quarry products; building stones, lime, cement, plaster.
Clay and clay products; bricks, tiles, pottery.
Porcelain and glass.
Acids, alkalies, bleaching materials, phosphorus.

Organic raw materials and their industries

Timber; structural, forest crafts, wheelwright, shipbuilder.
Agriculture; corn, flour-milling, barley, malt, hops, brewing.
Animal husbandry; animals for transport.
    Cattle; meat, hides, tanning, tallow, horn.
    Sheep; wool, woollen textiles.
    Milk and milk products; butter, cheese.
Special plants; hemp and flax, linen industry, ropes, cotton textiles.
    dyes; woad, saffron.
Oils, fats, and waxes.

Power and Fuel

Power – animal muscle, horse-mills, etc.
    wind – sail, windmills.
    water – water wheels, turbines, hydraulic engines.
    steam – reciprocating steam engine, turbines, locomotives, etc.
    gas, oil, electric power.
Fuels – timber – charcoal making, sawdust. Peat.
    gas and oils, coal and coke, electric, atomic.

Transport

Primitive transport – paths, bridleways, pack animals, fords and bridges, green roads.
Constructed roads, sledges, wheeled carts, bridges,
    turnpikes, county and national roads.
Rivers and canals, locks, inclines.
Boats, ships, docks, and harbours.
Tramways and railways, wagonways.
Bridges.

Accommodation[1]

Early mills as structures, wind and water-mills, horse-mills.
Factories and workshops.
Special structures, kilns, malt houses, shot towers, etc.
Warehouses.
Housing for workers, associated directly with their work.
Schools and cultural buildings connected with industrial training.
Railway and canal structures.

The evidence of past industries varies considerably as to its clarity and completeness. Much evidence of some of the earlier stages has been swept away in the course of later progress, while other industries leave little or no evidence of their existence, and recognizable remains are very rare. While the extractive industries of mining and quarrying leave great excavations and large accumulations of debris, these are not so permanent as one might expect. The nature of mining is such that later work either removes the earlier, or buries it under debris. Coalmine sites are now being cleared, levelled and turned into usable land or recreation areas at a steadily increasing rate. In the post-war years old quarries have been recognized as a gift of providence to harassed local government officials with increasing loads of domestic rubbish to be disposed of. Many quarries have already been filled, levelled, and grassed over, and the only microscopic grain of comfort for the industrial archaeologist is that in their depths there is now

[1] Many types of structures will be described along with their industry: for example, furnaces, kilns, and structures which are a part of a process and not primarily a sheltering structure, which gives accommodation but is not a functioning part of a process. This section could be extended to any length if one ventured into the spheres of architecture, town planning, housing, etc.

preserved a vast sequence of the trivia of the plastics age. The rebuilding of city centres is clearing old buildings and industrial sites at a rate which has emphasized but cannot exaggerate the urgency of recording in the urban areas. Our great reservoir of industrial archaeology is in fact in the rural areas, and those older remains partially or wholly buried to which excavation must be applied. These two facets of our subject, urban and rural, will appeal to different groups of workers, but they are complementary and of equal importance, and only when brought together will a comprehensive subject be achieved. Now let us look at the evidence which the different industries may have left.

mineral raw materials; mining sites

Mineral veins are normally very narrow fissure deposits, nearly vertical and of a lateral extent that may be a few hundred yards up to a few miles. Their outcrop at the surface, therefore, is a long narrow ribbon, a few feet wide, needing considerable skill and sustained search for its discovery. In hilly country, where most of the mineral veins are found, one method of searching out and occasionally of working veins was that of *hushing*. The *hushes* produced by this kind of working form permanent features on the hillsides, easily mapped but nearly impossible to date unless documentary evidence can be found. They may date from Roman times to the late nineteenth century, but the majority are sixteenth or seventeenth.

The hushes occur on steep hillsides where veins of ore have been suspected by ordinary prospecting, but where exact location is lacking. On the brow of the hill a turf dam is built with drainage or cut-off channels to collect water to fill it. When full, the dam is broken and the water pours down the hillside in a flood. The power of the torrent is enough to tear out soil and subsoil and to remove the broken and weathered rockhead. If necessary, repetitions of the flood will clear a deep gully down to the fresh rock and allow a careful search for any vein thus exposed. The fan of debris at the hillfoot may contain ore from the weathered top of a vein. Hushes may be as much as fifty feet or more in depth and of comparable width. Their nature is proved by remains of the dam and channels at the head, and the lack of a stream in them. There are many scores – and probably hundreds – of them in the Pennines.

If a vein has been encountered a second parallel hush some distance to one side can confirm the vein and give its direction of run, and so hushes frequently occur in pairs. A good vein may have been tested by a shaft sunk on it in the hush, and then by a *level* driven from the valley bottom to cut it in depth. This will generally be marked by a masonry-arched entrance and a spoilheap fanning out from it. A hush is not the work of a solitary miner but the work of a partnership, which would not expend all the required labour unless careful prospecting had justified a strong hope of success.

When the outcrop of a vein was found at the surface it could be excavated by a deep trench along its length, by *open-cast* or *open-cut* working. This was usually an early form of mining, though a very large twentieth-century example is being worked today in Derbyshire.[1] The oldest open cast is usually collapsed along the edges, and this with the debris formerly piled there partially fills and changes the original shape of the cut. Shafts are often sunk alongside such an open cast from which the vein is worked in depth.[2]

Bellpits, small shafts from the bottom of which workings were carried in each direction along the vein for short distances, were sunk close together so that their workings would meet. Debris from one shaft was usually backfilled into an older one, and the bellpits remain now, strung out along a vein like beads on a string, each of them a circular mound with a deep depression at the centre. They are seldom later than early eighteenth century and mostly they are much earlier, possibly as early as fourteenth century.

Later and deeper shafts are circular, oval, or rectangular in section, in the upper part lined or *ginged* with dry-built masonry based on the head of the solid rock, or on beams placed at the shaft sides as bearers. It is important to look around the shaft mouth for evidence of the means by which ore was lifted, and men descended and ascended. This can often be a good guide to approximate dating. With very narrow shafts, mostly seventeenth- or eighteenth-century, a simple *Jack roller*, a small diameter windlass running between two uprights, and lying across the diameter of the shaft, was used. Occasionally the stumps or sockets of the two uprights can be

[1] This is cutting across Longstone Edge where the Deep Rake–High Rake–Watersaw Rake is worked by open cast for two miles, to depths of 100 feet. There is some amount of backfilling of debris which will in a slight degree reduce the damage this work is doing to the landscape.

[2] In Cornwall, old workings on the course of lodes (veins) 'where the ancients have carried away the soft ground viz. the gozzany, flukany, or slovany parts of the lode, easily broken down' are called 'coffen' or 'koffen' work. In 1617 Carew speaks of ore being shovelled from cast to cast (steps in the excavation) and thus a long chasm is formed, called by the miners a Coffen.

traced. For men climbing a shaft, *stemples* were short timbers set across the corner of a rectangular shaft, or a *climbing shaft* was made, a narrow oblong or oval with footholes in the middle of each long side, the miner climbing by straddling across, one foot on each side. Larger shafts had ladderways, usually partitioned in one end of an oblong shaft. Both these remained in use well into the nineteenth century.

When deeper shafts were introduced they were made of greater diameter, and the Jack roller was displaced by the *horse whim*. This was a large barrel or drum on a vertical axis running in a footstep bearing set in a large boulder. The top bearing was at the centre of a cross beam carried at each end by posts and stays. Below the drum a cross arm from the axle carried at each end gear for a horse. A rope was wound on the barrel and carried over two pulleys at the shaft head so that as the horses walked round a circular track the ends of the rope were raised and lowered in the shaft. The horse track consolidated with gravel is usually between twenty-five and forty feet in diameter and this, and the central boulder with bearing, are the permanent remaining evidences (Plate 1). If an area had a copious stream which could be tapped for storage in a dam, then, particularly in the nineteenth century, a water wheel would be used for winding, which might be placed a few hundred yards away, according to the water supply, ropes being carried to the shaft top on pulleys. The stumps of the posts carrying the pulleys are often found leading from the shaft to the remains of the wheelpit. In the late eighteenth and nineteenth centuries there was some winding done by the steam engine, but this was by no means common except in Cornwall.[1]

Besides shafts, a common mode of access to mines was by *levels* where these could be driven from a low point in a valley so as to cut a vein in depth, or to drain the mine. Levels vary in their dimensions, the best being about six feet high and three or perhaps four feet wide. Some very early levels are much smaller, four feet by one foot six inches being known. The later levels are generally parallel-sided with an arched top in rock. Older levels are sometimes cut with a wider part at about shoulder height for a man wheeling a barrow, and these are called, from their shape, *coffin levels*. In levels driven before the use of gunpowder, pickmarks are often seen on the walls, the result of dressing with a pick, to a final smooth shape, after the rougher driving. Levels must only be explored by people fully experienced in underground work, as they are often places of great danger.

[1] The evidence for water wheels and steam engines will be dealt with in the section on power.

When *bouse* (the mixed ore, minerals, and stone) is brought out of the mine it has to be *dressed* to separate the ore and prepare it for the smelter. It was only in the later nineteenth century that the dressing was brought into covered buildings, so much of the evidence of earlier dressing is in the open around the mine. *Deads*, rock not carrying any wanted mineral, was dumped around the shaft mouth to make the spoil heaps which give a rough idea of the extent of working and the composition of the veins worked. Hand picking then separated obvious lumps of ore and rich lumps of mixed rock or spar and ore. The bouse was dumped in *teams*, large storage structures rectangular or bowl shaped with an opening at the bottom through which the bouse was raked out. On earlier sites the bouse was tipped in a heap from which it could be raked onto the top of a low wall with a very heavy flagged top. There, as from the bouse team, boys or women sorted out ore and broke down the rest with flat hammers called *buckers* to about the size of peas. Heaps of broken deads, in pieces at most only a few inches in size, mark the site of this *bank* or bucking floor and the wall or the teams are a very common remaining feature.

The next dressing to separate rock and ore, after the early sixteenth century, was done by shaking in water on a sieve, so that ore sank to form a bottom layer and the lighter top layer of deads could be scraped off.[1] The richer material could be sorted in a stream of water running down a sloping trough which left the heavier ore at the top and washed the rock debris away. Early *buddles* were sloping, paved areas with stone sides, and usually between about fifteen and twenty-five feet long. In the nineteenth century buddles were made of timber, but the circular buddle, built of carefully masoned stone, came into use in 1826. This is a circular tank, about fifteen feet in diameter, and two or three feet deep with a conical bottom, with a central boss from which the fine slurry was distributed through two revolving arms. These buddles went through a long evolution and in the nineteenth century both sieves and buddles were elaborated and mechanized. In all cases the ore was crushed before buddling, either by hand with the bucker, or by *stamps*, a number of heavy rods shod with cast iron, which were set vertical in a frame and lifted and dropped in turn, by water or steam power. They fell in a box in which ore was fed to be crushed and partly washed by a stream of water. The site of a set of stamps can sometimes be recognized. In the nineteenth century crushing rollers were introduced, driven by

[1] The sieve after 1810 was hung on a lever by which it was jerked up and down in the water. This arrangement in its many modifications was a *hotching tub*.

water power, but they were generally located only on the very large dressing floors (Plate 31a). One form of crusher occasionally met with was worked by a horse. The remains are rather like those of a whim. There is a circular path around which the horse walked, pulling the outer end of a horizontal beam, the other end of which was pivoted on a short upright central pole. Between horse and pole, a large crushing wheel, of stone usually bound with an iron tyre, and about five feet in diameter, ran on a circle either of massive flags or of iron plates three feet wide, crushing ore fed beneath it. Remains of both circles and rollers are sometimes found. All dressing required a constant supply of water, so water courses were cut, sometimes a mile or more in length, to bring water from a remote bog or stream. It was the miners' most precious commodity, without which dressing was not possible.

The evidence of dressing floors, apart from structures and water courses, is seen in the spread of low heaps of fine crushed debris and a spread of *slimes*, the finest rock flour and mud washed from the last stages of dressing. The cleaned and separated ore is a *concentrate*, its ore content expressed as a percentage, and this was taken to the *bing-stead* at the smelt mill, usually a row of storage compartments in which different partnerships could keep their ore separate (Plate 31b).

Tools are sometimes found among the mine debris, and these are fairly simple. The picks are small, short-handled, two-pointed for softer ground, but for hard rock having one point and a hammer end. They are straight, not curved like a navvy pick. The point could be set in a fine crack and the hammer end struck with an ordinary heavier hammer. Steel *wedges* were set in holes cut with the pick point, then driven in to split the rock. Later a longer wedge was driven between two side 'flats' forming a *plug and feathers*, set in a drilled hole. The remains of smaller diameter, smoother holes usually indicate the use of blasting powder. On the dressing floors buckers, cole-rakes, and *spalling* hammers, square-faced, are the commonest tools, though nowadays more buckers are to be found in neighbouring villages, in use as door stops, than on the mines.

The shaft and level working will apply to most mines of metallic ores. There are a few exceptions, however, which used different methods. Some copper ores are diffused through a great body of rock, like the ores at the Parys Mine, Anglesea, where workings are open cast but on the scale of a large quarry. Diffused copper ores at Aldersley Edge were worked in irregular caverns, and some iron ores are worked in the same ways. From the earliest times tin ore has been washed from the sands and gravels of many Cornish streams, but little permanent trace of this work remains. It consisted of turning over the river gravels to get at the lower layer where the ore tends to concentrate, and the river, after the working finished, has usually turned and re-turned the gravels beyond recognition.

After winning and dressing, all ores except gold have to be smelted to extract the metal, and in this process there is a great variation in ways of treating the different ores. The basic process uses furnace conditions to convert an ore to the oxide of the metal, if not already an oxide, and then reduce it to the native metal. The impurities which are present in small percentage in the ores or dressed concentrates are converted into a *slag* by the addition of lime or some other flux in the furnace. The slag is run off and is rejected, or treated a second time in a *slag hearth*, a furnace designed and regulated to extract a little more of the metal which always remains in the first slag. Each type of furnace and each process used for different metals produces its own characteristic slag. The recognition and study of slags is therefore a most important part of the techniques of field archaeology. The necessary analysis of slag specimens, however, can only be carried out by a competent metallurgist in his well-equipped laboratory. The discovery of slags will be the first important step to the location of smelting activities.

From pre-Roman times until the sixteenth century the common method of smelting lead ores was in the *bolehill* or *bloomery*. For iron ores too, these were used, but the Romans introduced *low-shaft furnaces* which have only been recognized in recent years and found by excavation. Copper demanded a more advanced technique than lead, and needed to be in the form of oxide for smelting. This was obtained from sulphide ores by roasting them.

Lead ore was the easiest of all to smelt and lead bolehills are common near all mining areas. As they required a good supply of timber, ore was generally carried from the vicinity of the mines to an area of well-wooded country, even a few miles away. In the fifteenth century ore was carried from Upper Weardale mines to 'les Bolehill' at Walsingham in the lower wooded part of the dale; Greenhow Hill ore was carried across Nidderdale to 'the baill hills in the Bishopside'. Thus boles are more likely to be found in old woodlands around a mining field than among the mines.[1] A bail hill

[1] In Derbyshire the mines are almost all on the limestone areas west of the river Derwent, while the bolehills lie on the Millstone Grit country east of the river and as far as the outskirts of Sheffield. R. A. Mott, *Bull. Hist. Met.*, 1967, No. 8, pp. 6-11, map 1.

or bole was essentially a shallow bowl furnace, a few feet in diameter, with a low retaining wall round it. A position was chosen to get the best advantage of winds for draught, and a fire of brushwood was used. Crushed ore sprinkled on the top of this was oxidized and as it fell into the lower enclosed part of the fire was reduced to lead. As lead melts at 327 °C., it was easy for it to flow out into a prepared hollow. The evidence of a bole is a circular area of burnt ground, nearly always with bits of charcoal and ore in a black soil, and more or less slag thrown out to one side. As boles for iron smelting are somewhat similar, though smaller, an analysis of the slag in the absence of pieces of ore will soon decide the nature of the smelting. The slags always contained some lead, even as much as twenty per cent or more, so were a valuable material for resmelting in more recent times. From many of the larger boles the slags have been carried away to be smelted in later and more efficient furnaces, so that it is usually the smaller boles that have survived. A place name will frequently give a clue worth following with a careful search. *Bale-hill*, *Bolehill*, *Tag Bail*, and similar names are surprisingly common, and a search of the large-scale maps can be very rewarding.

Bolehills were occasionally improved in the fifteenth century by the addition of foot bellows, and in the sixteenth by water wheel driven bellows, and these allowed boles to be built away from the windy hill crests, even down in the valleys on a stream side. A change came in 1565 with the *shaft furnace* and bellows (patented by William Humphray) introduced into Derbyshire. Burchard claimed that as early as 1552–3 he had used such a furnace in Derbyshire. The bellows-blown furnace quickly displaced the bole, and from it the *ore-hearth* was developed.[1]

The true smelt mill was developed to house the bellows and the hearth, and the remains of these two compartment buildings are recognizable. Bellows for the ore-hearth were too large for any but water-wheel blowing, so a whole site with features additional to the mill is to be looked for. After about 1780 small one- or two-hearth mills often had a short flue at ground level, running up rising ground to a stumpy chimney, the flue being not more than one, or perhaps two, hundred yards long, or in some one-hearth mills even shorter. The ore-hearth was rather like a large blacksmith's hearth, about six feet square, and is easily recognized. The molten lead was run into a *sumpter pot*, a cast iron hemispherical pan eighteen inches or

[1] For a detailed description of the ore-hearth see J. Percy, *Metallurgy of Lead*, 1870, pp. 279–93, and A. Raistrick and B. Jennings, *History of Lead Mining in the Pennines*, 1965, pp. 80 ff.

so in diameter, with a wide rim. These pots are found sometimes not far from a site, serving some farm use. Slag is thrown out in one place, and usually in the larger mills put through a slag hearth before going finally to the slag heap. In the first half of the nineteenth century large mills with many hearths were built, and the flues, mainly to secure the condensation and recovery of volatilized lead, became long and complex, even as much as two or three miles in a few cases.

In the eighteenth century the *reverberatory furnace* came into use in some of the larger mills, and the chief difference is to be seen in the larger foundations, about twenty feet by thirteen feet, with a fireplace at one end and a chimney or flue at the other, and the absence of bellows.[1] The flues are sometimes interrupted by condenser chambers, but these are not earlier than 1840 and have usually been inserted in an older flue when reverberatory furnaces have been adopted. Reverberatory slags are very different from those from the ore-hearth.

Many smelt-mills had an additional furnace for refining lead after the smelting. Most smelted lead contains a small proportion of other metals which are present in the ores. Silver is the commonest of these, being present in quantities from a fraction of one up to many ounces (Troy) in a ton of smelted lead. The recovery of this is one of the chief sources of silver in the world. The refining is carried out by *cupellation*, usually in a reverberatory furnace where the lead is remelted in a powerful oxidizing atmosphere. This is done on a bed of bone ashes which absorbs the lead oxide, litharge, so produced, but rejects the silver, which remains a cake of pure metal on the surface. The bone ashes with their charge of litharge are then treated as an ore and reduced back to refined lead. The structural remains of the extra furnace can usually be recognized.

Copper is much more difficult to smelt than lead, having a melting point of 1,083 °C. No early copper smelting furnace is known in Britain, but there are a few hearths which have been used as shallow bowl furnaces for melting and possibly for smelting oxidized ores. Some of the 'bun ingots' (circular and bun-shaped) are likely to have formed in the bottom of a primitive bowl furnace, but no field evidence is yet available. A bowl furnace using charcoal, with a strong bellows draught, could have smelted a few of the copper ores, and evidence of these must be kept in mind as a possibility when seeking out any smelting sites.

Copper mining and smelting on a larger scale only starts with the

[1] For drawings and all details see J. Percy, *Metallurgy of Lead*, 1870, pp. 319–25, figs, 105–11.

sixteenth century when German miners came to Keswick when Elizabeth I founded the Company of Mines Royal (copper) and the Company of Mineral and Battery works (brass). A simple blast furnace was in use until the reverberatory furnace, a century later, proved to be more efficient. Smelting involved roasting the ores, in the early days in large outdoor heaps which have left traces as patches of deeply burned ground, with slight traces of ore to differentiate them from iron sites. Smelting was generally done at a few centres and in mills with several reverberatory furnaces, each with its own tall chimney. Centres like Redbrook near Bristol, Keswick (only to the mid seventeenth century) and one or two in Cornwall were replaced by Neath and Swansea in South Wales, to which most ores were sent. Smelting involved five or more treatments in the furnaces, and much of the slag from one stage was mixed with the ore as flux for another, the final slags being markedly less in quantity than those produced in lead or iron smelting.

Tin ores were got from river gravels during the Iron Age and also in the Roman period. The ore, cassiterite, is in very pure pebbles or sand, and after the minimum of dressing it could be smelted. Like most other ores the early smelting was done in a bowl furnace, but these can only be recognized by the presence of particles of tin ore, or by the composition of a slag. Such tin smelting as was done in the medieval period was accomplished in the so-called *Jew's houses* which are numerous in the south-west. They consisted of a small furnace made of clay, about three feet high three feet in diameter at the top, and tapering downward. They were blown by foot or hand bellows and used peat fuel; molten tin was run out of the base into small rectangular 'block' moulds cut into granite blocks. The chief evidence is of course the presence of slags, moulds or mould fragments, and less commonly pieces of the hard burned furnace.

By the mid fourteenth century the *blowing house* was being introduced. This was a small, substantial stone house with a thatched roof. This enclosed a short blast furnace built of granite blocks, and blown by larger bellows powered by a water wheel.[1] The water-wheel pit and watercourse often give a lead to the blowing house. After the mid sixteenth century charcoal instead of peat was used for regular fuel, and fragments of this among the slags should be looked for. In the seventeenth century, ore coming from vein workings was more mixed, so *calcining* in a small square

[1] The blowing house usually had a set of stamps for crushing slag for resmelting. The leats to supply water to the bellows and stamps wheels are often the most prominent remains.

kiln was sometimes done before smelting. Sparkles of tin were carried off from the furnace during smelting and these, at first caught in the thatch and recovered by burning this, were later caught in a trap chamber in a chimney over the furnace. These various features make the identification of tin smelting places, up to the end of the seventeenth century, fairly easy. In the eighteenth century tin smelting, like copper, moved into large multifurnace smelting houses with reverberatory furnaces, and coal or culm fuel.

The ores of iron are very widespread over most of the country, and many outcrop in a form such that they can be collected by little more than *grubbing* from the surface. The smelting and use of iron was introduced to this country about 650 B.C. and an industry was well developed by the time of the Roman occupation. The ores occur in three main groups. Carbonates occur as nodules in the coal measures of all the coalfields and among the wealden series of the south-east. Haematites occur in Furness, West Cumberland, and parts of South Wales. Limonite is the principal ore of the Forest of Dean, and also occurs as the 'bog-ore' of the northern moors.

Most ores need some roasting, prior to smelting, and then the oxide ores can be reduced to iron at a temperature of about 800 °C. if there is a reducing atmosphere with abundant charcoal to maintain a sufficiency of carbon monoxide. The melting point of iron is 1,540 °C. and between these two temperatures the slag produced with silica impurities becomes liquid at about 1,150 °C. In primitive smelting, then, iron is produced at 800 °C. but is pasty, not melted, and mixed with slag. At 1,150 °C. much of the slag can be run out as liquid, and the iron can still be collected as a pasty, spongy ball or *bloom*. With reheating and gentle hammering most of the remaining slag is squeezed out of the bloom leaving a lump of very pure iron. Ore-roasting was done in exposed heaps, the smelting in a *bowl furnace* or *bloomery*, and the last stage in a *bloom smithy*.

Roasting areas will be recognized by the burnt ground, and distinguished as iron sites by the presence of iron ore or by association with a bloomery. The bowl furnace is simply a bowl-shaped hollow scooped in the ground or, very rarely, made in a rock. The pre-Roman bowls are generally between one foot and one foot six inches in diameter and were lined with clay. Fragments of this hard, beaten, and burned clay may be good evidence for a bloomery. Like the lead bloomeries, some were placed to be dependent upon the wind for draught, but as the required temperatures are much higher than those needed for lead, bellows were common in the Roman and later periods. The nose of the bellows does not make contact with the fire but delivers air into a *tuyere*, a clay nozzle in the side of a furnace. These break but are easily replaced, so that pieces of tuyere are sometimes found. Alternate layers of charcoal and ore were built up, and probably covered by a final layer of powdered charcoal. After the formation of the bloom, an increase in temperature liquefies the slag, and this is run out to a convenient hollow, producing a very typical *run slag* or *tap slag*. The furnace usually had a rough retaining wall, and this, collapsed, with a black soil rich in charcoal filling the bowl, and run slag nearby, is sure evidence of a bloomery. In the pre-Roman smelting there was no run slag, but slag accumulated with charcoal in the furnace bottom and formed *cinder*. The bloom smithy does not produce run slag, but makes cinder, very easily distinguished.

In the Roman period the bloomeries greatly increased in size and numbers, and some were worked for one or two centuries and accumulated slag heaps, some of them of hundreds of tons. Slags were so abundant that they were used for the foundations of some Roman roads. In some places the Romans introduced a form of *shaft furnace*, made of clay, about one foot in diameter and certainly, in one case, four feet six inches high. Tap slag, or run slag, was run out of these into hollows and so often forms round cakes a few inches thick.

The shaft furnace does not seem to have continued in use into the Dark Ages, when iron smelting continued to be done in the simple bowl furnace, which remained of relatively small diameter and shallow. What little evidence has been found of the Dark Ages and early medieval period suggests reduction in the scale of iron working, but the craft of the smith was highly respected and some excellent art work was achieved in addition to the day-to-day provision of tools and weapons. The Saxon monasteries fostered the art of the ironworker, but most of the remains are those of the smith, and not of the smelter. There are few undoubted Saxon furnaces and no evidence of any change in methods except an increase in the size of the blooms produced. The war and devastations of the Normans may have checked the industry but the coming of the Cistercians in 1128, with their great interest in wool and iron, introduced a period of expansion which lasted for a few centuries. Most of the new abbeys secured grants of mines and ironworks before the end of the twelfth century. As Bartholomew Anglicus said around 1240, 'Well-nigh no handiwork is wrought without iron; no field is eared without iron, neither tilling craft used, nor building builded without iron.'[1]

Mines showed the biggest change, as bellpits were used extensively where layers of iron ore lay not far below the surface. The bloomery was generally larger, and the charcoal-making areas better defined and more permanent. There was usually a wooden house or building (forge house, the bloomeries often being called forges), workers' houses, and stables, all these with a dam and provision for a water wheel making a compact industrial unit.

A vital change in ironmaking came at the beginning of the sixteenth century when the *blast furnace* was introduced from the Continent and almost at once put an end to the use of bowl furnaces. The blast furnace was a tall shaft furnace, fed with ore and fuel from the top and blown by large, powered bellows. It produced iron in a liquid state which was tapped at the base and so could be run out into moulds made in a casting floor of sand. This was *cast iron*, an iron-carbon alloy (2-4 % of carbon, while bloomery iron had only 0.1% or less) too brittle to be worked by the smith and needing refining to wrought iron by a process involving two more stages in *finery* and *chafery*. The iron was run from the furnace into blocks, or *pigs*, with larger ones, ten cwts or more, *sows*. The blast furnace required a much larger dam for its bellows wheel, and both finery and chafery had large wheels as well, so the situation of all was dominated by the availability of an adequate water supply.

The furnace was a very massive and strong masonry structure, so that unless deliberately demolished there is every chance of recognizable remains being found. The principal features of a furnace are the *hearth* or crucible, at the base of the *tunnel*, a tall stack shaped as two cones, base to base, the lower one much shorter than the upper one. The lower cone or inward slope is the *boshes*. Instead of two cones the section may be egg-shaped. This structure is set in a square masonry casing with a wide space between filled with broken stone, for support and insulation. The hearth is built of a fire-resistant stone, and the tunnel of fire-brick, or with a fire-brick lining. The early blast furnaces were about eighteen feet high. The hearth was not usually more than a foot wide and was of square section, and about three feet high to the boshes, which were rarely more than four feet high. The blast was blown in through tuyeres about the top of the

[1] Bartholomaeus Anglicus, *De proprietatibus Rerum*, Lib XVI, ch. 45 (English translation), 1582, p. 260.

hearth. The fuel was always charcoal. The furnace was usually built against a hillside so that a *bridge* could lead from the ore and fuel heaps onto the top of the furnace. In the course of smelting some unsmelted residues, stone from the wear of the furnace lining, hard slags, and some iron, ran together in the bottom of the hearth to form a very hard, resistant mass called the *bear*. This is very durable and usually remains on the site as evidence of a blast furnace even if all structures have been removed. There were improvements in furnaces in the seventeenth century – larger hearths and taller stacks. The usual timber tie beams used to give the furnace stack more strength were replaced by iron ties.

When a furnace site is investigated, besides the detail of the actual furnace there might be the tracks by which ore and fuel were brought from the mines and charcoal area; the provisions for storage and for washing and roasting ore; the slags which in a long-continued site might give information of changing methods. The position of water wheel and bellows link up with the water course and launders which bring water from the dam. The *founder* (the old name for the chief smelter) often had a small house at the furnace. The casting floor was a levelled space in front of the furnace, with deep sand in which moulds for iron casting could be made. There may be a recognizable tip of dirty casting sand. A little further afield, a quarry of hearthstone and a source of sand can be looked for.

The output of the late-sixteenth-century furnaces might be about one ton a week, but this was increased to two or three tons by the mid seventeenth century. Improvements were made in bellows and other detail, but nothing which will show much difference in the remains.

Cast-iron from the blast furnace was unusable by the smith, so its conversion to wrought iron was done in the *finery*, which got rid of most of the carbon. The refined iron was then reheated and forged into bars in a second hearth, the *chafery*. These two hearths, with their bellows, and the powerful trip or tilt hammer, needed a big and constant water supply for their water wheels, and so were usually built on larger streams than the furnaces required. The whole group constituted a *forge*. Storehouses for fuel, raw iron and finished bars, a house for the forge master and sometimes cottages for workmen, or accommodation for a further process made a forge into a small and compact industrial settlement. Water could generally be brought by a leat from the river or stream into a pond just above the forge, and many of these *hammerponds* are now almost the only trace of early forges.

The buildings of a forge have often continued in use as a tool forge or other iron-working place, and the original lay-out can in some cases be traced. Portions of the tilt-hammer may remain, and fortunately several are now preserved. An example is a forge at Churchill, Worcestershire, where just beneath the dam of a large hammerpond there are two buildings each with its water wheel, used for the forging of agricultural tools, and small forgings for many purposes. The remains of two fine tilt-hammers lie outside, and the records of this forge which go back for many centuries support the idea that here we have the wheels, hammer, and site of an early forge with finery and chafery in adjacent buildings.

During the nineteenth century the blast furnace underwent a very rapid evolution with the development of many ancillaries – steam- and electric-powered blowing engines, hot blast and its accompanying regenerators, the re-use of furnace gases and many others, which converted the simple furnace into the very much mechanized and vast complex of the modern blast furnace bank. The continued improvements have caused the removal of many plants even of the nineteenth century, and the industrial archae-ologist can do little more than photograph at once any early plant that remains, and search for and record photographs, drawings, and diagrams which are fortunately fairly abundant in the technical press.

The ores of zinc are not very abundant in this country, but they have been mined for two centuries or more. The ores are the carbonate calamine (or its modern name, smithsonite), the sulphide, blende or sphalerite, and the silicate hemimorphite. They are all vein ores and occur in the lower part of the zone of lead ores. Calamine has been mined since the Eliza-bethan Company of the Mineral and Battery Works, in 1568, who made brass by mixing calamine with copper and melted them together. Cala-mine was usually dried and roasted at the mines, and at two or three places in the Pennines the name Calamine House points, not to a dwelling, but a calamine roasting place. In 1738, William Champion succeeded in smelt-ing blende, a very difficult process, and a few years later his nephew used blende directly in making brass. Zinc ores were always closely associated with lead ores, so there is no difference in mining evidence beyond the occurrence of the minerals on the spoil heaps. The smelting is so closely associated with the brass industry that it will be dealt with under the brass manufactures.

In some ways gold is like tin – its commonest occurrence is in alluvial gravels, though it is also found as a primary deposit in quartz veins in some of the old rock formations. It has also occurred as a very rare trace mineral in some of the copper pyrites, from which it is extracted in small quantities. The quartz veining tends to be very irregular, so the gold workings are very irregular tunnels varying from the thinnest creepways to cavernous spaces. The quartz was got out in Roman times by using heavy iron hammers. The principal workings at Dolaucothy were two adits extending 160 feet into the hill, which were about six feet high and five feet wide. The gold-bearing quartz was broken down with hammers or pounded in mortars cut into the rock. Millstones for fine grinding were found at these mines, at a dressing floor with a supply of water brought from some miles away in a watercourse. The crushed quartz only needed washing to separate the gold dust, which could then be melted in a crucible at 1,063 °C., a temperature which could be achieved in a charcoal fire, using bellows. There is little definitive evidence of gold working to be expected except on the sites already well known at Dolaucothy and around Dolgelly in Wales, but one should still be on the alert for a chance find.

CHAPTER 3

Metal-based Industries

Most of the metallic mineral deposits, with the exception of iron ores, are found in the 'highland zone' of Britain – the mountains of Scotland, Wales and the Lake District, the Pennines and the South-West – while their products have been taken to a growing number of town centres in the lowlands to be manufactured. This trend has been particularly dominant since the start of the Industrial Revolution, when domestic industries were slowly replaced by work done in factories. The extractive industries have left their mark on what are still, in the main, rural areas, commons and mountains with sheep and cattle rearing as the continuing occupation which has not obliterated the evidence of working except to take down some of the buildings for making fences. In the towns, however, there are frequent changes in the uses of buildings, replannings, and extensions which sweep away the old features. Sites have been reused and remodelled, and especially in the last few decades wholesale demolition of older property is the normal prelude to the redesign of towns on a very large scale.

Many manufactures are based upon the use of machinery which, with the progress of technology and invention, rapidly becomes obsolete and is replaced. Processes change and new processes are invented so that the character of manufacturing includes a high degree of progressive change and replacement. For these reasons the evidence of manufacturing processes is in general much more impermanent than is the evidence left by mines and quarries. Machines are usually broken up for scrap as they become obsolete, and the chances of survival of any of them are slender. If early machinery has survived anywhere, its best chance of a continued existence is now to be found in its removal to an industrial museum. The urgency for accurate and adequate recording must be obvious both for machines, buildings, and any sort of structure and tool.

Because of these factors a section on the evidence of manufactures will be brief for the early periods, and for the present will demand very great powers of selection if it is not to become a catalogue of machinery or a description of technical processes. It is easy to recognize and describe the surviving evidence of an early chemical industry such as the alum trade, but impossible to do more than photograph some of the complexities of a modern chemical plant. To do more than that would require the special skills and knowledge of the chemical engineer and many other professional men. The above considerations might provide an argument for seeking a terminal date for industrial archaeology somewhere in the middle or later years of the nineteenth century, with an appendix of 'Industrial Recording' to carry us through to the present.

Many manufactures are housed in buildings the form of which is not determined by the processes carried out, or by the machinery being housed. The buildings which do take a particular form which is directly related to the work done in them, such as, for instance, to take a very simple example, the weavers' cottages with their special windows, or the later weaving sheds with their asymmetric north-light roofs, have a special significance above the small workshop-mill which may have housed any of a dozen trades which demanded nothing but floor-space and light.

For many of the manufacturing processes which must at least be mentioned, it will be only the rarest accident which will preserve visible remains of them except for tools, which thus acquire great significance. It is fortunate that most tools are suitable objects for preservation and display in a museum without demanding the large resources of room, capital, and staff needed for the preservation of a whole manufacturing process. While field work is still a first essential it can be profitably supplemented by research in business records, the numerous technical encyclopaedias of the seventeenth and eighteenth centuries, and the proceedings of professional and scientific bodies, where illustration and description might be found which will enable an interpretation of such scant field remains as are located.

Metal-based manufactures

Lead

Lead has a great many industrial uses, the oldest of which is the making of sheets and pipes. *Sheet lead* was cast on a smooth bed of sand into which patterns could be impressed when making sheet for ornamental tanks.

Plain sheet was in great demand in all ages for a roof covering and for lining baths and vats,[1] and after 1670 for sheathing boats. It was of course used in several alloys, of which pewter was the most important. *Pipes* were at first made by forming sheet round a mandril and soldering the long joint. Neither of these products needed much apparatus beyond a melting furnace and room in which to work. In 1670, rolls were introduced into this country for rolling sheet lead, and copper and iron sheet and bars, and rolling soon replaced nearly all the casting processes for making sheet. The demand for sheet was greatly increased by the development of the chemical industry and the chamber process for making sulphuric acid, while the provision of piped-water supplies to towns made heavy demands on pipe.

The only lead manufacture that has left a distinctive structure is that of shot casting. The method introduced in the mid eighteenth century was simply to drop molten lead from a height into water. The *shot tower* was about two hundred feet high and lead, at the correct temperature, was poured through a collander with the proper sized holes and from the proper height in the tower. The lead was melted in a furnace-heated vat, and a measured quantity of arsenic was added to it, which gave harder and better shaped shot. The shot tower, slightly tapering and usually built as an architectural feature, rising high above all surrounding buildings of the lead works, was usually a local landmark.

Other important products of lead were the oxide, *red lead*, and the carbonate, *white lead*. Red lead was made by remelting lead in a reverberatory furnace in a strongly oxidizing atmosphere, the furnace sometimes being circular and smaller than the smelting reverberatory. Traces of red lead around the remains of such a structure usually give a clue to its use. White lead is made in a way which usually leaves no structural clues. Lead was cast into thin sheets, a fraction of an inch thick, or, in the nineteenth century, into small gratings. These, in either form, were laid over the top or hung in a large earthenware pot holding a small depth of vinegar or sour wine lees. A great number of these pots were sunk in a foot or two of horse manure or spent tanning bark, which by fermenting produced a small but steady heat. A floor of boards across the top of the pots carried another similar layer of pots and manure, and this was repeated several times. The fumes of acetic acid from the vinegar converted much of the lead into the carbonate, the commercial *ceruse*, which was scraped off and the small amount of residual lead returned to the melting pot. The ceruse was

The great Roman bath at Bath is lined with sheets of lead.

washed, recrystallized, and dried. Apart from occasional finds of broken pots little remains to mark such a process. The process lasted eight or nine weeks. The beds were commonly about three hundred square feet, and the desired temperature was about 85 °F.

There are industries employed in refining lead for the recovery of silver and of trace impurities, such as antimony which makes lead very hard, but these use little but a reverberatory furnace or chemical means, and they leave few recognizable remains. The refining of lead for the recovery of silver, however, is usually carried out at the smelt-mills.

Copper

In the sixteenth century, copper was the basic material of the manufactures of the Company of Mineral and Battery works which made brass, beat hollow ware out of brass and copper, and made wire. To become the raw material of the coppersmith, the copper was beaten, or, in the seventeenth century, rolled, into plate of varying strengths. Most of the work was formed under the hammer on specially shaped anvils or *stakes*. For the heavier work a tilt-hammer might be used, driven by a water wheel, or, if of a light design, it might be foot operated. These hammers are common to many metal trades and can never be recognized as a sure indication of any one except by the size and shape of the head or other diagnostic evidence. Beaten ware was burnished, and buffing wheels were usually operated by a water wheel. Some hollow ware dishes, vases, and so on were spun on a lathe even as early as the Romano–British period. The drawing of *wire* by pulling thin rod through successive dies to a required thinness dates from 2500 B.C. About 1850, rolls were used for making wire, and in 1862 a train of rolls was introduced. This process developed and with the demands of electricity the making of copper wire and cable became a major industry, which is still expanding. The uses and manipulation of copper wire are now myriad and the associated machinery will present a major problem of recording.

The Romans used copper alloyed with tin to make a 'brass' for some of their coinage, and moulds for casting coin blanks, ladles, and remains of melting hearths have been found on some sites in this country. As the basis of the lower denomination coinage, copper has been used in ever increasing quantity up to the present. The earliest use of a copper alloy goes back to the early Bronze Age – about 1800 B.C. in this country.[1]

[1] For convenience, the making and manufacturing of bronze will be dealt with under tin.

Tin

Tin has been used since the prehistoric Bronze Age in its important alloy, *bronze*, and since at least Roman times in the alloy, *pewter*. After the remains of mining and smelting, the most likely evidences connecting tin with manufactures will be those of the trades using the alloys as their raw materials. Little is known of the actual discovery of bronze in the earlier periods, but being an alloy of which a very common form contains about ten per cent of tin with ninety per cent of copper, it could have been made by the accidental or intended inclusion of a proportion of tin ore when smelting copper ore. Bronze was being made and cast into various articles as early as the third millennium B.C., so that by the time the bronze workers reached these islands in the second millennium their art was very advanced and bronze was a regular article of manufacture and trade. The bronze workers appear to have been founders rather than miners and smelters, possibly importing their bronze and later collecting up broken implements and scrap to remelt.

The bronze was melted in a clay crucible and cast in stone or clay moulds. The art of casting is older than the smelting, having been developed with native metals at the beginning of the third millennium B.C. The temperatures for crucible melting would require the use of bellows in most cases. A few fragments of Bronze Age crucibles are known, but many complete ones have been found on Roman and later sites. The melted metal usually reacts with the inner clay surface and produces a layer of slag like a glaze, which can be analysed. The melted bronze was poured into a mould either of stone or clay, and these are fairly frequent remains in archaeological sites in the British Isles. The earliest flat bronze axes were cast in a shallow mould carved in a suitable piece of fine-grained stone. Many moulds were made for two or more axes on the one stone.

Two-part moulds were made in the middle Bronze Age, of sandstone or steatite (soapstone). The bulk of those known are from Ireland, which was the principal area in which the prehistoric metallurgists worked. In the late Bronze Age clay moulds were used, all of them two-piece and comparatively fragile, so that fragments of moulds are the common evidence. Several bronze two-piece moulds have also been found. Stone moulds too were used in the Roman and later periods and most of the tin smelted in the blowing houses was cast in granite ingot moulds until fairly recent times. The article to be cast will determine the date of a mould. The distribution of finished castings and their very great number are evidence of a widely organized trade. Hoards of bronze implements, both complete and broken ones, sometimes in numbers of a few score, along with occasional moulds and small lumps of ingot bronze show that many bronze founders were itinerant, setting up their fire in some place and casting implements for that locality. Practically all these finds both of implements and founders' hoards are accidental, but a detailed study of their distribution and nature will provide a picture of a very early but flourishing industry.

A special bronze is that known as *bell-metal*, which varies only a little in composition from twenty-three per cent of tin with seventy-six per cent of copper. In medieval times bell casting was a special trade carried on by skilled artisans who were usually itinerant. They brought their metal or metals with them and built a furnace in a place where a pit could be dug in front of it, in which the bell mould with its core could be set up. The melted metal was run straight from the furnace mouth into the mould. If the casting were successful then the new bell was tuned by filing it along the bow. Near many churches and cathedrals there are places still named Bell Field, Bell Garth, and so on, and occasionally overgrown hollows and mounds or spreads of ashes mark the place of the casting pit and the melting furnace.

By the seventeenth century some bell casters had taken permanent premises and filled in the time between bell jobs by making other bronze castings, usually small objects, buttons, buckles, ornaments, etc. A name may often be a clue to where bell founding has been situated. A very early name for a bell founder, which became a family name, was Belleyeter, derived from which we have Billiter Street in London. Some of the earliest cannon were cast of a bronze not much different from bell metal, but these were succeeded in the fourteenth and fifteenth centuries by cast iron.

Another very important alloy of tin is *pewter*, which from the Middle Ages onwards was made with twenty per cent of lead and eighty per cent of tin, the lead only recently being reduced in proportion, and in modern pewter being replaced by antimony. Modern 'pewter' is really a separate alloy, Britannia metal, with about ten per cent of antimony and a little copper to give hardness. The Romans used a great deal of pewter and the pewterer's workshop has been recognized on more than one site. As the chief apparatus is a melting hearth, crucibles, and moulds, the differentiation from some other metal working remains will rest chiefly upon the recognition of the articles produced.

A modern industry based upon tin is that of tinplate. From the medieval period copper cooking utensils had been tinned inside as a protection from corrosion by acid foods, but the development of thin, fine-quality iron sheet made possible the production of tinned sheet, soon known as *tinplate*, which could be used for food containers. In the twentieth century the canning industry has developed to enormous proportions. In 1665 Andrew Yarranton brought back from Germany the idea of plating iron, and two licences for making tinplate, neither of them taken up, were granted.[1] When these expired in 1720, John Hanbury started making tinplate at his iron works at Pontypool, but it soon spread to Neath and other places in South Wales, where forges making good charcoal iron and having water power sufficient for rolls were already established.

Until the production of mild steel in the second half of the nineteenth century, iron sheet was used, and the tinplate industry included its own iron rolling-mills. A *mill* included several furnaces, rolls, and power shears, where plates were made, and rolled down to a thickness of about one-hundredth of an inch. The rough black plates had to be prepared before they could be tinned, and this involved dipping into hot dilute acid to remove scale and oxide. After washing in water the plates have to be annealed, raised to a high temperature and cooled slowly (about forty hours) to get rid of the hardness induced by rolling. Cold rolling is then used to produce a good surface and even thickness, followed by another annealing. The plates were again pickled and dipped in oil as a flux before being dipped into the molten tin. This is done twice to produce a film, which is a surface alloy, not in any sense just a skin of tin. These many processes need sets of rolls, special annealing furnaces, and vats for acids, oils, and water. The remains of a tinplate-mill will thus be a very complex industrial unit, of a distinctive character.[2] The annealing furnaces are a modified reverberatory through which the plates, stacked in a sealed steel container, can pass without exposure to air or gases.

The remaining non-ferrous metal is *zinc*, and this is both a modern metal and one which is predominantly used in alloys. As a pure metal its main use has been as an anode in electric cells or batteries and in galvaniz-ing. Though calamine, the carbonate ore of zinc (now generally called smithsonite), was used in making brass, zinc was not smelted in this

[1] 1673 to William Chamberlain, 1691 to John Hemingway.
[2] Tinplate works were almost all in South Wales so their remains are not likely to be a problem to those not actually working in that area.

country before 1720, so there are no early zinc works to explore. Until metallic zinc was available, brass was made by roasting copper, calamine, and charcoal together in a crucible. The crucibles were grouped in a special furnace in which they stood on a perforated support above the fire and surrounded by the flames. Brass made in this way was used by the Romans in their coinage, but though coin moulds have been found no brass furnace of that age has been identified.

The first use of brass in relatively large quantities was in casting small cannon, though it never rivalled either bronze or iron. With the invention of the steam engine, the early engines from 1712 had their cylinders cast of brass until the Darbys in 1718 began to make them of cast iron, which was much cheaper. It would be difficult to distinguish a brass foundry from any other in which remelted metal was used.

The development of the sciences of astronomy and navigation, of watch- and clock-making, and the need for accurate measurement led, by the early seventeenth century, to the new craft of the instrument-maker, whose principal raw material was high-quality brass. In this activity the chief remains for the industrial archaeologist will lie among the tools and their products, which will mostly be the proper subjects for museum recording and preservation. On a similar scale of production, but developing numerically into a very large-scale industry, was the manufacture of a multitude of small Birmingham wares, anything from buttons and furniture fitments to articles for export to less civilized countries, designed to catch the eye of the primitive people and later of the less sophisticated traveller. Some very interesting early workshops are still to be found, with hand presses, moulds, and tools, and there is scope for persistent search and good recording.

An important new alloy of three-parts copper and two-parts zinc, called *Muntz's metal*, was adopted in 1832 to replace copper as ships' sheathing, but this offered nothing for the recorder different from the preparation and rolling of any other brass or copper sheet.

In the mid nineteenth century, zinc began to be used as a protective cover for iron in the process mis-called *galvanizing*. Iron tanks were generally galvanized, and eventually galvanized corrugated iron came along as a major industry. It involves reheating furnaces, rolling-mills, and cleaning and dipping tanks in which a bath of molten zinc can be maintained. All this has become part of normal iron and steel plants and will be difficult to sort out in terms of recognizable and definitive structures.

Zinc has had some use as zinc white (oxide) in paints, and a substantial use in pharmaceuticals as calamine lotions and zinc ointments.

Iron

It would be difficult to give an adequate account of the manufactures based upon iron and steel in less than a large volume. As iron and its first product, steel, along with fuel, were and are still the basis of the Industrial Revolution, it will be difficult to select a limited number of manufactures employing iron or steel during the last century and a half which are not more easily studied by the engineer and technician. Nonetheless, as the making and using of iron goes back to prehistoric times, there are at least twenty centuries before the opening of the Industrial Revolution which can afford simpler material for our studies.

The production of iron by the so-called indirect process of making cast-iron and then by further separate processes converting it to wrought iron or steel is the mark of the Industrial Revolution. Before the eighteenth century the direct process produced an iron bloom, usually of very pure wrought iron, which the smith wrought directly to the finished article. The early processes of iron manufacture are therefore mainly those of the blacksmith. However varied his product might be, his basic equipment will always be hearth and bellows, anvil and hammers, chisel, file, and tongs. It is the shapes and arrangements of these that will change to become distinctive of particular trades. This equipment, with the building housing it and place for stores and fuel, form the forge, and the forge is quite probably the earliest industrial building we shall encounter. Like the earliest pottery kilns, however, some of the forges were the temporary erection of itinerant craftsmen who worked in one place until the immediately local ores and fuel were exhausted, and then moved on.

The iron-maker, working either in a bole or any other furnace, produced slag, by which his workplace can be recognized. The smith in his hammering of hot iron produces the fascinating sparkles which are tiny fragments of 'scale', flakes of oxide which are hammered off the surface of the iron and burn as they fly through the air. The scale is trodden into the forge floor and is mixed with the refuse from the fires, ash and cinder, and nothing more clearly marks the position of an early forge than a small area or a heap of scale and cinder. The iron left in it will oxidize and in some cases rust the whole mass together as a ferrocrete. The smith from at least Roman times has used coal as a fuel, so that the debris of a forge contains coal ash or coke breeze, and not wood ash and charcoal.

The blacksmith's forge with its hand bellows is only the prototype of the larger forge with power-blown bellows which became the principal first unit in larger-scale working, and in making wrought iron from cast-iron in the eighteenth century. The blacksmith used his man as striker to wield the heavy hammer by his direction, but the man was replaced in the larger forge by the *trip-hammer*, or *tilt-hammer*. This became, from a very early date, an almost universal tool in most heavy metal working industries, until the invention in 1839 of Nasmyth's steam-powered hammer.

The tilt-hammer makes no use of the muscular strength of a striker but depends for its force only on the fall of a heavy mass of iron, the head, the power being used only to raise that mass repeatedly. The hammer head of cast-iron varies in weight but may be several hundredweights, and it falls onto a corresponding anvil. The strong shaft, or helve, several feet long and usually of ash bound with iron hands, is pivoted in gudgeons (heavy axle bearings) either at the remote end or at a point short of midway from that end. In each case a water wheel rotates a heavy, large-diameter shaft, which carries a series of three or more nogs (projections) on a single plane at right angles to the axis. In the first type of hammer, the shaft of the wheel is parallel to the hammer shaft and so set that, as it rotates, each nog in turn lifts the shaft then lets it fall. In the other type the nog shaft is at right angles to the hammer and the nogs depress the short end of the hammer shaft and so lifts the head. The shock and vibration of the hammer stroke is so great that all framing, structure, and parts of the hammer are of unusual strength, beyond that of almost any other structure. Occasionally parts of the iron bound shafts or massive framing are found near modern works, which are good evidence of an earlier forge. In the eighteenth century the tilt-hammer helve might be made of cast-iron, shorter but much more massive, thus increasing the force of the blow. Such hammers are still to be found preserved in old-established forges. They were generally operated by a steam engine and the helve was lifted at the extreme end beyond the hammer head (Plate 3b).

While the blacksmith's forge is primarily a local service, shoeing horses and cattle, making plough irons and cart fillings, and doing numerous repairs, the manufacturing forge usually has a more restricted range of product, but deals in continuous production in large quantity. So long as iron was produced in the bloomery the blooms of iron were taken direct to

the forge as raw material for direct working. However, the product of the
blast furnace, whether using charcoal or coke, was cast-iron and this had
to go through the *finery* to be converted to wrought malleable iron, and
then passed to the second forge, the *chafery*, to be shaped into bars or
sheets.[1] Cast-iron has a high percentage of carbon combined with the iron
(about 3.5%) and this makes it too brittle for use in a forge. The finery
gets rid of most of this carbon and makes the iron malleable. The finery is
like a large blacksmith's hearth, square in plan, and was usually lined with
five iron plates making a shallow box. A pig of cast-iron is fed slowly into
the reducing part of the flames, directed by the blast from the tuyere. As
the iron melts and falls into the fire in drops, the carbon is burned out and
the refined iron accumulates in the hearth in a large lump like a bloom.

The bloom, of about a hundred pounds weight, was hammered to get
rid of scale, and entrapped slag, and then forged into a bar two or three
feet long, with a thick knob at each end. This bar was the *ancony*. The
ancony was reheated in the chafery, to a higher temperature to sweat out
some of the remaining carbon alloys, and then forged into a uniform bar.
To produce the higher temperature the chafery bellows were usually
larger than the finery ones. The finery, chafery, and tilt-hammer were
usually housed in one building, and judging from the records this was
generally about forty feet by thirty feet. Commonly there were two finery
hearths and one chafery. The hammer had its own powerful water wheel,
and finery and chafery had wheels for their bellows, the chafery wheel
being larger than that for the finery. The processes produced some slag
and scale as well as cinder, but it was fairly common practice, if a blast
furnace were near enough, to return slag and scale for resmelting. Forge
slags can be recognized by analysis, but in the absence of other supporting
structures or definite evidence it is not safe to come to conclusions on
visual inspection alone.

The first product of the forge was iron bar forged to many sizes, including broad and thin bar or strip. The strip was then cut by hand into further
strips as narrow as the thickness which could be used for nail- or wire-
making. This hand cutting into very thin rod was highly skilled and
employed many men. About the end of the sixteenth century the *slitting-
mill* was in operation on the Continent and in this country Bevis Bulmer
had taken out a patent for a machine to slit iron plate. There are many
legends of the bringing of the secret from abroad, but from one source or

See above, Chapter 2, p. 32.

another the machine was developed, and before 1630 slitting-mills were in operation in this country.[1] One operation was to pass the hand-forged strips through a pair of plain rollers to ensure an even thickness. The mill had two sets of circular steel discs one set above the other, the one set of cutters running between the others with a contact similar to a pair of shear blades.

The provision of accurately cut rod of small size gave a great impetus to the nail-makers and wire drawers. The nail-maker worked usually at his home in a small smithy which needed only a hearth with hand bellows and an anvil. In the nineteenth century a development was the building by a master nailer of a row of small cottages with a row of smithies, one behind each cottage. Some museums have secured and rebuilt a complete nailer's smithy. The isolated nailer's smithy may date from the end of the sixteenth century, before which nearly all small nails were imported. The nailers' rows are almost all of the nineteenth century.

The expansion of the woollen industry had created a big demand for combs and cards for the preparation of wool. The wire for combs had been forged by hand for many generations and it was becoming difficult to keep pace with demand. The slitting-mill, however, produced rod suited in quality and quantity to meet this demand, and this was used in the wire-mill.[2]

A much heavier forge industry which remained almost domestic in the individuality of its forges was that of the chain-makers of the Black Country.

With increasing demands for iron the finery process for wrought iron proved slow and expensive, and another process, that of *puddling*, was invented by Cranage (1766), Onions (1783), and Cort (1784).[3] A reverberatory furnace of special shape was used and fed with broken-up cast-iron. When this was melted it was moved about and stirred with long pokers by the men called puddlers. This brought all the iron in contact with the air and gases of the furnace, and burnt out carbon and some other impurities. As the process was completed the iron became stiff and could be gathered in balls or *loops*, which were carried to the hammer to expe

[1] See Rhys Jenkins, articles in *The Engineer*, 24 May, 7 June 1918, pp. 445–6, 487–9.
[2] Wire drawing is said to have been introduced by Humphrey in the Company of Mineral and Battery works, *c*. 1566. This was only the use of the water wheel for what was previously done by hand.
[3] A recent study is that by G. R. Morton and N. Mutton, 'The transition to Cort's puddling process', *Journ. Iron and Steel Inst.*, 205 (1967), pp. 722–8.

the slag. Cort added rolls to his mill, some of which were grooved, and after squeezing through plain rolls, the grooved rolls reduced the iron to rod or bar of various sections. For some grades of cast iron a finery, more properly called a refinery, was used as a first stage before the puddling. A typical iron plant at the end of the eighteenth century might thus have blast and puddling furnaces, rolls, slitting-mill, and a foundry. The whole site would be five or six acres or more in extent.[1]

The blast furnace was the first furnace to produce liquid iron, so the *foundry* at first was directly connected with it. The product iron was run out into moulds made in a sand floor in front of the furnace tapping hole, or ladled from the fore hearth into moulds. The iron was then either in the form of pig iron which could go to the refinery, or of castings made on the floor. The foundry was concerned with making castings in a whole new range of goods – pans, cannon balls, railings, flat irons – as well as an increasing number of engineering and structural parts. For large objects like cannon, pipes and columns, and engine cylinders, a very deep floor of sand was used, where sometimes the objects were cast in vertical position. From 1718, the Darbys were casting engine cylinders in this way. Smaller objects were moulded in moveable flasks or frames which held the sand mould, and these were filled with iron poured from ladles.

During the eighteenth century foundries were separated from the furnace and used remelted pig iron, and this is now the general practice. For this purpose a special type of small blast furnace, usually called a '*cupola*', has been evolved, though at first the true 'cupola' reverberatory was used for remelting. Some early castings, such as firebacks and gravestones, had been done in shallow open moulds made by impressing a wooden model in the sand floor. More elaborate castings from closed moulds, however, depended upon skilled pattern making and moulding, and occasionally a find of old patterns can be a real treasure trove.

The later nineteenth century saw much mechanization in moulding and casting plants, which in the present century have become largely automated. Traces of a foundry are to be looked for in the remains of the melting furnaces and the foundry floor, and in accumulation of old foundry sand and worn-out lining bricks from the cupolas. Occasionally, flasks and patterns might be preserved along with some products of the foundry, but

[1] Puddling furnaces were very numerous. A list compiled for the Black Country in 1872 listed 2,155 puddling furnaces in operation there, and the commonest number on any one works was between ten and twenty.

usually the older foundry has been remodelled more than once and is gone beyond recovery.

Steel

Steel has been known and used in small quantities, from very early times, particularly for swords and knives. It was made by a process which became known as *cementation*, which in the Hittite empire, in the second millennium B.C., consisted of repeatedly hammering and heating iron bars in contact with charcoal. This converted the surface to a steel. This process came into common use in Europe through the Middle Ages, and was still used in the sixteenth and seventeenth centuries. The further hardening by heating and then quenching in water came later, but this also was known and used by the Romans. The use of steel was almost restricted to swords and cutting tools through the Middle Ages, and it was not until the seventeenth century that demand was greatly increased. Before the end of that century the modern version of the *cementation process* was in operation. Very high quality Swedish or Spanish charcoal-iron bars were imported. These were packed in charcoal in large fire-clay chests which were sealed off against the access of air. The chests were then raised to a high temperature and kept at that for several days, during which carbon was absorbed and the iron rod converted into steel. Because of its rough surface this was known as *blister steel*.

The furnace used for cementation is easily recognized. It uses the reverberatory principle. The clay chests are held under a domed clay roof so that the flames and heat of the fire are deflected down and around them. The chests were at one time about three feet square in section and about twelve feet long, so it was convenient to use four in a circular reverberatory chamber. This in turn was enclosed in the base of a tall brickwork cone, which may be as much as fifty feet high. A few of these furnace cones, rather like those of a glass house, still remain, and with the remains of the fire ashes, the reverberatory structure and occasionally fragments of the chests, they are unmistakable (Plates 5a and 5b).

Blister steel made in the forge or the cementation furnace was used for cutlery and edge tools, and these were fabricated in small forges which needed a water wheel to operate bellows and tilt-hammer. Sheffield, with its five swift rivers, and with good grindstones to be had in the neighbourhood, was a very early centre of cutlery- and tool-making. Many tools were made of wrought iron, onto which a strip of steel was welded for a cutting edge. There were scythe-mills where the blades were made in this way, and other mills where shears, hoes, and the larger tools were made, while the cutlery remained essentially a domestic industry. Some forges remain with their definitive water-wheel-driven grinding wheels and a tilt-hammer. The textile industry used large cropping shears for cloth finishing, and these, like the best cutlery, were of shear steel made by welding together small plates of blister steel which, after working under the hammer, have a better texture than the blister steel. The industrial archaeologist has a rich field among these small forges, and examples such as the Wortley Top Forge, near Sheffield, and other similar ones, are now being studied and preserved in many parts of the country.

In 1740, a Doncaster man, Benjamin Huntsman, finally completed a method of making fine steel by melting broken-up blister steel in a crucible which could then be poured as *cast steel*. The cast steel, broken up in turn, was remelted with the addition of small quantities of other metals, by which he made extra hard tool steels which were needed for cutting and working other steels.

For the bulk production of ordinary, or 'mild', steel, the greatest improvement was Bessemer's method of blowing air through molten pig iron of a suitable composition and burning out some carbon and impurities until the desired composition was reached. This method using a *Bessemer converter* became a commercial process in 1856. Soon after this the brothers Siemens invented a furnace using furnace gases in which a comparable process could be carried out in an *open hearth* rather like a large reverberatory. The linings of both Bessemer converters and Siemens open hearths were of silica refractories, so both were acid processes which could not use phosphoric ores. An open hearth was made with a refractory limestone (magnesian limestone) lining which gave a basic reaction with phosphorus and produced basic slag, which has great value as a fertilizer. Bessemers have now ceased to be used and are not likely to be met with except in the Steel Gallery of the Science Museum. Open hearths still operate and can still be recorded.

When the new steel processes were in full operation, they were feeding greatly extended *rolling-mills*, which were producing sections of all kinds: structural steel girders, rail and tram lines, boiler plate and armour plate, and a thousand varied sections for industry. Along with the rolling-mills the steel works now had forges with steam hammers and hydraulic presses and hammers under which enormous and complicated forgings could be made. Main crank shafts and other parts for engines and other requirements of heavy industry often weighed scores of tons. The plants, by the end of the century, were a complex of giant blast furnaces with all their ancillaries – blowing engines, regenerative stoves for the hot blast, banks of open-hearth furnaces, casting pits for steel ingots, the rolling-mills and forges, and great engineering shops for maintenance and for turning the rolls. The manufactures based on iron and steel after 1850 would take us into the whole range of engineering – mechanical, electrical and civil – a world of ever more numerous and complex machines and tools, into structures from bridges and skyscrapers, to tankers and submarines, far too many even to list. However, the technical press, the revolution in draughtsmanship and in the reproduction of drawings and records have made it almost unnecessary for the industrial archaeologist to venture into these highly specialized fields.

One nineteenth-century development in the metallurgical industries is that of the *alloy steels* and other alloy metals. The discovery that the addition of small quantities of manganese, chrome, nickel, and other metals such as tungsten and vanadium could impart new properties of strength, hardness, resistance to corrosion, and many other characteristics became the basis of a vast new industry. The role in the last few decades has almost been reversed. Instead of finding a use for new alloys, the new demands of strength, lightness, resistance to fatigue, and a score of other special properties in spheres such as the aeroplane industry have been met by the invention and development of suitable new alloys. These have brought into industrial use many metals besides the traditional ones – aluminium magnesium, cobalt, and so on – and other compounds such as tungsten carbide, of a previously undreamed-of hardness. All these are too new for 'industrial remains' of them to have been created yet, and the laboratories in which most of them have been created are distinguished more by their equipment and raw material than by any difference in basic structure.

CHAPTER 4

Non-metallic Raw Materials

Coal and coalmines

If coal was used in prehistoric times it must have been by accident, and it is not until the Roman occupation of Britain that we have certain evidence of its use. Both the ashes of coal and fragments of unburned coal have been found on many Roman sites, with clear evidence of its deliberate use as a fuel for both metallurgical and domestic purposes. It was dug from outcrops in many of the coalfields but nothing is really known about actual mining methods. The real beginnings of mining do not become clear until the thirteenth and fourteenth centuries. On Tyneside in the fourteenth century there are records of the demise or lease of a 'coalpit' for a year at an outright rent, but, in Yorkshire, Bolton Priory in 1290 bought sea-coal for their forges, from Colne in Lancashire.[1] Records of digging coal are abundant in the fourteenth and fifteenth centuries, but with the minimum evidence of how the coal was worked. No doubt the earliest mining was just digging along the outcrops of coal seams along the steep banks of the coalfield rivers, followed by shallow *bellpits* and some open cast work on the seams which underlay much of the ground just north of the Tyne. By the sixteenth century, bellpits in most areas were sunk deeper to reach the lower seams, and the Jack rollers for winding were finding difficulty in dealing with the weight of their great length of rope in addition to the coal they were lifting.

The early shallow pits would be bellpits, and though only a few have survived on the surface they have been uncovered frequently during modern open cast coal working, and in a few cases tools, a wooden sledge, and baskets have been found. If only the bellpit mounds have survived they may be indistinguishable at sight from medieval ironstone pits or

[1] This was bought as 'Carbon marin ad forgiam' along with steel for reaping hooks and knives and leather to repair the bellows. *Compotus* 1290–1294 and subsequent years.

early lead ore bellpits. However, an examination of the spoil will soon distinguish the typical shales and bits of coal, whereas the ironstone mines will show some traces of the ironstone nodules, and other mines will show traces of ores or gangue minerals from the mineral vein. It is something of a paradox that the open cast mining which is now going on in most coalfields will completely destroy all evidence of earlier shallow mining, but it does, in the process, uncover the earlier workings over great areas. We have learned more of the early coalpits by this uncovering than by any other method. This opportunity to examine ancient underground workings laid bare to the light of day will not recur, and it is essential that the keenest continuous watch shall be kept on all sites and that everything possible be recorded.

The bellpits crowded close together were too laborious for any great depth of working, and as early as the fifteenth century workings were extended from the foot of a deeper shaft, or made from a *drift mine* driven in a coal seam from its outcrop. To prevent the fall of the roof a method of working was evolved known as *pillar and stall* or *bord and pillar*, which consisted essentially in cutting out the coal in a rectangular pattern of roads, which left between them unworked blocks of coal, the pillars, usually of larger dimensions than the roads, to support the roof. In this method at best only half the coal was taken out, and in many cases as little as a quarter was won. Evidence of this way of working has been revealed on old sites both by the open cast mining and, in a few rare cases, by a pattern left on the ground by subsidence and recognized by air photography. Details of the method are well known, as it has been practised in some northern coalfields as late as the twentieth century. In mines where the roof was strong and nearly self-supporting, coal was extracted completely, but propping, both of timber and stone, was used near the actual working face and along the roadways. Sooner or later the old workings closed up and the subsidence so caused is marked by the large areas of marsh and flashes on the surface.

For deeper winding, *whims* similar to those used on metalliferous mines were used and evidence of these should be looked for. One of the most interesting types of field evidence associated with the collieries is the very widespread use from the seventeenth century onwards of the *wagonway* running from pits to loading points on a nearby river or less frequently to a landsale point. Horse-drawn wagons, as well as pack-horses, carried coal from the pits, but in the absence of good roads only small loads could be carried, and these in good weather. About the mid seventeenth century, wooden trackways were laid over which a wagon would run easily and carry a load of up to two tons. The greatly increased demand at the end of the century for coal in London, and for baking, brewing, glassmaking, and other trades, was an incentive for any pit which was well placed to enter the export market, and to make its wagonway to the loading staithes on the riverside. The great maze of wagonways is recorded on many maps of the nineteenth century, and on some eighteenth-century plans, but remains of the tracks are still visible on the ground in many places. After the introduction of iron rails (1767), stone blocks or cast iron or timber sleepers were used, and the stone blocks in particular often remain to mark the line of the wagonway.[1] (Colliery railways with steam locomotives will be discussed in the section on transport.)

An ever-present problem in the pits was that of drainage, and though evidence of early drainage tunnels has been uncovered in open cast working, the common method in the seventeenth century was to lift water from the pit either by chain pumps or buckets, in both cases using a horse whim. In the eighteenth century Newcomen's steam engine was applied to colliery pumping (first in 1712), and soon became widely used.[2] In the last quarter of the century the improvements of Smeaton and Watt made the steam engine more economical and efficient and spread its use over every coalfield. The remains of a few early engine houses can still be found, and a few of the late eighteenth- and early nineteenth-century engines are now preserved.

The nineteenth century saw the exhaustion of most of the early, shallow pits, and the steady development of deeper sinkings with the movement of new pits towards parts of the coalfields too deep for earlier working. The individual pits were fewer but far larger, a trend which has continued to the present day. Great mountains of shale and waste were accumulated and pits were surrounded by acres of railway sidings, stock and timber yards, and buildings including lamphouse, machine shops, stores, and offices, and, in the late nineteenth and twentieth centuries, such amenity buildings as pithead baths. Some collieries abandoned in recent years are therefore leaving for recording but few remains of anything of the eighteenth or nineteenth centuries. However, there are available for us numerous plans,

[1] See the splendid study by B. Baxter, *Stone blocks and Iron rails*, 1966 (Newton Abbot).
[2] See, for example, A. Raistrick, 'The Steam Engine on Tyneside 1715–1778', *Trans. Newcomen Soc.* XVII (1937), pp. 131–63.

drawings, and engravings. The collieries with their mass of buildings and headgear, wagonways, and braziers of burning coals proved attractive to many artists, so that illustration for the nineteenth century is abundant. The Northumberland and Durham field is perhaps uniquely fortunate in having the magnificent drawings of Hair.[1]

Some materials other than coal, which are associated with coal seams, may be worked at the same time as the coal and be used as the raw material of an associated industry. The Coal Measures consist mainly of shales among which there are bands of other related materials, including fine sandstones, some of which have the special properties required for good grindstones, as well as many famous building stones; several of the shale bands are suited for bricks for both common and special purpose; the floor of a coal seam is usually either a fireclay or a hard rock ganister, both very valuable refractories widely used for furnace linings; and also among the measures and usually not far above the coal seams, there are the famous ironstones such as the Black Band and the Tankersley and several others which have been the basis of great iron industries. The Coalbrook-dale Company had its own collieries and ironstone mines in the surrounding small coalfield, and from the same measures got the clays for its brickworks, and until very recently the refractory clays from which it made the firebricks for its various fireplace and stove linings, and at an earlier date for lining its furnaces.

The pits were often small, using whims for winding, and not very different from the coalpits. However, ironstone was usually weathered for many months on the open ground near the pit bank and then calcined in great heaps, the poor quality slack coal being used for this purpose. The weathering and calcining places can sometimes be recognized. Some of the shales brought out of the pits were weathered before pugging[2] for brick-making. The remains of the brick kilns are like those for any other brick-making. Ganister is a very hard silica rock of high purity and is ground with a small addition of fireclay to make furnace lining. To make silica bricks for use in the open-hearth furnaces a small proportion of alkali in

[1] T. H. Hair, *A Series of Views of the Collieries in the Counties of Northumberland and Durham*, 1844 (Newcastle). This has forty-four plates. It has recently been reprinted by David and Charles, 1969 (Newton Abbot). The volumes of journals like the *Illustrated London News*, the *Graphic*, and the technical press like *The Engineer*, and later, *The Colliery Guardian*, are also a good source for more recent illustration (Plate 15).
[2] Clay is pugged either by trampling or working in a special mill and so being mixed and kneaded with water to the required plastic condition for use.

the form of milk of lime is added to the ground ganister to form a bond for the bricks, which are burnt at temperatures between 1,200 °C. and 1,500 °C. The evidence of these manufactures should include, besides the high-temperature kilns, the grinding-mills for ganister, pug-mills for the shales and clays, weathering floors for shales, and occasionally calcining and weathering floors for the ironstone.

Tools and small remains from coal working include the means of lighting. Candles were used until repeated explosions of gas led to attempts to find a safe light. Between 1740 and 1750, Charles Spedding invented the flint-mill in which a dim light, thought to be safe though not always so, was got from a stream of sparks generated from a lump of flint held against a rotating steel wheel. Disastrous explosions in the northern coal-fields led to experiments from which emerged the Cluny lamp in 1813 and the rival safety lamps of Stephenson (the 'Geordie lamp') and Davy in 1815. Examples of these and their many subsequent modifications should be looked for and preserved in a museum. Old workings have yielded wooden sledges, wooden and iron shovels of their own characteristic shapes, picks, drills, and tools for packing shot holes. Examples of all these should be sought for in any museum in a mining area. Underground conditions and a full range of mechanical tools are beautifully displayed in and around the model coalmine at the Science Museum.

Quarries

Quarries must rank as the oldest type of extractive sites, and they precede the underground mining of materials, which in many cases was initiated only when open quarry methods of winning had reached exhaustion. Quarrying has commonly been associated with the winning of stone, but it is also applied to other materials – clay, sand, gravel, and even in a few areas to great bodies of ore such as the pyrite deposits of Huelva, Spain, or the copper of Parys Mountain, Anglesey. The methods of quarrying are largely dictated by the nature of the material quarried, and have changed less over the centuries than have methods of underground mining. Worked-out quarries have not usually been re-used for any other purpose until this last quarter century, during which civilization has threatened to drown itself under its own domestic refuse, and when most available quarries not actively at work are being filled with modern rubbish at an alarming pace.

Stone

In stone quarrying there is a fundamental division into two types of quarry which employ entirely different methods and skills. In getting stone for building, for heavy load bearing structures, or for art or ornamental work, such as statuary or building involving fine carving, every skill is employed to get the stone in suitable size and to handle it in such ways that none of its properties of strength, texture, or appearance will deteriorate, either in getting, in working, or on long subsequent exposure. Other quarries want stone in large quantity, to break up for road metal or aggregate or to burn for lime or cement, and if it is blasted out the more it is broken up the less work is needed later to reduce it to size. The skill here is directed to the use of explosives and mechanical means of getting and breaking in as large a quantity as possible. These two types have changed places over the centuries. Until the late nineteenth century most quarries were of the first type, but the development of concrete as a constructional material, along with the high cost of the skilled labour needed for working stone, has made all but a few obsolete. The modern demands for road-making and concrete aggregates, cement and so on, has increased the second type to output capacities up to and above a million tons a year, which compare with the old quarries as the largest textile factories do with the cottage hand-loom weaver. The interest for the industrial archaeologist lies largely in the first type of quarry and there is a rich field of recording here, if it can be done urgently before the increasing stream of domestic refuse overwhelms all our remaining quarries.

After the Roman occupation, during which many quarries were opened for the building of their forts and cities, the demand for stone did not become very general until the twelfth century, when castles and churches were being rebuilt in stone and a great programme of monastic building, which was to last for four centuries, was initiated. On a very local scale there was a rather specialized demand for millstones, an essential part of the innumerable manorial mills. The millstones were an intermittent demand, easily met from the local resources of most of the highland zone villages, but depending in other areas in much of the Midlands and South on trade and import. On the Millstone Grit moors of the Pennines, and on other fells where a suitable sandstone is found, there are very many places where a large boulder has been split to get a lump which could be dressed to a millstone. The initial splitting has been done with a row of iron wedges (perhaps partly steeled by the blacksmith), set in a row of little slots dug out with a sharp pick. These wedges, properly struck with a heavy hammer, would split the rock. The split face would always 'draw' to the lighter side if the weight of rock was not in close balance on each side of the wedges. The remaining boulder in most cases has a concave fracture surface, the lighter flake being taken off for the millstone. This was then shaped and trimmed on the ground where it fell, so that in front of the split rock there is a 'floor' of rock chips, large and small, sometimes to be found by stripping off turf or peat. The top edge of the split face of the boulder has its row of half wedge-slots. There is evidence in the six-teenth and seventeenth centuries of more careful selection of a suitable stone outcrop and the development of small quarries to use the soundest beds. The final 'dressing' (cutting and slotting the face) was done at the mill, by the miller.

In the seventeenth century the quarrying and shaping of millstones and grindstones assumed the proportions of important businesses, grindstones becoming one of Tyneside's important exports (Plates 6a and 6b), and many of the sandstones around Sheffield also taking on a national importance. Many of the sandstone 'edges' in most areas have traces of this trade in the broken or flawed stones abandoned during the making, and also, in some places, stones that have got away when being handled, and run to the bottom of the hill, have been left there.[1] This trade developed in the late nineteenth century on a large scale, with the advent of the popular press. Larger quarries specialized in pulping rollers for the woodpulp-mills of the papermakers and other commercial grinding requirements.

The building of monasteries and castles in the thirteenth to fifteenth centuries set the craft of the masons and quarrymen at a premium, and of the great number of quarries then made a sufficient number remain to be of interest to the recorder. The fabric rolls of many abbeys, and the monas-tic chartularies, provide abundant documentation, usually locating a quarry grant with precision. In many remaining quarries there is sufficient evidence of the way of working to reward a close study, which should always include a careful examination of the quarry scrap, which can always be got in fairly fresh condition by digging into a spoil heap. It is useful to remember that the tip grows round its end or circumference and that the oldest material is at the bottom of the inner end. On some of the scrap the marks of tools almost make a catalogue of the tools used and a

[1] The places where this evidence can be found, and the quarries traced above them, are far too numerous to list.

demonstration of how they were used. For good building stone, among other things, two qualities are essential. It is desirable that the rock shall have very clear set of bedding and joints, and that, in working it, it shall have the minimum of heavy hammering or the use of blunt tools. A heavy blow will start micro-cracks round the impact which in the course of years (and remember the stone was intended to stand for centuries) would allow the access of frost and weather and produce an ugly blemish.

With a well bedded rock, jointed into natural blocks, crowbars and wedges were the tools most in use to wedge off the blocks. In a modern quarry of high quality stone you will see a crane with a hook driven into a bedding plane, carefully easing a block off its seat. If the blocks are very large they may be cut down by wedging or sawing. In all this work the natural 'bed' of the rock is carefully marked and preserved so that the stone is built into its natural position. The stone is 'green' and full of quarry water, so it is often stored on a prepared part of the quarry floor so that the quarry water, full of salts, is replaced by purer rain water. Many stones harden as they mature so shaping is done before storing. The mason who cuts and shapes the stone is the *banker hand*, who has a platform of large stones for a bench on which to place the stone he is carving. Simple shaping to size of a repetition moulding like hundreds of feet of a string course or plinth, were cut to patterns supplied in wood by the architect. The masons' departments of many of our cathedrals preserve a fine collection of these old patterns.

From the quarry there are usually loading staithes with sledge roads to be traced to the nearest road, on which wains and oxen could carry the stone to a river for the longest arm of its journey. Some river staithes are known. Tools, tool marks, banker places, loading places, and (usually deep cut) sledge tracks, roads and river staithes are part of a single complex resting at one end on the quarry and on the other at some notable building or at an export wharf. This pattern changed very little over the centuries, and today quarries of good stone follow it closely, the principal changes being the introduction of saws for dimension stone, power cranes for lifting, and mechanical transport for the product.

In some cases, where a particularly good stone was available on a hillside or in a dipping seam where the overburden soon became too great to remove, the stone was followed underground and worked by mining. Such stone mines can be a very extensive maze of rooms and connecting passages and of pillars left to support the roof. In such a mine, the methods of working can be seen more clearly than in the open quarry, free of the effects of weathering and of overgrowth. This method of working is often found in slate quarries, as slate is generally found in narrow bands with very limited outcrop. At the slate quarries the sheds and floors where the slate was split and shaped, and the special tools used, are very different from the bank of a building-stone quarry. These methods apply not only to such slates as those of Wales, the Lake District, and other areas of ancient rock, but to the very thin-bedded sandstones which make the 'grey slates' of the Pennines, and to the several 'slates', the 'Collyweston' and others, of the Cotswolds and the south and east.

The largest quarry development has been the twentieth-century demand for aggregates and broken rock which are taken from the limestones, igneous intrusive rocks, and the very compact grits of the older geological formations. In these quarries the chief method of working is by blasting, and the principal machinery is that for breaking, crushing, and grading. Movement of the rock involves much mechanical transport, conveyors, motorized lifters and dumpers, and a high degree of engineering design and power equipment. In these quarries the inquirer becomes much more of a recorder than an archaeologist.

Limestone has been quarried for burning, first for making mortars and cements from Roman times, and later for use as a manure. The quarries can hardly be separated from the lime kilns to which they are an adjunct, and with which they will be more easily studied. In a similar way, clay, gravel, and sand quarries can be studied as accessories to brick- and cement-making, aggregates, and to the glass, foundry, and building industries. A special kind of quarry working has been developed in the china-clay industry, where the clay is washed down with powerful hydraulic jets, made into a very liquid slurry, and then pumped from the quarry for treatment on the surface.

In addition to the quarries concerned with large bulk production there are a few which have been concerned with special rocks of limited distribution, rocks used in the first case mainly for ornamental purposes, or rocks of very special quality. Such special materials are the so-called *marbles*, Frosterley, Purbeck, Dent, Connemarra, and so on, very special stones like that of Portland or Bath, and other materials like serpentine or gypsum (alabaster). The chief interest in the marble quarries, where they can still be found, will be the evidence of special methods of working and handling the rock. The so-called marbles are usually particular layers only, sometimes only a foot or two thick, in a series of limestone rocks. Their particular properties are that they will take a good polish, when they will have an attractive appearance. Such layers have a very narrow outcrop and are often followed in underground workings. If the strata are horizontal, as with the Dent marbles, then they form a narrow outcrop following round the contour of the fell sides, and have been worked from a string of small quarries. The rock was generally carried by sledges, leaving deep worn roads, to a water-powered mill where sawing and polishing was carried out. Remains of the mills are usually recognized by the marble scraps and sawn debris around them (Plate 7a).

Gypsum deposits occur in the red marls of the Keuper (Trias) series of strata at several places in the Midlands, and in the Vale of Eden and near Teesside in the North. It is the hydrated sulphate of calcium and the dehydrated form is anhydrite. In the oldest worked deposits near Derby it occurs in irregular nodules, or 'balls', which may be up to ten or twelve feet in diameter, occurring at a few horizons in the marls. In the early quarries at Chellaston and Aston, it was worked underground either from levels or shafts, and the workings wound about following from one lump to the other. Where it was found in surface quarries, lumps were properly exposed and then sawn in slabs. The rock is soft and any toothed saw easily cuts it. The white varieties and some white with red or green staining in it were used as *alabaster* from the fourteenth century for ornamental work, statuary and tombs, and later for fireplaces, columns, and other architectural work.

In the Trias deposits of the north the gypsum occurs more commonly in continuous beds and is usually associated with beds of anhydrite, often of great thickness. These are quarried on a large scale in the Vale of Eden, and mined in a very large modern mine at Billingham-on-Tees. It is used now for making *plaster of Paris* and also (at Billingham) as the main source of sulphur in their chemical work. Except by the strata there is little to mark a gypsum quarry as such. Where alabaster has been cut and worked, the scrap has usually been collected and sent to the plaster kilns.

Quarrying in the igneous rocks such as the granites and syenites is on the whole fairly recent. The absence of any regular jointing and the great hardness of the rock requires different techniques from those which can be used on the sedimentary rocks. Heavy machinery is needed for sawing and polishing for ornamental or architectural products, and even for the crushing for aggregate for use in the heavy-duty concrete flags for pavements.

Clay pits and gravel pits in the past have been small and very numerous. It is only in the last few decades that the huge quarries connected with brick-making and with gravel for concrete aggregates have been worked with dragline and other mechanical excavators, which generally have left behind them only flooded lagoons, at best landscaped for boating and water recreations, at worst an unusable drowned wilderness with nothing to record.

Chemical raw materials

Salt has always been a necessity of life, and as population increased the demand for salt not only as a savour but as a preservative for meat and fish made its preparation on a large scale necessary. From at least the Bronze Age salt has been prepared in the eastern Mediterranean countries by the evaporation of sea water. From about the fourteenth century it was an extensive industry in this country using sea water and occasionally inland brine springs. Not many recognizable remains are to be seen now, beyond the *saltways* by which salt was carried inland, and a few small harbours that owed their importance to salt, coal and lime. On the southern coasts, with a longer sunny season, sea water was put to stand (either pumped or carried) in shallow pools for several weeks, the gradual evaporation increasing the brine concentration. The brine was then finally evaporated in small lead pans over a wood fire. In the thirteenth century Tynemouth Priory had a joint grant of coalpits in the Tyne valley and salt pans at the coast, but in general coal was not used at the pans until the sixteenth century. The sulphur in coal was apt to corrode lead pans, so iron pans later replaced them. It took two and a half tons of coal to produce a ton of salt, so there was a migration of pans to the estuaries of rivers like the Tyne and Wear which flowed through a coalfield.[1]

The pans were naturally above sea level, so pumps were necessary for their filling. At some places, like Seaton Sluice on the Northumberland coast, a special harbour was built to handle the coal and salt (in that case about the middle of the seventeenth century, with glass-making added in

[1] It was noted by Sir Lionel Maddison that in the salt pans at Shields and Sunderland about 90,000 tons of coal a year was used, and Nef calculated that at the end of the seventeenth century more than 300,000 tons of coal a year were burned in England and Scotland in making salt.

the eighteenth), and continued until the salt trade declined. It is rare that any trace remains of salt pans beyond the name, but from the principal producing areas salt was carried inland, particularly to the Michaelmas fairs and markets, and sold at individual villages at a traditional place or stone, so that it is very common to have a Salt Field or a Salt Pie at many villages strung out on an ancient way called Saltergate, with Salterford, Salterhebble, Salterhill, and other 'Salter' names marking its whole length right back to the salt pans.[1]

Rock salt was discovered about 1670 and for nearly two centuries was mined in Cheshire and sent all over the country, particularly along the canals in the eighteenth century. The modern phase of salt production started when boreholes were put down into the rock salt deposits under-lying some of the Triassic areas such as Teesside and the Cheshire plain. It was possible with multiple bores to circulate steam or water into the salt deposits and pump it as brine back to the surface. Larger-scale and more efficient evaporating plants were built up in the late nineteenth and twentieth centuries.

Alum

Alum is a mineral substance of restricted occurrence and has been chiefly produced by the treatment of so-called *alum shales*, or in early times by the evaporation of water from springs which have percolated through alum-bearing rock. Until the sixteenth century the Pope had a world monopoly of the alum imported from the East, and that which had been discovered in Italy in the fifteenth century. At the end of the sixteenth century (1595) strata were discovered near Guisborough, North Yorkshire, from which alum could be manufactured. There was a demand from medieval times for alum as a mordant for making vegetable dyes more brilliant and per-manent. As the textile industry grew so did the demand for alum, so that the discovery of a way of preparing alum in this country at once relaxed the grip of the Italian monopoly and encountered a quickly increasing demand.

The alum shales are a section of the Lias series of rocks, and they out-

[1] The best study of the saltways for a large area is by W. B. Crump, *Saltways from the Cheshire Wiches* (Bristol, 1940). This was reprinted from *Trans. Lancs. and Ches. Antiquarian Soc.*, Vol. LIV, pp. 84–142, plates (maps) xxi–xxviii. An earlier account of great value is in English Place-Name Soc., vol. iv., *Place-Names of Worcestershire*, in which F. T. S. Houghton wrote a section on the saltways associated with Droitwich.

crop on the North Yorkshire coast from south of Whitby, northwards, as well as at inland areas on the north and east flanks of the Cleveland Hills. The shales are essentially aluminium silicates, but with iron pyrites disseminated in a finely divided form throughout them. Alum is a double sulphate of aluminium and potash or aluminium and ammonia. The problem of the alum-maker is thus to release the sulphur from the pyrites (iron sulphide) and combine it with the alumina. This was done by apparently crude but effective empirical methods. The coast both north and south of Whitby was the chief area of the alum industry from the last decades of the seventeenth century for over a century and a half.

A typical works was sited on an outcrop of the alum shale, preferably on steep ground on the cliffs. A quarry was opened and as it developed the works extended over its floor. The shale was broken small and then calcined. On a platform of brushwood the shale was spread lightly and the heap fired. As the shale contains some proportion of carbonaceous matter, and as the breakdown of iron pyrites is partly exothermic (a chemical reaction which gives out heat), the burning was maintained by building up the heap with some admixture of small coal. The heaps were large and piling may have continued for some months – a size frequently attained being 100 ft by 150 ft and occasionally as much as 50 ft or more high. The calcined shale was put into leaching tanks built in the quarry floor in numbers from a minimum of four up to twenty or so. These were often about 30 ft long, 15 ft wide, and 5 ft deep, lined with large flags.[1] After several days of leaching in a succession of pits, the spent shale, with calcining ashes, was tipped onto the sea shore for the tide to carry away. Some areas of these tips are still easily found below the works sites, which are now overgrown quarries.

The liquor from leaching was transferred to lead or iron evaporating pans,[2] where urine (for ammonia) or burned kelp (sea-weed for potash) was added. In these, over coal fires, the liquor was concentrated until the alum was made to crystallize on the sides and bottom of the pan by the

[1] The tanks were usually built upon terraces so that from the first leaching the liquor would run by gravity through the necessary succession to the evaporating house.
[2] On the Yorkshire coast lead evaporating pans were usually 10 ft × 4 ft 9 ins × 2 ft deep, but in Scotland, at Hurlet and Campsie, the evaporation was accomplished in a different way. A stone-built cistern, watertight with clay behind the stones, was made in the ground, 4 or 5 ft wide, 2 ft deep and 30–40 ft long. This was covered by a brick arch and made into a form of reverberatory furnace by a fireplace at one end and a chimney at the other. Evaporation was from the surface of the liquor to which fresh stocks were added from time to time. The remains of these are easily recognized.

addition of the potash or ammonia (kelp or urine), the mother liquor retaining iron sulphate, which was recovered separately as '*green vitriol*' or *copperas*.

In the second half of the nineteenth century the greatly increased demand for alum was partly met from two new areas. Some shales in the Coal Measures of Campsie and Hurlet near Glasgow were found to yield a good alum, and at Newton Heath near Manchester the calcined Coal Measure shales were treated with sulphuric acid after a short, fierce calcination. The Pendleton Alum Works soon became the largest single alum producer in the world. Many other methods were patented from time to time, some of them using aluminium minerals such as bauxite, cryolite, or alunite, but the only remains likely to be found outside the complex of a modern chemical plant are those of the Yorkshire and Scotch methods. At Sandsend, north of Whitby, the remains of a small port are still to be seen – wharves, warehouses, rail tracks, buildings, etc, all made for the alum trade (Plate 9b). The alum quarries have reshaped the cliffs at Boulby and Kettleness, where a few million tons of shale have been cut away. Other quarries with traces of the works will be found along the coast on the outcrop of the alum shale, and traces of mining remain at inland sites (Plate 9a).[1]

Arsenic was obtained in this country by roasting some of the arsenious ores of iron and copper and condensing the volatilized arsenic fumes. The principal ore used was *mispickle*, the sulphide of iron and arsenic ($FeAsS$) which occurs in both lead and copper veins. There are two ores of copper, tennantite and enargite (both sulph-arsenides), which are associated with some copper veins and which can yield arsenic when roasted. The production of arsenic has been almost entirely concentrated in Devon and Cornwall in the nineteenth century. Mispickle was particularly abundant at the Devon Great Consols mine, but was also found at many others. There was a demand for arsenic in some parts of the glass industry, in making enamels and in insecticides. The ore was washed, crushed to less than half an inch, and then calcined. The patent Brunton calciner was essentially a firebrick-covered circular iron plate revolving over a furnace, on which the crushed

[1] Ports for handling the coal were constructed at Mulgrave or extended as at Whitby. As more than three tons of coal were used there for the production of each ton of alum, the traffic from Sunderland and Tyneside was very heavy. Some of the shipbuilding at Whitby was employed in supplying coaster colliers.

ore was laid and stirred. The more general calciner was a firebrick-lined iron cylinder, up to fifty feet long, rotated over a furnace. Both required a power drive, either water wheel or steam engine, for the crushers and the kilns, and the foundations can be looked for. From the kilns the arsenic vapour was led off through a labyrinth of flues and chambers, where arsenic was condensed. The flues and chambers are built with stone walls two or more feet thick, and generally lie up a hill to a tall chimney designed to help the draught and to disperse residual fumes. The flues are very long and involved, at the largest works totalling over five thousand feet. After recovery from the flues the arsenic went to a refining furnace, and its vapour was condensed in tile-lined chambers in which it crystallized. This was then ground to flour.

Sulphur, which occurs native in Italy and Sicily, was only found in this country in the sulphide ores of metals and was lost in the calcination prior to their smelting. In the later decades of the eighteenth and the early part of the nineteenth century the demand for sulphur in the manufacture of sulphuric acid was vastly increased, as the acid was wanted for the developing alkali manufactures. Acid was made from sulphur imported from Sicily, but in 1838 a monopoly was created which forced the price beyond the economic limits. At one of the world's largest copper mines, Huelva, in Spain, thousands of tons of sulphur were burnt into the air as the first stage before smelting copper-iron-pyrites. Methods were developed in Britain of burning pyrites and either condensing the sulphur from the fumes or using it as sulphur dioxide in chemical processes for making sulphuric acid. At least ninety per cent of the pyrites used was imported from Spain. The cinder produced by the calcination was mainly iron oxide with from three to five per cent of copper and many rare trace minerals including gold. 'Wet' methods were devised for the recovery of copper and the separation of the other trace metals, and the remaining iron oxide was sent as raw material to the open-hearth steel furnaces.

During this century another source of sulphur has been developed in the large deposits of calcium sulphate, the mineral, *anhydrite*. This is mined and then calcined to give sulphur dioxide for acid manufacture, and calcium used in many forms in the chemical works. Nowhere in this country do we get native sulphur but derive all our consumption either from sulphide ores or from the sulphates of calcium. A still more recent development, in 1914, followed on the discovery of the salt and sulphur domes with which much of the American oil is associated. From 1954 the oil domes have become the principal world source for sulphur.[1]

The interest of the industrial archaeologist will rest largely with the early chemical works – traces of their banks of calcining furnaces and the batteries of lixiviating tanks sometimes remain in the older works.

[1] A further source, likely to increase, comes from the hydrogen sulphide which is mixed in many of the natural gas deposits. This has to be separated and methods of recovering the sulphur have been developed. By 1962 more than one and a half million tons of sulphur a year were being recovered from gas, and Canada was producing more than a million. With the discovery of North Sea gas, Britain will be producing more and more sulphur from this source.

CHAPTER 5

Manufactures Based Upon Non-metallic Raw Materials

The by-products of coal are very numerous but nearly all of them belong to one or other of three main groups–coke, gas, and the tar distillates. *Coke* was used in the mid seventeenth century in the preparation of malt, and in 1709 was successfully used to smelt iron in the blast furnace. For much of the eighteenth century the coke was made by burning heaps of coal in the open air on a levelled space, which could accommodate a number of heaps, and which is still sometimes marked by the name *Coke Hearths*, as at Coalbrookdale. The heaps were carefully piled and the burning was regulated by means of a cover of fine slack, wetted if necessary, and by using hurdles as a wind shield. About 1763, the *coke oven* was introduced, taking its name from its likeness to the older bakers' oven, and by 1800 it was in use in many parts of the Northumberland–Durham coalfield. It was a circular oven with domed top, of about ten or twelve cubic feet capacity, and with one door near which there was a chimney or hole in the roof. The oven was filled with coal, the iron door luted in (sealed with fireclay), the coal burning slowly with insufficient air to allow complete combustion. The ovens were built in banks, and as the domes were made higher they acquired the popular name of *beehive coke ovens*. Remains of these banks are now being cleared away at an increasing pace, but there are still some to be traced and recorded.[1]

The next change in the coke oven came with the invention of the Coppee vertical type, where a bank was made up of tall, narrow, vertical compartments, lined with firebrick, in which the coal was converted to coke. The main structure was of iron or steel, often with automatic loading and clearing, and with draw-off provision for the gases produced. The gas was sometimes used to heat the ovens or in other ways about the works.

[1] There is a bank at the Barlow Ironworks, Derbyshire, alongside the ruins of some blast furnaces.

In 1792, Richard Murdock lighted his house and office, at Redruth, Cornwall, with *coal gas* and thus initiated what rapidly grew into a major industry. In 1804 a gas plant was built in the Boulton and Watt factory at Soho, to produce gas which lighted the whole of the factory, and in the next few years the use of gas spread rapidly. In 1810, an Act of Parliament incorporated the London and Westminster Chartered Gas-Light and Coke Company. The remains of the gas industry belong, therefore, entirely to the nineteenth and twentieth centuries. For the production of *gas*, coal was brought to a red heat in retorts made either of iron or refractory clay, its volatile content was driven off as crude gas and the residual carbon was *gas coke*. The crude gas contained tar and many other substances which had to be extracted to make the gas usable as a good illuminant. All these were dealt with in purification plant, so that a typical gas works had a sequence of apparatus and a number of by-products. The coal was distilled in coal-heated retorts which were usually in unit banks of five. Raw coal was handled in many ways and the works generally had an interesting system of conveyors and hoists with, in later works, mechanical fillers for the retorts.[1]

The first stage in purification of the gas produced a crude mixture called *coal tar*. In 1845 Hoffman, then head of the Royal College of Chemistry, realized that coal tar contained a number of very valuable chemical substances which could be separated by distillation. The lightest distillate was a group – benzene, toluene, and xylene. Phenol (carbolic acid) and naphthalene came next; cresols (used in winter sprays, 'tar oil wash' for fruit); and anthracene left a final residue of pitch. In 1856, Perkin made the first *aniline dye* (aniline purple) from a benzene derivative, and following this a vast chemical industry sprang up based upon the coal-tar derivatives. Only the highly trained chemical engineer could deal with and differentiate the vast proliferation of distillation and fractionation towers and other magic-performing apparatus of the synthetic industries, stemming from coal tar derivatives and ranging to such extremes as TNT explosives, aspirin and saccharin, dyes, and hundreds of other products.

After the bulk of the tar has been extracted the gas requires further purification to take out ammonia and hydrogen sulphide and other impurities, the purified gas going finally into the gas holder. The deep circular

[1] The discovery and tapping of natural gas in the mid twentieth century has put an end to the coal gas industry and most gas works have been demolished. What little remains should be the urgent concern of the industrial recorder.

basal tank of the holder often remains among the ruins of an abandoned rural mill which for a time made its own gas. The small retort house and simple purifier have also been recognized and should be looked for in any mid-nineteenth-century site remote from a public gas supply.

Allied to the products of coal distillation there is a small group of natural tars and oils which for a time were developed as an industry. The group includes a few solid bitumens like the Elaterite (elastic bitumen) of Derbyshire, liquid bitumens (the Tar Tunnel) of Shropshire, and oils distilled from oil shales. Near the middle of the nineteenth century James Young, chemist at Tennants' Chemical Works, Manchester, was consulted about an oil seepage in a Derbyshire colliery, the New Deeps mine, Alfreton. He erected a refinery and for a time produced oils and paraffin. About 1850 he discovered the rich mineral shale at Boghead near Bathgate, Scotland, and started what became the considerable Scottish *oil shale* industry. Many other oil shales were discovered and crude oil was produced by their simple distillation. Paraffins and other oils were refined from this. By 1870, there were at least ninety works dealing with the oil shale produced by a considerable mining industry. However, American competition brought many of these to an end, though some industry continued with new and better plant. Remains of these old plants, with arrangements for crushing and distilling the shale, and possibly with provision for refining, ought to be sought out and recorded.

Quarry products

These are very numerous and some of the industries based upon them are very ancient. The raw materials of the stone quarry are fairly simple – dimension stone, and rubble, including crushed stone. In medieval times the actual quarrying of stone was regarded as semi-skilled labour done under supervision, and the skilled worker was the mason working in his lodge. Sometimes a lodge or group was hired to do a particular job, as when the sheriff of Yorkshire bought stone from Tadcaster quarry and then employed thirty-seven masons to make 606 stone balls for use in the catapults and balistae. In 1418, seven thousand balls were ordered from Maidstone quarries. The monumental mason of today who carves tombstones from a variety of imported stones is almost in the line of the medieval and later mason-sculptor who produced statuary, column capitals, and carved ornament to order and pattern, from stone sent to his lodge from a variety of quarries. A mason's workplace can be suspected where a layer of stone chippings and spoil contains a variety of stones from widely scattered quarries. In the *marble* and *alabaster* work, a good deal of the rock was sawn to slabs or blocks and then sent to centres like Nottingham and London, where stone carving was an established industry.

One of the older of the quarry trades which has left structural remains worth recording is that which took limestone and burnt it to *lime*. For this purpose only broken rock was required, which was generally burnt on the spot where it was quarried. It was an advantage if a cheap supply of coal could be had within reasonable distance, though the earliest kilns could be fired with wood. Roman lime kilns are known, in which they made lime for their builders' mortar. Most contracts for medieval building include provisions for making one or more lime kilns. Some of these were ten or twelve feet in diameter, walled round to three or four feet high, with draught tunnels at the base. Inside them a fire of brushwood was made and broken limestone added in alternate layers with the fuel to the top of the wall, and this was continued up to make a heaped top. The whole was then covered with sods and left to burn itself out. Once alight the process was exothermic and no further attention or fuel was required.

By the late thirteenth century, kilns were being built with a tapering bowl-shaped interior, with one or two 'wind tunnels' into the base, and containing lime, coal, and coal ashes when excavated.[1] Timber and brushwood, however, was still used where coal was not easily available, as at Oxford, where in 1229 the king allowed twenty-six acres of timber for the two kilns made for building the castle. In the sixteenth century lime was recognized as a good manure for sour land and local 'lime pits' became very common. In these a space was cleared, usually at the limestone quarry, and a shallow excavation made which might be ten or more yards long, half that width, and tapering to the bottom. Wind holes were cut to the bottom, and coal and limestone piled up in layers until a high heap was made which formed a great mound above the pit. The whole *pye*, as it was called, was then covered with sods, fired, and left to burn slowly for a week or two. Such pyes are now rare, but the sites of a few have been recognized, and at least one on a very much larger scale was still in action commercially until quite recently. They were in common use until the early nineteenth century.

[1] For example, O. E. A. Craster, 'A medieval limekiln at Ogmore Castle', Glamorgan, *Arch. Cambrensis*, CI (1951), pp. 72–6.

The late eighteenth century saw the Enclosure movement develop and the enclosure of much poor, sour land on the uplands. The *running kiln* became popular and many thousands remain to be recorded. Essentially this was a large, stone-built bowl, round about ten feet in internal diameter, parallel sided for eight feet or so and then tapering downwards rapidly to the bottom. There was a grate at the base for drawing out lime and ashes. The whole was contained in a very sturdy enclosing structure, a massive tower, perhaps eight feet thick at the side of the bowl, circular or square in section. A tunnel at the base led to the grate. The top of the kiln was below or at the level of a quarry floor, so that broken limestone was tipped in with the least trouble. Coal was brought from the nearest point and stored on the quarry floor. When the kiln was burning, limestone and coal were fed in alternately, and lime and ashes drawn at the bottom, so the kiln could work continuously for weeks on end.

These kilns were usually built and owned by a farmer and served, with only seasonal use, to improve or manure all his land. It is common in some limestone areas to find as many as twenty or more small kilns in one township and even a hundred or two on the upland edge of a single valley. The lime kiln should always be studied as the focal point of a larger complex: limestone quarry and kiln, coalpit and coal tracks (usually packhorse, sledge, or small cart) to the kiln, lime tracks from the kiln, often remarkably clear over poor-quality ground. As these kilns were farmer-built they have great diversity of detail, though following a common plan, and if a good kiln builder lived in an area family likenesses can be seen over the locality in which he worked.

The great days of the kilns were associated with canals and the building of the industrial towns. A canal which ran through limestone and coal country – for example, the Leeds and Liverpool – had banks of much larger running kilns built against the towpath side both in and near towns, or in the farming country away from the limestone. Coal and limestone were brought by the canal, and the lime was sold at the kiln mouth. This was an important part of the trade of some sections of several canals, and whether these kilns are recorded as canal accessories, or as kilns in their own right, they must not be overlooked (Plate 8a).

As lime came into greater demand in agriculture, industry and chemicals, towards the end of the nineteenth century, new and large-capacity kilns were devised and patented and set up in connection with quarries on a very large scale. The 'stone kilns' were replaced by high tower kilns, steel-built and lined with firebrick, continuously burning for several years and only laid off for renewal of the linings. Coal was the general fuel until the interest in reducing the smoke nuisance caused many to turn first to coke and then recently to oil-fired forms. A further modification has been introduced in the horizontal kiln. All these are associated with much mechanization of the quarry and of crushing, grading, and handling plant, which also often has the addition of mechanical hydrating and packing plant, after the burning.

Kilns were used for burning gypsum and the scrap from alabaster to make *plaster of Paris*, and this has now developed into a highly technical industry producing many varieties of plasters and plaster products. A similar development has taken place in the cement industry. The principal discovery in this was made in 1824 by a Wakefield builder, Joseph Aspdin, who was burning chalk with some small proportion of clay to produce a strong mortar. His material was fired at too high a temperature and produced a sinter or clinker. This, when ground up and mixed with water, was found to produce a very strong cement. Aspdin gave it the name *Portland Cement*, hoping that it might replace Portland stone. Instead, it initiated the era of concrete. Cement can be made by burning together, to a clinker, a mixture in proper proportions of any form of calcium carbonate, limestone, chalk, calcareous mud, with clay materials, either clay, shale, or clay mud. These ingredients, properly mixed, are burnt in special kilns, now mostly near-horizontal iron-built rotary kilns, and the clinker is ground to flour as cement. Apart from an existing kiln it is difficult to see what specific object of industrial archaeological interest will survive from a cement works.

Clays and clay products

Brick- and tile-making
The use of brick in building goes back to the civilizations of Mesopotamia and Egypt and later was an important part of Roman building practice. The Romans brought the craft to this country, using brick extensively in many of their buildings and making tiles their main roofing material.[1] After the withdrawal of the Romans in the fifth century, bricks ceased to

[1] Though there are a few pre-Roman Iron Age (Belgic) bricks known, and also fragments of glazed Saxon tiles from Winchester.

be made in this country but those robbed from Roman sites were incorporated in many buildings. It was not until the late thirteenth or the beginning of the fourteenth century that the art of brick- and tile-making was brought here from the Continent and that the trade of brick-making began again.

An important factor in brick-making is the very widespread occurrence of clays which with some preparation can be made into durable brick. Clays are particularly prevalent in the lowland parts of the country, where stone is often scarce or absent. The getting of clay is easy, not requiring any special skills such as the hardrock quarryman must use; it is generally a surface deposit, so on early quarry sites what is left is not likely to be more than a shallow area, probably tumbled and hummocky with reject gravel, which often occurs in streaks and patches in the clay, and must be got rid of before the clay can be prepared for use. In modern clay pits, mechanical excavators and dragline methods are used and areas of thick clay are worked in very large and deep quarries. In the Millstone Grit and coal measure areas, and to a lesser extent in some of the later geological series, particularly the Jurassic, shales are used for brick-making, and are an equally good material but needing more preparation for use. Many of these shales are mined usually by drifts from the outcrop.

To make a good brick the clay must have two constituents which might be got separately and mixed – a plastic clay to allow good moulding, and a sandy clay which will prevent the shrinking and cracking which a plastic clay would undergo on cooling after firing. The raw materials were made plastic by being kneaded together, trampled often by oxen, sometimes by men, wetted and worked until the suitable *dough* was made. This was then pressed into brick or tile moulds, turned out and stacked under sheds to dry and harden sufficiently to be handled and stacked in the kiln.

The part of a brickworks most likely to survive is the kiln, and this can be of many kinds. Before the eighteenth century, most brickworkers were itinerant, moving round the country to where building was required, taking a contract and hunting out and testing the nearest clays. When a satisfactory source was found, digging and moulding was started and, when sufficient 'green' (unfired) bricks were ready, a *clamp kiln* was started. A large stack of bricks was made with the fuel, usually of selected brushwood, packed among the bricks and between the layers, and the stack was covered and then fired. This method produced very uneven burning and a high proportion of wasters, and it is not difficult to recognize these in the field. A great improvement was the so-called *Scotch kiln*. Four walls enclose a square space like a small tower, within which the bricks were stacked. The top was open and a fireplace was made external to the kiln, at the base, and the heat drawn into and upward through the kiln which acted as a chimney. This gave a uniform temperature with very few spoilt bricks. A modern form of this *updraught kiln* is still used (Plate 8b).

The form of kiln which was to be more permanent, and more widely used than the clamp, was the *downdraught* pattern. This was built either circular with a domed roof or rectangular with an arched roof. The heat from the fire came in at the top and was drawn down through the stacked bricks to a flue in the base leading out to a chimney which provided the draught (Plate 10a). These kilns are still used for special quality face-bricks, engineering (high strength), and refractory bricks. In the mid nineteenth century, kilns on the Hoffmann principle were introduced, which were so designed as to be continuous burning over a long period. The kiln was built as a long succession of chambers – often about sixteen of them – with some communication between them. There was a tall chimney to provide an adequate draught through all the kiln. In one form the chambers were built in a circle, in another in two parallel sets. The fire started in one chamber, burned the bricks there, its heat travelling forward through the others, drying and preheating them. The cold air drawn through the last-finished chamber helped the cooling, and as the burning progressed forward through the chambers, the ones behind the firing (the fuel being fed to each chamber as wanted, from the top), were cooled sufficiently in turn for emptying and restacking. In turn, the fire came to these, so that by strict regulation of the communication between different chambers, some could be firing, some cooling and some emptying and refilling, in a continuous circuit. The remains of a kiln are generally sufficient to display its type and the abundant deposits of wasters are a guide to the products. Occasionally the track of a horse-mill may be found, the mill having been used for *pugging* the clay or grinding up shale. Mechanical brick-moulding was introduced in the later nineteenth century, but it is very rare for any of this machinery to be left on a site.

The shape of Roman bricks is easily recognized, as they were thin, and more like tiles. The commonest sizes were approximately 12 ins × 6 ins × 1¼ ins, or 18 ins × 12 ins × 1½ ins and some were square. They were burnt in stacks and, being thin, were burned all through, and so are particularly durable. When brick-making was reintroduced a different size of brick was made, and as it was related to what a man could conveniently grasp and handle it did not change much in later centuries except in thickness. The early bricks were generally two inches thick, later and modern ones about three inches. The other dimensions have remained near nine inches long and half that width. The early eighteenth century was the great period of brick architecture which was boosted by the *Act for the Rebuilding of the City of London*, after the Great Fire, and which really initiated the commercial brickyard on a fixed location. The size of bricks was regulated in 1571 and this speeded up the brick-laying and -handling; brick was cheaper to make by labour which was much less skilled than that of the mason-stone-cutter.

Tiles are of nearly the same composition as bricks and were usually burned in the same kilns, the bricks being so stacked around them as to shield them from temperatures which would cause warping. One can thus expect tile and brick waste on the same site. Tiles were, however, in use before the return of brick-making, their manufacture being encouraged by the Ordnance of 1212 prohibiting the use of thatch in London as a precaution against fire. Plain roof tiles were made alongside floor tiles, which became a dominant industry in the thirteenth and fourteenth centuries. The tiles were of a red body and patterns were made at first by impressing a shallow pattern into the unfired tile, with a carved wooden mould, and filling the impress with a white clay. This turned yellow under the glaze. Printed tiles were later made by impressing the wooden mould, which was dipped into a white or coloured slip, on the tile and so printing the pattern. Roofing tiles were far less common in the North and West, where good stone slates and true slates were found and where there was an abundance of good thatching reeds. It should not be very difficult to date a tilery if any fragments of figured or shaped tile can be found, and this will be of help where the remains of a kiln lack any specifically dateable feature.

The name Tilery – for example, Tilery Field, Tilery Lane, Tilery Hill, etc., and even in one case of total misunderstanding Artillery Field – has another connection. Following the enclosures of the early years of the nineteenth century and the war years of the second decade, much hill land was brought into temporary cultivation for oats, or made into good pasture. Besides the lime kilns already described much of the wetter land was drained by means of comparatively shallow tile drains. The 'tiles' are short earthenware pipes, three or four inches in diameter or of square section and not more than ten or twelve inches long, laid end to end without any sort of jointing. These were required in thousands, so that where a patch of clay of almost any medium quality was found a simple updraught kiln was built, and this and its shallow clay pits became the tilery. Broken wasters and the tumbled pit area are again the clue, and a neighbouring heap, or a spread of ashes, will often prove to be on the site position of the kiln. Variations from one maker to another often enable the area served by a particular tilery to be determined. Any modern excavation for drains, roads, pipes, or so on is liable to turn up the old drains.

The chief difference in a modern brickyard is the use of more machinery in preparing, moulding, and transporting bricks and material. Other improvements concern the kilns, though these have altered little in principle.

Pottery

One of the oldest uses to which clay was put is that of making pots. From the neolithic revolution pottery has been the distinguishing mark of all civilizations, and because of its indestructibility as a material potsherds are the basic material for much archaeological dating. The technology of pottery changed less than did that of almost any other craft over a period of several millennia. Three principal operations are employed in potting, one of which leaves very recognizable remains. The operations are getting and preparing the clay, shaping the pot, and firing in a kiln. The chief differences over the centuries are seen in the structural detail of kilns, though in principle the kilns remain true to one or two basic patterns.[1] Mechanization on any large scale was not applied to potting until the eighteenth or nineteenth century. The industry offers the same widespread abundance of material for the industrial archaeologist as does the iron industry prior to the Industrial Revolution. Because pottery was essential to every community it is equally common to the lowland agricultural settlements as to the highland hunter peasants. It was the ideal occupation at one and the same time for the one-man intensely localized craft, and for the producer-distributor serving a widespread area. The location of kilns is most frequently revealed by ploughing or drainage operations, as a kiln is surrounded by an area of wasters and broken pot, often running to thousands of potsherds. A kiln site is usually present

[1] Kilns were essentially a Roman introduction. Most prehistoric and some Roman pottery wa fired in bonfires.

where such potsherds are turned up regularly or in quantity, the precise position of the kiln often being marked by a patch of blacker soil existing at the stoke hole of the kiln and in the ash around and in front of it. Place-names are often a guiding clue – Potterfield, Potter Pits, Pot Lane, and so on, are common.

The earliest recognizable kilns are those used in the potteries of the Roman and Romano–British potters from the first to the fifth centuries A.D. The simplest form is related to the bowl furnace of the metallurgist, a bowl-shaped cavity in which the unbaked pots are piled along with fuel, covered either with clay or small fuel, then fired. Related to this is the clamp, a well piled heap of pots and fuel the burning of which was regulated by altering the cover, opening or closing holes to change the draught.

The kiln which is most characteristic of Romano–British sites is the *shaft kiln*. A vertical shaft usually made of clay has at one side of the base a tunnel leading into it from a stoke hole in which, and in the tunnel, the fire was maintained. In the base of the shaft there is some sort of pedestal or an arrangement of clay bars on which pots can be piled. The flame and heat of the fire is drawn through the pots by the draught induced by the chimney-effect of the vertical shaft.

Where a good clay is found the shaft kilns are found, usually in numbers, some sites having twenty or thirty close together. Mostly they seem to be built in a hole made to accommodate them, three or four feet deep. The shaft was at least this height, and its diameter a foot or a little more. The bars are of hard burned clay commonly arranged like the spokes of a wheel from a central boss to a ledge around the inside of the kiln. Fragments common on some sites suggest a covering dome of clay with a central chimney hole. The inside of the kiln was often damaged in the firing or loading, and before the next charge was relined with plastic clay which burned hard in the firing. The remains on a kiln site, besides a possible kiln, are abundant potsherds, and fragments of bars, kiln lining and dome, and ashes and fuel. The potsherds and broken pots can determine the date and duration of the kiln's usage.

The true Roman kiln is not very different from this. The kiln was set in a pit to which a sloping firing-hole is sunk. The kiln has a floor on which the pottery stands, eight inches or more above the floor of the pit. This floor is either perforated or built up with baked clay fire bars. The pots are piled in a dome-shaped heap and covered with a clay dome which has a central hole at the top to act as chimney. The flames from the fire can thus be drawn up through the piled pots, or the kiln can be completely closed, and the smoke then acts as in a smother kiln and can colour the pots.

A horizontal kiln was occasionally used in Roman times in which the pots were piled between walls enclosing an oval space, with a fire-hole at one end and a short chimney at the other. No doubt this structure was easier to make, but the shaft kiln was the more popular. In all these kilns brushwood seems to have been the regular fuel.

The Roman potters made full use of the wheel in moulding their pots, but when they withdrew at the end of the fourth century the wheel seems to have been forgotten until its reintroduction about the ninth century. In the Middle Ages, kilns were improved, although larger horizontal through-draught kilns were still used in many places. Some of these which have been excavated have the wall stones heavily burned and marked with green glaze which has run over them. This, and a greenish-yellow glaze, are very typical of the thirteenth and fourteenth centuries. It was made by sprinkling the pot with powdered galena (lead sulphide).[1] The ore was powdered on after the pot had been painted with a clay slip or with flour paste to which ore would stick. Some of the brighter green glazes contain a small proportion of a copper ore, the usual lead glaze being yellow. A common glaze used for centuries was that got by throwing salt into the kiln at the proper stage. The fumes or vapour of the salt settled on the surface of the pots and produced a fine transparent glaze.

The medieval potters revived the through-draft, horizontal kiln for their commoner ware, but for finer stuff used a domed furnace developed from the Roman type. On the Continent a high domed furnace was in use in the sixteenth century and became the common type in this country. The medieval kilns produced large numbers of jugs and dishes and general household ware, and usually had a distribution radius of a few miles, perhaps up to twenty.

The domed furnace remained in use for a long time, but in the eighteenth century was gradually replaced by one in which the heat from the fires was used as in a reverberatory furnace. This kiln had its firing place separated from the part holding the pots. The pots were now packed in seggars. These were small boxes of resistant clay, which could be covered either with a lid or by standing on one another. The soft pots were thus

[1] Some good-quality powdered ores were known as 'potters' ore as late as the eighteenth and nineteenth centuries.

kept entirely free of any direct flame or smoke and were in fact baked in the closed 'oven' of the seggar. The dome of the kiln reflected flame and heat down onto and among the seggars. This way of packing saved the soft, unbaked pots from being pressed out of shape by the weight of others piled above them, and gave a very uniform firing. This type of kiln was erected inside the base of a high conical or bottle-shaped building which shielded the kiln from wind and weather and left work room all round. These large potbanks are a feature of the potteries. They resemble in some respects the glass-house cones, but closer examination will show differences and of course the waste associated with them will be distinctive.

In the twentieth century a new kind of kiln has replaced most others. This is a horizontal tunnel kiln, usually fired by gas, oil, or electricity. In one type the kiln is loaded cold, the pots being ranged in seggars on small trucks which can be run into position, then the kiln is raised to the required temperature, variation along its length being possible. In the second type, the kiln is heated all the time with required temperatures spaced along its length so that the pots passing through on the trucks, at the proper rate, pass in turn through all desired stages.

There are several varieties of pot, among which the stoneware became probably the one most in everyday use. This was made from about 1700, using approximately one part of ground flint to four parts of clay, with a salt glaze. Porcelain, or semi-transparent china, was not made in this country until after 1768 when William Cookworthy discovered that the *Petunz* of China was indeed the mineral kaolin (china clay) which occurred in Cornwall. This, with ground flint, was the basis of the china industry which became a very important section of the pottery trade. Flint-mills have varied from the edge-runner horse-mill, the mill with coarse Millstone Grit millstones, and the ball-mill in which tumbling iron or steel balls in a rotating drum do the pulverizing, to very modern types. They are an adjunct of most potteries and their remains should be recorded.

It must be kept in mind that the flint-mill and the kilns are only two items in the complex which makes a pottery. There are mills and places for preparation of the various clays, raw material stores, sheds and wheels for shaping pots, sections for ornament and others for glazing, and usually there will be more than one firing kiln. Warehouses for storage and packing are also needed, with artist rooms and offices. Much later pottery was made in plaster moulds which need accommodation for their making and storage. A complete pottery offers a great diversity of interest.

Glass

The materials from which glass is made are sand, soda or potash, and lime, and these are heated together in a furnace until they fuse into a vitreous fluid which is cooled and again reheated in such a way as to prevent crystallization. It was made as a glaze for pottery in Egypt and Greece. Glass-blowing was developed by the Romans and the art of making and blowing was brought with them to Britain about the end of the first century A.D. Window glass was used by them in several of their larger buildings, which was made by the 'muff' method in which a large cylinder was blown, the ends cut off, then cut down one side, opened out and flattened. The kilns in which the glass was made are not known and most of it was certainly imported. Glass-making ceased when the Romans left Britain, but was reintroduced as a new craft in 675 when Benedict Biscop used it in his church at Monkwearmouth. Bede tells us that he 'sent agents to Gaul to bring over glass-workers, a craft hitherto unknown in Britain . . . they made the English people understand and learn this craft.' Glass remained a luxury article for a long time, but in the thirteenth and fourteenth centuries the demands of the churches for both plain and coloured glass enabled some glass-makers to erect glass-houses, the remains of which or their furnaces can be recognized and so become the proper study of the industrial archaeologist. Much glass, particularly coloured, was still imported, but plain glass was being made at a few places.

In the fourteenth century glass-houses were well established in Surrey (Chiddingfold), the Weald and at Vale Royal Abbey in Cheshire. In the same century, glass was being bought from the makers in Shropshire and Staffordshire. There were local makers at other places, but the real development of the trade came in the second half of the sixteenth century when so many medieval-type timber houses were being rebuilt in stone in the designs of which windows were an essential part.

Glass was made in clay crucibles accommodated in a furnace either of the through-draught type, or a covered furnace using something of the reverberatory principle. The through-draught furnace which was in use in the sixteenth century consists of two stone walls, up to eighteen or twenty feet long, parallel in their middle section where they have a rectangular space between them seven or eight feet long and a foot or more wide. The walls diverge at each end away from this, forming a splayed opening either of which would act as a wind funnel and a firing-hole. The walls are thick and substantial each side of the mid-space with a bank to

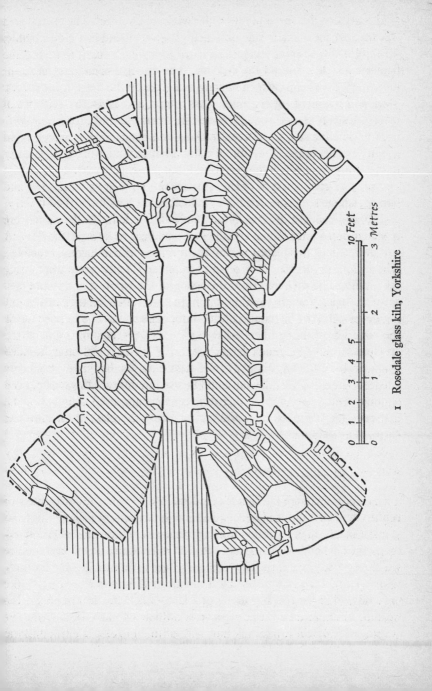

1 Rosedale glass kiln, Yorkshire

hold crucibles, then expand into wider wings to each end. The central area was the furnace on each side of which glass was made in a clay crucible. The fire of brushwood was in this space and the approach to it, and the flames could lick around the crucible. The crucible sometimes broke or molten glass was spilt, which remains as a glaze on the fire-burned stones. This, and fragments of crucibles, glass lumps, and ashes, are evidence of its use. Usually the glass was reheated in, or transferred to, a second furnace to be annealed, to prevent cracking and crystallization which rapid cooling would cause. This furnace was smaller, and worked at a lower temperature from which the glass could cool slowly (Diag. 1).

The more common type of later furnace was circular or rectangular and domed, a large structure divided by a floor, below which was the fire. Heat and flames from the fire rose through a central hole in the floor and were reflected down onto lidded crucibles or pots held in holes in the floor. A row of openings was placed around the furnace for handling the crucibles. The annealing furnaces were often rectangular. The furnaces were inside a building to be sheltered from the action of the wind, which would cool them and make the fire variable, and in the eighteenth century this building developed into the familiar brick-built glass cone. The furnace inside the cone was still in principle like the earlier reverberatory, though the crucibles were now much larger, generally called pots, straight-sided cylindrical and holding about a ton of glass each. As the furnace used only a natural draught, the tall cone could be used to increase this in the way a chimney would have done. Other furnaces were also used in preparing the materials for the glass melt, and for reheating the glass at intermediate stages of its shaping.

Chemical industries

The prime demand of the chemical industries arising in the late eighteenth century was for sulphuric acid, and although methods of making this from sulphur had been in operation from 1737 they were little more than laboratory methods, entirely inadequate to deal with the scale of manufacture which was necessary if the new demands were to be met. Roebuck's lead-chamber process as improved by Tennant in 1803 was able to meet the demand and is the real beginning of a large-scale chemical industry. Instead of making acid in large glass vessels Roebuck made large chambers of lead sheet, inside which sulphur, with a little nitre, was burnt and the sulphur dioxide was absorbed in water to form sulphuric acid. Tennant's improvement was to burn the sulphur in an outside furnace and feed the gas into the lead chambers. The acid from the lead chambers could be concentrated by evaporation in glass or platinum vessels. A new process for making sulphuric acid was found when in 1831 Phillips of Bristol used finely divided platinum as a catalyst which made sulphur dioxide combine directly with oxygen to form sulphur trioxide. This was dissolved in water to make concentrated acid. In 1852 the discovery that an oxide of iron would serve as a catalyst brought the new process within economic limits. The real extension of this method, however, came with a rising demand for stronger acid than the chamber process could produce. This was a concentrated acid containing an excess of sulphur trioxide, known as *oleum*, and largely used in the production of dyes.

Acid chambers were used until recently on many chemical plants, and although the value of the lead ensures its entire removal, foundations of banks and furnaces may still be recognizable. Prints and drawings are fairly abundant by which remains can be checked.

The prime demand for sulphuric acid was made by the growing *alkali industry* which was becoming necessary for the expansion of glass and soap making and in parts of the textile industry. The alkali industry followed the discovery by Leblanc in 1791 that common salt could be decomposed by sulphuric acid to produce sodium sulphate and hydrochloric acid. The sulphate of soda could be decomposed by carbon and calcium carbonate into carbonate of soda and sulphide of lime. These could then be separated by extraction with water. Leblanc's process was brought to England, and in 1794 John Losh joined in partnership with Lord Dundonald at Lemington on Tyne to make soda by the new process. Sea salt and sulphuric acid, mixed with clay to dry it, was roasted in a reverberatory furnace; then the product was lixiviated (to separate soluble and insoluble substances by extracting the soluble with water) to extract sulphate of soda. This was then heated again with charcoal. In 1823, Muspratt at Liverpool used the Leblanc process, then five years later, as a partner with Josias Gamble, a chemist, started the production of soda at St Helens, Lancashire, which was soon to become one of the largest centres of chemical industries. Alkali works were also established on the Tyne below Newcastle. One very intractable product was the so-called black ash residues left after the extraction of the soda. This accumulated in enormous heaps and set as hard as concrete, presenting the chemical areas with a problem of apparently indestructible waste heaps of calcium sulphide. These are the unmistakable evidence of alkali chemical industries, the remains of the works themselves being not much more than furnaces and extraction tanks.

The large quantities of hydrochloric acid liberated in the first stage of the Leblanc process were a great nuisance, until in 1836 Gossage added towers in which a descending stream of water absorbed the gas and made a commercial hydrochloric acid. The process which gradually replaced the Leblanc was the Solvay ammonia-soda one in which carbon dioxide is passed into brine saturated with ammonia, when sodium bicarbonate is precipitated. This is changed into soda by heating it and the carbon dioxide given off is returned for use in the first part of the process. It was this process which was adopted and developed by Ludwig Mond who with his partner John Brunner built up the great chemical industry later to become I.C.I.

Hydrochloric acid from the Leblanc process was used on lime to make bleaching powder, which soon became a great industry serving the demands of the textile manufacturers. In 1870 a new process for the bleaching powder was introduced. In this the hydrochloric acid gas was oxidized and the chlorine liberated by means of manganese dioxide.

Sulphuric acid was finding many industrial uses, one of which has left very evident remains. This is the manufacture of *phosphorus* for superphosphates, fertilizers, matches, and many other products. The process consists essentially of the treatment of bones or the mineral apatite (calcium phosphate) with hot sulphuric acid, the bones being first de-greased with hydrochloric acid. This produces soluble phosphoric acid and insoluble calcium sulphate. The calcium sulphate (gypsum) was sometimes used in the manufacture of fertilizers. The phosphoric acid was distilled with ground coal or charcoal in special clay retorts. These were commonly cylindrical, about forty-eight inches long and eight inches in internal diameter, ranged in banks of twenty-four rather like coal gas retorts. They were made of a good hand-picked fireclay mixed with 'grog' (burnt fireclay). The retorts had a life of only about six weeks, and then were rejected and accumulated in very large numbers. In some areas, like Oldbury, they were extensively used as building bricks would have been, and walls and other structures made of them remain to be recorded. White phosphorus was produced which was very poisonous. Heated in a closed iron container it could be converted to the safer red phosphorus. About 1890 a method of fusing apatite, silica, and carbon direct, in the electric furnace, was adopted, the phosphorus then being condensed from a gaseous state. This process produced quantities of slag, some of which was widely used as road metal, and some remains in intractable slag heaps of calcium silicate.

In all the industries so far described it is clear that the commonest process has been the application of heat in an intense form to raw or prepared material. This has been done in furnaces or kilns, and any proper appreciation of the apparatus and remains of the industries will require a knowledge of furnaces in a great variety of forms. Though very variable in detail, however, furnaces belong to one or other of a very few basic types until the late nineteenth and the twentieth century, when the introduction of gas and oil as fuels, and heat supplied by electric arcs, and electric induction, have required very different designs.

The simplest furnace is, of course, the bowl in which fuel and material to be heated, roasted, or melted is mixed together and sufficient draught is supplied by the wind by updraught or by bellows. These were applied to smelt the ores of most of the metals, to pottery, and, in an elaboration, to the lime kiln. The clamp is not much different, except that fuel is piled systematically in heaps with materials to be baked or roasted, as in the roasting of iron ores to rid them of sulphur, alum shales, and some other materials, or as a method of baking pots or bricks. The burning was slow with a carefully controlled access of air.

The more easily recognized shaft furnace had a square or cylindrical vertical shaft high enough to cause a sufficient induced draught when burning. Fuel and ore, or other materials like bricks and pots, might be mixed in the shaft, or the fire might be separate in a prepared stoke hole at the base. The chief development of this type was in the increase in size of the shaft, both of diameter and height, and the application of a forced draught by means of bellows or (later) blowing engines. This type developed into the large blast furnace, almost restricted to the smelting of iron, and the so-called foundry cupola for remelting metals for casting.

Associated with most furnaces there are many ancillary structures connected with the fuel supply, the blast, and the movement of material into and out of it, the whole being a great interrelated complex of which a few surviving parts can give a clue to the rest.

CHAPTER 6

Organic Raw Materials and Industries Based Upon Them

This group of materials and industries forms a strong contrast with th ones so far discussed. Raw materials fall naturally into two groups mineral substances, which are entirely expendable and incapable of re newal; and organic, plants and animals which are characterized by th power to reproduce and multiply. The continuation of industries base upon mineral materials depends upon the constant discovery and exploita tion of new deposits, the recovery of used material or the discovery o substitutes. While the mineral group depends upon mining and quarryin which are non-repetitive at any site, the organic materials depend upo the use of land or water for the breeding and cultivation of repeate generations, all of which can be subject to selective breeding and improve ment. In this group the basic occupation is agriculture, animal and plan husbandry. The location of the various mineral deposits is fixed and im movable, but plants and animals can be moved from one location t another and the environment in which they live and grow can be altere and improved. The dominance of furnaces, heat treatment, and compli cated machinery in the world of mineral products is replaced by the sim pler tools of cultivation and harvest, the grinding and extracting mill, an the processes of food preparation. Most organic material is perishable, an what remains for the industrial archaeologist is mainly the structures an tools of the farmer, such marks and patterns of husbandry as remain on th land, and the apparatus of the industries such as tanning and milling an textiles which are secondary to the primary agriculture.

Probably the first organic material to be used by man, apart from th food gathered to be eaten, was timber. This must have provided weapon and structural pieces for his first shelters. Some of the stone axes wer hafted in wood, and large timber was used for the dug-out canoes of whic many specimens remain. The most extensive use was in house buildin and many examples from the twelfth century onwards are still to be found in cruck and timber-framed buildings. The crucks were formed of the two halves of a suitably curved tree trunk or large branch, split or more often sawn down the mid-plane to give matching right- and left-hand members. These stood with feet apart, meeting at the apex to carry the ridge tree. Two pairs of these which were braced across by a tie which formed an 'A' frame, were connected laterally by purlins. In the sixteenth and seventeenth centuries rebuilding in stone the massive cruck timbers with the mortices for purlins and pegholes for fastening were often re-used, and because of their partly curved shape, and the evidence of the mortices and pegs, they are now in many cases attributed by local legend to ships' timbers from the Armada. In a barn recently measured, one complete cruck was built into the gable, and ten other single cruck legs were recognized, used in the boose (cattle standings) lintels of doorways, and roof timbers. There was thus the evidence of a five-bay medieval building, and its position in relation to the remaining cruck was easily determined from the remains of its foundations. Much of the structural use of timber about buildings can be dated.

Other uses for timber give rise to many industries. Small timber, willow and ash, is made into hurdles, baskets, tool handles, rakes, and so on for agriculture. Beech and some other woods are turned for chair legs and other furniture parts. Larger stuff is selected for the wheelwright and the shipwright. The sawpit cuts out planks, battens, and spars, for the carpenter and joiner, and some special timber goes to the bobbin-maker, the clogger, and some to the turner who made platters and trenchers. The cooper demanded his particular selection of timber for his job, and the list of craftsmen for whom timber was grown and cut could be extended to great length. Many of these crafts were carried on in the woodlands, or on their fringes, and some, like the hurdle-makers, charcoal burners and chair-makers, depended upon coppice wood. Few of these crafts, however, left remains which can be recognized, other than their particular tools, unless they had moved, as many of the bobbin-makers did, into small workshops with a water wheel for power. The charcoal burners left their mark,[1] and so did the saw-mill, though this tended to be downstream like the bobbin-mill, where water power could be relied upon. Except for the abundant bloomeries and forges of the Middle Ages, and some very minor crafts,

[1] These will be dealt with in the section on fuel, see below, p. 121.

the forest has been occupied primarily for growing, cutting, and transporting timber for industries outside its area.

The wheelwright and shipbuilder used the heaviest timber, making selection of individual trees whose trunks and branches would cut, as far as possible, with the least shaping, to the curves and dimensions they wanted. At both the wheelwright's shop and the ship yard, the sawpit with its large and heavy frame saws is a constant feature, while the joiner and carpenter usually had a smaller sawpit with lighter saws. Sometimes the remains can be traced of a steam box where smaller timber was bent to a particular shape, the hoops for hay rakes, the spikes for thatching and so on. This will be a primitive stove and small boiler supplying steam to a trunk or chest in which the timber is placed until it becomes pliable.

In the nineteenth and twentieth centuries the vast demand for newsprint and the expansion of coalmining created demands for softwood timber which was never characteristic of our native woodlands. Coniferous planting spread and now the Forestry Commission manages several million acres as a regulated crop. The demand for timber pit props is declining but soft woods are being used more and more for cellulose pulp for paper and as a chemical raw material. There is little for the industrial archaeologist in this development except perhaps in cutting and handling tools, and in transport. When a crop is taken the ground is re-ploughed and a new crop planted, so that gradually any older remains on the ground, unless specially protected, are eliminated.

Agriculture

The essence of agriculture has been the production of food, and it has been the first occupation of man, personal to himself and his family, for an unknown time before it became the occupation of a community. Tillage and animal husbandry were the occupations of the majority of the people in the early historic periods; the growth of groups segregated from this to special occupations, and the growth of the monastic, court, and urban communities, with markets and fairs at which they could buy the foods they no longer produced, brought agriculture within the definition of an industry. Corn-milling had been an activity of the family with its quern (hand-mill for grinding corn), and then of the miller within the manorial mill, until the arrival of the merchant and the market. Surplus corn, following greater skill and increased productivity, could be collected by the travelling buyer or sent to the nearest market, and so could become the raw material of the miller working to produce flour and products especially for market sale. It is difficult, if not impossible, to distinguish an industry from the normal agriculture of an area except perhaps by the larger size of farms and mills, until in the case of mills they begin to be built at ports or other foci of transport and distribution. In the case of brewing, the barley crop, and later the culture of hops, the oast and malt houses are a recognizable industry, but nothing in the cultivation of a field of barley could indicate that it was not a part of the village agriculture, producing its crop for local consumption.

The industrial archaeologist can take note of lynchets,[1] medieval plough rigs, field patterns, and boundary ditches, with many other features eminently suitable for field study and recording, but where these cease to be the illustration of social history and become the materials of industrial archaeology it is difficult to determine. So far as agriculture is concerned, the industrial archaeologist will find his most rewarding material in ancillary industries which are based upon the products of agriculture, like flour-milling, brewing, leather working, and so on, or in the production and treatment of a few special crops such as woad, and such structures and apparatus as are concerned with their preparation for use.

The almost universal stone querns for corn grinding are found in most prehistoric settlements, from the saddle quern of the neolithic peasant to the rotary quern introduced to Britain by Iron Age B people between 100 and 50 B.C., and all its developments through later periods. The quarrying and shaping of querns was industrialized by the Romans, especially on the Continent, but many outcrops of rock in this country were quarried and querns were manufactured and spread over wide areas. Place-names indicating these quern localities are very common – Quernmoor, Quernhow, Whernside, and so on. It is safe to assume, however, that querns, with few exceptions, were articles only of domestic use.

Corn-milling

For several centuries the *corn-mill* was a common feature of almost every manor in the country. In the Domesday Survey many hundreds of mills are mentioned, and this number greatly increased during the next two or three centuries. A small proportion of the later mills were windmills but by

[1] Ridges or terraces of soil made or accumulated in areas of prehistoric or early to medieval ploughing.

far the largest number were water-powered. Taken collectively, these mills represent an industry worthy of the attention of the industrial archaeologist, even if it is particularized into a vast number of local units. These local units have a minimum set of parts in common, only varied in detail by local topography. The general location of the water corn-mill is on an available stream, and often at its lowest point within the manor, to secure the maximum water flow. The stream was usually tapped into a dam to secure both more equable flow, and increased head and storage for a dry spell. Into and out from the dam there will be leats (watercourses) to fill the dam and serve the wheel. Where rivers rather than streams are concerned a slant dam would be built across the river, but as rivers were usually boundaries between manors a dam often rested its ends in different parishes and was a lively source of dispute. Chancery, Star Chamber, and other records of the disputes sometimes include details of the structure of the dam. At the mill there is the wheelpit and inside the mill the gears and shafting to turn the stones. There is room here for several alternative arrangements. The tail race from the wheel back to the stream is often the best preserved part of the watercourses. Even where the mill building has disappeared, dam, watercourses, wheelpit, and fragments of broken or discarded millstones remain to be discovered.

Associated with most mills there was generally a kiln to dry the grain, particularly oats, to a proper state for grinding. An interesting evidence of the former presence of a kiln, not necessarily near the mill, would be parts of stones or tiles used for the kiln drying floor. In the stone areas of the north the kiln was a small square building with a dividing floor, the basement containing the fireplace. The kiln was often built against a hillside so that each floor could be entered from its own ground level. The floor of the kiln room was often made of long narrow stones set side by side like the joists under a floor, but touching, so that grain would not fall through. Each side of each stone beam has channels cut in it close together, deep at the base and very shallow at the top. These corresponded in adjacent beams, making a floor with a regular pattern of funnels leading heat from the fire up to the narrow-slitted floor on which the corn was dried. When the kiln was abandoned these beams were useful building stones, and many can be seen in gateways and walls, as lintels, and in various uses in and about farm buildings. In the clay country large square tiles, spanning between flat iron bars, were used. The tiles are deep, for strength, and have a close-set pattern of conical holes from the base to fine holes at the top surface. Broken fragments of these are common around old kiln sites.[1]

The position of a corn-mill is usually at a ford or bridge to which ways converge from all parts of the manor, as tenants had to carry corn to and from the mill for themselves and for the manorial lord. Tenants also, as manorial dues, usually provided all millstones, and repaired the mill, the dam, watercourses, and the kiln. In contrast, however, with the water-mill is the windmill, which was usually located on a hill to catch all available winds.

In the eighteenth century the first attempt was made to apply the steam engine to turn a corn-mill, at the Albion Mill in London (1786), but it was not until the end of the century that this source of power was used on any large scale, and water wheels remained in general use right into the early years of the twentieth century. Attempts to use rollers instead of stones started during the late eighteenth century, but between 1833 and 1870 combined roller and stone-mills were used. The first all-roller mill was Radford's Albert Mill, Liverpool, of 1870. By that time the steam engine had divorced corn-mills from the necessity to be located on a stream, and newer mills were dominated by transport both for raw corn and for distribution of their products. Railways and canals were important, and as more and more corn was imported mills were built near the points of import. The new type of mill of a size beyond any previously built is typified by Vernon's, built at Liverpool on a valuable site on the margin of the largest dock, with a deep-water berth and the railway termini as well as the large grain warehouses alongside. This was designed to yield 12,000 sacks (280 lbs each) a week and became the prototype of the modern mill. Nonetheless, devoid of its machinery, this new mill would offer less evidence of corn-milling than many a small mill several centuries older.

Barley, which forms an important section of the crops grown in this country, is prepared in the mill for malting, not by grinding, but by husking, separating in such a way as to preserve the grains. Beer is a fermented infusion of malted barley, flavoured with hops, and its different varieties – ale, porter, stout, etc. – depend upon the differing flavours and colour of the malt used and the strength of the brew. The key to the brewing is thus in the malting, which is done in a *malthouse* or *oasthouse*. These are among the most distinctive buildings of the agricultural areas and adhere closely to type (Plate 11). Three processes are involved in making malt: the selected grain is steeped in large wood or stone cisterns; the steeped grain

[1] In some areas perforated cast iron plates were used with a coarse harden stretched over them.

is then spread on a wooden floor to germinate; at the correct stage the germination is stopped by drying in a kiln. The malthouse has thus three sections. The cistern house calls for no special comment. The *couching* house needs floors of large area on which the barley can be spread in a thin layer, and to save time and help production there may be three or four floors, each with barley started at a different time. The barley stays on the floor, being turned and moved, for a period which may be from nine to fourteen days, and as temperature and air regulation is essential each floor so used has numerous small window spaces filled with louvres or doors. This makes a very characteristic building. At one end of this is the kiln or kilns.

The *kiln* is tall, with a lower furnace room, a perforated floor above it on which the malt is dried, and then a high tapering building square, except in the oasthouses, where it is usually circular, rising high enough to secure the proper draught to carry the heat through the malt. The top of this has the large movable cowl and the attractive wind vane to keep its eye in the wind.

The *brewery* where the malt is used to make beer varies in its arrangement with its size. In the small public house, the country house, and even in some town houses, the *brewhouse* was generally no more than a range of cellars or, more commonly, a group of outhouses in the yard. The apparatus in these included tubs, a copper for boiling sufficient water, and a store for barrels. The commercial brewery was a large industrial building on which the processes involved in brewing tend to impose certain recognizable features. The two essentials, malt and water, usually start at the top of a building, with malt hoppers and water tanks. In most large breweries the water is pumped from a well or borehole, and as some waters are preferred to others, as getting better flavour or colour from hops and malt, there is a concentration of breweries, as at Burton-on-Trent where water is pumped from the Bunter Sandstone. Some of the older pumping engines are worth recording. With the development of railways the malthouses have moved alongside the breweries in the larger centres like Burton.

From the top floors of the brewery the malt passes through the crushing-mills to the mash tub, and the wort (liquor) can then run by gravity to the boiling and fermenting rooms, and then to the barrelling at ground floor. The typical brewhouse is thus tall and narrow, associated with a group of lower buildings which house extensive stores, stables, offices, and cooperage. The craft of the cooper is a very essential adjunct, as there are many vats and thousands of barrels to make and repair. Many smaller market town breweries date from about the end of the eighteenth and early nineteenth centuries, and the larger commercial ones from only a little later.

Related to the breweries but forming a distinct industry is that of the distilling trade. This trade began in the mid seventeenth century, but it was only in the early eighteenth century that it became really established. Its main apparatus was, of course, the still, and occasionally an old still and its condensers has survived. Most large distilleries are modern, or at least post-1880, and have little which can demand the attention of the industrial archaeologist. The coppersmith will be in evidence as a craftsman in all brewing and distilling centres.

Animal husbandry

A very large part of farming is devoted to animal husbandry, especially in the highland zone of the country where arable farming is minimal and where sheep and cattle account for the greater part of the work and produce of the farms. Nonetheless, in the arable areas horses and oxen were essential animals for transport and ploughing, and also for power, until displaced by the traction engine, the motor-car and lorry, or by electric power. Until the end of the Middle Ages the ox was the animal bred for and used in the plough; it was powerful, docile, its pace was suited to the job, and it worked well in a team. It was used in treading the corn in threshing, it could pull the cumbersome and heavy wains, and at the end of its life it provided meat (however poor the quality), hide, and bone. There is, however, little to record of the vast numbers and many generations of oxen other than documentary references. Ox-place-names are, however, very common, many villages having an Ox Pasture, and some towns such as Oxford, Oxton, Oxenhope, Oxborough, and so on recording for us the ford, farm, valley, town of oxen. Ox yokes, goads, shoes, and a few other incidentals have survived in museums but the principal memorials are documentary (Plate 12a).

The horse has a more varied history than the ox but it has left little for the industrial archaeologist beyond the stables which gave it accommodation, the harness and shoes it wore, the carts and machinery it moved, and the mills in which it worked. Its memorials are chiefly in the museums or in such monuments as the 'cross-over' bridges and tow paths built for its use on the canals. However much its history is a part of the story of industry it will stand in relation to it very much as do the nameless occupants of a fine 'weavers's cottage' or the forgeman of a seventeenth-century forge – we can record and preserve cottage and forge but the persons who made and used them are only names, known or unknown. Like the ox, the horse has left us an even greater abundance of place-names – Horse Close, Horsehead, Horse Pasture, and so on – and the reminder of his value in many horse fairs of great antiquity such as the Brough Hill Fair, still an exciting gathering of horse lovers and horse traders. In spite of his usefulness for over two thousand years, the horse has only an indirect place in industrial archaeology and a kind of important anonymity which can perhaps be expressed best in the words of Masefield:

> Into this barn horses have dragged corn
> Each summer for five hundred anxious years.
> Full many a hundred horse shoes have been worn
> To bright, thin streaks, upon the ash-pit hurled
> In homing harvest safe amidst these piers ;
> The old horse in the old barn stands forlorn,
> The warhorse of the war that saves the world.

Sheep

The sheep is probably the oldest domesticated animal used by man, and from the neolithic period onwards sheepfolds of one type or another are a commonplace of settlement sites. They all cater for the same needs – a place to gather, count, and check the flock or a place to shelter them. As the basic function has hardly changed, so the shapes and construction show little difference from age to age, except that some are near a stream with a dipping pool, and other modern ones have an artificial dipping trough. Every village community had a number of sheep on the commons and waste, and, as forests declined, sheep replaced pigs as the common grazing animal. The rapid rise in the wool trade in Tudor times brought a great increase in the flocks of sheep and the enclosure of some arable land for sheep pasture. In the late eighteenth century breeding and better feeding improved the sheep stock, first for more wool, then for meat. With all this long story, however, there is practically nothing for the industrial archaeologist to look at and to report.

The opposite, however, is the case with the industries to which sheep gave rise. The most important was the textile industry using the sheeps' wool, and part of the leather industry using the skin. Minor industries used the bones and tallow, and in the Middle Ages the ewes' milk was made into cheese. Later the flesh was used as meat. The main discussion will, therefore, centre on the industries which use the products of sheep and not on sheep husbandry itself.

Woollen textiles

Most Romano–British and Roman sites in this country provide evidence of textile manufacture in the number of spindle whorls, loom weights, weavers' combs[1] and other evidence of the spinning and weaving of cloth. In West Yorkshire there is still earlier evidence in the remains of a woollen garment or cloak wrapping a body in an Early Bronze Age burial, 1600–1400 B.C., the cloth being of worsted yarn which had been dyed. It is known that woollen cloaks made by the native population were a regular item of trade with the Romans.[2] The Romans had a cloth trade of their own, as there are sections for fulling cloth and for dyeing preserved in some of the villas. Cloth-making continued, as every community needed clothing, through the Dark Ages and the Norman period; and in the Poll Tax returns of 1379 several villages have a cloth-making colony, two or three weavers, a fuller and dyer – and in some of the towns the immigrant weavers are taxed with names based on their trade or origin, Peter Challoner (shalloon weaver) or John Brabaner (John of Brabant), and others who came over here to help improve our industry. The monasteries, particularly the Cistercians, were great flock masters and had by the end of the twelfth century developed a big wool export industry with Flanders and Italy. The most convincing evidence of this is their widespread sheep granges in the fells and such splendid buildings as the Cellarium at Fountains Abbey, made to hold their annual wool crop.

The rising wool trade was an affair of merchants feeding a great export organization, the Staple, and having little connection with the manufacture of cloth. The monasteries made the cloth requirements of their community by the labour of their lay brethren and tenants, and the common people did their own spinning and employed a travelling weaver as need arose. Clothes were made to last and were inherited from one

---

[1] Though not, so far, in the south-east.
[2] It has been suggested recently that weaving combs of the pre-Roman Iron Age may have been used for plucking sheep.

generation to the next. The first process in the cloth-making to break away from the cottage worker was that of *fulling* in the woollen section. Long staple wool was woven up into worsteds, but short wool made woollens. After weaving the woollens could only be made serviceable by a considerable pounding in water and a detergent, which got rid of grease and oil and felted the short woollen fibres together into a strong web. In the earlier centuries this was done by men trampling the cloth in tubs, the method of the Roman fullers. This process was 'walking' and gave us the surnames Walker, Fuller, and Tucker, and the name of the walk-mill or tucking-mill (fulling-mill).

It was this process of fulling that was the first to be mechanized. Fulling stocks operated by a water wheel were introduced in the thirteenth century from Italy. The stocks changed little until the nineteenth century, except in the refinement of detail, from the early types. These were falling stocks which, like the later ore stamps which may have copied them, had vertical shafts with wooden feet, lifted by nogs on a water wheel shaft, and let fall into a box containing the folded cloth in water and a detergent, fullers' earth. The second type of stocks had shafts with the wooden foot swinging like a pendulum on a horizontal shaft above the box for cloth, water and detergent, in such a way that the mallet, lifted by the nogs, swung down and hammered the cloth at the lowest point of the swing against the end of the box. These were called driving stocks. Some fulling stocks of the eighteenth century survive, and many mills which started as fulling-mills in the fourteenth or fifteenth centuries are incorporated in later structures.[1] Deep-cut green tracks and roads lead down to the fulling-mills, which usually served an area wider than the corn-mill, and were at or became a fording or bridge point on the stream. It is fairly common to find fulling-mill and corn-mill side by side, and even in some cases combined in a single structure.[2]

In the mid sixteenth century another process in cloth finishing was in part mechanized and transferred to the fulling mill – the raising of the nap on cloth. This had been done with teazels fixed on a hand frame with which the cloth was brushed. The *gig-mill* was a large drum with frames of teazels covering it and revolved from the same shaft and wheel as the

[1] In the sixteenth century the fulling processes became divided, the swinging stocks being mainly employed for scouring and cleaning new woven cloth. After drying and 'burling' (sewing in broken threads) it went back to the mill to be fulled in the falling stocks.
[2] This was the so-called 'double mill', fairly common in the North.

stocks, so that later fulling-mills may contain traces or remains of a gig-mill.

Until the second half of the eighteenth century all other processes in cloth manufacture were carried through by hand – cleaning, combing, or carding, spinning, weaving, and tentering the cloth – but they have left traces for the industrial archaeologist to hunt out and record. From the very source, the wool clipping, come the *shears*, little changed in form from those used by the Romans, and the *wool weights*. Those made of stone are the more common, usually cylindrical or perhaps tapering slightly upward. The base is flat, the top rounded with an iron ring leaded in for lifting. A number, and, rarely, a date may be carved on the side. More elaborate weights cast in lead or iron were flat, triangular, or shield-shaped, with a provision to be carried on a strap. These usually belonged to the merchant buyer and carried a device in decoration on one flat side. *Cards* and *combs* also changed little, and seventeenth-century examples are to be found, along with a few earlier ones, as evidence of the early wire industry as well as the early woollen trade. As in the case of salt, one of the most permanent evidences is the network of green tracks, used by the broggers as they went about collecting or taking out wool and yarn to and from a few special markets. These are especially abundant and well pre-served on the highland zone, as in the Pennines from Halifax, in the Lake District to Kendal, and in Wales.

While the bulk of the work was done in the cottage homes, a number of yeoman-clothiers emerged in the sixteenth and seventeenth centuries, having enough trade to employ a few men or apprentices in their own house. To them we owe many fine seventeenth-century buildings, and occasional groups of small cottages with a common loft where combing and weaving was done collectively. The feature of these buildings is still the 'weaving windows' – long mullioned windows in the top storey with many lights, five and more, even up to twelve in some cases – against which the handlooms were set. The spinning remained essentially a cot-tage occupation for the 'spinster' women. After weaving came the journeys to and from the fulling-mill, then the final process of tentering on the tenters near the weavers' homes. The *tenters* were parallel bars set with tenterhooks to hold the cloth by the selvage to dry and stretch.

The changes that turned woollens from a cottage occupation to a factory industry came slowly as news of the textile inventions in the cotton manu-factures in Lancashire spread across the Pennines to Halifax and Huddersfield. The first inventions to be adopted were Kay's flying shuttle and Hargreaves's 'spinning jenny' which in its earlier forms could be used in the cottage or in the weaving loft to keep up with the increased demands for yarn. In 1775, Arkwright had invented a carding machine, which was at first small enough to be hand operated. By 1780, the machine was sufficiently developed for the *scribbling-mill* to appear. This was a small mill with water-wheel drive, where the wool was first *carded* then *slubbed* and wound on cops[1] ready for the weaver. The remains of scribbling-mills are to be found in many of the upland streams in the woollen area (Plate 20a). Where mills are found in the lower courses the ingenuity and patience of the industrial archaeologist will be taxed before he can disentangle corn-, fulling-, and slubbing-mills, particularly as a few examples have been all three in turn, and some larger ones have housed more than one process at the same time in different sections.[2]

These combined fulling- and scribbling-mills are the points about which the final mechanization grew. The first steam engines were brought to them (1794) to supplement water wheels, which were becoming overloaded and failing in dry seasons. Warehouses were added to several of them. As the other cotton inventions in Lancashire became known, power looms were adopted and the steam engine freed the new mills from the inadequate streams. The movement was generally into the main valleys along the canals, which could now offer transport for coal and goods and water for the engines and processes. By the early years of the nineteenth century the steam-driven factories (mills) housing many processes were appearing, and rapidly became the normal pattern of the new textile industry. The small water-powered mills were slowly abandoned and should be recorded, with their water-power complex and the tracks and early bridges so intimately associated with them.

Changes in agriculture and mining started the immigration of rural populations towards the factories and the towns which grew up to accom-

[1] The loose wool from the carding machine was joined into a continuous thin rope by children called 'pieceners'. This was then fed to the Slubbing Billy, which stretched it and gave it a slight twist so that about eight inches of cardings became about seventy inches of rough yarn. This was wound in large balls called 'cops', or bobbins, ready for the spinner.
[2] For example, in 1786, Little John Mill in Brighouse was leased as a 'fulling mill, scribbling and carding mill'. By 1828, it had become a wire-mill. Brighouse Lower Mills were sold in 1816 and were listed as 'all those powerful and valuable Fulling and Scribbling Mills'. They had three water wheels, seven double falling stocks, three double and one single driver swinging stocks for the purpose of fulling cloth; also seventy inches of cards for scribbling and carding wool. Eight blocks for wire emphasize the dependence of cards and combs on wire works.

modate both the population and the ever-increasing mills. In recording the growth of the textile industry it must always be kept in mind that we are also recording the transformation of a rural population, with roots in the soil and the countryside, into a population whose new generations were to be brought up in a new and strange environment, that of the town and the mill. These changes in human environment must be recorded with as much care as is given to the changing processes and to the machinery and transport.

Cattle

Cattle, like sheep, were domesticated certainly by the neolithic revolution, and Iron Age man had become a herdsman as well as a shepherd. Meat, milk, and hides were an important part of the economy when the Romans arrived in the country, but as the Roman troops were largely vegetarian their towns and forts have little provision for cattle and their requirements of leather were met by the native population. These requirements were large, for the soldiers wore leather jerkins and breeches, and their boots, tents, and shield covers were also of leather. Of the carcass only lard was wanted by the Romans. Through the Dark Ages and medieval period the position of cattle in agriculture was much inferior to that of sheep, and even for milk and cheese the ewes were used.

A change came in the status of cattle when scientific breeding and winter feeding almost coincided with a rapid growth of population in the south and a demand for meat which the southern farms, mainly arable, could not satisfy. In Scotland cattle breeding had been more dominant than in England, and by the opening of the seventeenth century the country was a reservoir of stock with a moderate export trade to Flanders, both in barrelled beef and skins. The Borders with England, because of the raiding that went on across them, were a wild and unsettled country. After the Union and particularly in the mid eighteenth century much of the Scottish cattle was diverted to the English markets, along the great drove roads crossing the lowlands and southern uplands from the great cattle Trysts at Falkirk and coming down to big cattle fairs in England. Besides meat, the hides were of value to the leather industry and many tanneries and associated trades developed around this greatly increasing cattle trade.

Leather

The tanning of hides to make leather is a very ancient craft, and was practised by the Celts to supply Roman demands. Most early leather was made by drying or salting skins, but by post-Conquest times oak bark was being used on cattle skins, and alum and oil on the skins of horses, deer, and sheep. Tanners were given a monopoly right to purchase hides in the markets, so that it was natural for the leather industry to settle in the principal market towns, where it may be a very old established trade. Indeed, the 1579 Poll Tax returns show leather workers in most towns which had cattle markets or fairs. Tanning took a good amount of water, and so the older tanneries are near streams, rivers, or wells. The amount of oak bark needed led to an actual trade in getting, drying, and grinding bark.

In the tannery the first requirement was a large number of vats. The tannery at Mieux Abbey in 1396 used fifteen of them, and a commercial tannery usually had many more. By the seventeenth century the vats had mostly been replaced by stone-lined pits occupying a large 'tan yard'. These were permanent and some still remain. Hides to be dressed for the best leather (for shoe soles and uppers) were always from cattle. They were first soaked a few days in a pit of milk of lime, then washed until all trace of lime was removed. This softened the skin and the hair and much of the fat was then scraped off with a two handled tool like a large, blunt spokeshave, the hide being laid over a convex sloping board, the beam. The scrapings went to the plasterers and tallow-makers. After two or more days in a very dilute sulphuric acid to open the pores, they started their long progression through the pits of bark liquor. The first pit has weak, almost spent liquor, but successive pits were stronger until at the last the hides were piled with fresh powdered bark between them, in a strong infusion of bark. At each pit the hides were regularly moved about and turned. The whole passage took about a year, so, to keep up a reasonable output, several sets of pits were needed. Alongside the pits was a wide flagged area on to which the hides could be dragged to drain or handle, and so a set of tan pits provided a very unique and durable structure. When the tanning was at last completed, the skins were hung in sheds to be dried by the circulating air, and when dried they were passed to the currier.

The currier treats the rough tanned hide by soaking and shaving with keen knives of special form, to reduce it to an even desired thickness. After drying, the leather is impregnated with tallow or oil. Surplus grease is again removed and the leather squeezed, rolled, or subject to other treatment to secure the toughness or flexibility needed for its intended use. There are other methods used in tanning skins other than those of cattle,

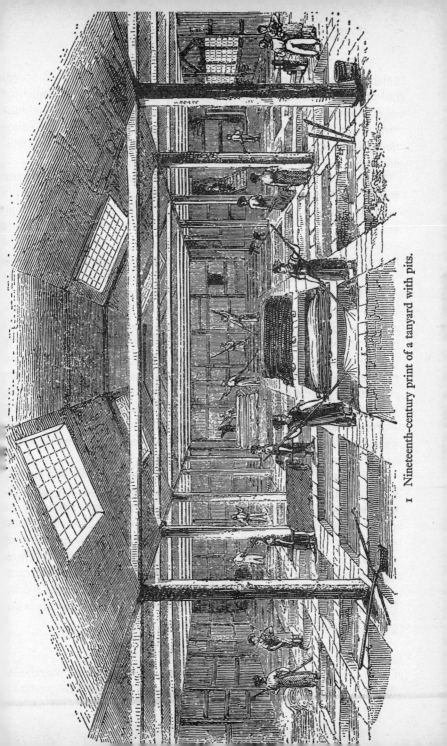

1 Nineteenth-century print of a tanyard with pits.

most of them taking much less time, and using vats, not stone pits. It will be obvious that the tanning of ordinary leather offers little scope for mechanization. Machinery has been introduced on the currying, for thinning and splitting skins, and many different processes have been introduced for making fancy leathers from unusual skins, even of fish, lizards, and so on.

Both tanning and currying need a large accommodation for drying and this is generally provided in one or two storeys above or around the tan yard. The drying rooms are long and narrow with a large area of the long walls made up of louvres to allow maximum air circulation. These are generally large and almost continuous, easily distinguished from the louvres of a malting floor, which are smaller, like ordinary windows, louvres replacing the glass.

Industries based upon leather tend to be in the nature of crafts, the best known of which are those of the shoemaker and the saddler and harness-maker. Until the later part of the nineteenth century these have been the trades of the individual skilled craftsman, working in his own shop, or perhaps in twos and threes, leaving no special structure, and with only his methods and his tools to be recorded. These crafts are eminently the subjects for the craft museum, where a whole workshop is a suitable subject for reconstruction. When shoemaking, saddlery and other leather working trades were mechanized and moved into the factory they really passed out of the sphere of the industrial archaeologist into that of the industrial and technical historian.

Besides leather, cattle have provided other raw materials, though none has given rise to very distinctive buildings or apparatus. Fat from the slaughterhouse and the tannery has been boiled down and refined by the tallow refiner, who was usually at the same time the candle-maker. Bones have been used and treated for the preparation of glycerine, phosphorus, bone-meal manures, and for various objects such as buttons and knife handles. Horn was long used for drinking vessels, scraped thin for lantern windows, or made into spoons, snuff boxes, and other small objects. Again the use of horn was largely the work of craftsmen and their tools and products will be preserved in most museums.

Milk

Cows, sheep, and goats have always been valued for their milk, though from the Tudor period onward in this country the cow has become the animal bred for milk production. The chief milk products are still butter and cheese, and they were important as early as the twelfth century, when many monastic farm accounts show substantial weights of them sent with great regularity to the parent community. At the Kilnsey Grange of Fountains Abbey, with its huge flocks of a few thousand sheep, cows were kept to supply milk for the lambs, so that the more prized ewes' milk could be reserved for butter and cheese-making. It was in the seventeenth century that cows' milk became the principle raw material for cheese.

Cheese- and butter-making have left more visible remains than most farm crafts. In the house there is the dairy, with its long slate or flag shelf with the holes in which the 'leads' stand. These are the large bowls, once of lead, in which the milk stands until the cream rises. Skimmers and other utensils are still seen in the house, and in the dairy a churn, occasionally a dash churn or an early rotary. The large pans, and the massive presses for making the cheeses, are still numerous, but are essentially material for the museum. Cheese factories are a creation largely of this century, and except for their vats and other equipment they differ little from any other small factory.

Special plants

Flax has been grown for the fibres it yields for linen textiles as well as for linseed oil. The preparation of the fibres does not involve any complicated process. The whole stem has a woody centre around which the fibres are ranged, held by a resinous substance. This has to be got rid of and the fibres separated and cleaned from the woody part of the stem. The first is done by retting. This is steeping in water long enough to allow some fermentation of the resinous part, and its removal. *Hemp* has been grown, but not to the same extent, for its fibre, which is coarser and stronger and is used for ropes, sailcloth, harden and sacking, and for some of the rougher hard-wearing cloths for working clothes. Most hemp, however, has been imported, but nonetheless it is the basic raw material of an important industry.

The complete retting of flax may take a few weeks and creates an offensive smell as well as polluting the streams in which it was practised, so that in many villages where flax was grown bylaws in the seventeenth century compelled the regulated use of troughs. Stone troughs four or five feet long, two feet wide or so, and up to two feet deep were made in the grit areas, and many of these are still to be found, usually moved into some large garden or stable yard. After retting, the flax stems were tied in bundles, dried, and then scutched. The seed was removed usually before, but sometimes after, the retting, and the oil extracted in a press, the residue being oilcake, a very valuable cattle food. The scutching bruises the stems and breaks the woody part so that the fibres can be properly separated. About the middle of the eighteenth century scutching machines came into use and *scutching-mills* with water-wheel power were built, this development taking place in Scotland and being spread from there into northern Ireland and later into England. The scutching produces long fibres for spinning and a proportion of very short, broken fibres called *tow*. These are separated by hackling, a process similar to wool combing. Both the long fibre, called line, and the tow are spun and then woven, the line producing the best-quality linen. There were many difficulties in spinning line by machinery, not really solved until Marshall of Leeds built his model mills in 1788, and used steam power. The introduction of power looms was later than in cotton and wool, due to difficulties arising from line being less elastic and more easily broken in the weaving. After weaving, the chief remaining process was bleaching, little different from that applied to other cloths, particularly after the introduction of bleaching powder and chemical bleaching in 1785.

Hemp was never grown to the same extent as flax but was imported. Its treatment was similar to that of flax but its coarser fibre was used in making sacking and the coarser linen known as huckaback. Much hemp was used in rope-making and this industry has left its very distinct remains in many places. The great length needed for spinning and laying rope gave us the *rope walks*, which can often be recognized even if their usage is altered. The hemp industry eventually concentrated around Dundee, where another industry – the manufacture of jute – arose from it. Linen spinning and weaving were well established in and around Dundee, with forty mills in the town by 1825 and with power looms adopted for weaving by 1840. The linen was displaced by jute in the second half of the century.

Jute is harsher than flax, but its treatment is approximately the same, and it is woven up for sheeting, sacking, carpets and rugs, and other coarse fabrics. Another industry was introduced in the mid nineteenth century when *linoleum* was first made. With the great expansion of small housing in the industrial towns this soon became a major industry round Kirk-caldy. The linoleum is a cement of linseed oil, resins, and cork, keyed onto a foundation of jute canvas, while its companion product, *floorcloth* or *oilcloth*, is a tough cloth made from the linen tow, sized, and printed. All these industries involve large mills, but like all the textile mills there is little but the machinery they house to differentiate them one from another.

Jute was an imported crop from India on which substantial industries were based, and the same is true of *cotton*, never grown in this country but giving rise to a vast sector of the textile industry. In small quantity cotton was imported from Cyprus and the Levant in the sixteenth century, but it was not until the second half of the seventeenth century that the manu-facture of cotton materials was recognizable as an industry with some potential for growth. It was at first largely concerned with the making of fustians. In 1733, Kay of Bury, Lancashire, had invented a flying shuttle which speeded up weaving. This at first found more users among the Yorkshire woollen weavers than it did in Lancashire. It soon created a crisis by the spinners' inability to keep pace with the new demands for yarn. The great mechanical inventions which changed the whole industry followed: in 1765 Hargreaves's 'spinning jenny'; in 1769 Arkwright's 'water-frame'; and in 1774 Crompton's 'mule' spinning frame. The power loom followed in 1796.

These various inventions transformed cotton from a cottage industry to a factory occupation dependent upon power, at first that of water wheels and later of the steam engine. The succession from small water-powered mills in the higher streams of the Pennines to the steam-driven mills set along the lowland canals is paralleled on both sides of the Pennines in cotton and wool, and offers a rich field for the industrial archaeologist to work at. The development of the very recognizable cotton-mills of the nineteenth-century boom years, the great weaving sheds with top lighting, and the equally architectural woollen mills and warehouses, form an important chapter in the architectural history of industry. The developing complexity of textile machinery takes it out of the range of the industrial archaeologist into that of the engineer and technician by the middle of the nineteenth century. It is with this era of large mills that the major period of industrial housing is associated, and neither can be profitably studied without the other.

The last process in much of the textile trade is that of *dyeing and finishing* the cloth. Some wool is dyed in the yarn before weaving for complex patterns, and for knitting wools. The finishing may include a final cleaning, raising a nap, smoothing, folding, and everything necessary to prepare it for the market. Dyeing, before the introduction of the coal-tar and synthesized dyes, was based on the use of special plants. Generally the colours were duller and less 'fast' – that is, they were liable to fade with age and sunshine. The principal plants were woad, madder, went, and weld, all grown to some extent in this country, and, later, indigo and some dye woods among which the most used was logwood, all of them imported.

Woad is known to everyone by name, for classical writers claimed that the natives of Britain stained themselves blue (though some say green, and others black) with woad and went naked. It is more likely that the blue woollen cloaks which some of the natives traded with the Romans were dyed with woad. Woad was cultivated as a crop, then needed much preparation. The plant (*Isatis tinctoria*) was stripped of its leaves, which were reduced to a pulp in an edge-mill. Two or three rollers travelled round the bed of the mill, each pulled by a horse. The rollers were sometimes of stone, between four and five feet in diameter, with deep, sharp-edged grooves cut across the edge. Other woad rollers were made of two large timber wheels connected by close-set iron bars two or three inches square with similar spacing, set parallel to the wheel axis, at right-angles to the trough in which they ran. These wheels cut up the leaves and reduced them to pulp. The pulp was made up, by hand, into balls not more than four inches in diameter. These were carried to tall stacks of slatted racks in an open shed, so that air could have free circulation among them. When the balls were dried and hard they were sold in this state to the dyer. The balls were broken up with wooden hammers, put in heaps, wetted and allowed to ferment. When dry again it was pounded and sieved and then was ready for use. The most characteristic remains of the woad industry are the special edge rollers of the mill, and, more rarely, the remains of the drying houses.

Madder (*Rubia tinctorium. L.*) was well known in India and the Near East, from early times, as a red dye. It was brought to Europe as roots in which the dye is found, but in the sixteenth century the plant was brought to Holland and in the mid seventeenth century it began to be cultivated in France. It was also grown in parts of Britain but in the later nineteenth century it became cheaper to import it and its cultivation died out. The madder root is boiled in the dyeing vat with a calcareous water. There is no process in the growing and preparation of madder which is likely to have left tangible remains, so its history will be almost entirely documentary.

Went and *weld* are the Dyers' Green-weed (*Genista tinctoria*) and Dyers' Rocket (*Reseda luteola*); both are important yellow dyes, the weld being largely used with indigo to make a green dye. *Indigo* was imported from India, being derived from a whole group of Asiatic plants. It was introduced in Europe in quantity about the middle of the seventeenth century. The indigo gave a brighter and faster colour than woad, and so gradually replaced it. Woad, however, was still used in combination with indigo for promoting fermentation in the indigo-woad vat, and its preparation, though now on a minute scale, is not yet extinct. While these dyes, except woad, left little in the way of distinctive structures or apparatus, another dye, *logwood*, imported from America, was treated in the special mills made for its preparation. It came into use for a black dye about the mid seventeenth century. It was imported in logs, about three feet long, which were cut from a tree which grew to thirty or forty feet. The bark and outer wood were stripped where it was grown and the logs were selected from the heart wood. In the mill the log was fed against a set of rotating blades, which cut it into small chips or reduced it to very coarse small pieces by a rasping action. After proper drying the chips were ground to powder in an edge-mill under grit millstones about four feet in diameter. The power was usually provided by a water wheel. The last logwood-mills only finished working within the last ten years. Other kinds of dyewood were also treated, so that some mills had two or more sets of edge stones.

The *dyehouse* in which cloth was dyed was a fairly distinctive building. At first and for a long time it was built near the head of a stream, as it required a soft and pure water, though not in the great quantity taken by the wheel of a scribbling-mill. The dyehouse needs only one storey and its work is mostly carried out in a series of large vats standing on a flagged floor. There are one or more 'coppers' for heating water, and some accommodation for drying dyed cloth and yarn. Some of the vats may be stone troughs built in the floor. The roof usually had a row of large ventilators. A grinding-mill was used in some dyehouses where logwood chips were ground, and many of these were horse-mills. Recording an early dyehouse is often easier than deciding what some other textile buildings have been.

Paper-making is linked with the textile industries through its principal raw material (until recently), rags. The earliest and best papers consisted of a web of pulped linen fibres, sized and pressed together in thin sheets. As the trade increased, other materials – cotton, woollen, silk, and other rags, and more recently wood pulp (cellulose fibre) – have been used, along with straw and other cellulose wastes. The process is in theory very simple but demands considerable skill of its operatives. Selected rags are cleaned and shredded in machines with armed rollers, or beaten to shreds and pulp by hammers very like those of the fulling stocks. A water wheel was the common source of power. The pulp is usually bleached at an early stage and, if necessary, given a second pulping. This pulp is filled into vats, brought to the proper consistency by adding water, and then, in hand-made papers, the maker dips a frame with a base of fine wire mesh or gauze into the tub, and lifts it out full of pulp. After shaking and draining over the vat, the web of fibres left on the wire is turned off onto a sheet of felt. The felts and paper webs are subject to great pressure in a press, then dried and pressed again without the felts. The sheets of paper are finally dipped in size[1] and squeezed and dried again. They are given a finished surface by pressing between copper plates or rollers. The rollers and pulping machines need power, but nothing else will leave any special trace. The mechanization of paper-making in the nineteenth century was achieved by the introduction of a continuous machine which followed all the hand processes in due order. The new feature was a continuous wire web onto which pulp was spread. Successive squeezings, rollings, and the sizings followed in the same train, and the paper then went through a continuous drying section. This produces a continuous roll of paper which has then to be cut to the various desired sheets. The greatest change has come with the incredible demand of newspapers for newsprint. This could only be supplied by turning to the use of woodpulp drawn from the major forests of the world. The many kinds of paper available make little difference to the maker, the processes for all being very similar.

Oils, fats, and waxes are remaining products of agriculture which were handled in many small industries. The pressing and processing of oils and nuts has now become an important part of many of the modern food industries, such as the margarine industry, nut oils and nut butters, cooking oils and special preparations. From the animal fats some cooking fats

[1] A gelatinous solution used to stiffen textiles or paper, etc.

are made, but the bulk goes to the tallow refiner, the soap boiler, and the candle-maker. Wax goes into candles and polishes. Only the soap boiler, and possibly the candle maker, carries on a self-contained industry.

Soap is essentially a potash or soda salt of one of the stearine group of fatty substances. Fats or oils are treated with a caustic lye, either soda or potash, and other additives, and after boiling a soap is formed which can be put into moulds to set. Soda makes hard (bar) soaps and potash produces soft soaps. There is very wide variety in the type and quality of soap that can be produced, but all are made with the mixing and boiling vats as the principal apparatus. We are left again with an industry that leaves few identifiable structures, or which, in its modern form, is absorbed within a great complex of chemical processes and plant outside the scope of the industrial archaeologist.

CHAPTER 7

Power and Fuel

The two inanimate things which were to give man a degree of mastery over his environment and make industry eventually possible were fire and mechanical power. Tools were made by primitive man to extend the effectiveness of his hands and to arm them to accomplish desirable tasks which were otherwise beyond his strength. The hand armed with a stone axe was capable of cutting down a tree which its strength alone could not uproot. A stone pounder could crush, break, or shape another stone. Tools augmented muscular power and machines applied power to advantage. The discovery of the wheel along with the power of the lever and wedge held out all the promise and potential of our present age of mechanisms. Fire gave to man another range of power which enabled him to change the character and properties of the natural materials around him, and even to create new properties in them. Fire could loose the metals from their ores; change plastic clay to rigid pot; soften metals until they could be shaped and moulded; foods could be cooked and made more palatable. Water could be turned to steam and more and more complex processes could be achieved through the application of fire. For these reasons, in a scheme of industrial archaeology, a section on power and fuel would seem to follow naturally the studies of raw materials.

Mechanical power is essentially the capacity to move things – to shift a large weight, to move a cart or a ship, to rotate a grindstone, to energize a machine – these effects are all achieved by the expenditure of energy, which must be directed from some natural source and applied and controlled for the task in hand. The natural energies available to man are those of his muscles and the muscles of other animals, the pull of gravity whether in a falling object or the pulsing ocean tide, the energy of the wind and of moving water. More sophisticated energies are those of solar heat, the expansive power of steam and gases, of chemical changes, of lightning and electricity, and the more esoteric energy stored in the atomic structure of matter. Man's material progress has been tied to a steady recognition and harnessing of these sources of energy.

Very simple mechanisms were discovered at an early stage in man's development. The appreciation of the lever is seen in the Egyptian balance of the mid fourth millennium B.C., which also initiated precise measurement; the shaduf, lifting water from Egyptian wells, was employing the same lever, as were also the oar-propelled boats. Wheels had been attached to a sledge before 3500 B.C. and by the third century B.C. the many-spoked wheel was being made up to six feet in diameter. The modifications which turned the wheel into a pulley or a windlass during the first millennium B.C. was only one of the further mechanical advances which were available to the Romans and which made their achievements in engineering and construction possible. The steps from using these simple machines which could be hand operated to seeking an external power which could do the work were not long delayed. The hand quern was made larger and more efficient, and in Pompeii and Rome it was arranged to be turned by a horse or a donkey, thus creating a *mill*. The windlass and capstan were moved by men, and though the capstan became a horse machine in the form of the whim, the foot-mill (horizontal tread-mill) remained a man-driven machine into the sixteenth century. Of these inventions at least the hand quern, the lever, and the roller were known to the natives of this country before the end of the neolithic period, and the wheeled chariot was brought by the Iron Age invaders.

The muscular power of the horse or ox has been used in direct pulling ever since the invention of the sledge, the wheeled cart, and the plough and has remained an important part of our transport systems until the recent decades of this century. Industries like brewing, with a constant and large delivery of its products over a local area, usually have large stabling accommodation connected with them, and this was particularly so in the Victorian period when the use of, and pride in, horses was probably at its peak. Some of the stable blocks achieved considerable architectural merit. The shoeing smith, the harness-maker and the wheelwright were all tied to the service of the horse as much as were the horsekeeper and stable hands. These occupations make a tight network over the whole industrial transport scene and will be better studied as part of such a complex, the connecting strands of which are the roads, rather than being looked at in isolation.

The *horse-mill* appears to have been introduced into Europe before the sixteenth century, at which time the horse whim for hoisting ore and working pumps was in wide use on the mines in Saxony and was used by the German miners in this country. The common principle of the horse-mill is that of the whim – the horse walking round a circular track rotates a central vertical axle by means of a radial connecting pole. To the shaft or pole, apparatus is connected and so is turned by the horse. There are three important types; in one the central vertical axle is keyed into gears which transmit the rotation to a horizontal shaft which can convey motion to machines at a distance. This is seen in most farm horse-mills which turn threshing machines, churns, turnip choppers, or such in a barn against the outside of which the mill is built. This horse drive was also used in some early corn-mills and other grinding-mills.

In the second type a large winding drum is mounted on the vertical shaft, as on a capstan, and this constitutes a *whim* used in mine winding, pile driving, or some forms of crane.

In the third type the radial arm is itself an axis on which one or two large wheels revolve, their edge running on a circular track or in a trough. Simple examples of this type are seen in the small ore-crushing-mills, remains of which are found on some of the Derbyshire lead mines. In these one arm extends from the centre pivot to the horse gear and has an edge-running wheel, three or four feet in diameter and several inches broad, iron-bound, revolving on it and running on a track of heavy flags. These single-wheel mills had many other uses and are widespread (Plate 126). Small ones with a nicely carved circular stone trough were used for bruising gorse for cattle food, for cider making, for bark and logwood grinding in tanneries and dyehouses. The larger mills are worked by two horses and have a cross arm with a horse at each end, and two much heavier wheels. The woad-mill has already been described, and the modern mortar-mill (now almost extinct) is an example of the 'mechanized' mixing-mill. Gunpowder-mills use this type of two-wheel mixing-mill adapted to a special job and with a special remote drive arrangement.

There are many varieties of these mills and a detailed survey of an area will usually reveal the remains of examples, large and small, mainly nine-teenth-century, and often found on farms. In the later examples cast-iron gears and shafts often have the founder's name cast on them and a search in directories should then give a fairly close date for the mill or its renewal. A few of the earliest textile-mills used the horse whim with transmission gear to drive the spinning jennies, but they were displaced by water wheels which soon gave their name to Arkwright's water frame.

Wind power

The next natural power which we can consider is that of the wind. The earliest use of this is the direct thrust of the wind on the sails of a boat, but the use of wind power in industry is limited to its employment through windmills. The windmill was more restricted in its usage and distribution than the horse-mill but draws attention by its attractive and even romantic appearance. Originating in the East and eventually coming to Europe via the trade routes, it seems to have come to England from Holland, some two centuries or more after the Conquest. There are drawings of a wind-mill among the scenes depicted in the Luttrell Psalter which was made between 1320 and 1340. In 1434, at Tivetshall, Norfolk, a carpenter con-tracted to build a new windmill in four months and to have for his work the materials of the old mill, nine and a half marks, and a gown.

There were only two types of windmill before the introduction from America, about 1850, of the multi-vaned, all-metal wheel seen on so many farms and isolated houses. The older types were the post-mill and the tower-mill. The *post-mill* is merely a rectangular housing for the stones with the driving shaft from the sails at the top of the mill and its necessary train of gears. The whole is balanced and pivoted on a vertical pole in the centre and usually has a long tail pole out at the back, reaching to the ground a short distance away. This allowed the whole mill to be turned when it was necessary to bring its sails into the wind (Plate 13). The centre pole is generally set on two cross beams making a crossed foundation, or the ends of the beams rest on four solid blocks of stone or brick, which with the turning ring are good evidence of the former existence of such a mill. The *tower-mill* has a rigid structure of stone, or brick, or timber, to house the stones and all machinery and gears, with the driving shaft, at the end of which are the sails, accommodated in a cap or attic storey which can revolve on a track set on the top of the tower walls. In later mills there will be a vane and wheel opposite to the sails, to secure the movement on the track so that the sails always face the wind. It is usually the shaft or tower of this type of mill which survives, and some have been preserved by being adapted as dwelling houses after the machinery has been removed. Most of the remaining mills are not earlier than the eighteenth century, but fortunately several have been preserved and some of them are in full working order.

Among survivals some older mills retain part or all of their wooden gear. This is always of interest and some of the larger wheels, the driving and the wallower wheel, an occasional lantern, and even a bevel wheel are superb examples of the wheelwright's craft. The interior of a mill offers the photographer many dramatic subjects.[1] The distribution of windmills is not uniform, the great majority being found in the eastern lowland zones, where the country is too flat and the streams too sluggish to attract the water-mill.

A few windmills of the tower type and practically all of the American multi-vane type have been used for pumping from relatively shallow wells and drains, and the newer ones with their crowded metal wheel on a spidery steel tower are a common sight around more scattered farms.

Water power

The water-driven mill is of greater antiquity and has far wider and more varied uses than the windmill, and may occur in almost any district. Watermills were used by the Romans and through the Dark Ages, so that at the time of the Domesday Survey more than five thousand mills were recorded. Through the following centuries water wheels were the prime source of power until the coming of the steam engine, and through the nineteenth century they remained in common use, with a few still working today. The industrial archaeologist must, therefore, be prepared to recognize and record the evidence of water wheels from any historic period and in connection with any industry.

Water wheels operate on three main principles:

(*a*) those with a horizontal wheel and vertical shaft in which water impinges on radial blades or vanes on the wheel and pushes it round by the velocity and volume of the striking water. These are *impulse* wheels. These wheels in general were early, primitive, and small, and some remain today in the Hebrides. In the eighteenth and nineteenth centuries and to the present the principle has been developed and has given rise to *impulse and reaction* wheels and turbines, among which are some at work in the largest hydro-electric power stations in the world.

[1] The books and papers of Rex Wailes, especially the exciting book, *Windmills in England*, 1948, by Rex Wailes, provide a complete guide to windmills.

(b) the plane of the *undershot* wheel was vertical with its axle horizontal. Boards or blades set radially on the circumference dipped into a running stream in the lowest part of the wheel's revolution, and were pushed by the running water, giving a turning moment proportional to the push on the area of blades submerged, the push of the stream and the effective radius of the wheel. These were in general use by the Romans and were most effective where a swift, large-volume stream was available.

(c) the wheel which was to become the general and most efficient type was the one described as *overshot*. These came into use in the twelfth and thirteenth centuries and their characteristic is that water is led quietly to the top of the wheel where it fills shaped compartments made by the blades in such a way as to hold the water for about a third of the revolution before it is dropped out into the stream. It is the attraction of gravity on the mass of water held in the 'buckets' which provides the greater part of the turning power. There have been many modifications in the position on the wheel circumference at which the buckets are filled, and in the shape and construction of the buckets, but the wheels remain essentially a gravity machine. There are many advantages other than purely mechanical. One is that the wheel is no longer bound to a stream, but is best operated from a dam which can store water brought to it, sometimes over long distances by a watercourse or leat, and that water can then be turned onto the wheel only when wanted, and can be regulated in quantity. The velocity of the stream has no significance for the wheel, the size of the dam can compensate for a stream of small volume, and its storage can also keep the wheel turning in a dry period (Plate 14a).

On rivers it was the custom from at least the thirteenth century to establish mills on the banks and to get a head of water for the wheel; a dam was built across the river, often on a longish slant, with a watercourse from it to the top of the wheel. As the dams were an obstruction to any form of navigation they were the subject of very frequent quarrels, and much detail about them, their history and construction, can be had from proceedings in the various courts. In the attempts to improve river navigation these old-established mill dams were one of the greatest problems.

Most wheels have now disappeared but much can be deduced from the pit in which the wheel worked, and from the dam and the watercourses that fed it. The ordinary overshot wheel ran with its lower half in a shaped pit with the bearings of its axle on the sides, so that in a way, allowing for some clearance, the pit is a cast of half the wheel – its length and breadth, less nine inches or a foot, will be the diameter and breadth of the wheel. As the water is in open buckets on the circumference of the wheel, too quick a speed of rotation would throw it out by centrifugal force. To work at its best and not to lose water the velocity of the rim of a wheel should not exceed twice the square root of its radius. Thus a wheel ten feet in diameter would have its rim velocity four and a half feet per second (to the nearest reasonable fraction). As the circumference will be about thirty-two feet, it should only make about eight revolutions a minute for maximum efficiency. A wheel of forty-five feet diameter would make only about four revolutions a minute. The water should come onto the buckets at half the speed of the wheel, so the size and depth of water in the goit along with the rim velocity will allow the amount of water per minute to be calculated, and therefore the power of the wheel can be obtained to a reasonable approximation.

The relatively slow motion of large wheels, ideal for pumping, demands the interposition of multiplying gears if they are to drive, say, textile machinery.[1] The drive was taken either from a spur wheel on the shaft, or, in later wheels, from a gear circle on the wheel spokes or rim, and this drive position will be seen, in the absence of the wheel, by the position of holes for shaft journals in the building wall against the wheel. This rather lengthy explanation is meant only to emphasize that more precise details can be had from the remains of a wheelpit and its goit than from almost any other industrial remains (Plate 14b).

The breast wheel is a late improvement in which water was fed on to the wheel at a small height above the horizontal diameter, and the wheel ran in a fairly close case which retained water in the buckets to a lower point in the turn. The major work on wheel efficiency and design was done by the engineers Smeaton in 1752 and Fairbairn, and is summarized in a work which should be the handbook of all industrial archaeologists interested in the mills of the nineteenth century.[2]

In the early days of the steam engine it was not infrequently the practice to use a steam engine to pump water from a mine and use the water on a water wheel for the winding. Another common arrangement was that used at Coalbrookdale Furnace where the bellows were moved by water wheels and a steam engine pumped the tail water back to the dam for re-use, thus increasing the value of a rather small supply.

During the nineteenth century the *water turbine* was invented,[1] in which the reaction of a jet of high-pressure water was the turning power. This gave the means of very much higher powers and speeds than the largest wheels could supply. There have been many advances in turbine design, and the Pelton wheel, a high-pressure wheel with a jet of water striking on curved buckets, and these combined to produce the high-speed turbines of the modern hydro-electric stations of many thousands of horsepower. Some of the modern turbines have a vertical shaft, and approach as much as 150,000 horsepower, compared with a probable maximum of 250 horsepower for the largest water wheels of between fifty and seventy feet in diameter.

Hydraulic engines

During the eighteenth century an invention for the use of water power, which became of great importance in metalliferous mining, was that of the hydraulic engine. The familiar elements of the steam engine – cylinder, piston, and valves – were retained, but high-pressure water was used instead of steam. In many mines a drainage adit driven from the lowest available level in a nearby valley left a large part of the mine below that level undrained. If water could be diverted to the top of a shaft which intersected the adit, then a pipe could carry the water to a hydraulic engine at the adit level and would have the pressure due to the depth from the surface. Such an engine worked pumps to lift water from the lower level to the adit. The first such engine was made by Westgarth Forster on the Allendale mines in 1765. They were applied in many mines both for pumping and for winding on underground shafts. There was no cost of fuel in raising steam, and the engines, which were very robust, required the minimum maintenance – indeed, some ran for several years, unattended. Several remain underground but are often reached only by difficult and dangerous access.[2]

A machine related to the hydraulic engine so far as it involves cylinders

[1] In 1827, in France.
[2] One has been fully recorded and described, that in the Sir Francis level, Swaledale: *The Engineer*, XLIV, 1880, and *Proc. Inst. Mech. Engineers*, Apl. 1880, and also *Northern Cavern and Mine Research Soc. Memoirs*, 1966, pp. 21–8, Plates 5–10.

and pistons is the Bramah press, widely used in industry in the nineteenth century. This was based upon the fact that the pressure in a liquid is the same in all directions. Bramah in 1796 patented an arrangement of a high-pressure pump with a piston of small diameter and connected this with another cylinder of far greater diameter. The same pressure was exerted on each square inch of the large piston as was by each square inch of the much smaller pump piston. In this way the effective 'lift' of the large piston could be many hundred times the pressure of the small pump, though the distance moved would be less in proportion. For baling wool, for compressing all sorts of materials for packing, and for heavy forgings requiring pressures of several thousand tons, this press was an invaluable tool.

Steam

Although Hero of Alexandria about 150 B.C. had made an aeolipile which involved the principle of the reaction steam turbine, the real invention of the steam engine belongs to the end of the seventeenth century, and in its reciprocating form became operative in 1912. The elements of the steam engine are simple: a boiler to make steam, a cylinder in which a piston is moved by pressure of the steam, and transmission to apply this movement to do desired work. The early engines using steam were called *atmospheric*, because steam was turned into a vertical cylinder under a piston, and then condensed by a jet of cold water, creating a vacuum. The pressure of the atmosphere on top of the piston then drove it to the bottom and so pulled down one end of the pivoted beam to which the piston was attached. The other end lifted pump rods which moved down again as the next lot of steam counter-balanced the weight of piston and atmosphere. Boilers were crude and ill-made, the steam being used only at about five pounds per square inch pressure. Few of these early engines remain, but examples are preserved in the Science Museum. Until 1769, when Watt patented his separated condenser, few engines had been used for anything but pumping. Other improvements were made which converted the engine into a powerful and economic prime mover, so that by 1800 there were nearly five hundred such engines at work in England.[1]

The conversion of the up-and-down movement of the engine beam to a rotary movement presented a difficulty during the long time in which the

[1] The greatest improvement was the use of the pressure of steam on the piston in a closed cylinder. This changed the engine from an atmospheric to a true steam engine.

use of the crank was blocked by a patent not being used, but held sterile by the inventor. However, Watt's 'sun and planet' movement made rotary motion possible in time to allow the steam engine to become the principal source of power in many industries, particularly the textile. Beam engines have been in use in many older mills, in furnace blowing houses, and in pumping stations until this last twenty years, during which one after another they have disappeared (Plate 15). Nothing that has replaced them has the beauty of their sweet, steady motion and their silent power. The turbine and the electric motor vibrate with power, but to a man brought up on steam nothing can ever equal the sweet running of a well-cared-for steam engine, either beam or compounded horizontal.

The chief remaining evidence of a *beam engine* is the tall engine house, which no other engine needed to quite the same extent (Plate 27). The cylinder base foundations at one side of the beam support, which in older engines was often a powerful wall or the gable wall of the house, are monumental. Cylinders of seventy, eighty or even one hundred inches diameter and up to ten or eleven feet stroke need both massive support and powerful holding down. Thus a cylinder block foundation with bolt holes and the like, can reveal much about the engine. The spacing of cylinder to the beam or to the flywheel-shaft bearings can tell us of the beam length, and if the engine house still stands an engineer's eye will read on its many marks a fairly good and reliable description of its engine. The boiler seatings can tell of the size and kind of boiler, so an accurate and detailed recording of foundations and walls, and of every mark and hole and corner on them, can provide a script which can be read by an engineer.

The great change in steam engine design came when the beam was replaced by the connecting rod, the cylinder was laid horizontal, and high-pressure steam was used. In 1802 Richard Trevithick went to Coalbrookdale to have a high-pressure boiler and engine built and tested, and this was entirely successful. His small pumping engine and cast-iron boiler worked at 145 lbs per sq in pressure with a cylinder only 7 ins in diameter and 3 ft stroke. This proved to be a powerful, quick-running engine, and high-pressure engines on these principles found a very wide application in industry. In 1804, still at Coalbrookdale, he built the world's first locomotive to run on rails, and five more were built almost at once.[1] This work

[1] The accounts for these experiments are in the *Horsehay Account Book* or *Settling Journal*, Oct. 1798–Dec. 1808, preserved at Coalbrookdale, and are quoted in full in A. Raistrick, *Dynasty of Ironfounders*, 1953, reprinted by David & Charles in 1970.

opened a new era in steam engine practice. The new engines were quickly improved and increased in size, with a steady development of higher speed and shorter stroke. Many changes were made in boilers, and one type which can be recognized from the remains of its foundations is the circular haystack boiler. A good exercise for any industrial archaeologist is to spend time in the Science Museum learning what these early engines and boilers of all types are like, and studying particularly what they need in the way of foundations and other structures, which are more likely to persist than are the engines.

Between 1870 and 1880, great improvements were made, and high-speed engines were in greater demand both for ships and for the emerging electric power generating industry. Many of the new engines were vertical, high- and low-pressure cylinders were 'compounded', new types of valve gear were used, and the water tube boiler was becoming more general practice. The remaining invention which provided steam power on a different principle was that of the turbine, patented in 1884, in which a single rotor shaft was fitted with blades developed on the same principles as those of the later impulse water wheels but reacting to the flow of high-pressure steam. Turbines were applied to ship propulsion and electric power generation and became the dominant engine of the first half of the present century. All these later changes of the nineteenth and twentieth century are fully documented in the technical and professional press of mechanical engineering, so that the recorder needs only to recognize the type of engine and refer for all details to these sources.

In 1876, after a period of experiments, an entirely new type of engine appeared when Otto produced a practicable engine in which gas was exploded in the engine cylinder instead of steam being admitted to push the piston. The *gas engine* at first used 'town's gas', but soon producer and water gas, made by passing steam over red-hot coke or anthracite, and waste gas drawn from the blast furnace were used, and fuel costs greatly reduced. The further development in the early years of this century was in engines which used volatilized oils, petrol and the heavy diesel oils as fuel, and with these engines available motor transport followed. The term archaeology applied to these later inventions has somewhat of a ludicrous flavour, and we leave them in the domain of the recorders of engineering and industrial history, reserving the industrial archaeology to the earlier material which precedes the technological revolution.

Fuel

Wood

One mark of the neolithic revolution by which man climbed out of the mesolithic was the use of fire, and the increasing sophistication of the applications of fire to more complex processes marks our increasing civilization.[1] The earliest natural fuel was timber and this still remains a principal fuel over much of the world today. At an early period the partly burned wood was seen, on re-use, to burn with much less smoke and with a good wind to give a hotter fire. This new fuel, *charcoal*, though made from wood, needed preparation. It was used in some early metallurgy and on occasions when a smokeless fire was desirable, and the craft of charcoal-making assumed importance. The early iron industry made great demands for charcoal, so that in former forest areas the remains of charcoal 'pits' or 'hearths' are sometimes to be found.

For the best *charcoal* some trees were preferred above others – oak and beech in particular. Timber was cut at the season when sap was lowest and then was seasoned for about half a year. The wood was cut, piled, and measured in cords; hence the name *cord-wood*, the cord being a heap 4 ft by 4 ft by 8 ft long. Charcoal was made on a 'hearth' or 'pit', a levelled circular place about twenty to thirty feet in diameter. Around a centre pole the logs were piled, by various methods. In essence these consisted of leaving a space like a small chimney up the centre, and arranging the logs in very carefully placed layers around this, leaning inwards. A hemispherical pile was built in this way, to the diameter of the hearth, and then covered with a layer of turf and earth dug from the immediate circumference of the pile. A well preserved hearth thus settled down as a very shallow circular ditch round a central area in which fragments of charcoal and burnt earth make a black or reddish-black soil. The number of hearths in a charcoal-making area was very large and the chances of survival of one or two are fairly good (Plate 18a).

The finished heap was lighted by dropping a shovelful of fire in the central 'chimney' which gradually spread outward through the pile. Proper burning was regulated by opening or making up holes in the earth cover. The process of 'coaling' was complete in twelve to fifteen days. By volume the charcoal made was about sixty to sixty-five per cent of the volume of wood, but by weight only between fifteen and twenty-five per

[1] It is now believed that fire was known well back into the Palaeolithic period.

cent. The devastation of forests was tremendous until in the seventeenth century coppicing was adopted. In this method sufficient woodland was leased to allow a division into sections. One section only would be cut each year and a few lordlings (mature seed-bearing trees) left to regenerate. This section might then have fifteen years growth before its next cutting in rotation. Evidence of this is abundant in leases, and can be recognized in many woodlands and plantations (Diag. 2).

In lead smelting in particular another fuel sometimes called *white coal* was used. This is small wood which has been barked and dried so as to drive out all sap. The drying was done in kilns, which as permanent structures are very common in some areas. They are usually a bowl-shaped hollow dug into a hillside or on level ground, about ten feet in diameter and seven or eight feet deep. They are lined with drystone boulder walling and have an entrance or firing-hole sloping down into the bowl. Large branches were laid as a floor over the bowl, the edge often being raised in a low bank. On this floor smaller stuff was piled and brushwood and loppings burned in a fire in the bowl beneath. The heat and smoke from the fire drove out all sap and left a fuel almost ideal for ore hearth smelting. The wood ashes from the hearth were sold to the soap boilers. These structures are called *elling hearths*, and they occur in many mining accounts as 'to building a kiln, 5s.' or indirectly as so many loads (often many hundreds) of kiln wood and also as wages paid for elling. They were in use to the end of the eighteenth century. They became obsolete as the reverberatory furnace displaced the ore hearth and coal became the general fuel.

Peat

In the mountainous areas, particularly of the Pennines and of Wales, peat was widely used as a fuel for ore hearth lead smelting. On the peat grounds there is no certain way of distinguishing an actual peat cutting as industrial rather than as domestic except that the small mills rarely used more than the top few feet of the peat, and the bottom, heavy compact peat, which was difficult to dry, was left. In domestic cutting the peat is usually 'bottomed', as these dense lower peats have a better fuel value and being slow-burning are ideal for banking up a fire overnight. Peat was tried in iron smelting but was not strong enough to support the weight of ore in a blast furnace, and though patents were taken out for smelting iron with peat they did not prove successful.

As peat cutting was a seasonal event a smelt-mill using it had to provide

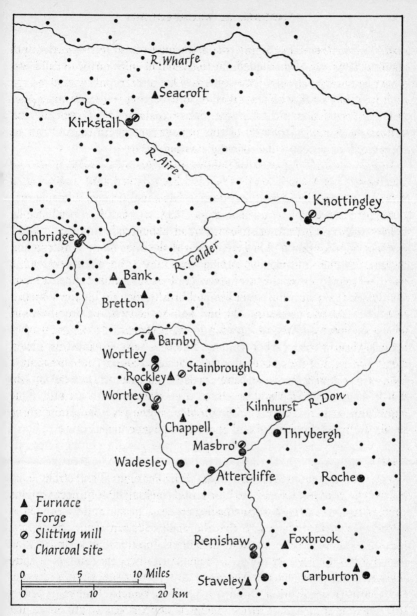

Furnace

Forge

Slitting mill

Charcoal site

R. Wharfe

Seacroft

Kirkstall

R. Aire

Knottingley

Colnbridge

R. Calder

Bank

Bretton

Barnby

Wortley

Rockley

Stainbrough

Wortley

Kilnhurst

R. Don

Chappell

Thrybergh

Masbro'

Wadesley

Attercliffe

Roche

Renishaw

Foxbrook

Staveley

Carburton

0   5   10 Miles
0   10   20 km

2   Distribution of furnaces, forges, and charcoal burning sites associated with the Spencer Group, South Yorkshire, c. 1725

a storage which could accommodate a whole year's supply, and this was generally done in a large shed with one side an open colonade of pillars to allow plenty of air circulation. Such sheds are often very big, one at least being 390 ft by 20 ft, with several others of comparable dimensions. Some coal was used along with the peat and so coal sheds can generally be recognized near or in the mill. Roads to the peat ground remain now as green tracks or as deep-cut sledge tracks (Diag. 3).

Coal

Most coals contain impurities, particularly sulphur and phosphorus, which have a very deleterious effect upon the quality of iron produced in contact with them, making it brittle when hammered, either cold (cold short) or hot (hot short). This prevented the use of coal as a substitute for charcoal in the iron-making blast furnace until the discovery that it could be 'refined' by coking. Some coals in being mined produced a lot of dusty slack along with the larger lumps which were desirable for domestic coal. The slack was used at the salt and alum works, where a slow-burning fire was acceptable.

Coals vary in their carbon content over a wide range and this affects their properties and uses. The highest carbon coals are the anthracites, which are relatively scarce, and the next group with a little less carbon has a wide range of steam coals, needed for use in boilers with high draught. These are hard coals of high calorific value, giving off the minimum of smoke and tar. Anthracites and the best steam coals, because of their higher density and less bulk, were the best coals for ships' boilers all through the nineteenth century, and in the twentieth too until displaced by oil. There is a restricted range of coals which make good and strong coke which can support the very heavy loads of ore in a tall blast furnace without crushing and can so keep open sufficient passage for air and gases. These cokes react with the ores and the iron and are essential for all modern furnaces. Domestic coke is softer and is mainly produced in the gas retort, but with the change over to natural gas its place is being taken by manu-factured smokeless fuels.

Some of the coal properties are regional so that one thinks of South Wales for anthracite, Durham for metallurgical coke, Yorkshire for domestic 'bright' coal (bright looking, clean to handle and burning brightly) and steam coals, and most coalfields for one or more special varieties of coal. This tended in the eighteenth century to encourage particular industries

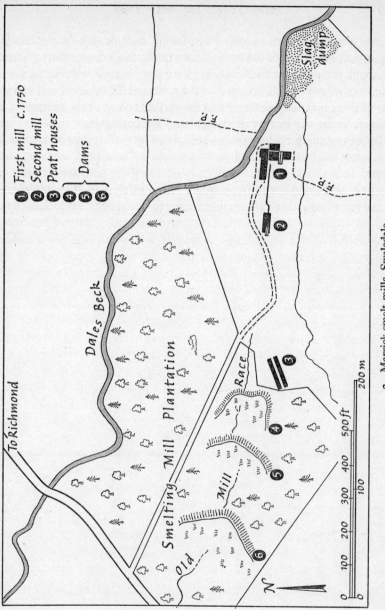

3 Marrick smelt-mills, Swaledale

To Richmond

Dales Beck

Smelting Mill Plantation

Slag dump

Old Mill Race

Mill Race

① First mill c.1750
② Second mill
③ Peat houses
④⑤⑥ Dams

①
②
③
④
⑤
⑥

0   100   200   300   400   500 ft
0   100   200 m

N

where certain qualities of coal were found, though this special localization disappeared with the development of the modern transport system. Although the different coalfields may have slightly different methods and traditions of working determined by the nature of the coal and coal seams, few of these make any difference to the surface layout or the remains of a colliery. These will be very much alike in all the coalfields.

In the twentieth century oil has become an increasingly important fuel, displacing coal in more and more sections of transport, heating, and power. It has an abundant literature in which all the processes of getting, refining, and using are fully recorded. It can safely be left to its professional recorders rather than finding a place for it in industrial archaeology.

CHAPTER 8

Transport

We have postulated as one element of an industry the distribution of its products to customers, and this involves transport, carriage by a variety of ways and means whether on land or water, by which the carrier can travel. In all the realms explored by the industrial archaeologist there is no remaining monument to compare with the thousands of miles of transport structures which still form a very tangible network over all our country.

Footpaths and bridle roads are often of great age, arising as soon as communities needed to get in contact with one another. The bridle ways often form part of important networks between markets and fairs, and some of these networks have been part of the necessary equipment of industry. The most important older ones are the pack-horse tracks by which goods were carried by trains of ponies over great distances of thirty, forty, sixty miles or more. At Richmond, Yorkshire, as early as 1440 a complaint was made that traders were being diverted to new markets. The burgesses declared that

> merchants and others were wont to resort thither from Lancashire, Cumberland, and Westmorland, with merchandise of grain, victual and other goods every Saturday in the year as well as conveyors and carryers of grain and bread . . . along with Lonsdale, Craven, Dent and Sedbergh in which no great quantity of corn was then grown, for which the inhabitants of those parts made their chief provision of grain in Richmond market . . . .

The trade at these markets was more than provisions, as tolls were collected also on wool, cloth, hides, iron, lead, coal, wines, woad, salt, and many other products of distant industries.

A pattern of pack-horse roads can still be traced from Richmond, spreading across the Pennines to the Lune valley and the west coast as well as eastward to the North Sea coast. Part of this pattern is concerned with the corn trade and part with the trade in woollen yarns and hosiery, both of which continued for three or four centuries.

The textile industry of Halifax can only be understood in the sixteenth to eighteenth centuries when the vast network of ancient ways has been explored which drew wool to Halifax or took it to put out for spinning in most of the cottages in the Pennine Dales. The *badgers* who carried corn and the *broggers* who dealt in wool along these routes, carrying their packs on the backs of *jagger ponies*, have left their name on many a Jagger Lane, Badger Gate, Brogger (sometimes altered to Bragger or Braggart, or even Boggart) Brow, all of which a patient survey will fit into the patterns of medieval and later industries. The number of pack ponies moving about the countryside was considerable: at Kendal in Westmorland, in the eighteenth century, for example, 354 pack-horses a week, in different gangs, were operating continually from the town. The hosiery handknit-ters alone at that time sent 28,600 dozens of stockings a year to London. Such a gang was advertised in 1728 as –

A Gang of Good Packhorses, containing eighteen in number, with their accoutrements and Business belonging to the same, being one of the ancient Gangs which have gone with Goods from York, Leeds, and Wakefield to London, being the Horses of Thomas Varley.

The pack-horse roads could go fairly directly across the fells, the gradients being no hindrance to the ponies. On the breast and brow of the hills the tracks cut deep into the turf and became gullies for heavy rains. In time they may become ten or more feet deep, and unusable in bad weather. Another one was made alongside and then abandoned in its turn. This set of deep-cut tracks winding over the brow of a hill is excellent evidence along many of the pack-horse ways. On the moors, where soft ground has to be crossed, big flagstones were laid and the track became a single-width paved causeway. In some areas of the lowlands similar paved ways mark a pack-horse road. In the hill country a network of tracks crosses the high moors and to help in bad weather, and to mark the way, 'crosses' or 'stoops' were erected. These are rough stone pillars, often set at a point which can be seen from a distance, or at the crossing or branch-ing of two tracks. Their names can be of great interest. Badger Stoop, Porridge Stoop (site of wayside oats market at the meeting of several ways), Lancashire Lad and Lancashire Lass (on a track leading eventually to that county), Hollow Mill Cross, Mid Causey Stone, and so on, through scores of names, all with significance for the track they mark. To those of us who walk the moors today, these are familiar landmarks, known from childhood and the names taught to us by father or grandfather and passed to them from some pedlar or drover forbear.

Closely related to the pack-horse ways are the monastic ways between an abbey and its outlying granges. These varied greatly in length but some extend for scores or even more than a hundred miles – as, for instance, the road from Fountains Abbey in Yorkshire to its farms and grange in Borrowdale in the Lake District. These were in part roads on which ox wains could carry the wool crop or stores, and in part droving roads along which their flocks could be moved. The purpose of many of these ceased in part with the dissolution of the monasteries but many stretches of them remained as useful roads, and research on the ground can usually trace the whole original line. Alongside these roads and on prominent points crosses were erected, partly to protect but chiefly to direct travellers, and although few complete crosses remain, the great socket stones are very common. Many are named and some occur in accounts of the boundaries of property from the thirteenth century. All the names should be sought out and recorded and efforts made to preserve the socket stones, which were often built into the foundation of enclosure walls in the eighteenth century.[1]

The oldest constructed road system is of course that created by the Romans, a system which in large part still remains. Parts of the Roman roads are visible across the high moors, parts have become the foundations of modern roads, long stretches were adopted as parish boundaries in the pre-Conquest years, and can now be detected on a large-scale map by the ruled length of hedge or bank, and some parts have become buried and await a casual discovery. Along these roads the products of Roman industry were carried, and indeed the success of the Roman industries has been attributed to the excellence of the system of communications between all parts of the country and the ports. The roads have been well recorded[2] but vigilance can still be repaid by the discovery of new fragments which can fill in a doubtful line, or by the finding or noting of a milestone or other feature.

[1] In Craven, Yorks, the socket stones of two crosses, known only by name, Weets Cross and Nappa Cross, were discovered as foundations in enclosure walling. They were got out, replaced in their original position and refitted with shafts. They can now be seen from miles around.
[2] The Ordnance Survey map of Roman Britain is the basic reference, and such books as those of Margery (I. D. Margery, *Roman Roads in Britain*, 2 vols, 1955, 1957) and others will fill in a great amount of detail.

The Roman roads remained an asset to the country, even to the present, and in many areas influenced the pattern of Anglo-Saxon settlement. A use for many lengths of these roads was found from time to time – as, for instance, the great cattle droving road from Scotland which used the Roman road across the wild and treacherous Bewcastle Fells and the Maiden Way over the Cross Fell range, or the heavy traffic of the early textile industry along the Blackstone Edge road over the Pennines between Yorkshire and Lancashire. The Fosse Way from Bath to the Humber has in great part been in constant use for more than fifteen centuries.

An industry of great extent but not of very long duration was that of the cattle drovers who brought the wiry Scots cattle down to the growing fairs and markets of England, in response to the ever increasing demands for meat. The trade flourished throughout the eighteenth century but declined in the nineteenth. The cattle were driven by tracks which avoided the common roads and towns and crossed the wilder parts of the un-enclosed hill country, where streams could be forded near their source, and grazing could be had along the way. These *drove roads* are a distinct feature of the northern parts, little studied as yet but certainly worthy of research.[1] The roads run with the minimum diversion from a north to south line, avoiding all towns except the few with large cattle fairs. On a few of them there are inns, now mostly reverted to farms, near meeting places of the drovers, and a few still keep the name, 'The Drovers'. The drove roads are wide green tracks, maybe a hundred feet or more in places, with a fine green turf resulting from a century and more of trampling and grazing. Stances or overnight resting places are near a spring and are an area of an acre or so where a hundred cattle could lie under the eye of the drovers and their dogs. Some great fords like those of the Solway near Rockcliffe have found a place in literature but most of the drove roads are still to be written up.[2]

There are some other early roads worth investigation. The monasteries, besides bringing their wool from the granges to the mother house, after sorting it, sent it to some port for export. The port was often convenient to a fair, as at Boston, Lincolnshire, to which many northern monasteries sent their wool. The quantities were considerable: in the case of Fountains

---

[1] Haldane, *The drove roads of Scotland*, is by far the best textbook for the subject. One for England and Wales is by K. J. Bonser, *The Drovers, who they were and how they went*, 1970.
[2] Diag. 4 shows the pattern of the drove roads down a part of the north Pennines. Similar roads are to be found coming across and out of Wales.

11   Oast houses, Kent.

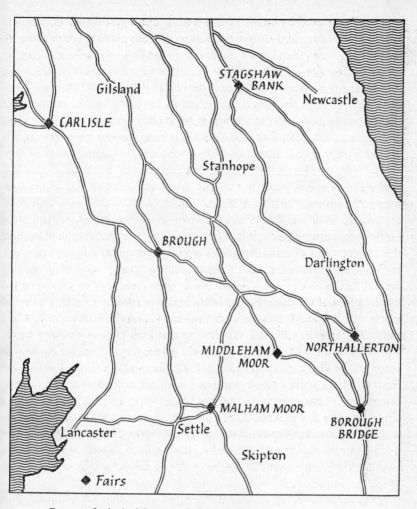

4   Pattern of principal drove roads down the Pennines.

Abbey, in 1315, their wool crop was about twelve and a half tons. For all the Yorkshire abbeys and priories the export in that year was 693 sacks of 364 lbs in a sack. Similar amounts of wool were sent from the Cotswolds and from Salisbury Plain to the port at Southampton, and Bristol, Chester, Hull, and other ports had a comparable trade both monastic and secular. In the Middle Ages there was a big export of lead, much of it carried long distances to the ports, by pack-horses, but occasionally by ox wain. In 1365, for instance, twenty-four fothers,[1] about twenty-five or twenty-six tons, was carried in ten ox wagons by 'high and rocky mountains and by muddy roads to Boroughbridge, about 20 leagues', from Caldstanes in Nidderdale (Greenhow Hill). Lead from Swaledale was carried some forty miles to York for shipment, but most of this journey could have been on the Roman road. Similar tracks and roads go from each mining field to an embarkation point on a river, and many fragments can be seen which a careful survey could piece together. An eighteenth-century road of this kind, for pack-pony carriage, is the *Lead Road* from the Alston Moor and Allendale smelt-mills across the fells along the south of the Tyne, to a wharf at Ryton at the head of the tidal part of the river Tyne. This road and wharf were for long a vital part of the organization of this great industry and cannot be neglected by the industrial archaeologist. It is more than thirty miles of monument to a past great industry. There are many such industrial roads in the country but they are very inadequately recorded.

The roads of the country had fallen into a sad state of disrepair by the late seventeenth and early eighteenth century, and the growing industries were hampered by lack of good transport and the slowness of communication. A major change in the attitude of the country to its roads was accomplished by the establishment of the Turnpike Trusts. The change moved the onus and cost of maintenance of main roads from the inhabitants of each parish to the users of the road, through a system of tolls. The first Turnpike Act was passed in 1663, but the eighteenth and early nineteenth century was the great period of Turnpike construction. Between 1750 and 1830 about eleven hundred Turnpike Acts were passed. Many of the early Turnpike roads can be traced on the late-eighteenth-century maps and in the road books, but along their lengths there are many diversions to be noticed, both from an older line to cut out bad gradients, and where the Turnpike line has since been improved.

Of structures connected with the roads the toll houses are the most striking, at positions where formerly there were gates across the road, only opened when tolls had been paid. The architecture of toll houses is very varied, from hexagonal with gothic pointed windows to the plainest wayside cottage, but all had some provision for the display of a list of the tolls due on a board or plaque attached to the building. They are often called

[1] The common measure of lead and lead ore.

Bar House, or combined with a placename, Cottingley Bar, Leeming Bar, or such in the north, but in some parts, particularly in the south, they retain the names of gates, Strap Lane Gate, Cranmore Gate, and so on. A surprising number of toll-bar houses have survived but are coming into danger now from the extensive road widening schemes in all parts of the country.

For the use of the stage-coaches and posting houses it was necessary to have the road measured, and for this purpose milestones were erected. These, again, are very much subject to local fashion. Many in the north and west are square or triangular stone pillars with names and distances cut in the faces, often in very handsome and distinctive lettering. Guide stoops or milestones were ordered to be erected by the justices of the peace under an Act of 1698, and in an amending order of 1738 it became compulsory to state distances to the next market towns. One must determine what mile was used, and remember that the customary mile, usually just over one and a quarter statutory miles, and in some instances more than this, remained in use in some parts far into the eighteenth century. The Turnpike construction also often led to the widening of bridges, and so all bridges should be examined with care, especially underneath, and fully recorded.

The Turnpike Trusts were not entirely disbanded until the formation of the County Councils and their assumption of power as the statutory Highway Authority in 1888. All the roads which were heavily used in the nineteenth century were improved or maintained by Trusts, and only a few actually created by them. The largest group of new roads was that designed by Telford for the Scottish Highlands. In 1803, he was commissioned to plan better communications through the Highlands and in the course of eighteen years he supervised the making of 920 miles of new roads, which because of the mountainous country had 1,117 bridges along them. One of his best-known roads is the present A5 London to Holyhead, with two famous bridges, the Conway Bridge and the Menai Straits road bridge upon it. Bridges form one of the most varied groups of structures, of all ages and of individual design and they are connected not only with tracks and roads, but with canals, and railways. Bridges are among the more permanent structures, many of the road bridges being several centuries old, still in use and of considerable importance.[1]

A discussion of bridges can be conveniently deferred until other forms of transport have been described; see below, p. 141.

Water Transport

Rivers and canals

Prehistoric man discovered the art of making a boat which could support him in water, at first by hollowing out a log as a 'dug-out canoe'. Useful at first for crossing rivers or fishing on small tarns, it was inevitable that early civilizations would quickly improve the structure of boats until they could be used for shore-line exploration and then for travel on the sea. Large streams and rivers were a barrier to inland travel and the establishment of a ferry with its attendant boat was only possible on occasional busy routes and was very rare except as an act of piety along some of the pilgrim routes to important medieval shrines.

Boats and ships, however, quickly became an essential adjunct for trade, and inland trade routes came down to convenient points on the rivers, from which the journey across the sea or along the coast could be started, or from which river boats could carry goods to the seaports for transfer to the sea-going ships. The conveyance of lead from the Pennines to Borough-bridge on the Ouse has already been mentioned. For a few centuries the lead was carried by river boats to York or Hull for trans-shipment overseas. Similar use was made of most of the large river estuaries, and towns at the head of the tidal or navigable part of the river became ports. Boats and ships were improved and built to larger sizes as trade increased, and some rivers silted up or had shifting mudbanks.[1] It was inevitable therefore that rivers in great use should become the subjects of 'improvement' schemes.

As well as the mudbanks and shallows, many rivers were impeded by the dams erected for the larger water-mills on their banks. These were usually manorial mills, with very powerful rights and claims on the water. The passage of the dams was provided by staunches, a gap closed by re-movable planks which allowed a temporary flow of water on which a few boats could pass. Many river improvement schemes were hindered by such dams, as well as by a very winding course, so that it was inevitable that the idea should arise of cutting a new course around such obstruction, thus canalizing the river.

Between 1660 and 1702 a large number of Acts of Parliament concerned with the improvement of existing river navigations had been obtained, and most of them included powers to improve the course of the river by dredging, by straightening, and by the removal of obstructions. Some of

---

[1] Most of these small river ports had a life of intense activity before being completely abandoned

these straightenings and some of the replacement buildings for those removed as obstructions are still easily recognized and recorded. The Acts
usually also included power to buy land to make wharves and build warehouses. Few of the locks built under these powers have been seriously
altered and many of the wharves are still surviving with their buildings,
although their usage may have changed with declining canal traffic. A few
of the earlier riverside wharves can be found which in their time were the
transfer points of important industrial traffic from land to water transport.

A short canal had been cut to improve the approach to Exeter from the
sea in 1564 to 1566, and this had included three pound locks to enable
boats to pass weirs which were built without staunches. These were the
first pound locks to be built in this country, although their use was well
established on the Continent. The earliest canal in this country, that is an
artificial cut as distinct from an improved river channel, was the Caerdyke,
cut by Roman engineers from the river Nene at Peterborough to connect
it with the river Witham at Lincoln. The Fossdyke later continued this to
Torksey on the river Trent, thus linking three navigable rivers. In the
seventeenth century some canal-like drains were made for the drainage of
the Fens, but the earliest canals in our modern sense, cut only for the
carriage of goods, were made in the mid eighteenth century in Lancashire.
The St Helens canal opened to traffic in 1751 and the more famous Bridgewater canal to Worsley opened in 1761. These initiated the canal era which
gave us a wonderful network of canals to serve nearly the whole country.
After a recent period of decline there is now renewed interest and possibility of a revival.

The construction of the canals was a major engineering feat carried
through during two or three generations by a handful of outstanding
engineers and a magnificent body of tens of thousands of highly skilled
navvies and a group of masons and carpenters. It was a triumph of hand
labour achieved almost entirely by the power of human muscle and with
the minimum of mechanical aids. There were three major requirements of
materials: clay for the puddle on which the water-tightness of the canal
depended, and stone and brick for the construction of locks, bridges, warehouses, and other ancillary buildings. In the effort to keep transport to a
minimum, clay was got wherever a good quality was encountered along the
line of work. In the lowlands, brick fields were established, and in the hills
where the locks and tunnels were situated quarries of suitable stone were

opened or existing quarries contracted to supply it. Occasionally the tunnels provided large quantities of stone of a satisfactory quality. Sometimes, as at Bradford, large quarries on adjacent hills were connected to the canal by a tunnel and tramway, and as that section of the canal was completed and filled stone was delivered at the canal bank and carried on the canal for work along its course. Some of the quarries are seen along the canal-side, and others have the traces of tramways or sledge tracks to a stone wharf, and these are essential features in the recording of a canal.

For the industrial archaeologist, the features for recording will be all those which can be connected with the construction and the operation of the canal. Quarries and brickyards, masons' and carpenters' depots, and, if they can be traced, navvy camps must be looked for. Of structures, the locks are the most intriguing, but of equal importance are the towpath and the lock-keepers' houses. To operate the locks and not to drain the canal, make-up water is supplied to the top level pound, and this almost always involves the provision of one or more reservoirs, or of a big pumping installation. One canal reservoir in high country opened a quarry of splendid stone on a neighbouring common, to build a masonry dam. Sledgeways and roads connect the quarry and reservoir sites, but another memorial remains because with the money made and the quarries provided for them the commoners could afford to present all the stone required for building a village school. The pipe-line may involve structures on its route to the canal, and there can be quite elaborate provisions for regulating flow into the canal.

Some canals were allowed to take springs or streams which they intersected, but frequently the canal companies had to provide culverts to carry the stream under the canal bed. Some of these are excellent pieces of mason work. Aqueducts carried canals across valleys or over rivers, and tunnels took them through the hills. Some canals used inclined planes instead of a steep flight of locks, and boats floating in troughs were in places lowered or lifted by a hoist between canals at different levels. Some wharves have cranes and other equipment, and to a careful observer the canal soon appears as the string along which a vast number of interesting structures are displayed. Profitable areas for intense study of almost every phase and structure of canal work are the great canal terminals. The whole port of Gloucester, the great depot at Stourport, the town of Goole and a large number of transfer points between canal and river, canal and rail, or canal and road offer not only canal material but an architecture – offices, houses, stores, stables – and an element of town planning all of which is part and parcel of the canal system.

One aspect of canals which as yet has not been given the attention it deserves is the use of canals underground, almost entirely in the course of mining. The greatest and usually the only quoted example is the forty-two miles of underground canal which, as a part of the Bridgewater Canal, penetrates through the collieries at Worsley. Gilbert, who was connected with the Bridgewater Canal, and was later associated with Walton and Smeaton, planned with them an underground canal in the Tynebottom Mine in Alston Moor, where the famous Nent Force level, designed by Smeaton, with a few miles of its course used as a canal, was already being made. Examples are found in all mining fields, but their exploration is dangerous and must be left to the experienced members of the mining and caving groups who are doing splendid work in underground recording.

Most of the boats used on the canals were built at yards along the canal-side, but though most of these yards have now gone the positions of some can still be found, and some are now used as saw-mills or carpenter's shops or for other light industries. On some of the improved rivers or canal junctions larger boats were built, and some places like Selby on the Yorkshire Ouse developed a shipbuilding industry. Tugs and coasting vessels were often built in such inland ports.

Tramways and railways

Wagons running on rails were known in this country only at the very beginning of the seventeenth century, though they were illustrated in use in some Continental mines in the sixteenth century by Munster (1550) and Agricola (1556). The earliest precise reference in this country is found among the manuscripts of Lord Middleton at Wollaton Hall, Nottingham, referring to his colliery in 1597 and mentioning 'railes and bridges', and in 1610 speaking of his coals, 'and we will bring them down by raile ourselves, for Strelley cartway is so fowle as few cariadges can passe'. Here is clearly stated the original reason for the wagonways. Conflicting claims have been made for the area of their full adoption, one being a set of 'tylting railes', from a colliery at Broseley, Shropshire, to the Severn, laid in 1606, but the general documented conclusion must place their first full use on Tyneside in 1671. They were 'constructed entirely of square

wooden frames or rails, laid in two right lines on wooden sleepers' according to Robert Stevenson.[1]

The earliest wagonways were rapidly developed into a great system
linking the Durham and Northumberland collieries with the wharves
along the banks of the Tyne and Wear. One of the most striking of the
early ways was that from Tanfield Moor, about seven miles south west of
Gateshead, to the Tyne at Dunston. Along this line one of the earliest
railway monuments still surviving, the Causey Bridge, or Tanfield Arch,
was built over the gorge of the Causey Burn. The arch has a span of 103
feet, is 60 feet high, and semi-circular. Its architect was a local mason,
Ralph Wood. There is a sundial on one pier and the inscription 'Ra. Wood,
mason, 1727'. A fine map of wagonways was published by John Gibson in
1787 and subsequent maps show an amazing number running to the Tyne
and Wear.

The wagons were drawn by horses, and the ways terminated at the
staithes (coal wharves) on the river banks, where later the coal 'drops'
were built. The tracks of many of these wagonways are still to be found
not only in the North but in all the coalfields, generally running in fairly
direct lines, with shallow cuttings or embankments. In 1767, the Coalbrookdale foundry produced the first iron rails to replace their twenty
miles or so of wooden wagonways, and the use of cast iron rails spread
rapidly over the whole country. Many early rails were carried on stone
blocks set under them at regular intervals. Chairs were pegged to the
blocks, at first with one spike, later with two, though the earliest plate or
angle rails were pegged without a chair. The remains of these 'stoneways'
are abundant.[2] In the nineteenth century some of these tramways used
cast-iron sleepers into which the rails slotted. Chairs, lines, sleepers, culverts, short tunnels, and bridges are common features of the hundreds of
miles of wagonways to be recorded (Diag. 5).

Allied to the coal wagonways are the quarry inclines which, fitted with
narrow gauge rails and wagons, remained in use between many hill-top
quarries and valley roads or rails into this century. A feature of many of
these is a brake drum by which the run of full trucks descending and pulling up empties was controlled. Tramways, of course, became a common
feature of mines of all kinds, and rails, chairs, points, and other features

[1] R. Stevenson, *Report on a proposed railway from the coalfield of Midlothian to Edinburgh to
Leith, 1818.* This was Stevenson, civil engineer, not Stephenson of the early railway.
[2] A fine survey is now available: B. Baxter, *Stone Blocks and Iron Rails* (Newton Abbot), 1966.

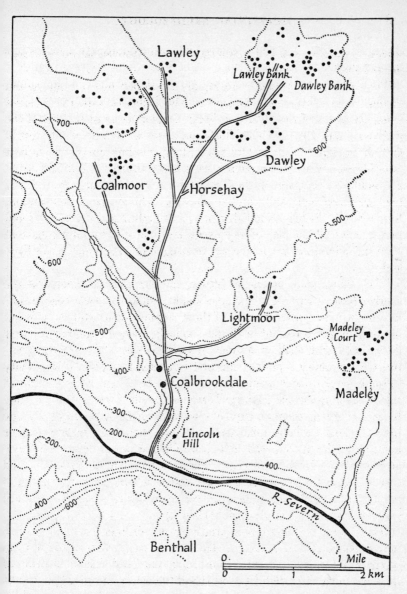

5 Tramways between ironstone and coal pits, and the furnaces at Coalbrookdale, *c.* 1750

are regularly seen; and short lengths of line emerge from the mines and serve the dressing floors and stock yards. These light railways provide a rich field of study with almost infinite variety. The loading and unloading arrangements and transfer stages between mine or quarry tramway and the transport at either end often include cranes, winches, and sometimes tipplers, of great interest (Diag. 6).

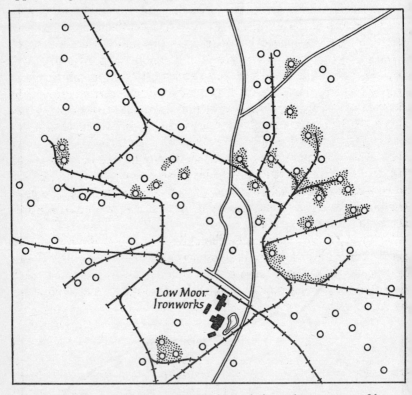

6   Low Moor ironworks – ironstone pits, coal pits, and tramways, *c.* 1860

The steam locomotive which transformed the tramways into railways as we know them had a comparatively short prehistory in such experiments as those of Cugnot and Murdock, to produce a road vehicle propelled by steam. The new era started in 1802 when Richard Trevithick went to Coalbrookdale for the tests on his high-pressure boiler and pump, and, having proved them, proceeded to build the first locomotive to run on rails. Six were built in rapid succession before he made a partnership with

John Urpeth Rastrick to produce others more in the form which became the familiar pattern. Many locomotives were built and were used on iron tramways at iron works, and on some of the colliery wagonways. It was under the influence of George Stephenson, when engineer at Killingworth Colliery, Northumberland, that the locomotive was improved to an economic machine.

Many early railways were built which still used some horsedrawn lengths, combined with stationary engines to haul trucks up the inclines made for each hill. Some combined locomotives on part, as on Hetton railroad, County Durham, one of Stephenson's early contracts, where in the length between colliery and river there were five self-acting inclines, five inclines with stationary engines, and three locomotives on level stretches. The Stockton and Darlington Railway at first combined locomotives, horse-drawn coaches, inclines, and a stationary engine. Before the Manchester and Liverpool railway of 1830, most lines offer this mixture, and some of the inclines since abandoned are still to be found and recorded. A splendid set along the Stanhope to South Shields railway, County Durham, are still to be seen; the line used horses on ten and a half miles, nine stationary engines on eleven miles, locomotives on nine and a quarter miles, and self-acting inclines on three miles.

By 1840, the railways were well established, many of the stations and goods yards built, and the familiar adjuncts to be found everywhere. There has been a tremendous interest in their running for all this century, with flourishing societies for their study and preservation, along with a fine literature, so that there is little need to enter into more detail.

Bridges

One group of structures that is common to the roads, canals, and railways is that of bridges, which, though all related, have a seemingly endless variety, from the simple treetrunk spanning a small stream to the startling magnificence of the two Forth Bridges. The simple *clapper bridges* with flagstones spanning between crude piers, built in the stream, are very difficult to date, as they carry nothing dateable about their structure, and they are so simple that they have been built in almost any age where the material has been available. In mining areas there are some excellent eighteenth- and nineteenth-century examples.

The use of the arch was brought to Britain by the Romans, who built bridges along their main roads, occasionally using the arch, though their military bridges were more often of timber trestle structure. Fords were made to serve for the general crossings on rivers until the Norman period, when under the influence of the church the maintenance of roads and bridges was regarded as an act of piety. Not only individual benefactors, but most monasteries, gave money for the building of bridges, and a surprising number of those built from the thirteenth to the fifteenth centuries survive in bridges still carrying important classified A and B roads. The original bridge has, of course, been widened, usually when the road was Turnpiked in the eighteenth century, and again in the motor age. All this can be seen on the underside, where different masonries can be distinguished side by side, and where often the additional width is built to a different curvature. There are mason marks and differing constructions to be noted, and often a long history of a bridge can be deduced, reaching back to the monastic period, and some documentation may be found in chartularies and compoti from the twelfth century onwards.

A second great period of bridge building began with the Highway Act of 1555, which provided for the state of bridges to be inspected by, or reported to, Quarter Sessions, and levies for their repair to be raised on the Wapontakes, Hundreds, or Counties. Many new bridges were built in the early seventeenth century which can be documented in the Quarter Sessions rolls, and in the occasionally surviving Book of Bridges which some counties kept. Most of these were still built with semi-circular arches with two, three or more spans, and massive pillars and starlings in the river bed. The pressure of the dawning Industrial Revolution turned attention to the redesigning of bridges, and in France a 'Department of Bridges' was formed.[1] Perronet introduced new arches, elliptical, segmented, and other forms, which enabled the span to be greatly increased without adding much to the height. A new period of bridge building followed his discoveries.

In 1779, the completion of Darby's cast-iron bridge over the Severn, at Ironbridge, started the modern period when more and more bridges were built of metal. This usage can be followed through bridges of the Ironbridge pattern, through those adhering closely to stone prototypes, to new

---

[1] *Corps des Ponts et Chaussées*, established in 1716, was followed by the *Ecole des Ponts et Chaussées* in 1747. The first director of the Ecole was Jean-Rodolphe Perronet (1708–94), who was one of the greatest of scientific designers of bridges, and who worked out the theory of many curved arches which replaced the semi-circle.

girder designs, and to suspension bridges, which are really material for the historian of civil engineering rather than for industrial archaeology.

A group of early bridges deserving study are those over smaller streams, built for the pack-horse traffic. These are built high enough up the streams to be a single span structure, and are only wide enough for the passage of man and ponies. Some date from the fourteenth century. They are mostly in remote areas but are an essential part of the early pack-horse ways, are usually the product of local masons, and are in need of careful and detailed recording (Plates 19a and 19b).

Canals demanded a multitude of bridges — to carry roads above them, rivers beneath them, culverts - crossover bridges, and small bridges, often hand-operated swing bridges, on country lanes and farm occupation roads. All these vary in design both from one canal to another and in the slightly different circumstances of each one. There is a vast area here which is probably best studied as a part of the canal story. The railways provided their own bridges over the canals, rivers, and valleys and the study of these will likewise be a part of the railway story.

Bridges have been built in many thousands, and it would be impossible to make a proper concise study of them, except in terms of engineering design, or in direct connection with the roads, canals, or railways of which they are an essential part.

CHAPTER 9

Accommodation – Buildings and Structures

The provision of shelter for himself, his animals, his tools and his machinery has been an occupation of man from very early times, and with developing civilization buildings for purposes other than just shelter have been made, connected with his intellectual and spiritual beliefs. The industrial archaeologist's interest will lie mostly among the secular building, leaving the religious and monumental to the studies of the architect except in so far as their actual building involved the masons' and other industries. In what we may regard as secular building there is a rough-and-ready division into those buildings which are primarily made only for shelter, and those which are functionally a part of an industry, designed specifically for a particular purpose which has dictated their shape and design, strength and internal arrangement. This contrast can perhaps be seen in two examples. In a steel works and in many heavy engineering shops, the furnaces and machinery are protected from the weather by a building which is little more than a wind-break and rain-shelter. A steel frame clad with corrugated iron sheets is characteristic. In sharp contrast with this is the water corn-mill with its wheelpit and watercourses, or the windmill with its sails, both with the strong floor carrying the stones, the whole structure designed to assist the work of the mill. The mill could not stand free of its massive structures and still work inside a purely shelter building which surrounded but had no necessary connection with its constituent parts.

In the building industry there is a cleavage in the post-Conquest centuries when the masons and stone-getters were almost all of them engaged on the castles, abbeys, cathedrals, and churches which were the principal large buildings of the Middle Ages. Domestic building of anything beyond peasant hovels was done by the carpenter. The more substantial cruck buildings lasted into the sixteenth century, and it was in the towns that the newer-style timber-framed buildings replaced them in the fifteenth and sixteenth centuries. The end of much of the military and ecclesiastical building in the early sixteenth century liberated the masons and stone-layers for secular work. It was these people and their apprentices who built many new bridges and who built stone houses for the merchants and yeomen who were benefiting by the general prosperity of the Elizabethan period.

A major change in construction accompanied the change to stone in domestic building. In the cruck and the framed structures, the walls were in fact only screens between the structural members carrying the load. In the new houses, the stone walls were load bearing, massive for stability and limited for openings to the spaces left between the piers directly under and supporting the roof trusses. However, the houses of whatever size were more directly related to the individual domestic needs and fancies of their occupant than dictated by an industry. True, merchants might use one room of their house as a shop or small workshop, but it is not until the seventeenth and eighteenth centuries that housing appears which might properly be called industrial, and the bulk of industrial housing will belong to the nineteenth century.

In earlier chapters, many structures have been mentioned which in their design are adapted to one particular industry or industrial process only. Many such buildings can only be adapted to a different use with difficulty, or even not at all. The most obvious example of this is seen in the lime kilns which have been unused in most cases for a century but of which few have been removed and for which no subsequent use has been found beyond that of a receptacle for farmers' rubbish or for land clearance stones. This is fortunate for the recorder as it has ensured the persistence of a sufficient number of accessible examples to allow of both local and regional studies. Windmills are similarly industrial buildings whose whole design is linked to a specific purpose. A few tower-mills have been gutted and turned into dwellings but they remain unmistakably a mill and cannot become anything but an eccentric house. Shot towers, furnaces, kilns, and some other industrial buildings are of this very restricted class.

A second group of buildings, however, have a wider possibility of varied usage. These are usually concerned with the textile industries, spinning or weaving, or other processes, where what is required is room and shelter for numbers of similar machines in a building in which they can be supplied with power. The actual manufacture carried on can and does change from time to time so that it is common to find that a factory has had a succession of owners making very different products but all with the basic needs of space and a source of power. This kind of building is perhaps best exemplified in parts of the textile areas of the North, where the 'room and power' system gave support to the small manufacturer. A factory was equipped with an engine and transmission shafting and the floor space could be rented in small or large lots with an inclusive rent for space and power. A man could start with two looms driven from the common shaft, and take more space as his business grew. Through this system some factories housed a great variety of small manufactures. This illustrates the essential minima of a factory, a building substantial enough to carry and house safely a great number of machines and workers and to have an adequate power supply.

These factories were only arrived at by stages under the pressure of inventions which speeded up processes in the textile manufactures, coinciding with a rapidly expanding demand for goods. These stages in the progression from the spinning wheel used in a cottage to the cotton-mill employing hundreds of spinners, and similarly in the other textile processes, have left much evidence for investigation and recording. The eighteenth century, which saw in its first decade the change from charcoal to coke in smelting iron ores, a change sometimes taken as the beginning of the Industrial Revolution, saw also some vital changes in parts of the textile manufactures. Wool and linen for some centuries had been woven on hand looms in hundreds of cottages, and exceptionally in workshops. Jack of Newbury at the end of the fifteenth century had gathered his weavers and apprentices together in a workshop which later would have been called a factory. It was sung of him in a popular ballad:

> Within one room, being large and long
> There stood two hundred looms full strong.
> Two hundred men, the truth is so,
> Wrought in these rooms all in a row.

The ballad also mentions boys and a hundred women busy carding. The numbers are certainly much exaggerated, but even allowing for that, Jack had organized a factory comparable with many early eighteenth-century ones except for the provision of water power. He was not alone in this kind of organization; others who employed large numbers of workers in one building were William Stumpe, clothier, who occupied part of Malmesbury Abbey as his workroom, and Tucker of Burford, both in the mid sixteenth century.

In the fifteenth and later centuries there was a great stocking knitting trade in the Pennines with Kendal and Richmond as collecting centres. Hundreds of people knitted stockings by hand, and both men, women, and children knitted. In 1589, William Lee of Calverton near Nottingham invented a machine, a *stocking frame*, on which stockings could be knitted. The machines were slow to be adopted, but by the middle of the seventeenth century frame-knitting was established in Nottinghamshire, and a little later in parts of Leicestershire and Derbyshire, while handknitting continued in the North. The frame remained essentially a domestic machine until well into the nineteenth century, there being one or occasionally two in a cottage. The machine was intricate and needed good light for its operation, and knitters' cottages commonly had one window enlarged, against which the frame could stand. The intricacy of the frame slowed down its adaptation to a power drive, so that even in the early nineteenth century the industry was still domestic. Many families, however, had acquired or rented up to three and occasionally four frames and the 'frame window' had lengthened to accommodate them. Cottages had been built with the characteristic window either on the top floor under the eaves, and running the whole width of the cottage front, or on a ground floor room specially set apart as a work room.

This development is exactly paralleled in the woollen areas, where the cottage handloom needed light. In this case, the machines were almost always on the first floor, and, with two or three looms, the long five-, six- or seven-, or even ten-light mullioned window became the mark of the *weaver's cottage*. These definitive houses were a little earlier than those in hosiery manufacture, and are found in buildings of the seventeenth and eighteenth centuries (Plate 20b).

A development found in both woollens and hosiery was that of the *shop* or *workshop*. It was found convenient for several men to work together either cooperatively or under a common master. Some groups of three or four cottages had a common attic over the whole group, while others had a separate large room built at the end or back of the row, where perhaps a dozen looms or frames could work. These purpose-built workshops were mainly of the eighteenth or very early nineteenth centuries, and are very easily recognized and recorded. A development on the Pennines was the fold – a group of such cottages built around a quadrangle with a common attic workshop in which combing, carding, spinning, and weaving were all carried on. Many of these folds became the nucleus of later mills. A large proportion of the weavers' cottages are scattered on the hillsides, not in hamlets, but often having a few acres of intake land around them, enough to form a small holding which supplemented the earnings, often rather meagre, that were got from the loom.[1] They form an important intermediate and overlapping group with the early factories.

The small textile-mills are found on streams among the Pennines, the Welsh hills, in the Cotswolds and other wool-growing areas with quick-running streams. They are usually small buildings, tall for their area, two- or three-storeys high. The water wheel may have been against the gable either inside, or, more commonly, outside the building. From the pitwheel on the water-wheel shaft, a vertical shaft distributed the power to each floor through bevel gears. It was easier both to make short shafts for a compact mill and also to find room alongside a hill-country stream for a small area multi-storey mill, than for a spreading one-storey structure requiring greater lengths for a single shaft carrying the whole load. In a late-eighteenth-century sale of a small cotton-mill in the Pennines, the schedule specifies the water wheel, pitwheel, vertical shaft, naked tumbling shaft on each floor (three), dam, goit, and waterway. This schedule with slight modification would fit hundreds of these early mills, intermediate between the hand workshop and the factory.

In the iron trade nail-making was always of great importance and the variety of nails immense. It was a craft which lent itself to a cottage industry structure in which each nailer could make his own type of nail for which he generally had a steady and assured market. The nail smithy was very compact, accommodated in a tiny building, a lean-to, against his house, requiring little more than a small blacksmith's hearth and an anvil. His store of rod iron could stand in a corner, and a few barrels housed his production. One feature of the nailers is that they tended to congregate in particular hamlets or sections of a village, the isolated nailer being very rare. This was because his requirements of rod iron were not enough to merit transport from the forge unless several could make up a load between them. The nailer was a specialist, so there was little rivalry among them and the dealer could collect a satisfactory and well assorted load from a group that an individual could not have supplied.

---

[1] Plans and illustrations of frame-knitters' cottages and shops will be found in D. M. Smith, *The Industrial Archaeology of the East Midlands*, 1965. The weavers' cottages and folds are illustrated in W. B. Crump and G. Ghorbal, *History of the Huddersfield Woollen Industry*, 1935 (Huddersfield).

In the nineteenth century some master nailers had prospered sufficiently to build *nailers' rows* in or near the iron-making centres. These were terraces of cottages, and behind them a corresponding terrace of small nail forges, one to each cottage. Several of these persist, but many are being lost under slum clearance, so the task of recording is now quite urgent. The machine-made nails have at last made the nailers' shop obsolete, except perhaps for a very few specialties such as climbing nails for expeditions, though even these are now being replaced by other forms.

Factories

Overlapping much of the development of the weaving and hosiery shops, a new type of organized manufacture was introduced in the silk trade. Silk spinning and weaving was brought to Spittalfields by Huguenots migrating from the Continent after the Edict of Nantes in 1685. In 1702, Thomas Catchett started silk throwing in Derby, using Dutch machinery in a mill for which the engineer George Sorocold made a thirteen and a half feet diameter water wheel placed on the river Derwent. This venture was not a success, but a London silk merchant, Thomas Lombe, and his brother, John, who had seen silk throwing machinery at work in Italy, obtained a patent in 1718 for the use of this machinery. They built a larger, five-storey mill alongside Catchett's mill, and this had a twenty-three feet diameter water wheel for power. The new mill was in work by 1721 and soon employed three hundred people. These two mills were the first of the new style *factories*, and Lombe's multi-storey block was the prototype for a vast progeny of mills in all sections of the textile manufactures – cotton, wool, and flax. Lombe's patent lapsed in 1732, and many mills were then built in Derby, Stockport, and Macclesfield.

The greatest development of the factory was in the cotton spinning section of the textile industry. The invention of the flying shuttle by Kay made it almost impossible for hand-spinners to keep pace with the weavers' demands for yarn. In the 1760s, Lewis Paul and John Wyath had attempted to spin yarn with rollers but were not commercially successful, although their rollers were incorporated in later forms of spinning machines. The successful method was invented by James Hargreaves in 1764 but it was a few years before his *jenny* was being made and sold. Richard Arkwright and John Kay, a few years later, made a spinning frame to be driven by a horse or by water power. Arkwright moved to Nottingham and with two partners built a mill in 1769, which employed about three hundred people, and was driven by a horse-wheel. The mill was four or five storeys high on a similar plan to Lombe's. The horse-wheel was a whim driven by six horses, with its wheel twenty-seven feet in diameter, toothed on the rim and driving a vertical shaft in gear with it. A horizontal shaft took off through bevel gears on each floor. This horse-mill was replaced in 1790 by a Boulton and Watt steam engine.

The available streams around Nottingham were not large enough for the developments which Arkwright had in mind so he moved to Derbyshire for his next mill, which was built at Cromford in 1771, followed by a second one in 1777. His success was such that he built in succession five more mills. Mills were multiplying at a great rate but fire was proving a real hazard. In 1793, Jedediah Strutt, for a time a partner with Arkwright, built a fireproof mill at Derby, six storeys high, with floors of shallow brick arches carried on wooden beams supported by cast-iron columns. In 1797, Charles Bage built a flax-mill at Shrewsbury on similar principles but with the added safety of cast-iron beams instead of wood. This was the first completely fireproof mill. Strutt then built, in 1803, his famous Belper North Mill on this completely fireproof design. By that time cotton-mills were being built in Lancashire and woollen-mills in Yorkshire, driven by water power and located on the lower course of the larger streams, or on the main river banks. Two factors, however, changed the pattern at the turn of the century. The steam engine began to replace the water wheel, and its dependence on coal supplies led most new mills to be built near the canals, which now made a fairly complete network through the growing industrial areas. The power loom followed the spinning inventions and along with machine combing made larger demands for power in larger mills.

Many of the earlier mills can still be found, a few occupied by some kind of rural industry, many in partial ruin, and most only as foundations with traces of wheelpits or engine and boiler foundations, roads, houses and other features to be recorded (Plate 21a). The general pattern which was functionally sound was adopted over most of the British Isles and good examples are to be found in all areas where there has been a textile industry. The flax-mills belong mostly to the mid or late nineteenth century. Some other industries, like paper and printing, adopted many features of the textile-mill. Mills are numerous enough to form a vast subject in themselves. Many of the early-nineteenth-century mills have architectural merit, and their associated buildings, power arrangements, and houses reward careful study. A powerful and reliable stream may have several mills upon it and an industrial settlement which has grown up around them.

The mills were built at a time when enclosures were causing many labouring families to leave the land and look elsewhere for a new employment. This supplied the labour force for the new mills and made the rapid industrial expansion possible. With the smaller mills the housing of this migrant population presented a difficulty which in its early stages could be met by the erection of a row or two of cottages near the mill. These 'mill cottages' were a constant feature, a part of the whole mill complex, until the problem became too great for the mill owner and the speculative builder stepped in. A few of the mill owners built good and substantial cottages, many of which are still used. Some of Strutt's cottage rows at Belper are a case in point, while many small and remote mills still have their row of half-a-dozen cottages or more, or their housing grouped round part of a quadrangular 'yard' with the mill making one side.

Some industrialists built a new hamlet or village. Arkwright, in 1784, started New Lanark in connection with the mill he was building there, and this was continued and extended by Robert Owen and included schools for children and social facilities for adults. Perhaps the most complete of many of these schemes was the rather late one by Titus Salt. He decided to remove his work from Bradford to a site on the banks of the river Aire where the Leeds and Liverpool Canal and the Midland Railway both crossed his proposed mill site. Lockwood and Mawson, the architects, were advised by Ruskin and Millais. The result was the creation of a unified new village and mill, under the name Saltaire. Here, mills, housing, schools, institute, chapels, hospital, all the services of a community of about three thousand people were integrated in a single excellent architectural design. The mill opened for work in 1856 and is still in full use. This magnificent mill has a link with the very earliest ones, in being designed for Lockwood and Mawson by the engineer, Fairbairn, so that all its arrangements, including power and transmissions, are part of a unified whole.

When weaving was transferred to the mills a separate feature, the *weaving shed*, was added. This accommodation for the looms is one storey only with a roof made up of asymmetric ridges, where possible running east and west. The steep side of each ridge is to the north, and is glazed, so ensuring a uniform north light and excluding direct sunlight. Apart from a very definite architectural style adopted in the nineteenth-century cotton-spinning mills of Lancashire, carried out in red brick which makes them recognizable at a glance, there is usually very little to indicate the precise use of an individual mill. While the mills are dominantly a textile feature, other industries – paper-making, printing, clothing, flour-milling, boot and shoe-making and a few others – have adopted the mill-type of building, but these are mainly of the late nineteenth century.

There is one other type of industrial building which is varied and spread over the whole industrial scene – the warehouse. Raw materials and finished goods, vastly increasing in quantity as industry developed, had to be accommodated in suitable stores both at the place of manufacture and at points in transit along the various lines of transport, for distribution and for import and export. This building is the warehouse, ranging from the one or two rooms of the small, individual mill, to the vast structures of a busy port. The essentials of any warehouse are safe storage with adequate facilities for receiving, handling, and quickly moving goods in and out. Cranes, trucks, conveyors, and special means of handling and moving materials will be the bulk of the equipment of a warehouse.

The warehouse needs the maximum storage space for its goods, combined with easy handling. Before the appearance of the fork-lift bogies in the twentieth century, all piling up of goods was done by manual strength. Because of the difficulty of piling, say, bales of wool, weighing more than three hundredweights each, on top of one another, warehouses were designed with floors of great area spaced at relatively small heights so that an empty warehouse gives the impression of a vast but low room. The area of floor needs rows of pillars, usually of cast-iron, to support it. Many warehouses are of the fireproof construction introduced by Strutt at Belper and Bage at Shrewsbury, so that the ceiling is a series of flat arches of brick carried on cast-iron beams on the supporting pillars. These warehouse interiors can be very impressive, and can offer much interesting and varied detail in the cast iron members, pillars, capitals, brackets, and beams. The lowness of individual storeys allows many of the larger warehouses to be of five or six storeys, a structure reflected on the elevation by the rows of vertically close-spaced windows.

A feature of the wool warehouses, which because of the bulk and large quantities of the wool are large and imposing buildings of four, five, or six storeys, is the row of landing doors, one above the other, usually in the gable of the building. These are tall double doors, opening without balcony or stage into space above the road or yard beneath them. In the peak of the gable the jib of a crane or hoist projects, with the blocks and hooked and weighted rope ready to be used in hoisting the wool sacks to the required floor. The simplest of these hoists are horse-operated. A pulley is mounted near ground level, so arranged that it can swing round to any angle to the wall. A rope reeved through a block on the jib, brought down and taken through this ground pulley, is hitched to a horse. When the load is hooked to the ascending rope, the horse walks away along the side of the street or across the mill yard, and the load goes up (Plate 22a).

There is a great variety to be observed in the hoists, some hand-operated from any floor, some with a mechanical drive which is controlled from alongside any of the doors. It was a boyhood thrill, when living in the woollen areas, and walking along the banks of the Leeds and Liverpool Canal, to watch for the sacks of wool being hoisted and to see the ware-houseman, three or four storeys above the canal, his left hand holding the control rope of the hoist, stretch out at seemingly impossible angles to snatch the sack with his sack-hook and pull it safely in at his door.

Occasionally at the canal warehouse another form of hoist, a true crane, is used. The vertical member of the crane is held against the warehouse wall in a footstep and top bearing, with its horizontal jib stayed by a large diagonal strut or by iron rods. Swinging out from the wall a load can be picked up directly from a barge on the canal, and the crane is so placed that when the load is high enough the crane swings it round exactly into the landing door. Sometimes the cranes have manually-operated blocks or else a power winch in the warehouse. All are worth recording, some being of the late eighteenth century, some of the early nineteenth, but all are of extreme simplicity and very robust construction. These and the many hoisting devices would be a rewarding study and it might be worthwhile recording and comparing the differences found along the different canals and at warehouses where different goods were the dominant load (Plate 23a).

Every mill and factory has its own warehouse either as part of the mill or as an essential ancillary building. Ports, canal wharves, and railway loading points have the biggest concentrations, and there are the manu-facturers' and traders' wholesale warehouses in the larger cities. In the second half of the nineteenth century the display warehouse was added – premises in London or a large city where a stock of a producer's wares could be inspected and bought by the general public. Some of these, like Wedgwood's London warehouse, became fashionable places for the leisured public to visit and as places where dealers could see actual products rather than studying the figures in a catalogue.

Some of the most interesting and attractive warehouse groups are to be found on the canals and at the ports. A town like Stourport was built entirely around the junction of a canal and river, and most of its buildings are concerned with the canal operations (and now with a very considerable pleasure boating industry). The town as it stands is almost a living museum of canal working. Docking basins surrounded by fine warehouses, offices, houses, workshops, and factories are all built to serve the canal. At this point on the Severn there was in the mid eighteenth century a solitary ale house, used by a few Severn hauliers. In 1772, when the Staffordshire and Worcestershire Canal was completed, a new town sprang up at the canal and river junction. Not only warehouses but boat-building yards, and a considerable foundry, were established, and the place soon became one of the principal distributing centres for goods to and from the whole West Midlands. A comparison can usefully be made with Bewdley, a few miles up the Severn from Stourport., Bewdley was an earlier port for river traffic, with a large trade in corn, provender, iron, and other goods brought from a wide area, for transfer to river transport. The goods were carried by packhorse trains or wagons to and from the river wharves, which are still a feature of the town. There are fine warehouses, blocks of stables, blacksmith and farrier businesses to be found among the buildings of the town, and it is clear that all its history has been tied up for centuries with transport on the river (Plate 18b).

Goole is another town, the creation of the Aire and Calder Navigation Company who built docks, warehouses, boat-yards, offices, and a town, around the terminal of their canal, in the early years of the 1820s. Almost every town or city reached by canal has its block of warehouses around a dock or group of wharves, and these show much variation in style and design according to the chief goods carried. Some are designed for the corn and food trades, some for wool or cotton, some for timber, and so on. All have a complement of cranes and hoists, and in some the canal basin is extended under the warehouses so that loading and unloading can be done out of the weather. This can still be seen in the old canal warehouses at the splendid canal-head at Shardlow, Derbyshire. Some canals have been abandoned in this century and their tracks filled in, but the buildings

1 Horse whim on a coal pit. Water-colour by Paul Sandby, *c.* 1785.

2a   Modern blast furnaces at the Appleby-Frodingham Works, British Steel Corporation, Lincolnshire.

2b   Part view of the Billingham chemical plant of Imperial Chemical Industries, Durham.

3a Trip hammers at Abbeydale Industrial Hamlet, Sheffield.
3b Helve hammer, Kirkstall Forge, Leeds. Made in the works about 1730, this hammer was in use until 1918. It was powered by a cast-iron undershot water wheel.

4 Iron Forge at Tintern, Monmouthshire. Engraving by B. T. Pounce after a drawing by Thomas Hearne, 1790.

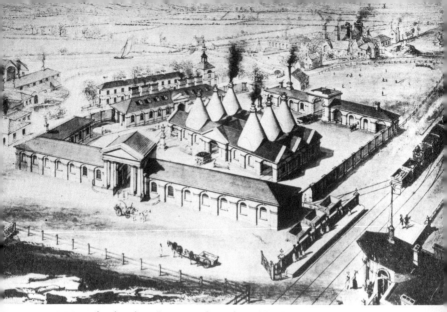

5a Architect's drawing for a steel works with six cementation furnaces, Sheffield.

5b The same cementation furnaces just prior to their demolition in 1970.

6a   Embsey Moor. One of the Stone Ridge quarries, sixteenth and seventeenth centuries, Yorkshire, W.R.

6b   Pulping rollers and old steam crane at Kenton quarry, Gosforth, Northumberland, 1932.

7a   A stone saw. Engraving from Pyne's Microcosm, 1803.

7b   Wheelwrights constructing a mill. Pyne's Microcosm, 1803.

8a   Lime kiln, Toft Gate, Pateley Bridge. This was a large commercial kiln built in its quarry, with a flue from the top to a stumpy chimney some distance away; Yorkshire, W.R.

8b   A Scotch kiln: the Tilery, Rilston, in course of excavation, 1971. This shows half of the square tower, and four of the stoke hole arches. There were eight in the complete kiln; Yorkshire, W.R.

9a Old alum quarries at Ravenscar, Yorkshire, N.R. Trace of the incline from inland quarries is clearly seen.

9b Remains of wharf, Sandsend, near Whitby. Built for shipping alum from various parts of the Mulgrave estates. Extensive buildings were being demolished when this record photograph was taken in 1948.

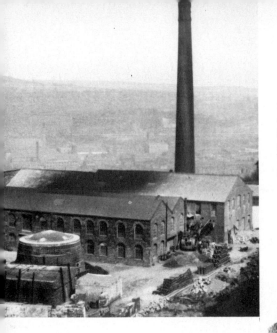

10a   Brick works at Wrose, Airedale, with a rectangular and two circular kilns of down-draught type, 1930, Yorkshire, W.R. Now demolished.

10b   The glass cone at Catcliffe, Yorkshire, W.R.

Opposite page : 11
Oast houses, Kent.

12a   Team of oxen ploughing. Pyne's Microcosm, 1803.

12b   Horse-mill with edge
runners. Pyne's Microcosm,
1803.

13   Bourn post-mill, Cambridgeshire.

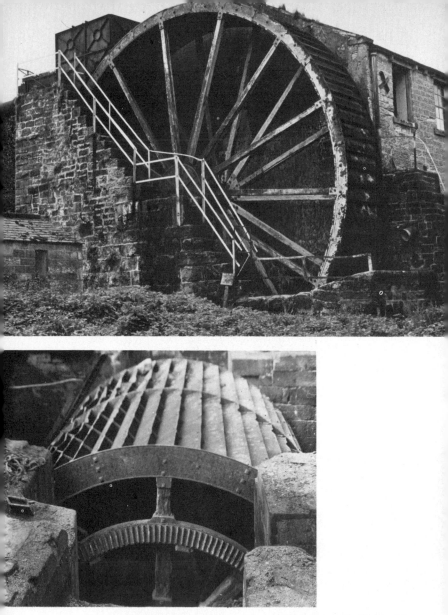

14a Overshot water wheel at Foster Beck flax-mill, Nidderdale, built 1864. Yorkshire, W.R.

14b Small-diameter, broad-faced wheel at Linton cotton-mill, Wharfedale, demolished in 1912. Yorkshire, W.R.

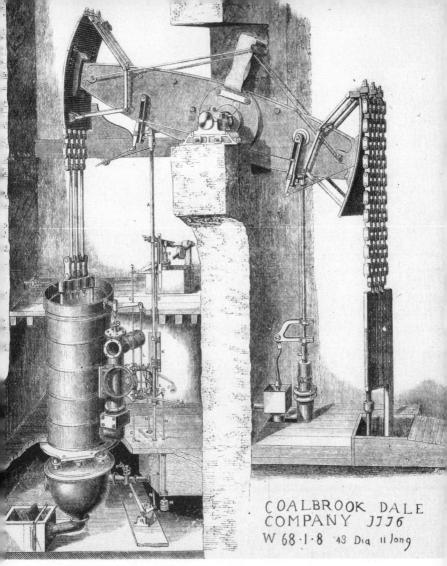

COALBROOK DALE
COMPANY 1776
W 68·1·8 43 Dia 11 long

15   Atmospheric engine made at Coalbrookdale in 1776, Shropshire,
still working in 1880.

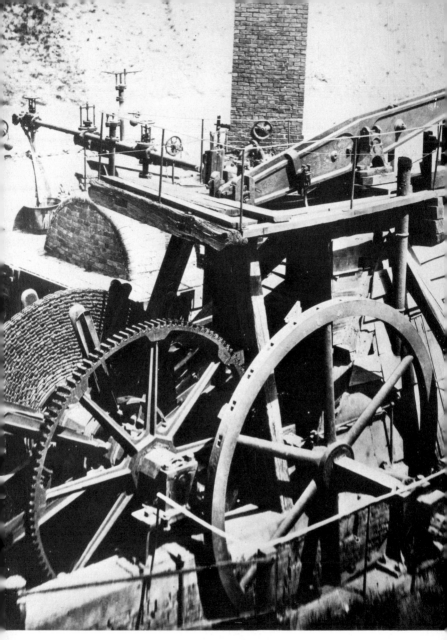

16   Heslop engine made at Coalbrookdale at work on a pit at Lawley, Shropshire, winding with a flat chain.

17a Levant Mine on the cliffs near St Just, Cornwall, in 1895. It worked until 1930.

17b Thackthwaite Mine, Wensleydale, about 1910. Remains of bouse teams, bucking floor, hotching tub, and sieve.

18a Charcoal burning, Wyre Forest, 1934. Typical charcoal burner's hut in the background.

18b Stourport harbour, Worcestershire.

19a Sunk road and bridge over the Ribble at Stainforth – part of a fifteenth-century pack-horse road, Yorkshire, W.R.

19b Pack-horse bridge at Oardale, near Harrogate. This was the early form, parapets being usually a much later addition.

20a Scribbling-mill, Upper Clough House, Merrydale, Slaithwaite, built in 1785. The seventeenth-century farmhouse and the early eighteenth-century cottages have weavers' windows and are a typical weavers' colony; Yorkshire, W.R.

20b Weaver's cottage, Bottoms, Almondbury near Huddersfield; seventeenth-century, with an addition at right.

21a Grassington Low Mill, Wharfedale, *c*. 1790. Typical rural mill. Corn-mill then extended for worsted spinning, then silk, saw-mill, furniture and turnery, finally a poultry battery. The right-hand approach formerly carried the goit for a water wheel inside the building.

21b Abraham-Darby Furnace, Coalbrookdale, at an early stage of the excavations in 1956, Shropshire.

22a   Canal warehouse, wharf, and crane, Leeds and Liverpool Canal, Skipton, 1780, now a sports supply centre.

22b   Dent Head viaduct, Settle to Carlisle Railway, 1875.

23a Pattern and moulding shop cranes, Coalbrookdale, *c.* 1800.

23b Pit wheel, wallower and crown wheel, at Newby Bridge water corn-mill. The wallower is a lantern wheel, Yorkshire, W.R.

24 Roman smelted lead pigs from Charterhouse, Somerset. Antoninus, A.D. 138–161, Vespasian, A.D. 69–79.

25 Morwellham Harbour on the river Tamar, Devon, *c*. 1870. The track of the incline from the Tavistock Canal can be seen, and the broad wharves with light rail tracks, where copper ores were stored for loading.

26 Engine house, Botallack Mine, Cornwall. One of the most spectacular of the pumping engine shafts near Lands End.

27 Five Rise Locks, Leeds and Liverpool Canal, Bingley. Lock-keeper's cottage at the foot of the locks on the left; the mills in the distance are all built on the canal side.

28   Abbeydale Industrial Hamlet. Restored as a Sheffield City Museum.

29 Grassington Moor smelt-mill chimney being repaired by members of the Earby Mines Research Group, June 1971. An earlier repair (1968) can be seen at the foot where vandals had tried to fell it.

30a   Octagon smelt-mill, Arkengarthdale, in 1923, now demolished; Yorkshire, N.R.

30b   Water wheel at Octagon Mill.

31a Ore crusher and wheel at the Providence mine, Kettlewell, *c*. 1924.

31b Providence crushers, 1960, now removed to the Craven Museum, Skipton.

32 Fourteenth- or fifteenth-century frame house being rebuilt at the Weald Museum, Chichester.

around the wharves and termini are still in use and much remains to be recorded.

There is another group of fine buildings which is being very properly recorded and this is the general class of *exchanges*. Many of the larger country towns have their corn exchange, and the cities can provide wool, cotton, cloth, coal, and other exchanges. Most of them are architectural features and in their internal arrangements are often of great interest. Nonetheless, they are concerned only with the buying and selling of goods and raw materials, a part of commerce which may be as essential to industry as are the banks, but which has no part in the actual production industry. Whether these buildings should be included as part of industrial archaeology is open to question. Perhaps they should join much more that, in the opening and exploratory years of the subject, has been included, but which might now seem to belong more properly to an organization for preservation and recording of social and economic history rather than industry.

On this borderline of recording a case can be made out for taking notice of early industrial housing. In the development of the factories there was a progressive, though very slow, improvement in working conditions. The dim, crowded, and unhealthy factories were replaced by later designs with more window space, safer placing of machinery with respect to the operative, and better sanitary conditions. The rapid expansion of industries and the mass influx of workers to the towns by the opening of the nineteenth century created an acute housing problem. Rows of identical houses built to minimum standards and at minimum cost were multiplied around the factories. These became a vital part of the environment in which the worker lived his life, divided between home and workplace, and with very little time to spend beyond those two. This housing, as a very essential part of the industrial environment, deserves study and recording as much as the factories. The housing previously mentioned, that put up by the employer as part and parcel of his factory, should have the priority in these studies, and the great rash of speculative industrial housing might well be left in part to the care of the social historian.

Some nineteenth-century building is so closely connected with the building of the new and larger mills that it can claim a legitimate place in the overall picture of industrial development. Like Saltaire there are whole sections of some towns which were built by employers for their workpeople. Of these Swindon, built alongside the railway workshops, is an example in which the standard of the housing and layout is still acceptable. The mining village of Nent Head, Cumberland, was created by the London Lead Company in the years following the concentration of their smelt-mills and mines in Alston Moor, with this valley head, five miles from Alston, as their headquarters. The first cottages were built in the high valley (the lowest point of the village is at 1,450 ft OD) near to the smelt-mill, soon after 1753; then by 1820 a new village centre was planned and built nearby. The houses of the new village were built in blocks of two or four, the overmen, doctor and schoolmaster in the semi-detached houses, smelters and miners in the blocks of four, but the two and four blocks alternated so that foremen, smelters, miners, doctors, and other professional and official people were neighbours and there was no segregation of the higher paid. Market hall, public wash-houses, co-operative stores, reading room and band room, church, chapel, and schools were all part of the general plan. The main building was along the hillside adjoining and overlooking the dressing floors, mine shops, and mine entrances, and not far from the smelt-mills. This was a great convenience, given the height and the wildish climate of the high Pennines. Examples such as this cannot be studied apart from the industries which created them.[1]

In the textile towns the connection is not so direct, though when a large mill was being built a number of streets of houses were generally built by a speculative builder, forming a single area as near as possible to the mill. These close-set rows of identical houses in parallel streets stand out on any plan of the town, and in their early days the uniformity of the houses was matched by the uniformity of the occupation of the tenants at the neighbouring mill. One characteristic of most of these areas of industrial housing is a total lack of public buildings, shops, churches, and so on, within their area, these being clustered either around the periphery or provided by the old town to which the area is added. The occasional small corner shop has generally been made from a dwelling house at some more recent date. The earliest industrial housing usually has no pretence at a garden but in the later years of the nineteenth century a narrow strip was added before each house, more of a token than a viable garden. It would be reasonable to include in industrial archaeology studies of such housing blocks, which, when built, were almost entirely occupied by industrial workers from factories close at hand. The demand for the houses was provided by the coming or expansion of a particular industry. It is possible

[1] This village is described in A. Raistrick, *Two Centuries of Industrial Welfare*, 1939.

that housing schemes such as Bournville, Birmingham, New Earswick, York, Port Sunlight, Bromborough, or other model villages built by a single industrialist should come into the category of industrial housing, but each would need a detailed and individual study.

Canal structures

The very extensive canal system we still possess has many bridges and aqueducts dating from the late eighteenth century, and these deserve as much attention as the warehouses. Among the earliest are the Barton Aqueduct over the river Irwell on the Bridgewater Canal, and the Seven Arches near Bingley, Yorkshire, carrying the Leeds and Liverpool Canal over the river Aire (1774). These aqueducts are entirely of stone and the canal channel is lined with puddled clay. In 1796 cast-iron was used for the first time to form a canal trough across the river Tern at Longden in Shropshire, an aqueduct still standing but now dry. The combination of stone and cast-iron came with Telford's great Pontcysyllte aqueduct near Llangollen, with its cast-iron canal trough carried on nineteen 121-feet-high stone piers, one of the finest canal monuments in the country. Coming down the scale from these almost national monuments there are hundreds, even thousands, of humbler bridges, many of them meeting local conditions with ingenuity and worth careful recording.

Railway structures

The railways have a large variety of buildings connected with them, many of which are now becoming obsolete since the introduction of diesel and electric traction; and in the vast reorganization of the last few years, still in progress, nearly all the fine engine houses, watering standards and pumping houses, turntables and other structures have disappeared. With the closing of many short local lines, some of them of early date, stations, bridges, warehouses, marshalling yards, and other buildings and grouped structures are being demolished and the necessity for an intensive campaign of recording is obvious. Fortunately the body of railway enthusiasts is still growing and sufficient manpower should be available to secure a nearly complete recording before it is too late.

The structures most familiar to the travelling public are, of course, the stations. These vary in their materials – timber, brick, and stone – and some use cast-iron in the platform structures, particularly the roofing. The larger termini are important architecturally and structurally. Many of the smaller rural stations are almost entirely timber-built, though, if there is a station master's house attached, this is likely to be built in brick or stone. The buildings of the different companies differ in their elaboration, design, and arrangement, but as a whole they are being well recorded by various local societies. Nearly every station has a goods yard with a warehouse, stone- or brick-built, and many country stations had cattle docks with pens. The Victorian Society has listed sixty railway stations which it considers worthy of preservation. These naturally tend to be the larger stations, though a few smaller ones of special historical (Wylam) or architectural (Beal) interest are included. On the whole, however, the selection has been made on architectural merit and not for importance in the history or development of railways.

Among imposing structures which were built by the railways, some of the finest are the bridges and viaducts. Cast-iron was used at an early date, and wrought-iron a little later. One of the earliest viaducts was that which carried the Manchester-to-Liverpool line over the Sankey Brook. In the north of England there are some fine stone viaducts, several of them on the Settle-to-Carlisle portion of the London, Midland, and Scottish line and dating from the 1860s. The fine viaduct at Batty Moss, Ribblehead, makes a splendid feature although it is set as neighbour to the natural giants of Ingleborough and Whernside. The Dent Head, Arten Gill, and Armathwaite viaducts and many others on this line, though late in railway history, need careful recording now that the line is threatened with closure (Plate 22b). One of the largest cast-iron span bridges is the Albert Edward bridge near Ironbridge, Shropshire, designed in 1863 by John Fowler, and cast at the Horsehay works of the Coalbrookdale Company. This, although dwarfed by the cooling towers of the new power station alongside, still retains its impressive dignity.

Some of the railway bridges such as the Forth, the Menai Straits tubular bridge, the Saltash viaduct, Devon, and many others are national monuments, but the public attention attracted by these larger works has distracted it from the hundreds of smaller bridges which include among them many worthy of recording and preservation. There is little need to elaborate the detail of more railway structures, as they are at present receiving more attention from the preservation groups than almost any other monuments of the nineteenth century.

PART TWO

A View of
Industrial Archaeology in Britain

CHAPTER 10

Prehistoric and Roman Industries

In Part One attention has been directed mainly to the materials of industrial archaeology and to a suggested scheme for their study. The natural raw materials with the industries based upon them have been placed in a related order, and the processes necessary for their winning, preparation, and manufacture have been described in order to indicate the type of structures likely to be associated with those activities. In much of the field of industrial archaeology it is the remains of these structures and processes that provide the evidence of past industries and industrial sites. It is the abandoned and often largely forgotten sites which call for the skills of exploration, recording, and interpretation, the efficient application of which will be materially helped by a knowledge of industrial processes. It is clear that this calls for a large measure of teamwork and for an early recognition of the person with the right technical knowledge who should be brought in to share the recording and interpretation.

During the last century, archaeology has approached near to becoming an exact science. The archaeologist can uncover and investigate fragmentary remains, can usually interpret them in terms of the life and activities of a community, and, by relating them to other comparable finds, can re-create a picture of life in a past environment which can be accepted with a considerable degree of confidence.[1] If industrial archaeology is to justify its name, then the methods of archaeological interpretation should be applied to the remains of industries, whatever the period of time to which they belong. Archaeological work has opened up the evidence that true industries have flourished even in the later prehistoric periods, and unless industrial archaeology is going to insist on the presence of machinery and mechanical power as the trademark of its studies it must give, and can profitably give, far more emphasis to these earlier phases of industry, and

[1] We owe much of this new attitude to the teaching of V. G. Childe, particularly to his *Prehistoric Communities of the British Isles*, 1940, and *What happened in History*, 1942.

must cease to place its main emphasis (except quantitatively) on the last two and a half centuries.

The methods of archaeological exploration will be applicable not only to the earliest sites of industrial activity but to many which fall within the period of the Industrial Revolution. With many sites of the nineteenth century good photography and some measurement can accomplish a satisfactory recording and it is often possible to collect a series of early photographs, prints, or drawings which will demonstrate the later history, buildings, and equipment. There are, however, a multitude of early sites which are not easily seen on the ground. They are buried under accumulations of rubbish, or may have been levelled and covered by later building. In such cases only the strict application of archaeological techniques will ensure a full and correct recording of the site and allow some assessment of the industry they represent.

An example of this argument is Panningridge Furnace, Sussex. The De L'Isle and Dudley MSS include detailed accounts of the working of a furnace in the sixteenth century at this site which was identified by fieldwork, based upon the documents, by D. W. Crossley of Sheffield University. He decided that it would afford a chance to obtain some close-dated sixteenth-century slags, and the plan of an early furnace, built in 1542. Exploratory trenches were cut through difficult waterlogged ground in 1964. One trench cut an area of slag heaps, and sherds of sixteenth-century pottery confirmed the date. Subsequent extended excavations in following seasons discovered the foundations of a furnace, with the remains of its water wheel and bellows, and continued excavation showed that this furnace had been abandoned and a second furnace built partly over its site. The physical structure and the succession in time of the two furnaces, their wheels, bellows, dams, slags, and ancillaries, were strikingly interpreted from the fragmentary remains uncovered. These results illuminate, or are illuminated by, the very full manuscript accounts of the furnace working.[1]

A case has already been stated for taking more serious account of the earlier industries, even from Roman and pre-Roman times, and so a number of specific examples of the exploration and interpretation of a

[1] D. W. Crossley, in a series of interim reports of the excavations given in the *Bull. Hist. Metallurgy Group*, from I, No. 3, 1964, to IV, No. 1, 1970. When Crossley's full account of these excavations, combined with his work on the manuscripts, is published, it will soon become a classic of true industrial archaeology.

variety of sites, comparable with the work briefly outlined on Panningridge Furnace, will be discussed from all periods. If these examples are chosen in an approximate chronological sequence, both the development and continuity of industries might be apparent, and at the same time methods of investigation and interpretation will be illustrated. Such a view of industrial archaeology will do little more than suggest the richness of the earlier field for investigation, which the insistence on 'with special reference to the Industrial Revolution' has largely overlooked.

Prehistoric

The period chosen for the start of these descriptions is the neolithic revolution, the opening of the New Stone Age, when man moved from hunter-food-collector communities into farmer-food-producer groups. This was no sudden change, but was accomplished slowly in this country around the middle of the fourth millennium B.C. A prime activity for the farmer was the clearance of forest, and for this efficient stone axes were required. Flint implements had been in use all through the Old Stone Age, but for tree felling, finer axes, still of flint, were chipped to shape but then ground and polished to a sharp cutting edge. A few hard, fine-grained stones besides flint were discovered, and the great demand caused an industry (with the main elements of a modern industry) to be created. Miners got the raw material; axe-makers shaped and polished the axes; traders carried them all over the country.[1] We will look at two examples of the axe industry – the flint axes of Grimes Graves, Norfolk, and the fine stone axes of Great Langdale, Westmorland – and see that the finding and working out of these ancient industries has a very proper place in industrial archaeology.

The two examples chosen are by no means the only mining sites of neolithic date in the country, the making of axes and the mining of flint and stone for this purpose being now known in many areas. The origin of the industry is not known with certainty. The type of pottery associated with the Windmill Hill culture, introduced by an immigrant group at the beginning of the third millennium B.C. from the Continent, has been found at Grimes Graves and several other mining sites, but the mining did not start until about 2000 B.C. It is still a matter of conjecture whether the

[1] In 1953, the efficiency of these axes was demonstrated when three men, using actual Neolithic axes, cleared 600 square yards of silver birch scrub in four hours. One axe felled 400 trees without resharpening. S. Cole, *Neolithic Revolution*, 1959.

Windmill Hill folk evolved the idea of mining flint, or whether the idea was introduced by immigrants of a second group. Whatever the true explanation, the fact is that mines are found on many sites both on the flint areas of East Anglia and the Downs and the uplands of the older rocks, all having a date in the neolithic period between about 2500 and 1700 B.C. There is little to choose in date between the Langdale axes and the Grimes Graves axes, though the site of Grimes Graves has been known for a very long time and was the earliest to be fully studied.

In an area of about thirty-four acres in the corner of Weeting parish, Norfolk (TL 817898), about five and a half miles north-west of Thetford, there are a vast collection of shallow pits and depressions, long the subject of speculation, until in 1870 excavations by Canon Greenwell in two of them demonstrated that they were shafts, forty feet deep, with low galleries radiating from the base. In the galleries picks of red-deer antlers were found and plenty of evidence that they were indeed flint mines. A large area at the surface was a flint dressing floor with flakes, broken axes and reject material showing that there axes had been roughed out of the flint and some had then been ground and polished. Subsequent explorations between 1923 and 1939 (mainly by A. L. Armstrong) and a complete review of the site has shown that there are between seven hundred and eight hundred pits and over one hundred chipping floors in the thirty-four acres. The date has been the subject of some controversy, but in 1933 it was demonstrated beyond doubt that the mines were of neolithic date, and later radio-carbon dating has suggested the range of the pits as between 2330 and 1740 B.C.

In 1931, the Ministry of Public Buildings and Works took the custody of the site, and two pits were cleared and made accessible to the public as being typical of the whole site; and indeed every feature of the mines can be studied in them. The shafts, which are sunk through the chalk to reach a particularly good layer of tabular flint, range from forty feet deep at the south-east part of the site, but because of the dip of the chalk only thirty feet at the north-west. From the foot of the shaft galleries radiate or form a complex maze, one shaft having as many as twenty-seven galleries or connections to other pits. The galleries vary in height, occasionally being five feet but more commonly between two and two and a half feet. Some are seven feet wide with room for two men to work in them, but most are only two or three feet, and provide work room for only one man. The principal tool was made of red-deer antler with all tines but one cut off. These have been used as ordinary picks on soft chalk layers, but on harder chalk they were probably hammered into the joints and used to lever out the lumps of chalk, to uncover the flint 'floorstone' layer. Estimating by the number of picks found in the various excavated galleries, it is suggested that through-out their working life the mines used up about 50,000 picks. The shoulder blades of large animals made shovels, and for the harder flint in some places polished axes of other tougher stone than flint were used. The chip-ping floors are marked by small areas of flint chips, the debris being some-times as much as five feet thick.

The distribution of the polished flint axes is not known, as those actu-ally made at Grimes Graves cannot yet be distinguished from those from many other sources. It appears from the numerous other mining sites that the flint axes were mainly for local use in the east and south-east, and that it was the axes of special quality stone from the Lake District, Wales, and Cornwall that had a wide trade value over much of the country.

For many years numbers of polished stone axes made of a fine-grained greenish-grey rock have been recognized in specimens from various parts of the country to be of the same material and workmanship and so of the same origin. Another group of axes of a different rock, but all of similar character, was also known and the rock was recognized as being an igneous rock of rather special type and restricted occurrence in North Wales. In 1919, the source of this rock at Graig Llwyd, Penmaenmawr, was explored and axes in many stages of manufacture were evidence of an 'axe factory' from which the axes had been distributed over much of the south between the Severn and Hampshire.

In the Lake District, Professor D. M. S. Watson had, many years ago, found a place on Stake Pass where there was a quantity of chips and flakes of the same rock as the grey stone axes, recognized by that time as being a volcanic tuff from the Borrowdale Volcanic Series, and suggested that axes or other tools had been made there. This tuff occurs in the Langdale Pikes, and makes large screes running below the crags of Pike of Stickle from about 2,000 ft OD down to 700 ft OD. In October 1947, Brian Bunch and his wife, climbing on the great scree of Mickleden, recognized a partly-made axe and a large quantity of flakes of the well-known axe rock. In June 1948 they returned to the site and found that the scree contained an abundance of flakes and large numbers of roughly chipped axes in various stages of manufacture. Research in following years has clearly demon-strated that here, and on a few other smaller sites round about, there was a large industry engaged in roughing out axes by chipping, getting the stone from the innumerable boulders on the scree. The position, exposed high on the mountain-side, makes it certain that the axe-makers worked only seasonally, deserting the site through the cold and stormier part of the year.

None of the axes found at the Langdale sites was polished, but a neolithic settlement on the shore of Ehenside Tarn, near Beckermet in West Cumberland, seventeen miles away, was excavated during the early 1870s when the tarn was drained and proved to have been a large habitation site of people, with hearths and cooking pots, who made many objects in wood, and hunted, and who occupied the site permanently. Among objects then discovered which now assume great significance were rough axes from Langdale, as well as partly and wholly polished ones. Blocks of the local red sandstone had been used for the grinding and polishing. It is now clear that suitable stone was got and 'roughs' chipped out on the Langdale screes in the summer season and then carried to Ehenside and other coastal sites, where they were ground and polished to their final condition.[1]

The skill of the Ehenside folk in using wood is shown by the occurrence on the site of a beautifully hafted Langdale axe. From the polishing sites the finished axes were distributed over the country. Some were carried east on to the Pennines and down to the east Midlands. Many went down into the Severn basin and spread southward among the neolithic settlements right down into Hampshire. A few reached the Isle of Man and Scotland. The bulk of them appear to have been carried either by sea, along the western coasts, or by the great route across the Pennines into Yorkshire and the eastern and south-eastern areas. The more of these axes being recognized, both found and recognized in collections, the clearer it becomes that we are dealing with a well-organized industry, getting its raw material, manufacturing and distributing its finished products. The date at which this industry flourished is linked with the recognized forest clearance, of which there is good biological evidence, and which was achieved between 2500 and 1500 B.C. The axes, as a very useful and efficient tool, were probably made and traded for a further 500 years or more.

[1] There are three important papers on this industry and its products: B. Bunch, and C. I. Fell, 'A Stone Axe Factory at Pike of Stickle, Great Langdale, Westmorland', *Proc. Pre-hist. Soc.*, 1949; R. G. Flint, 'Stone Axe Factory Sites in the Cumbrian Fells', *Trans. Cumb. and Westd. Arch. and Ant. Soc.*, 2nd. ser., 62, 1962; J. Davies, 'Some Recent, Prehistoric Finds of Lake District Origin from the Yorkshire Pennines', *ibid.*, 63, 1963.

The neolithic period was brought to a gradual end by the coming of people, the first waves of whom came from the Mediterranean via Ireland, and were workers in bronze, and perhaps builders of the megalithic stone monuments and tombs. They were soon followed by the spread of the so-called Beaker folk from the Rhine provinces and neighbouring parts of the Continent, who brought with them the use of more sophisticated bronze articles, a trade which crossed to England then continued westward into Ireland. Along the early route bronze axes and gold ornaments were brought to the neolithic traders, and travelling metal-workers brought metal with them, set up their forges and cast new implements in their temporary settlement. This trade was very widespread, but throughout its duration it was characterized by itinerant workers, as was the later bronze working coming in the other direction – into England from the Continent. This was a trade or industry carried on by an army of individualists, in which the many remains are only the traces of individual workers and very small events in its total distribution.

The addition of iron to the exploitation of bronze and gold brought in the Iron Age, and during its later centuries, perhaps from 300 B.C. onward, iron-making became fairly widespread, though localized at numerous small centres. Lead mining, pottery, weaving, and other crafts were practised, but, as in the Bronze Age, the industries were still very localized and not much different from the domestic stage of later industries.

Roman

True industries with localized and organized workplaces were reintroduced by the Romans, who also took over, organized, and expanded the small-scale efforts of the native population. Lead mining, based almost entirely on native-worked sites, became under the normal Roman custom an Imperial industry with a large and important export section. Iron-working and pottery both became large industries feeding a very substantial internal demand, not only of the occupying Roman army, though this was considerable, but of the Romano–British and native population as well. The greatest factor in this rapid industrial development was the splendid road system by which the products of industries in almost any part of the country could be carried quickly to the Roman towns and forts, as well as to the ports.

Lead mining

Soon after their conquest of Britain the Romans organized the lead mining
and smelting which was already an activity of the Celtic Iron Age people
on a small scale. They organized mining in many areas – the Mendips,
Flintshire, Shropshire, Derbyshire, and Yorkshire. The finding of no less
than eighty pigs of their smelted lead, which had been lost in transit to the
ports, for export, indicates an industry of large extent. The first pig to be
recorded from Mendip was found before 1544, which by its inscription is
dated to A.D. 49.[1] The location of the Roman mines, in spite of other finds
of lead objects, was not known until the early years of the nineteenth century. In 1818, the Rev. John Skinner and Sir Richard Colt Hoare were
walking the Roman road from Old Sarum to Uphill, and where it passed
the village of Charterhouse their attention was taken by an area of mounds
which suggested a settlement. Skinner says, 'a considerable tract of ground
was covered with squares, circles, and other irregularities. In digging we
turned up, beneath the blackest soil I ever saw, abundance of pottery,
from the fine Samian to the coarsest species, iron nails, scoriae of iron,
etc. . . .' Skinner revisited the site in 1819 and learned that Roman coins
and other things were often found in the area. The enclosures extended
over sixty or seventy acres. His visits continued and his digging turned up
many small objects. In August 1822 he saw three pigs of lead which a
farmer had dug up earlier that year, but these were later melted down.
Skinner made further excavations in 1824, but kept no measured notes
such as would be made today (Plate 24).

In 1846, a hoard of about nine hundred Roman coins ranging from A.D.
200 to 284 was dug up at Charterhouse, then in 1853 another pig of Roman
lead was found, from A.D. 49. Further information other than casual finds,
however, comes from the time in which the hillocks of debris and slag left
by old miners were being reworked, about 1867. The soil of the field where
they were working was impregnated with lead, and lumps of ore also were
found, and remains identified as those of primitive furnaces were uncovered. Notice of these finds in the archaeological journals attracted
many visitors, one of whom left a useful description of the area. There is a

[1] The Romans cast their lead in oblong pigs in moulds tapering slightly to the base. Inscriptions
impressed into the base of the mould were reproduced on the pig, in relief. The first Charterhouse pig to be found has the inscription TI.CLAVD.CAESAR.AVG.PM.T.R.VIIII.
IMP.XVI.DE.BRITAN. This means '(the property of) Tiberius Claudius Caesar Augustus,
Pontifex Maximus, holder of the Tribunician power, for the ninth time, Imperator for the sixteenth time. From Britain.' Its date is therefore A.D. 49.

shallow valley, Blackmoor, just north-east of Charterhouse, with a stream running part way down it until lost in swallow holes. The two fields where most discoveries had been made were thick with slag and mine refuse with a good deal of charcoal. The foundations of huts, and among them furnaces, one of which was built of sandstone and had lead ore and charcoal adhering to the inside, are evidence of a smelting area. The evidence for a mining and smelting settlement is quite convincing, but a full and skilled investigation of the site is still very desirable.

More pigs were found at Charterhouse, making seven in all. The lead industry was very extensive, the lead going from the various mining areas by several routes to three principal ports: Brough on Humber, Runcorn, and Southampton. Possibly some of the Mendip lead was taken to Uphill on the Bristol Channel, though some of the pigs were carried to the east and probably to Southampton. The number of pigs found along various Roman roads, and remains on the mining sites, show that industries comparable with Mendip were located in the other areas already mentioned. Some of the pigs have the district of their origin in their inscription, as LVTVD, Derbyshire, and DECEANG, Flintshire. The fact that eighty pigs have been found, which had been lost in transport, indicates that the industry was on a large scale. The commonest weight of a pig is about 200 Roman pounds – that is, about 175 lbs. As the lost pigs could only be a very small part of the production, the total must have been considerable.

Iron working

Iron was widely used in the Iron Age, particularly in the first century B.C., and ironmaking continued in the overlapping centuries of Roman occupation, much of it carried on by the native Romano–British population, some of it under Roman direction, and some distinctly Roman. Simple bowl furnaces occur on all the Iron Age sites, but on some Roman sites the shaft furnace was introduced. The ironmaking was generally carried on in industrial settlements rather than on isolated sites, and two examples will illustrate the general character of the Romano–British industry. The Iron Age furnaces were small and isolated and each would serve the needs of a very small group. It is difficult to distinguish the furnace of an early iron-maker from the heart of a smith, and in fact some sites may have alternated in their use.

A site which, without being spectacular, will illustrate some of the methods of industrial archaeology is that of Bardon, Sussex, discovered and studied by H. F. Cleere, who since 1960 has spent several seasons in excavating the area. During the first century A.D. the Romans took over some of the British iron-making sites and soon had several furnace-forge complexes at work in the Weald, between Hastings and Battle. Very large heaps of slag accumulated around these, but unfortunately for the archaeologist most of these slags have been quarried away during the nineteenth century, for road making material, and many were used in the furnaces of the seventeenth century. As the woods of the south-east were being steadily depleted, expansion of the industry in the second century moved to the central Weald around East Grinstead, and to the Forest of Dean.

The Bardon site in the parish of Ticehurst is on the south bank of the river Limden (TQ 663294). At that point there is, on the riverside, a slag heap and bank of refuse about a hundred yards long. During the last fifty years, bits of Roman pottery and other objects have been picked up from time to time. In 1960, Cleere began with an excavation on the western edge of the site and on the tip, and the pottery which he found confirmed a date of about A.D. 140 to 220 for the occupation. An eight-acre site has been recognized by the occurrence of black soil and slag fragments, but as most of it is at present under grain cultivation the large central area has not yet been uncovered. In determining where to dig, a thermo-magnetic survey was made of one available field, and magnetic anomalies shown by this were found to correspond with features in the site. Soil resistivity methods have also been used and an air survey made which have outlined a main building which can be excavated when that portion of the site is eventually put down to pasture. These modern archaeological techniques have been used to guide the excavation and to increase its efficiency.

In several seasons it has appeared more and more likely that this is the site of an iron-working community settled in and around a villa. Crop marks near the centre of the site indicate a rectangular building which could be the villa yet to be explored. Although no smelting furnace has so far been discovered, the excavated material includes two types of double tuyeres, and fragments of single tuyeres which are evidence of bellows-blown hearths or furnaces. Several furnace bottoms about one foot in diameter confirm the smelting, but nothing has yet been recovered which can indicate whether the furnaces were of bowl or shaft type. Two stone-lined structures, eight feet long, one foot wide, and one foot high were lined with clay and have been burned at a high temperature. Associated with one is an area of red, roasted ore fines, so that these structures may be interpreted as ore-roasting ovens.

Along with an abundance of pottery, there are numerous box-tile fragments, building debris, floor tesserae, and tiles, indicative of a building, probably part of the suggested villa. Three of the tiles carry the stamp CL BR, which would associate the site in some way with the Roman fleet of Britain (*Classis Britannica*). Roads are associated with the site, going to the east, west, and south, and are metalled with slag. There are several pits and post holes, and the fragments of a timber building which overlays part of one of the roasting hearths. The stratigraphy of these deposits shows three short periods, the roasting hearth followed by the timber building. This had then been destroyed by fire and rebuilt. Pottery showed that all this was within the period A.D. 140 to 220. Much more will be learned when the central area is excavated, but the work so far has recovered an industrial site, has proved its nature and its dates, and has demonstrated again the value of archaeological techniques in exploring the earlier periods of industrial archaeology.[1]

Among many other Roman iron-making sites, Ariconium is one which recent investigation is proving to be a true industrial settlement. Ariconium was a Roman town in south Herefordshire on the edge of the Forest of Dean. It is at Bollitree, in the parish of Weston-under-Penyard, and three miles east of Ross on Wye. The site is marked by a great extent of ground where black soil, with burnt clay, iron slag, and Romano–British pottery are found wherever the ground is disturbed. The site was in part excavated in 1924,[2] and it became evident that near a Roman settlement there had been a Romano–British villa settlement, around which there were extensive industrial remains, the whole covering about 250 acres. The sloping ground on the west side of the settlement proved to be a vast heap of iron slag with the significant name of Cinderhill.

Excavations connected with the site in 1959 and subsequent years carried out by H. P. Bridgewater[3] have revealed on a part of the area only 34 ft by 72 ft the remains of six furnaces. The remains suggest shaft-type furnaces with a slag-collecting pit. In one case there was a large mass of

[1] H. F. Cleere and H. P. Bridgewater, 'The Iron Industry in the Roman Period: the Bardown Site', *Bull. Hist. Metallurgy Group*, No. 6, 1966, 1–4. Also Cleere in 'Bardown Roman Bloomery, Sussex', *ibid.*, Vol. 2, No. 1, 1968, 55; 'Excavations at Bardown, Sussex', *ibid.*, Vol. 3, No. 1, 1969, 26; 'The Roman British Industrial Site at Bardown', *Sussex Arch. Soc.*, occasional paper 1.
[2] G. H. Jack, *Transactions Woolhope Naturalists' Field Club*, 1924.
[3] *Transactions Woolhope Naturalists' Field Club*, 1924, H. P. Bridgewater, 38 (2), 1965, 124.

bloomery slag. The general conclusions are that bloomeries, and possibly some bowl furnaces, had been replaced by shaft furnaces. A charcoal store-pit was found but no distinct trace of an ore roasting place. It is suggested that the ore was roasted at the mines, which were almost certainly those known to be on Wigpool Common. Pottery associated with the furnace site indicates a main working period in the second century A.D. The size of the slag heaps suggest that the excavated furnaces are only a small fraction of the working area still to be investigated.

This pattern of an industrial settlement adjoining a Roman site is seen at some other places, the first to be properly recognized being that at Wilderspool, near Warrington, Lancashire. This site was discovered by T. May and excavated between 1895 and 1905. T. May examined an area of three acres within which he described the foundations of dwellings and workshops, with the remains of many furnaces and hearths. Some of these he thought were for iron-making, some were glass furnaces, three were potters' kilns, and others he described just as 'heating furnaces', or as being possibly connected with brass-making. A re-examination of May's descriptions and drawings shows that some of the iron furnaces were true shaft furnaces of eighteen to twenty-eight inches diameter, and that some were bowl furnaces. The glass furnaces are doubtful. A crucible furnace may have been for bronze making or melting, as fragments of a crucible found on the site have bronze adhering to them. Without going into detail it is quite clear that Wilderspool was in fact an organized industrial settlement, with people working at more than one industry within it.

Pottery

Our knowledge of the Roman pottery kiln has been considerably increased by the partial uncovering of the working area of a group of pottery makers at Cantley, two and three-quarter miles south-east of Doncaster. The development of a housing estate was the occasion of this important discovery in 1953. When wall foundation trenches were being cut for the new houses quantities of Roman pottery were turned out. Later, when sewer trenches were being made by mechanical excavators, a number of structures made of baked clay were cut into. These were eventually recognized as a possible kiln field, and, with the goodwill and assistance of Doncaster Corporation, rescue excavations were organized by Doncaster Museum and the Ministry of Works. It was impossible then or later to excavate the whole site, but in the localized patches that were dug twenty-nine pottery kilns were uncovered, sufficient to suggest a pottery on a large scale.[1] The associated pottery suggested that the kilns were working between the mid second century and the third quarter of the third century A.D. Twenty-seven of the kilns were of the normal shaft type, while two others were an unusual variant. A bowl furnace for smelting iron was also found on the site. No habitation sites were found, suggesting that this was an industrial estate outside the Roman town of Doncaster, or with a separate housing area not yet discovered.

From time to time, kiln fragments were turned up or structures were cut into by the mechanical diggers, so vigilance had to be constant and excavation often had to be hurried so as not to hinder the contractors in their programmed work. Taking the better preserved examples along with information gathered from the more severely damaged kilns, an accurate picture can be formed of this type of kiln. The body in all cases was formed of clay and had two main features, a shaft and a firing flue. The remaining shafts show that the circular wall was generally about 1 ft 3 in thick with an internal shaft diameter of 3 ft to 4 ft, with its height 3 ft or probably more. A flue enters the bottom of the shaft and projects at right angles for 2 ft or 3 ft. The flue in different kilns was sub-rectangular, arched, or tri-angular in section, with very thick clay walls and a height of up to 1 ft 4 in. About 1 ft 6 in or so above the floor the internal wall of the shaft has a ledge and on the centre of the floor there is a central, moulded mass of clay, the central plinth. Baked clay bars, still in place in some of the kilns, span from the plinth to the ledge, like the spokes of a wheel, forming a grid on which the unbaked pots were piled. On top of the shaft wall a domed top with a central smoke hole was formed of pressed clay. When the kiln was loaded, the fire was made in a fire-hole at the external mouth of the flue, the induced draught being sufficient to draw flames and heat through the whole kiln shaft. There is evidence that the inside of the shaft occasionally needed relining with clay to make up for wear.[2] The kilns all seem to have been made in excavated holes as deep as the furnace was high, possibly to shelter from strong wind and so make a stricter regulation of draught and temperature possible. The products of the kilns were three main types of domestic pottery – the mortaria, which are large bowls for grinding pulse; shallow dishes and wide-mouthed bowls; and a variety of jars. All are of a

[1] Many more have since been uncovered; about forty are now known.
[2] The various excavations are recorded in the *Yorkshire Archaeological Journal*, XXXVIII, pt 3, 1954, 403–12; pt 4, 1955, 53–645; and XXXIX, pt 1, 1956, 32–47.

hard, sandy fabric, grey or grey-buff, though some of the mortaria shade towards brick-red. The mortaria have a slip coating. The products are like those of other large potteries of third century date in the east Midlands and along the Lincolnshire–Nottinghamshire border, and no doubt now that the characteristics of the fabric and shapes are known in detail examples will be recognized in museum collections and from other sites, and the area which this pottery served will soon be known.

One of the important centres of the pottery industry of the later part of the Roman occupation was in the Romano–British settlement around the fort of Malton in the North Riding of Yorkshire. One of these potteries is that at Cranbeck, which was discovered in 1935 by a group of boys from Bootham School, York, and excavated by them under the guidance of Philip Corder. Two pairs of kilns and a great amount of pottery was found. In 1935, three Bootham boys[1] made a search of the fields south-west of the first Cranbeck site discovered earlier, and found an area where potsherds and fragments of baked clay occurred in quantities which suggested the site of a kiln. Road operations were imminent across the site, and so intensive collecting was undertaken as the work proceeded, but two electricity pylons made an island which for a time was undisturbed except for trial pits to prove the ground. The boys saw that in one pit there was a layer of ash and potsherds, so permission to excavate was obtained. This excavation eventually cleared a paired kiln in remarkably good preservation and this was fully recorded before the mechanical navvy removed the whole site.

The kiln consisted of a large firing-hole from which two flues diverged at a wide angle, about 120°, leading to the two kilns. One flue was 3 ft 1 in long, 1 ft 1 in wide at the stoke hole, widening to 2 ft at the middle and closing to 1 ft 6 in at the kiln. Its floor was on rock, and the side walls were built of thin oolite slabs, nine courses high, cemented with clay which was burned black. The furnace was 2 ft 6 in high, and had been repaired or remade more than once. The second kiln was very well preserved and its building was clearly of two periods; its diameter was 3 ft 6 in and its flue 4 ft 6 in long and 2 ft 2 in wide at the stoke hole. No roof remained to the furnaces, but debris of baked clay was evidence that a clay roof had been used when the kiln was burning. It is suggested that the pots were stacked on vent-holed platforms.

The date of the working life of the kilns was approximately A.D. 370-c. 395. The pottery from Cranbeck is of an unmistakable type and was very

[1] R. S. Harland, G. B. Walker, and D. H. Waller.

widely distributed, being found at sites over the North of England from mid-Yorkshire to the Roman Wall, and from coast to coast. The quantities found are large, and all the evidence points to a very large and well-organized industry.[1]

Evidence now abundantly demonstrates that there was a widespread pottery industry in Roman Britain, well organized about several centres. The distribution of pottery types shows that, while some have a regional distribution, other types were spread over most of the country. Some of the more important centres already explored and described are those at Castor, near Peterborough, the Yorkshire potteries of Cranbeck, near Malton, and Holme-on-Spalding Moor. Other potteries were near Farnham, Surrey, at sites in the New Forest, and at several other places. Potteries of large size were sometimes attached to and served the needs of large towns like Wroxeter, Shropshire, or were connected, like those at Holt, Denbighshire, with a legionary fortress. This was supplier mainly to the fort and city of Chester.[2]

It appears that lead mining, iron-making, and pottery were widely spread and well-organized industries in the Roman period. Many other industries were practised – glass and textiles, metal working, leather, and others – but most of these were dispersed among the settlements almost entirely on a craft scale. Judging by the results of excavations in the last quarter century it seems certain that there are still many true industrial sites of Roman date to be discovered.

Agriculture

The remains of Romano–British agriculture are to be found over most of the country, the commonest being field systems, the querns for grinding corn, and less commonly the kilns for drying it. Among the smaller objects associated with these areas are occasional plough irons. The field systems form the so-called areas of Celtic lynchets, roughly rectangular fields, many almost square, defined by banks of turf and gravel. Some of the banks are claimed to be the result of continued ploughing over a long

[1] P. Corder, 'A Pair of Fourth-century Romano-British Pottery Kilns near Cranbeck', *Antiquaries Journ.*, XVII, 392–413.
[2] The pottery industry in Roman Britain was so extensive and important that there are excavation reports in all the archaeological journals, and only a very detailed bibliography could list them. Only two examples have been quoted here to illustrate the interest and material for study which the industrial archaeologist can find in these reports. No attempt has been made, nor could it be made here, to give an adequate account of the industry in Roman times.

period, but many, particularly in the North, are seen to be constructed with a core of stones, often carefully placed. The more extensive areas of fields are associated with settlement sites which can be called villages, though they are more comparable with our small hamlets, in which there are huts, some circular and some rectangular, the remains of roads among the fields, and small cattle pounds or sheep folds. Small remains from these villages, particularly those of the Highland zone, include evidence of a textile industry – shears, loom weights, spindle whorls and weavers' combs and brooches and toggles are found which were dress fastenings. The third and fourth centuries are the period most abundantly evidenced by pottery, but many settlements contain a smaller amount extending into the fifth century.

The very detailed mapping of such lynchet groups with some excavation in the village area can be regarded as sound industrial archaeology. There was a trade between the natives and the Romans in corn, woollen cloaks and cloth, leather, skins and furs, and some of these products, like the lead, were in sufficient quantity to be exported. There was some trade the other way as Roman pottery, more elaborate than the native ware, is found in many of the settlements. Some of the villages continue earlier Iron Age sites and were expanded when the contact with the Romans was made; and some of the later rectangular houses and the corn and pottery kilns may also be the result of this contact.

A typical group of Celtic lynchets and its associated settlement was excavated in 1932 by the members of the Brighton and Hove Archaeological Club, directed by Dr Cecil Curwen. This excavation was on Thundersbarrow Hill, north-west of Southwick near Brighton (TQ 229084), where a Romano–British settlement abuts upon an early Iron Age hill-top complex and is shown by abundant pottery to date to the period between 150 and 400 A.D., the earlier camp having been occupied at two periods approximately in the fifth century B.C. and in the first century B.C. to the first century A.D. The large area of Celtic fields lies all around the camp, and though the fields vary a good deal in size many average in length from about 250 feet to 350 feet. Besides clay pits and storage pits there were two very complete grain-drying furnaces or kilns of a type which has been found on Roman and Romano–British sites at Silchester, Caerwent, Malton, and several other places.

The kilns are dug into the solid chalk and are almost identical. The drying chamber in which the grain was spread is about 7 ft square and 2 f

6 in deep, walled with carefully cut blocks of chalk. There is a flue going under its whole length along the central line, and this is a trench in the chalk two and a half feet deeper than the floor of the chamber, walled up to a width of 2 ft, and 11 ft 6 in long. It was covered with flags. It starts in a large firing hole and rises slightly to a 'T' junction at the remote end which spreads to the full width of the chamber. This 'T' end is also flagged over, but there must have been a vent in some position to create the draught through the kiln. The fire had used moderate-sized branches of hazel, poplar, and oak, and had left a deposit of soot and charcoal in the flues, among which there were a few grains of wheat. Fragments of fourteen querns were found in the settlement, in which no doubt the parched grain was ground.[1]

A Romano–British settlement in Yorkshire, on Knowe Fell, Malham Moor (SD 881672), was excavated in 1965 and 1966, and, like the Thundersbarrow site, an earlier Iron Age site had been taken over and in it two later Romano–British rectangular houses had been built. The site seems to have been a small pastoral farm associated not with Celtic lynchets but with a complex of cattle and sheep pounds. The fact that the remains of four querns came from the two rectangular houses, and none from the older settlement, suggests that no attempt had been made to grow corn. In fact, as the settlement is at an altitude of more than 1,450 feet OD corn would never have ripened there. The querns and pottery of fourth-century type in the two houses suggests that the occupants may have traded hides and skins for corn with the Romano–British farmers around the Gargrave villa in Airedale.

The older settlement has two circular huts of 20 ft and 18 ft diameter, with very massive boulder walls, and the floor about 3 ft below the general surface level. These huts were connected by gravel and turf walls to a series of five enclosures, the largest about 40 ft by 30 ft and the others about 20 ft, which were sub-rectangular. In one of these one corner had very dark soil which contained small pieces of iron slag and scale, which most likely came from a blacksmith's hearth and not from a bloomery, of which there was no trace. In another of these enclosures one of the rectangular houses was built, cutting partly into the bank; and the second house, just outside the enclosures, had destroyed part of a bank connected with the earlier settlement.

[1] A very detailed account of this excavation is by E. C. Curwenn, 'Excavations on Thundersbarrow Hill, Sussex', *The Antiquaries Journal*, XIII (1933), 109–63.

The rectangular houses were of similar type, one 26 ft by 12 ft inside, and the other measuring 19 ft 6 in by 9 ft 6 in. Each had very massive walls using many large stones set on edge as an inside lining, backed by heavy boulder banks, and the inside was paved with very large and fairly regular flags. One had a partition with a wide opening in it cutting off rather less than one third of the length at one end, and at that end a small rectangular annexed room, not opening out of the main house. There was a well-made hearth sunk in the floor of the larger room, and near it, on a carefully built pedestal of stone, a whole quern was in position for use. Near the hearth and also in the smaller section of the house parts of other querns of Romano–British type were found. A fragment of a quern came also from the other house. Very little pottery was found, but sufficient to suggest a fourth-century date was found in the large house. Judging by the small amount of fallen stone, the walls had not originally been much more than 2 ft 6 in high, and the greater part of the building would have been of timber or wattle.

In a very much larger settlement near Grassington (SE 008654) the same mixture of round huts with apparently intrusive rectangular houses is associated with over two hundred acres of Celtic lynchets and with a 'village'-type stone-built habitation area which has yielded a large collection of remains, mainly of the third and fourth century, and in which the chief buildings are rectangular houses almost identical with those on Knowe Fell. It is a common occurrence in the northern parts to find an early Iron Age or Celtic site about the first century B.C. to A.D. having within it a later occupation of the third and fourth century, with rectangular houses and plenty of evidence of textile activities, cattle pounds, and other structures which might indicate a form of ranch pastoral farming combined with a varied trade with the Romans.

CHAPTER 11

Dark Age and Medieval Industries

After the departure of the Romans from Britain there were many centuries during which the industries which had flourished under them lingered on in a sadly diminished state. Such working as there was attained little more than a purely domestic scale. Much of the iron needed by the Saxons was imported, and smiths attached to the households of the more important lords made only small quantities for their own use. In the case of lead, there are very few records, and those are all connected with the Saxon monasteries – an occasional gift of a lead coffin, or the covering of the small church at York with lead. There was a little glass-making reintroduced to the country by Benedict Biscop of Durham, and there were a few potteries.

Iron-making
The iron industry seems to have reached its lowest point under the Normans, but a revival came with the settlement in the twelfth century of the Cistercians who were skilled in the iron and wool industries. Their abbeys, more numerous in the North than elsewhere, soon secured grants on the Pennines, in the Lake District and in North Yorkshire, giving them the right to dig ores of both iron and lead, and to take wood to make charcoal for the smelting, wherever the ores were found within their grants. The iron ores of the coal measures, the hematites of Lancashire and Cumberland, and many of the ores in the secondary rocks of the Midlands were worked before the end of the twelfth century, and similar ores in the Forest of Dean and the Weald – and, in fact all over the country – were soon being used. Iron was made for the monasteries' own smiths for plough irons, ox shoes, tools, nails, and all ordinary requirements. Some iron was sold in the markets and much was paid as rent. A bloomery would sometimes be granted by a landowner for the return of a number of blooms out of every lot made. Where ores existed, this was an advantage for the landowner, ensuring his own supply of iron.

The monastic iron-making followed two general patterns. Many leases were granted allowing a monastery to have a number of moveable 'forges' within a forest area. Usually the lease included all dead wood and the right to make charcoal for the forge, but not to sell it. Some forges were more permanent, and had permission to erect huts and to put fences around them so long as the fences could not trap the deer. When the wood at one place was exhausted, the forge moved on to another part of the forest. The essential parts of a 'forge' were a bloomery and a string hearth, both little more than bowl furnaces made in the ground. They were blown by foot bellows. There was usually a hut for the workmen, and possibly a store, and the whole was fenced round. There was nothing that could not be abandoned and little to carry away except tools and bellows and perhaps a few timbers. A lease of 1309 is for 'one forge with two furnaces which may be moved from place to place for making iron where convenient'.

A second type was the grange, usually a farm settlement with permanent buildings and a staff employed in a specific job. Some granges were for arable or dairy farming, some were sheep farms, but others were more industrial. Several had iron-making as their occupation. The Yorkshire abbey of Fountains had sheep granges on the limestone area of the Pennines, but also had the grange of Bradley, near Huddersfield, which before 1177 was granted part of a wood, and dead wood, for making charcoal, and all the ironstone they could find there. They were allowed to make roads and a bridge, and to fence round the grange. On the outcrop of a group of coal measure ironstones, running roughly south from near Leeds to Sheffield, many of the Yorkshire monasteries secured grants, and Rievaulx, Byland, and many other communities from a distance had their mines and furnaces (bloomeries) along this area. After the Dissolution of the Monasteries this became the location of the great South Yorkshire iron industry. Some of the bellpits and bloomery sites remain from the monastic working but most of the structural remains are of the later charcoal furnaces. The monastic bloomery sites are very abundant in all parts of the country where iron ores are found and are marked by slag heaps and bellpit workings, not easily dated in themselves but usually well documented in the chartularies and leases.

The most active period of monastic iron-working was the two centuries from very soon after their settlement to about the middle of the fourteenth century. After the tragedies of the Black Death, and the recovery in the later decades of the century, iron-working became more and more a

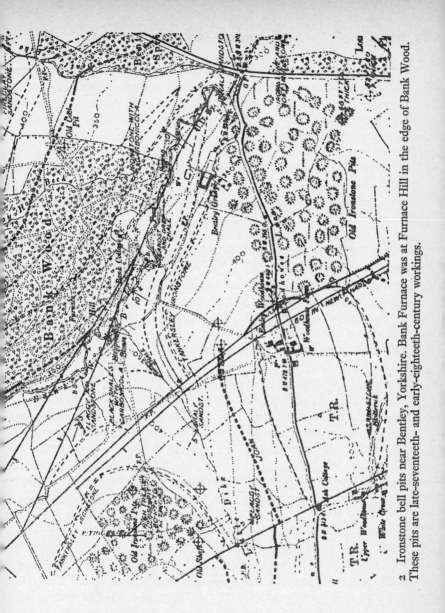

2   Ironstone bell pits near Bentley, Yorkshire. Bank Furnace was at Furnace Hill in the edge of Bank Wood. These pits are late-seventeeth- and early-eighteenth-century workings.

secular industry, some of the monastic sites even being leased to secular workers. There are many examples of this new generation of bloomery forges, of which one will suffice. They were generally more substantial than the monastic sites, with more permanent buildings, and mostly placed where water power could be had for the bellows.

Byrkeknott, Co. Durham All the medieval iron was bloomery-made, and so the evidence of bloomeries is fairly abundant, particularly in the form of grants made for forges or bloom smithies, and as bloomery slags. Actual structural details of the bloomeries are scarce and can only properly be recovered by the excavation of a site in an unusually good state of preservation. When such an excavation can also be supplemented by a documented description of the working, tools, and other details of the bloomery, then a valuable addition is made to our knowledge of iron-making at that time. These fortunate circumstances are found in the Byrkeknott bloomery in Weardale, Co. Durham. In 1899, G. T. Lapsley, in the course of searching out sources for a history of the county, came across a document in the Public Record Office, which was one year's accounts for the working – from November 1408 to November 1409 – of Bishop Langley of Durham's bloomery at Byrkeknott.[1]

In 1950, Dr R. A. Mott, in the course of a paper on early iron-making read at the summer meeting of the Newcomen Society, at Sheffield, gave descriptions of the working of Byrkeknott bloomery, based upon a re-translation of the accounts (which are in Latin). From his extensive knowledge of early iron-making he gave, from this document, an acceptable picture of what the bloomery must have been like, although its precise location was not then known. With H. C. Wilkinson, he made a strong plea that an attempt should be made to discover the bloomery, and gave arguments for its positioning on the north bank of the Bedburn Beck or on the nearby Harthope Beck where slags could be looked for. The roll which Lapsley transcribed states that the bloomery was built at Byrkeknott-by-Bedbourne and that it took water from Heribourne.

The next chapter in this story opened when Dr Tylecote of Newcastle University made a fresh analysis of the roll, with both historical and field research in the Bedburn townships. Hatfield's Survey of the area in 1345–87 gave the names of the tenants in both South and North Bedburn and

[1] G. T. Lapsley, 'The Account Roll of a Fifteenth-Century Ironmaster', *Econ. Hist. Revue*, 1899, 34, pp. 509–29.

these included some names which occur in the bloomery accounts. Bed-burn today is the South Bedburn of the survey, and along with a hall and a few cottages has a mill which was called Bedburn Forge early in the nineteenth century. This name had led Lapsley to the suggestion that this was, in fact, the site of Byrkeknott bloomery. Tylecote, however, found that from early in the fourteenth century it had been a fulling-mill, and later a corn-mill. Further, the mill race was about half a mile long, which is too long to be fitted with the bloomery race which was built and stone-lined by a mason and four labourers in only thirty days. There was, how-ever, a ruined mill less than half a mile away, on the Harthope Burn, with a watercourse of about a hundred yards. Other features supported the idea that this was the likeliest site for Byrkeknott bloomery, although the name Byrkeknott cannot now be found.

Harthope Mill (NZ 108322) is on the west bank of the Harthope Burn about two hundred yards above its junction with the Bedburn, a tributary of the river Wear. The present buildings on the site are a partly ruined corn-mill with another building at each end now converted into cow sheds. Behind the buildings there is a mill pond, the bottom of it about fifteen feet above the mill floor. Some slag was found near the mill and there seemed to be a likelihood that the mill in fact covered the site of Byrke-knott Forge. This could only be tested by excavations, which were, there-fore, made within the old mill, and these, taken with the account roll, were sufficient to prove that this was indeed the forge of 1408. The complete forge could only be uncovered by more extensive excavation, but the account roll is sufficiently detailed for an adequate picture of the forge at work, and the excavations so far have proved the location and local detail.[1]

The buildings on the site, according to the roll of accounts, were the forge and four huts, the huts being of timber with turf roofs, having being built in four days by the carpenter. John Dalton supervised the building of the forge and lived in one of the huts, the bloomer in another. In the forge there were two hearths, the bloomhearth and the stringhearth, and they were of a size to produce and work a bloom of 195 lb weight. The carpenter made the water wheel, sluices for the pond, and launders to the wheel. The position of the wheelpit and part of the tail race were found. Tools were made by a smith in West Aukland, and included hammers, axes, rakes, scales, sieves, etc. Dr Mott argued from the total weight of

[1] The excavations are described in R. F. Tylecote, 'The location of Byrkeknott. A 15th-century melting site', *Journ. Iron and Steel Inst.*, April 1960, pp. 451–8.

iron tools that the forge had a trip-hammer, but nothing to prove or dis-
prove this was found, though it would appear that the wheel was not
always sufficient for the bellows of both hearths, and could not have
worked a hammer in addition.

Under the floor of the ruined corn-mill, in which two bottom grinding
stones remained, there was a levelling fill of eighteenth-to-nineteenth-
century black earth with bits of coal and potsherds and fragments of iron
among it. This layer covered a thinner one of hard, highly ferruginous
clay, stained or burned red, and resting on a pebbly subsoil. This layer
contained a considerable amount of slag, iron-ore nodules, and charcoal
and covered about 250 square feet of the excavation. A stone-lined hollow
in part of this area might be the site of the bloomhearth. Stratified in this
layer were sherds of fourteenth-to-fifteenth-century pottery confirming
the date. For the working of the forge a year's stock of ore, 341 tons, was
brought by November, by wains from mines three miles to the south-east,
and about thirteen tons of charcoal was made in Bedburn and Blackbank
Parks weekly and brought to the forge by a train of twelve pack-horses.
About six blooms of iron (195 lbs each) were made each week, the total
produced in the year being 24·3 tons. It is estimated from analysis of the
ore and slag that about 326 tons of slag would be made in the year. The
blooms were reheated in the stringhearth, hammered to squeeze out as
much slag as possible, and then cut into twelve pieces of approximately
sixteen-and-a-quarter pounds each. At one time, twelve wainloads of old
bloomery cinder were brought from a nearby site at Hoppyland, where
there must have been earlier bloomeries. This could have assisted the
bloomery process by helping to reduce the amount of iron lost in the
slag.

The investigation of Byrkeknott is an excellent example of the coordi-
nation of historical research, field work, careful excavation, and competent
technical interpretation, all these being the elements of good industrial
archaeology. Most of the details of this forge were confirmed by the
excavation, and although the whole area cannot be dug because of the
buildings still in use, we now have a well-documented account of a forge
in 1408, the physical structure of which has been demonstrated.

In the last years of the fifteenth century the bloomeries began to be displaced by blast furnaces, which were better able to meet the increasing
demand for iron, and which were later built by many of the secular landowners who purchased monastic estates at the Dissolution. The change

from bloomery to furnace is well documented in many places and an example mainly dependent upon documents can be taken from Rievaulx Abbey, and one based more upon excavation from the Rockley Smithies, South Yorkshire.

Rievaulx was one of the earliest Yorkshire Cistercian communities, being settled in 1132. Among its early grants were some of iron ores and wood, and among its many iron-working sites (some on the coal measure belt already mentioned) it had a bloomery near the abbey and one in Bilsdale, some five miles to the north. At the time of the Dissolution, the bloomery south of the Abbey, at the place called the Forge, was working, and in 1540 the new secular owner rebuilt it. The dam on the river was increased and there were three water wheels: one worked the bellows for two bloom hearths, another those for the stringhearth, and the third those for a trip-hammer. The forge now made a bloom of about three hundred-weights. The second forge at Laskill in Bilsdale was rebuilt on the same pattern and rented to a tenant. Ore for both forges was exposed and weathered for six months at the mines and a regular supply of charcoal was secured by coppicing. Twenty plots of woodland were marked out, each sufficient to provide charcoal for one year, and these were felled in strict rotation. The output was then about forty-five tons of iron a year.

In 1576, a blast furnace was built near the abbey, where abundant slags remain, with a casting house, a finery, and store houses, and a new floodgate was made on the river, the forge or finery continuing on the old Forge site. Output was steadily increased from just over 1 ton a day in 1591 to $1\frac{3}{4}$ tons a day in 1603, when for a time peat was dug and used along with the charcoal fuel. In 1616, the furnace was again rebuilt with a new casting floor, furnace, and bellows house, and a cabin for the furnace man. The furnace by 1613 was producing around 280 tons a year, though there was a serious decline later and the furnace was finally abandoned in 1647. The furnace was away from the river but close to the canal, which had been cut in the twelfth century to carry stone for the building of the abbey from quarries further up the valley. Most of this canal and some river diversions and the position of the furnace and the forge are still traceable on the ground.[1]

[1] An excellent account of the canals and their history has been given by J. Weatherall, 'Rievaulx Abbey', *Yorks. Arch. Journ.*, XXXVIII, 1954, pp. 333–54. Details of the bloomeries and furnace are found among the Rutland MSS at Belvoir Castle and have been discussed by H. R. Schubert, *History of the British Iron and Steel Industry*, 1957, various references.

Stone

The Romans seem to have been the first to quarry stone systematically from its outcrop and to cut it to defined shapes for use in their buildings. Many Roman quarries are known, in some of which inscriptions remain on the quarry walls. Most of the quarries are adjacent to the place where the stone was used and there is no evidence of what could be called a trade or industry connected with them. They seem to have been worked only for the immediate local use of the stone. Although there was some building in stone in the post-Roman period, it was rare and it was not until the twelfth century that widespread stone building began. In many of the contracts for bridge or church buildings, in the post-Norman period, and through the next few centuries, generally made with a master-mason, the mason was bound to get the stone as part of his job. The contract for Catterick Bridge, Yorkshire, in 1421, for instance, gives to the three masons making it the duty of getting the stone in two specified quarries 'within the bounds which it is most profitable to the foresaid work'. The quarriers were to hew the stone and scapple it (trim to shape) and the masons provide transport to their lodge where the stones would be worked to their final shape. From the twelfth to the fifteenth centuries the monasteries in the upland parts of the country mostly found stone for their building close to their chosen site, but for those in the lowlands stone was often to be got only at a distance and gifts of a quarry were of great value and benefit. Often, where a suitable stone was found, more than one monastery was given leave to work, and in some such locations there were often many quarries side by side on the same outcrop, some monastic and some secular. It was in these large quarry-aggregates that an industry was developed – stone was quarried and shaped, transported and used or sold over a wide area. For some centuries there was a flourishing industry in Caenstone brought from France to this country for use in buildings over much of the south. Many good building stones were worked and sold in comparable fashion from several geological horizons in this country. Some retained their preeminence up to the present century – Purbeck (Jurassic), Bath (Oolite), Anston and Huddleston (Magnesian Limestone), and many others.

Two examples can be taken, ecclesiastical and secular, in which documentation and fieldwork together can recover much of the organization and working method of quarries started for particular buildings, but which developed a wider industry. The first is the case of York Minster for which the Fabric Rolls[1] give a vast amount of building detail. York, being in the centre of the clay plain of the Vale of York, had to turn to hills east or west for stone. The Magnesian Limestone of Tadcaster, some twelve miles to the south-west, had been used by the Romans and was proved to be of good quality and a fine texture and colour. Near the town there was already the old quarry, and when the enlargement of the Minster was started, Robert de Vavasour granted to the Abbot and Convent full and free use of his quarry at Thievesdale, just outside Tadcaster, to take sufficient stone for the enlargement and repair of their church. They were granted free passage along the cart road for wains carrying the stone to the river wharf at Tadcaster from which it was taken by boat down the Wharfe and up the Ouse to York. From later references it is known that the stone was taken to St Leonard's landing in York and then by sledge to the Minster yard. Thievesdale quarry is in an extensive outcrop now called Jackdaw Crag (SE 465416), and grants were given to several other communities in the thirteenth century. The canons of Howden had a quarry there adjoining the king's quarry; and Selby Abbey, Drax Abbey, and Marton Priory also had quarries in the crag.

The Minster also used stone from other quarries at Huddleston Delf near Sherburn in Elmet (SE 462334), near Bramhope, and at Stapleton near Pontefract, all in the Magnesian Limestone. The Huddleston quarry soon became the main source of stone, and, being much further from the river than Thievesdale, transport presented problems from time to time. The Cock Beck runs not far from Sherburn and joins the Wharfe near Tadcaster. This was used occasionally to carry stone on rafts but its course was very winding and its volume of water not very great. However, in 1415, the Dean and Chapter paid for the construction of a stone wharf at Kettleman Bridge, where the Cock Beck runs into the Wharfe, and payments were made for carriage of stone 'from the Minster quarry at Huddleston to Ketilbarnbrigg super aquan de Querff', and then by boat to York. Much of the carriage to the wharf was by wains and practically all the carriage was by roads.

The Archbishops of York had the manor of Cawood on the Ouse just below the junction of the Wharfe, from before the Conquest. Much of the land here was fen, liable to almost continuous flooding, and in the thirteenth century the people of Cawood and tenants of Healaugh Priory, which had part of the fens, did a considerable amount of draining, the

[1] Fabric Rolls of York Minster were published in *Surtees Society*, Vol. 25.

main drain being known as the Bishopsdyke. This extended nearly to
Sherburn and started not far from Huddleston quarries. The dyke was
straightened and deepened and some stone was carried on rafts to a wharf
at Cawood. Alongside the dyke a good road was made which became the
principal route for the stone. Accounts are numerous and set out in the
following way:

1416 For carrying 285 fother of stones in wains from the
         quarry at Huddleston to the staithe at Cawood   £13.10.0

For carrying 282 fother of stone by boat from Cawood to
         York, John Blackman, Shipman   108s. 4d

For sledding stones to Cawood 20 days Wm. Totty   20. 5. 0

Another account includes 'for sleddying the stone from St Leonard
landing to Minster yard'.

Stone was measured by the fother – about twenty-one hundred weights–
or the damlade – about ten tons – this last appearing to be a measure only
used in Yorkshire.

For the working of the quarries, lists of tools indicate that the stone,
which is well jointed, was got up by crowbar and cut with wedges. The
rough blocks were scappled with axes, and then passed to the mason who
finished them to dimension blocks or moulded them to a rough mould or
template. A quarry list of 1399 (Stapleton, getting stone for the Minster)
names 10 iron wedges weighing 100 lbs, 2 kevelles (heavy axe-hammers –
in Yorkshire dialect, to give a person or a thing a hard hammering is to
'kevell it'); 4 iron brocheux (broaches, i.e. chisels for heavy work), a puly-
ing axe (axe-hammer), 2 iron mauls, and 3 iron gavelocks (crow bars).
Other fifteenth-century lists include very heavy crowbars, 'great' iron
hooks, wedges and scappling pickaxes, with steel for 'steeling' tools – that
is, welding steel points and edges onto wrought iron bodies.

The quarries were relatively small areas within the larger whole to which
the name, Huddleston or Thievesdale, was applied. In 1371, the Clerk and
Mastermason of York Minster spent a day selecting a quarry and arranging
for three roods to be cleared for working. On another occasion fifteen
roods were to be cleared. A large quarry was 120 feet long and 8 perches
broad. The quarries were used intermittently through the succeeding
centuries to the present for occasional stone for repairs, and now they

present a large area of overgrown quarry refuse, and old faces, with a few working places. Taken along with their various transport routes, there still remains a valid picture of a fourteenth-to-sixteenth-century industry. Some stone was obtained from the Stapleton quarries near Pontefract, but transport to York was longer and more difficult. Stapleton was a commercial quarry and sent stone to many parts of the country – its stone was used in St Stephen's Chapel, Westminster, at Windsor, Rochester, the Tower, and Westminster Hall, and in 1417 ships fetched Huddleston stone from Cawood and Stapleton stone from Pontefract.

A good example of secular quarries are those which were first associated with Skipton Castle, West Yorkshire, and which later became a commercial industry. The Norman castle of Skipton, first built of timber, was rebuilt in stone as a keep and bailey, and then in the early years of the fourteenth century extended and strengthened by Lord Clifford, named as 'the chief builder of the most strong parts'. The stone of the older work can be recognized as from Embsay Crag, a massive outcrop of Millstone Grit, two-and-a-quarter miles north-east of the castle. The extension of enclosures and cultivated ground and modern roads have covered most of the original tracks from this quarry (Diag. 7). In the fifteenth century both repairs and some extension of the castle were carried through, and new quarries were opened for this work which remain and can be studied. The location is given in some of the accounts for 1437 when a tower was being added and payment was made for 112 cart-loads of stone from Staynrig to the Castle. The whole work was in the charge of a master mason (*capitalis latumis*) called Bellerby, and two other masons, Robert and Thomas Hammond. Lime was brought from Bolton and Addingham, although there was limestone at Skipton which for the last two centuries has supported a large quarry industry. A crane for lifting stone to the top of the tower was borrowed from the Prior of Bolton.

A search soon located Staynrig, and the remains of extensive quarrying from the fifteenth to the seventeenth centuries were found spread along about a mile of an outcrop of Millstone Grit along the south-west edge of Barden Fell. In this case documentation is fragmentary, but field evidence is clear, and the close inspection and mapping of a few square miles of the fell revealed the unspectacular remains of an early quarry industry entirely of pre-eighteenth-century date. This had originated in the building and extensions of Skipton Castle, but had persisted to serve the local domestic replacement of timber houses in the late sixteenth and the seventeenth

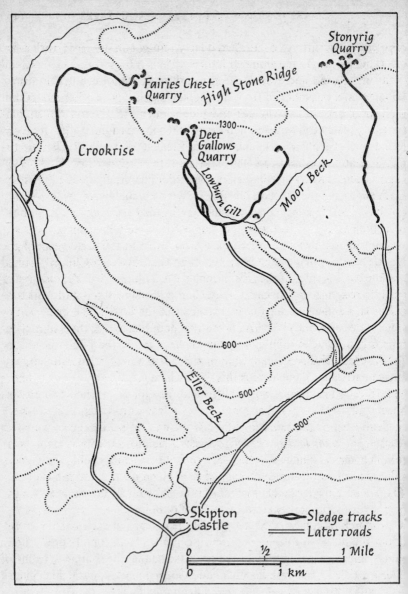

7 Skipton Castle quarry roads

centuries. One quarry of fine millstone continued working to the early years of the nineteenth century (Plate 6a).

Skipton Castle is built on high limestone rock, on the west side of which the Ellerbeck has cut a deep and narrow gorge. In the side of this gorge there are three old quarries which have provided rough stone and rubble for the castle building at many periods. Two miles to the north. Embsay Moor forms the south-west corner of Barden Fell, a high moorland (up to more than 1,600 feet OD) of Millstone Grit, the Embsay Moor part being mainly of Skipton Moor Grit, a sandstone of fine quality with beds varying between fine grained building stones and coarser beds which make excellent millstones. The Skipton Moor Grit forms a high craggy south-western outcrop at Crookrise (SE 898559) and runs approximately east, making the southern part and the steep southern face of the fell. The High Stone Ridge and Stone Ridge Plain (Stoney Ridge or Staynrig) form a noticeable feature. Stone Ridge is crossed by an ancient track coming up from Embsay, which in many parts is deeply entrenched and in some places strengthened across soft ground by being built up with quarry stone. It leads through a maze of quarry spoil heaps, on the Ridge (SE 007564), which mark the Staynrig Quarries.

The wide spreading heap is soon found to be made up of a large number of separate heaps each connected with a single small quarry, where perhaps three or four men might have worked. The quarries have a face rarely more than eight or ten feet high, not very deep but extending laterally twenty or thirty feet or more. There is evidence of breaking the stone by wedging, and there are 'banks' – built-up tables where the stone was trimmed to size. These are often surrounded by small chippings, but after a few centuries of overgrowth some digging is needed to get a full picture. There are loading places at the head of the main track and short dragways to this from the individual quarries. This would suggest that each quarry was the working place of one mason with two or three labourers to get the stone under his supervision, and to do the moving and carrying. The general average of worked and partly worked stones remaining is a cubic foot, and this was the 'standard' size for 'stones' at many medieval quarries.

To the west of this main quarry there are several others along a low outcrop of the grit. In these, larger and special stones were obtained, such as window sills and lintels, and larger carefully shaped stones which might have been used for quoins and the like. One quarry was getting millstones there are still eleven finished or part-finished ones and fragments of broken ones to be seen). All these rather scattered quarries have connecting causeways to a general loading place at the head of a massive sledway, deeply cut, built up in soft ground, and with huge abutments at a deep beck which it crosses. Among these quarries there are one or two which still have at their banking places a few stone mullions and sills of late-sixteenth and seventeenth-century type, and one quarry has the ridge stones for the seventeenth-century stone-slate roofs (Plate 6a). These quarries continued in use or were opened for the great domestic rebuilding of the sixteenth and seventeenth centuries. The greater part of the stone for the rebuilding, however, was taken from new quarries at Halton Height, on each side of the road from Embsay to Barden, along which carting was so much easier.

Another area of ancient quarrying lies under Crookrise at a hollow called Fairies Chest (SE 868561). Here a stretch of high crags have below them a tumbled mass of very large detached boulders often ten feet or more in size. A great many of these have been split by lines of wedges, the earth-fast part of them being left. Drag roads go here and there – in places to a part of the crag where prominences have been wedged off. The usual bankers' tables and loading places are all about, but there is no evidence that the very extensive quarrying has used any but the naturally detached stone.

From all three quarry areas the very deep-cut sledge tracks, often built up at the sides and over soft ground, lead down to the low ground, but they are then lost except as the line of later winding roads into which they have been converted. While the earlier quarries are nearly all connected with castle, abbey, and church building, the general replacement of timber by stone in the smaller houses, starting in the sixteenth century, created a demand that was only met by a very large number of local quarries, remarkably alike in their arrangement and method of working, which together form a very large industry. The location of eighteenth-century quarries was often different, as transport and large-scale production became dominant factors in the choice of quarry sites.

Pottery

In the post-Conquest years the demand for pottery, particularly for plain cooking pots and jugs, grew quickly, but the main demand came in the fourteenth century. Wooden trenchers and both turned and cooper-made cups were in general use, but for cooking, earthenware was essential. Potteries of the fourteenth and fifteenth centuries were established over

most of the country and many of them served several markets and distributed their wares over a moderately wide area. In the last few decades a
number of these local potteries have been investigated and one, out of
many, can be taken as an example of investigation, the methods of which
fall within the scope of the industrial archaeologist.

The Tolson Museum, Huddersfield, like most other museums, was
frequently asked to say something about a few sherds of pottery turned up
in a garden or a field, or by other accidental find. In the spring of 1960, a
quantity of early sherds which had been turned up in a recently ploughed
field were brought to the museum. On examination of the actual site, a
procedure which is always advisable and sometimes rewarding, a number
of burnt stones and pieces of burnt clay daub suggested the presence of a
kiln. Permissions being duly obtained, the Museum were able to organize
a proper excavation after the harvest in the years 1960-2. The excavations
revealed three kilns sufficiently complete to afford a knowledge of their
structure and working, and they provided an abundant suite of pottery
which enabled expert studies to be made of it.[1]

The site, between Upper Heaton and Colnebridge (SE 180195), three
miles north-east of Huddersfield, is on an exposed slope of the Colne
valley side, near a small tributary stream and near an outcropping stratum
of fireclay. Trial trenches where most of the potsherds were found soon
defined an area about thirty feet square in which three kilns were recognized and eventually completely excavated. The three kilns, varying in
their degree of completeness, when studied together afforded a detailed
picture of their structure and operation. The overall length of a kiln is
about twenty feet, and has three recognizable sections. The middle kiln
part is an oval, about eight feet long and five feet wide at the middle. At
each end this part narrows to a flue some three feet wide, one being used
as a chimney flue and the other as the fire-hole. These are 'through-
draught' kilns of a common medieval type. Among the debris, curved bars
of hard-baked clay were recognized as flue bars, used to bridge the flue
between the fire-hole and kiln. Portions of burnt clay daub which have
hand impressions on one side and the impress of grass and rushes on the
other are part of the kiln cover. Small clay cylinders about five inches in
diameter and the same height are props for spacing and supporting pots in
the kiln.

[1] The excavations and the study of the pottery has been recorded in T. G. Manby, 'Medieval
pottery kilns at Upper Heaton, West Yorkshire', *Arch. Journal*, CXXI (1965), pp. 70-110.

When in use, soft pots were piled in the central body of the kiln and secured and spaced with clay wedges. The sides of the kiln are low stone walls which carried a covering roof, probably grass and rushes on a framework of branches, sealed with wet clay pressed on. The flues were formed with stones and covered with the flue bars and a clay seal. The whole kiln was finally covered with turf then fired in the windward firing-hole.

Three-quarters of a ton of pottery was found, in which there were the remains of 2,700 recognizable vessels – of which eighty-three per cent were cooking pots, fifteen per cent pancheons and jugs, and the rest various bowls, jars, and other shapes. The fabric is hard and compact with coarse quartz grit which gives a rough and recognizable surface. It is a buff colour with a light green lead glaze on all but the cooking pots. Splashes of glaze have run onto them and onto the stones of the kiln. The kilns were working in the early fourteenth century, as is shown by the occurrence of their pottery in other dated sites, and by supporting documentation. Now that the pottery types and fabric are so completely known, its distribution becomes clear. The common everyday cooking pots were sold through local small markets within six or eight miles, and served much of Calderdale and the Colne valley. Jugs and other glazed ware have been found as far as thirty-five miles away. The occurrence also at some of these places of pots of Cheshire types has led to the suggestion that some more special types were carried along the salt roads and by other medieval trade ways. This is one of a rapidly increasing number of medieval kiln sites being excavated all over the country, and as all of them have some special feature of texture or glaze in their products, due to the local materials and individual working, similar studies to this are now building up a picture of a very widespread and large-scale industry. This is a case where the cumulative work on a large number of sites can, if results are coordinated, become a contribution of national significance.

This excavation throws light on the dilemma over the content of industrial archaeology. The Upper Heaton excavations were carried out by an expert and experienced archaeologist and its results were published as a contribution to archaeological knowledge. The long suite of pottery and its typology, and the comparison with material from other sites, was offered largely as a contribution to the prime dependence of archaeological dating on the recognition of strictly dated pottery sequences. The excellent account of the kilns was a contribution to the explanation of the nature of the fabric, and also to assist the interpretation of structures which might be encountered in other archaeological digs. How does the industrial archaeologist fit into this picture? To him the excavation has thrown further light on the technology and products of a late-medieval industry. The distribution of the pottery in the surrounding country has provided clues to be followed in exploring the transport network of the period, the movement of pedlars, and the exchange of manufactured goods and traffic through local markets. It is another piece in the jigsaw of a dispersed but essential industry; a glimpse of the humbler possessions of a peasant population and of their manufacture.

The integration of this piece of work with similar work over all the country, whether carried out by the true archaeologist or one calling himself an industrial archaeologist, and the synthesis of a country-wide industry with the development of its technology out of this diverse material, may be the function which the industrial archaeologist can fulfil. In the case of iron-making, bloomery sites from Roman and later periods are being discovered more and more frequently, and excavation and recording are steadily increasing our knowledge. Each site has its own little variants in its response and relation to its particular and immediate environment; each site is a satisfactory exercise in exploration and recording, but more and more these sites are seen to conform to a few general patterns. It would appear reasonable to assign to the discipline of industrial archaeology the task not only of taking part in these explorations and recordings, but of seeing them as part of a much larger whole. In the Industrial Revolution and far more so in the present century our thinking is dominated by large, almost self-contained industry, which, although its plant may be spread over a few different centres, is still a single entity. An outstanding example is perhaps I.C.I., which we rarely think of in terms of a group with chemical works, plastic and artificial fibre concerns, and far more constituent sections than one can specify, but give it an individuality whether we are speaking of its directorate, its policy, plant, or products. A little of the principle of this overall view could be applied by the industrial archaeologist to the pre-Industrial Revolution industries. In their early stages, industries will be made up of the sum of a large number of discrete and independent small units, but none the less it will be correct to speak of the bloomery-iron industry if this wider view is taken, or of the fourteenth-century pottery industry, or even, perhaps, of the neolithic stone axe industry with its scattered independent production centres but its overlapping country-wide distribution lines.

Glass

An early glass industry was located in the Weald and several glass-house sites are known. An early glass-house is documented in the parish of Chiddingfold before 1351, for in that year 1290 lbs of 'white' glass was bought there for the two chapels of St George, Windsor, and St Stephen, Westminster. About a dozen sites of this early period have been recognized, but all are on a small scale. It was not until 1567 that a second and large-scale phase of manufacture started in the Weald, which continued until, in 1615, the use of wood for glass-house fuel was forbidden by proclamation and the industry moved to areas where coal was available.

Of the early furnace sites only two give much detail of the furnace structures. One is located at Blunden's Wood, Hambleden (SU 974374), and was found in 1959 by N. P. Thompson and completely excavated by the Surrey Archaeological Society before the site was stripped by bulldozers in the process of brick-clay working. E. S. Wood was in charge of the excavation and has given a fine and detailed account of all that was found. The site was first seen as a mound about 16 ft across and with an average height of about 2 ft, with a smaller mound near it. The large mound proved to be the main furnace and the second mound a smaller one. The large furnace proved to be almost complete, of through-draught type. A central flue with a hearth at each end was 10 ft 6 in long and 1 ft to 1 ft 10 in wide; on each side of the middle portion was a shelf or siege, a built-up platform making a bench on which crucibles for melting the glass were stood. The sieges were each 8 ft long, 2 ft 3 in wide and 2 ft high. On each siege there was a pair of slight hollows in which crucibles could stand. Glass scum overflowing from the crucibles had covered the sieges and run in a large mass into the flue. Around the siege structure on each side was an outer cavity between it and an outer wall. This cavity might have been left for insulation. It was suggested, however, although no recognizable remains were found, that the furnace had been covered by a barrel-shaped roof of stones and clay, erected over some kind of timber frame which would burn away as the clay was burned hard.

The second kiln was round rather than rectangular but had similar parts, a flue between two sieges, though the fireplace was now at the mid-point of the flue. It was square and there was evidence of a tuyere suggesting that the fire was kept up by forced draught. These furnaces agree closely with the general type of most post-Conquest glass furnaces in the arrangement of two sieges with a flue or fireplace between them. On this and many other sites fragments of crucibles were found in large numbers, a common size of the restored crucible being about 10 to 12 in in diameter, and the same height, and rather bucket-shaped. There is some suggestion in accounts that the clay for them may have been brought from Stour-bridge.

The very complete excavation report by Wood has preserved the Blunden's Wood furnace details for us in an examplary recording.[1]

The salt industry

An industry which had a long life was that of making salt, a necessity for the whole population, and until the seventeenth century required in regular supply by every household, rich or poor. The preparation of salt by the evaporation of brine was well established in Anglo-Saxon England and remains today as the chief way of manufacture. The apparatus used has not been of the kind that would survive, consisting only of shallow pools or pans in which brine from either sea or salt springs could be con-centrated to the strength at which it could crystallize. Some of the still active evaporation plants in Cheshire can give a good idea of what the general form has been, as they have changed little except in size.

The remains of this industry belonging really to its distributive side are on a very large scale, and provide an admirable field for the application of industrial archaeological recording. Two excellent examples of this kind of work are available,[2] and one of these will serve to demonstrate what can be done. Comparable methods can be applied to the study of other road systems connected with past industries – the snuff roads from Kendal, the cotton roads across the Pennines, wool roads in the south, and many others. These may at first appear to lie outside the scope of industrial archaeology, but if that subject is intended for the exploration and recording of past industries then the methods of the distribution of the products of specific industries are an essential part of the whole industrial picture.

In discussing the Cheshire 'wiches' (Nantwich, Middlewich, North-wich, etc.), J. Tait said that they 'formed little manufacturing enclaves in the midst of an agricultural district, and they were neither reckoned as manors, nor as appurtenant to manors'. They belonged jointly to King

[1] Eric S. Wood, *Surrey Archaeological Collections*, Vol. 62, 1965.
[2] W. B. Crump, 'Saltways from the Cheshire Wiches', *Trans. Lancashire and Cheshire Antiquarian Soc.*, LIV, 1940, pp. 84–142; and F. T. S. Houghton, 'Salt-Ways', *Trans. Birmingham Archaeol. Soc.*, I, iv.

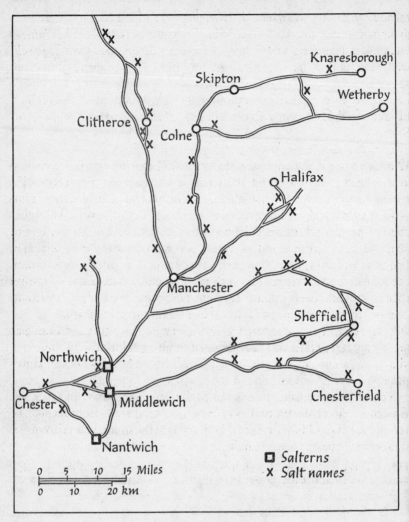

8   Mid-Pennine salt roads

Edward and Earl Edwin, in the pre-Conquest valuation. Salt was for sale at all of them to all-comers, but varied tolls were levied on customers from different shires. Over much of the northern counties, place names including the element *salter* occurred, and in his study Crump soon saw that the names lay along a limited number of roads radiating from Cheshire. These roads he called the saltways. He soon discovered a road from Northwich to Chester which goes by Tarvin, where it crosses *Salters Brook* by *Saltersbridge*. It is joined by a road from Nantwich which comes by *Salterswell*, while a third road, part of this group, from Middlewich, has a *Salterswell* and in part is called *Saltersway*. This road also goes east from Middlewich into Derbyshire, by *Salters Lane*, *Salters Ford*, *Salters Stick*, or a branch by *Salters Knowle*, *Salters Barn*, *Saltersgate Lane* and *Psalter Lane*[1] to Sheffield.

Saltways have been traced from Northwich to Manchester, and to Wigan, as well as the ones mentioned above. From Manchester there are several roads, all marked by salter names, all used in part by turnpike roads, but all having considerable stretches which are now only bridleways or green roads. The salter names are mostly documented from thirteenth- to fifteenth-century deeds, but in the Midlands they occur in Anglo-Saxon charters as well (Diag. 8). The saltways must have developed from pre-Conquest trackways, and probably reached their greatest use in the sixteenth and seventeenth centuries. Along the roads, or not far from them, there are names connected with this trade, of which *Saltfield* and *Saltpie* are the commonest. Both indicate places where salt was sold or stored. The Saltpie, however, was a definite building, and many examples are to be found either as foundations of small buildings on the edge of a village or near a cross-roads, or as a small but very sturdily built storeplace.

The whole investigation has revealed the existence of a medieval industry and its extraordinary transport network of tracks, roads, bridges, resting places, and selling locations. This can surely claim to be one type of industrial archaeological research.

[1] This is a confusion of name occurring in several places, where the original use of the road is forgotten, and its name preserved verbally. Several Psaltersgates, Psalterfields, etc. have arisen in this way.

CHAPTER 12

Prelude to the Industrial Revolution – the Sixteenth and Seventeenth Centuries

The sixteenth and seventeenth centuries are not an easy period for the industrial archaeologist, as they were a time of vital change in the scale of industries, of the introduction of a new technology, and the appearance of large capital concerns and monopolies. In many ways it was a time of transition during which industries organized on the medieval pattern came to an end and their place was taken by larger organizations which fore-shadowed or led into the new pattern of the eighteenth and nineteenth centuries, which has been called the Industrial Revolution. Many of the small units typical of sixteenth-century industry were replaced in the later years of that century or in the next by larger structures often operating new processes, and these either destroyed or completely covered the earlier sites. In the iron industry some of the new-type blast furnaces were built over the levelled remains of a bloomery and some of them used the comparatively rich bloomery slags as raw material to supplement their ore supplies. We shall never know how many bloomery structures have dis-appeared in these ways, but the frequent discovery of robbed sites suggests that they were many. It was chiefly the larger and later bloomeries of the sixteenth and seventeenth centuries that disappeared, though some of the long-worked Roman sites in the Weald and the Forest of Dean were extensively robbed of their slag both for smelting and for road-making. Larger pottery kilns in the seventeenth century were sometimes built on the levelled remains of their predecessors, though fortunately most of the new potteries moved to new sites, as they depended more upon selected raw materials brought from distant sources, and so were related more to the means of transport than to immediately local clays. It is this fact – that the new and larger industrial sites are fewer in number and have been established often in relation to transport or other new factors – that has left some of the old sites abandoned but not destroyed.

On the whole, the sixteenth and seventeenth centuries are a period during which the transition was achieved from industries with methods and organization which had changed little in the thousand years or more since Roman times, to the new methods and inventions which foreshadowed the Industrial Revolution. In the iron industry the transition from bloomery to charcoal furnace to coke blast furnace was not made in three clearly separated jumps: there was a considerable overlap. Bloomeries were still working in one place while in a neighbouring area charcoal furnaces were making iron. When coke smelting had become the general practice, a few charcoal furnaces were still in blast. Thus some of the transition techniques and structures can still be found within the period of the Industrial Revolution.

Fortunately these centuries are transitional in another sense, in that documentation is becoming more abundant and for some of the new industrial sites there is at least a skeleton of manuscript material, leases, accounts and occasional correspondence or licences against which, as a background, the physical remains can be studied. In the Industrial Revolution the documentation is often the larger and fairly complete section of an industrial history, and the physical remains are a fleeting and fragmentary supplement. In the sphere of the non-ferrous metals the transition, at least in organization, was more abrupt. The mid-sixteenth-century Chartered Companies, the Society of Mines Royal, and the Company of Mineral and Battery Works, with leases and privileges covering very large areas of many counties, were an innovation in lead and copper mining, in brass-making, and even in iron wire-drawing.

In the opening years of the reign of Elizabeth I, the demand for metals increased rapidly and many explorations for new sources and experiments in better ways of getting and of manufacturing them were being made by a group of people working in large partnerships and not as isolated individuals. The use of water power was becoming general, and in the mining areas of Saxony and other continental fields it had been applied to many processes in the dressing and smelting of ores in which new kinds of machinery were being used. Agricola's great book on mining[1] had provided a rich atlas of these new machines and methods, and stimulated those interested in mines to invite skilled men to this country to explore our mineral fields and to organize their development. Daniel Heckstetter came to this country in 1563 to search for all kinds of ores throughout

[1] Georgius Agricola, *De Re Metallica*, Basle, 1556.

Cumberland, Westmorland, Lancashire and Yorkshire, Gloucestershire and Warwickshire, Cornwall, Devon, and Wales. Following these explorations two companies were formed which would incorporate the help of German experts in their operations and make it possible to get German workpeople to direct the work. Elizabeth granted a Charter to each company, which was to be a joint-stock of twenty-four or thirty-six shares of which a majority was held by English partners. The companies were those already mentioned; the Governor and Company of Mines Royal, and the Governor and Company of Mineral and Battery Works. The Mines Royal were primarily concerned with mining, smelting, and refining copper, and the Mineral and Battery works with making brass and brassware, and with drawing iron wire. Both charters were issued in 1568.

With large capital and with skilled and experienced workmen the companies introduced a new scale into industry. The Mineral and Battery Works, established on the estates of the recently dissolved Tintern Abbey, comprised a wire mill, 50 ft by 30 ft, with four water wheels for wiredrawing, two forges, and two annealing furnaces. The new smelt-mill of the Mines Royal company, at Keswick, Cumberland, was 78 ft by 54 ft, and had three smelting furnaces. In a letter to Cecil, Thurland described it as 'such a notable and substantial melting-house for the trying and refining of our ore that the like is not in all Germany'. When in work it was producing twelve to fifteen hundredweights of refined copper daily.

At the mines in the Newlands valley, south of Keswick, stamp-mills, dressing floors, houses for workmen, stores, etc. were built, along with water wheels and watercourses; and shafts were sunk and adits driven at many places. Although the ventures experienced many and serious difficulties, the mines and mill were worked more or less continuously until they were destroyed during the Civil War in 1651. They have been worked at many subsequent periods and it is now an almost, but not quite impossible, task to distinguish the work and remains of the earliest period. Nonetheless this might be a worthwhile task for a dedicated industrial archaeologist with the necessary mining knowledge. Some of the adits and shafts of this period are known both in the Newlands and the Coniston areas, and there are extensive details and accounts of their work, and the names and approximate locations of many of them are mentioned in the Company's Journal.[1]

[1] Many of these accounts were translated and published by W. G. Collingwood, *Elizabethan Keswick*, Tract Ser. VIII, *Cumb. & Westd. Ant. & Arch. Soc.*, 1912.

The Company of Mineral and Battery Works established their wire-mill in the estates of Tintern Abbey, but for a time were in difficulties through the unsuitable nature of the iron they were able to get locally. This led them to build their own furnace, seven miles from Tintern, at Monkswood, where their finery was able to produce an osmond iron suitable for wire-drawing. At the same time the Company built a furnace within the abbey ruins, for making brass, but again they came up against difficulties in the quality of the zinc ore (calamine – the carbonate of zinc) which was worked on the Mendips. Around 1580, after various troubles, the wire works were leased until 1591 to a partnership in which Richard Hanbury was the dominant spirit. The works were leased and re-leased, time after time, to varying partnerships which worked them along with other interests – iron furnaces, tin-plate, lead, zinc, and brass – all in the new pattern which became that of the Industrial Revolution. The Tintern ironworks under various ownerships continued to the beginning of this century.[1]

The Company of Mines Royal also opened lead mines in Cardiganshire, but, after an initial period of less than twenty years bad management had reduced the mines to a poor and dangerous state, and following the example of the Keswick mines they were leased to one of the English shareholders. The mines were put in order, and soon, at the Cwmsymlog mine, the strike of a vein rich in silver was made; but after the death of the partner they were again neglected, then once more leased to an adventurer, Hugh Myddleton. He demonstrated that the mines could be drained by pumps driven by water wheels, and deep shafts which he sunk proved that in this area the veins were not impoverished in depth. After more changes, another technical innovation was made by Bushell, who leased them in 1636. He found the mines watered up but drained them by driving adits or 'soughs' into them from the lowest practicable level in the valleys, a method quickly adopted in other fields. The sough was used by Vermuyden at Longhead mine in Derbyshire (SK 293564) in 1636, and later in the Dove Gang mines which were drained by the Cromford Sough (SK 295567) about 1672. There were at least four other large soughs being driven in Derbyshire at the same time. Bushell also made advances in

[1] The very detailed history of these chartered Companies is given in M. B. Donald, *Elizabethan Monopolies*, and W. Rees, *Industry before the Industrial Revolution, incorporating a Study of the Chartered Companies of The Society of Mines Royal and of Mineral and Battery Works*, 2 vols, 1968, Cardiff.

smelting and refining lead, and in ventilation in the mines. Some of Bushell's adits can still be seen.

The Civil War brought troubles for all the mines, and the recession was felt until late in the century. In 1663, the Company of Mines combined with that of Mineral and Battery Works, but the new Company took little part in the further development of the field. Towards the end of the seventeenth century some of the privileges of the Society of Mines Royal were transferred to a group which at the beginning of the eighteenth century became the London Lead Company.

The Companies had some difficulties over the claims of the Crown on some of their mines as mines royal,[1] but the Mines Royal Acts of 1689 and 1692 freed all mines of lead, copper, and tin from claims by the Crown, even if gold and silver were found in the ores. The effect of these Acts was to remove a fear which had been a powerful restraint against the development of mines – that if silver were found in the lead or traces of gold in copper, the mine would be seized by the Crown and lost to the owner of the land. Because of this, many mines had been 'concealed': deposits known to exist were not worked or false returns of the nature of the ores were made. The passing of the Acts initiated a period of exploration and expansion in which the miner could have the assurance of working his discoveries without fear of confiscation. The London Lead Company in the early eighteenth century was able to implement its greatly improved smelting and mining techniques and to send large quantities of silver to the Mint, without the fear that might have prevented it in the seventeenth century.

In the sixteenth century restrictions were placed on the use of timber for the manufacture of iron, which drove some of the Sussex ironmasters to move into Wales, where the valleys of Glamorgan and Monmouth were still wooded and charcoal could be had with less difficulty. In the development of iron smelting in the charcoal blast furnace in Wales Hanbury of the Tintern works took an important part, driven by his need for iron of the osmond quality. He built the furnace and iron-mills at Monkswood in 1568, but also had shares in, or connections with, Trevethyn (Pontypool), Abercarn (in the Ebbw Vale), and Machon (on the Rhymney river). In the seventeenth century two more furnaces were built to supply the Tintern

---

[1] A 'mine royal' was defined as any mine in which the value of gold and/or silver occurring in it exceeded the value of the base metal. Such a mine was claimed as belonging by royal prerogative to the Crown and could be taken as such from the owner.

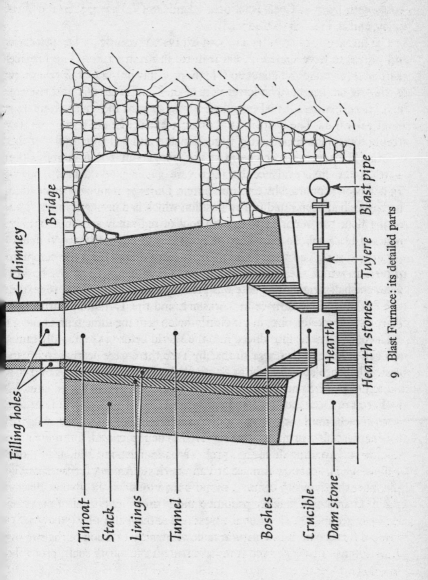

9 Blast Furnace: its detailed parts

Filling holes

Chimney

Bridge

Throat

Stack

Linings

Tunnel

Boshes

Crucible

Dam stone

Hearth stones Tuyere Blast pipe

Hearth

works with iron: at Coed Ithel near Llandogo (ST 527027) in the Wye valley, and at Trellech (ST 487048).

The furnace at Coed Ithel has been excavated recently by Dr Tylecote, and proves to have some unusual features in its structure.[1] The furnace shaft is 24 ft square and about 20 ft high, probably only a foot or two short of the original height. The lower part of the shaft is circular and rises to high boshes,[2] where it makes an awkward join with the square tunnel at about 11 ft 6 in. The hearth is not distinct but is just the bottom of this steeply conical lower portion, 2 ft in diameter, and widening to 8 ft at the boshes. The tuyere had come in at the side, about 1 ft 6 in above the hearth, and there is evidence that the tuyere opening and the hearth opening had been supported by cast-iron lintels. During a relining at some time the boshes had been lifted from a position which had been 2 ft lower. The casting floor was revealed as about a foot of red sandy soil on about six inches of black soil. In a drainage gully on part of this area three 'runners' from the casting bed were found. The furnace differs from the common pattern, in which the crucible would have been distinct and the boshes below the half-height. The date was possibly a little earlier than 1652, the date of the Rockley furnace in Yorkshire, and the Yarranton Furnace at Sharpley, Worcestershire, but it clearly belongs to the same type as them.

The blast furnace, introduced into the Weald before 1540, rapidly came into general use in that area so that by 1580 there were nearly seventy in blast. Their use spread early to South Wales and to Shropshire by 1564 and to Derbyshire and Yorkshire by the 1580s. They were not adopted in the Forest of Dean, however, until 1612, and the Furness area did not use blast furnaces until the beginning of the eighteenth century. Not many of these earliest blast furnaces have survived to be recognized, but there may be a few still awaiting discovery, probably as foundations, similar to those of the sixteenth-century furnace at Panningridge. Among furnaces surviving from the sixteenth century, in more than foundations, that at Blaencanaid, Glamorgan, is fairly primitive and is probably typical of many of this early group. The site is on the west side of the Taff valley (SO 035042), with the furnace built in a natural hollow. Some excavation of the site by D. M. Evans in 1965 showed it to have had a 12 ft square shaft, probably

[1] R. F. Tylecote, 'Blast Furnace at Coed Ithal, Llandogo, Mon. , *Journ. Iron and Steel Inst.*, 1966, 204, pp. 314–19.
[2] The part of the furnace where the expanding bottom section meets the contracting upper part.

12 ft high, built against the bank to allow easy charging. The hearth was circular, of 1 ft 9 in diameter expanded to 4 ft at the boshes 6 ft up. The lower part of the tunnel above the boshes is still to be seen. The fore opening to the hearth is 3 ft high and 1 ft 6 in wide. A stream within 20 ft of the side of the furnace, with a partly flagged channel, suggests that the bellows were operated by a water wheel.[1]

The blast furnaces did not completely displace the bloomeries for more than a century, so that during the seventeenth century bloomeries were producing rod and bar iron while blast furnaces not far away were making pig. The forge and smithy were developed in which some of the pig iron could be converted to wrought iron rod and bar, and a small part of the iron was cast direct from the furnace. Cast-iron guns never took more than about a tenth of the furnace output, the most abundant early castings being pots, firebacks, fire dogs, and grave slabs.

During the seventeenth century some bloomeries had expanded to large working units with permanent buildings and water-wheel-blown bellows, with a bloom-hearth and string-hearth, and sometimes with other hearths for working up or smithing. A large bloomery sometimes made its iron for the use of a wire-mill, and some of the largest were being operated in partnerships which included woods, mines, bloomeries and smithies, wire-mills and nail forges. Many smithies were engaged in the edge tools manufacture – scythes, sickles, axes and hoes, knives and bill hooks having a large and steady market throughout the country. This was the emerging pattern of much of the industry of the eighteenth century, when a group of charcoal furnaces owned in partnership would distribute their pig-iron to forges in the same group, which in turn provided bar and rod to smithies and mills, with only the surplus production finding its way to the open market.

The recent excavation of a seventeenth-century bloomery site in Yorkshire illustrates all the steps in an industrial archaeology investigation. In 1964, when the planned route of the new road between Sheffield and Barnsley was known, Sheffield City Museum and the Hunter Archaeological Society jointly examined the ground that would be covered to record all sites of interest before their destruction. Among these was an

[1] Details of this and other furnaces are given in D. Morgan Rees, *Mines, Mills and Furnaces. An Introduction to Industrial Archaeology in Wales*, 1969. This is a book that *must* be read and studied by everyone who wishes to record the archaeology of mines and minerals. It is a splendid example to be followed.

area at Rockley Smithies on which a bloomery was documented which had been replaced in the mid seventeenth century by Rockley Furnace, which is a scheduled Ancient Monument. A complete excavation of the site was arranged with the help of a grant from Sheffield City Museum and the Ministry of Public Buildings and Works, and a team of volunteers from the Barnsley group of the Yorkshire Archaeological Society and of the Wheelwright Grammar School, Dewsbury, under the direction of Dr D. W. Crossley of Sheffield University, excavated for three seasons – from 1964 to 1966 – and produced complete plans and reports on a water-powered bloomery and all its associated finds. The site is now covered by the road works, but is preserved in the five published reports.[1]

Rockley Smithies furnish an example of the replacement of bloomeries by a charcoal furnace, and their excavation and interpretation are a good example of industrial archaeology in action. Six miles south of Barnsley (SE 340023) the cottages known as Rockley Smithies lay on the route of the proposed motorway. In the nineteenth century this group of buildings had been associated with a forge and workshop for agricultural tools and colliery tramway work, but nearby deposits of slag which was of an early type suggested a possible bloomery site or the finery of the nearby Rockley Furnace which was working from 1652 into the eighteenth century. The exploration of a site about three hundred yards long on the south side of the Rockley Brook uncovered an area where slags were concentrated. At that part an area about forty feet square contained the remains of three water wheels, a bloom hearth, a string hearth, a reheating hearth, and some traces of a fourth hearth, the purpose of which was not clear. A dam and watercourses were also uncovered. On the north-west part of the site there was an area where ore had been roasted and where from time to time the site had been levelled up with bloomery slags. Pottery found in these layers ranged from fifteenth-century in the lowest to mid-sixteenth-century in the upper layer. There was evidence of a sixteenth-century bloomery, although the excavations did not extend far enough to uncover any hearths belonging to it. The main site at one place is cut into these deposits and so must be of a later date.

The main site was remarkably symmetrical and complete, cut into and

[1] D. W. Crossley, 'The bloomery at Rockley Smithies, Yorkshire', *Bull. Hist. Metallurgy Group*, No. 8, 1967; and D. W. Crossley and D. Ashurst, 'Excavations at Rockley Smithies, a water-powered bloomery of the sixteenth and seventeenth centuries', *Post-mediaeval Archaeology*, 2, 1968, pp. 10–54.

levelled in the natural clay of the site. A small dam held up a pond fed from a powerful spring three-quarters of a mile away. The pond was about an acre in extent and the dam was a clay and gravel bank, revetted with stone. The placing of the smithies in a hollow cut into the original surface gave the dam an increased effective height. Below the dam there were two wheelpits, their water coming to a common tail race, stone-lined and covered with strong timbers, some of which remained in position. The wheels had stood between the two bellows chambers, in one of which some of the timber carrier sleepers with mortice holes remained, with traces of a similar frame in the other. These were built on a floor of slag and cinder. The wheelpits contained potsherds of the second half of the sixteenth century, but both pits had been altered at some time. The early wheel in the north pit had been a 3 ft-wide breast wheel, but the pit had been narrowed to take an overshot wheel, 1 ft 6 in wide and 10 ft in diameter, part of which was still there. The wheel remains in the pit bottom were covered by slag in which was some pottery of about 1620.

About 1620 this wheel had been abandoned and its pit filled and paved over, and the second wheel altered and enlarged so as to serve both hearths. Near this there were the remains of a third wheelpit and hearth, but their purpose was not clear. There were also two small reheating hearths without bellows, and near them an anvil base. There was no trace of a wheel which could have served a trip-hammer. The site was therefore that of a bloom smithy with bloomery and string hearth, water-powered bellows, and smaller smithing hearths. There was evidence of a mid-sixteenth-century bloomery replaced by the more elaborate bloom smithy at the beginning of the seventeenth century. This was altered during the early seventeenth century and abandoned by the mid seventeenth century. It is named as derelict in the Royalist Composition papers of 1643.

Charcoal furnaces had been built at Wadsley Bridge and Kimberworth, not far away, before the end of the sixteenth century, so there was a long overlap of bloomery and blast furnace in this part of Yorkshire. About 1652 a blast furnace was built near the bloomery site, and continued in work until the late eighteenth century. This was the Rockley Furnace, now owned and being restored by the Sheffield Historical Tools Society. In 1652, Lionel Copley leased three acres of ground on which to build his furnace, paying £5 ground rent, and 55s. 0d. for every ton of iron made. There was an unusual condition that Rockley, the lessor, should have liberty to make forty tons of iron a year with Copley's utensils. In 1705, the heiress of Rockley sold the Manor of Rockley with the site of Rockley Furnace, the site of Rockley Smithies, Rockley Mill and kiln, Great and Little Smithy Woods, all the ironworks, smithies, and furnace in Rockley and three acres of land where the Old Furnace stands.

The furnace still stands, a square shaft built in sandstone, 20 ft square and still 15 ft high. It is lined with fire-resistant sandstone cut into blocks shaped and fitted with great precision. The hearth is not present. In 1696 it had been brought into a partnership with Chappell, Barnby, Upper and Nether Bank furnaces, Kirkstall and Colnbridge forges, and Stainborough Smithies. This was the nucleus of the Spencer partnerships which dominated the south Yorkshire iron industry in the early part of the eighteenth century. The furnace, by the end of the century, was making between three and four hundred tons of iron a year. It was worked in the same way and pattern as the others in the Spencer group, and the accounts for each year include items for getting, leading, and making the hearth, for mending and dressing the bellows, for casting pigs, and for sinking pits, getting ore, making charcoal, and all the numerous other items of the year's work. Between 1699 and 1705 charcoal was being made at and carried from forty-three different places, mainly to the north-east of the furnace and up to twelve miles distant.

Barnby is another example of a bloomery site being followed by a charcoal furnace. This substitution was being made at many bloomery sites which came within the Spencer partnerships and its associates. At Barnby (SE 287087) Thomas Barnby had a bloomery which he leased in 1635 to John Thornton for a payment of one quarter of the iron made, and one bloom of iron for every nine seams of charcoal taken from his woods. The leases passed to Major Walter Spencer who, in 1650, was described as 'of Barnby Furnace', when John Spencer, son of Randolph Spencer of Criggon, Montgomery, came to be his clerk. The accounts for 1657 include payments made in 1656 for 'pounding the water' and to a mason for getting the hearth stones for the New Furnace. This suggests that Spencer had replaced the bloomery by a furnace before 1650 and had then built a new furnace in 1656. The accounts relating to the Spencer partnerships show that between 1650 and 1690 charcoal blast furnaces had replaced bloomeries on all the sites in which they were interested, and that all these furnaces were built to a similar pattern. The annual repairs follow the same pattern for each furnace – making the hearth and repairing the bellows being an annual charge, with, at longer intervals, repairs to the furnace, laying (cleaning) the watercourse, repairing the dam and the wheel, and other lesser items.[1]

Steel

At the beginning of the seventeenth century a little steel was being made both in Wales and the West Riding, in the bloomery, but after 1614 the cementation process was used. Bars of iron embedded in charcoal were heated for ten to fourteen days in pots or chests in a furnace of beehive reverberatory type. Further cooling in the furnace for seven to ten days produced 'blister steel'. This method was well established in the Forest of Dean. Ambrose Crowley was making steel at Stourbridge using pots or chests of Stourbridge Clay, and imported Swedish iron. His son introduced the industry to the Newcastle-on-Tyne area about 1700. The steel production was not very large and much of it was used by the scythe smithies, where narrow strips of steel were welded onto iron bodies to make scythes and other edge tools. These smithies developed in the eighteenth century, often making their own steel.[2]

Coal

During the sixteenth century little progress was made in coalmining: methods and the size of pits had not changed much, although the pits had vastly increased in numbers and were scattered over all the coalfields. The first real changes came at the end of the century, by which time the first rails for the use of carts carrying coal to the river bank were made, an example which was followed experimentally during the early years of the seventeenth century. The biggest coalfield was that of Northumberland and Durham adjoining the valley of the Tyne, from which area coal was sent to London and also exported to the Continent. In the seventeenth century the coal trade on the Tyne was closely linked with salt-making and glass, and gave rise to shipbuilding, later to become a major industry on the river. The demands of the ships for easier loading led to the establishment of staithes along the river wharfage and the making of harbours at various places along the coast. The rapid growth of the coal industry in the seventeenth century destroyed or covered much of the earlier work by its debris, and the subsequent centuries, with the expansion of towns and

[1] The large collection of Spencer MSS is now in Sheffield City Reference Library.
[2] A typical surviving example will be described in the next chapter, see p. 233.

industries, has left little to be seen. However, there are fragments still to be traced and there is sufficient material both in manuscript and on the ground for the industrial archaeologist to find this a very demanding and rewarding area for research. One material evidence, typical of some others now largely destroyed, is Seaton Sluice, and much further research and preservation must soon be carried out upon it.

Salt

The salt industry in the west of the country has already been described by the network of saltways spreading over the mid-Pennines from the Cheshire wiches. There was an equally important production of salt along the north-east coast, the remains of which, besides a few inland saltways, include harbour works. These are also connected with the coal trade and emphasize the way the two industries were closely related. The principal salt pans were at Whitley, Cullercoats, Hartley, Blythe, and Amble, from three to thirty miles north of Tynemouth, associated with small collieries, all sending some coal as well as salt southward by sea. The growing export of coal from the North-East to London was carried largely by shipping based on the fishing villages and towns on the coast south of the Tyne, and not by ships local to Tyneside, though these gradually took a much larger share of the traffic during the seventeenth century. In 1612 a list of ship-loads of coal carried from Tyneside to London gives the following as the origin of the ships carrying most, with a long list of other ships which made only a few journeys: from Ipswich 363, Kings Lynn 298, Yarmouth 258, Newcastle and Shields 206, Hull 167, London 136, and Harwich 136. The same year, 1612, the shipmasters jointly refused to come into Hartley and some other small coastal loading points for coal, because there was only a comparatively small quantity, the loading facilities were very poor, and the coast was dangerous. Boats normally employed in the coal trade could sometimes be hired to take salt to London and to the fishing centres along the coast, but when Delaval, in 1600, tried in London and in Yarmouth to hire boats to carry his salt from the coast north of the Tyne, the difficult state of the loading place at Hartley was too well known and he was un-successful. For this reason he sent his salt by inland carriers to Blythe, where there was a better harbour. The salt pans at Hartley and a little further south at Cullercoats continued in a small way, but pans at Shields on the Tyne, with the advantage of good shelter for shipping and a great number of collieries on the Tyne as a source of coal, expanded and took much of the trade. In 1635, the salt-makers there were incorporated as the Society of Saltmakers of Shields.

The earlier salt pans had been scattered along the coast at places where timber for fuel was cheap, and the pans actually in use were small, made of lead from the Durham lead mines. Their location is often indicated by place names: for example, Howden Pans, Hartley Pans, Pan Bank, Pan Rocks, and many others. The lead pans were replaced by pans made of iron, the earliest in the north being installed at South Shields in 1489. As the salt pans increased on the Tyne, and at Blythe at the mouth of the Wansbeck, due to the advantage of the extensive coastal shipping from their harbours, combined with the abundant coal, small pans ceased at many points on the coast, with only Cullercoats and Hartley continuing to work on any scale. Their best period came about the latter half of the seventeenth century when coal prices and the demand for coal were increasing on the Tyne and making it more expensive to get pan coal. At Cullercoats and at Hartley the general trend throughout the country for landowners to invest in coalmines was illustrated. At Hartley and Seaton, adjoining manors belonging to the Delaval family, the Delaval pits were opened or deepened, and at Cullercoats, Lady Percy shared the cost of dredging the harbour and building a pier, for the sake of the coal shipment from her collieries. This benefited the salt pans and made it possible for this trade to expand. Sir Ralph Delaval, in 1661, replaced the ancient and difficult landing place at Seaton by a new harbour, with a stone pier. The pier was frequently damaged by storms and the harbour silted up badly. The old landing place had been dry at low tide but the new harbour had water at all states of the tide. To get rid of the silting, Delaval fitted his harbour with sluice gates which were closed by the pressure of the incoming tide, and not opened until a point in the ebb tide allowed the pressure of the impounded water of the Seaton Burn, accumulated in the harbour, to open them. As soon as this occurred, the great mass of water rushed out, sluicing out the silt and clearing the channel. This method was very effective for nearly a century though there were many times when the sluice gates were severely damaged by storms, and occasions when the silt banks became too heavy for the sluicing stream, and had to be dug away.

If, to complete the story, we look into the eighteenth century, Sir Francis Drake Delaval a hundred years later improved the harbour by making a new and more direct cut through the high sandstone cliffs, in line with the Seaton Burn, improving the new sluice to hold more water to achieve a more powerful scouring. A wagonway brought coal to the harbour, from which there was a considerable shipment of good-quality coal to London, while the small coal was used for the salt-making. Glass works were added, and a bottle factory planned. The colliery was troubled with iron pyrites in some of its coal, so this was brought to the high ground around the harbour and a copperas works established. Houses and offices were built around the harbour and in Hartley, the whole forming a true industrial estate. These industries persisted into the nineteenth century, then collapsed in face of the growing Tyneside competition. However, the harbour and sluice are there as permanent memorials to this venture; glass slags, remains of tanks and buildings, traces of the wagonway, colliery tips, and other evidence of the activities is still to be seen on the ground. The size of the industry at Seaton Sluice at its most flourishing period can be judged from the returns of coal and salt. In the four years 1754 to 1757, inclusive, before the full improvements were completed, 26,653 chaldrons of coal (a chaldron was then 53 cwt) and over 3,700 tons of salt were produced, by far the larger part of it for the east coast fisheries and London.

Alum

Some of the earliest works are those along the Yorkshire coast, which have left a large range of quarries at Boulby (NZ 739201), Kettleness (NZ 832160), Sandsend (NZ 860138), and Peak (NZ 970018). The area at Boulby is at present being excavated by an industrial archaeology group from Teesside, under the direction of K. Chapman. The very extensive remains of the alum works have been located in the quarry, which makes a vast ledge in the face of the vertical cliffs, 250 ft above the shore. Among the tumbled heaps of landslipped material and quarry waste there are fragments of masonry, and a long watercourse in part stone-lined and stone-covered, occasionally tunnelling beneath landslip heaps – all these along with other remains being involved in a largely overgrown wilderness. Among this chaos the excavators located the remains of several partly burned heaps in which the method of piling with alternate layers of shale and small coal can be seen. Below the heaps and between them and the cliff edge there is an extensive set of leaching tanks, rectangular and finely built in cut masonry, with connecting conduits taking the liquor to deep, circular storage tanks. From these a stone-lined conduit carried the liquor along the cliff edge nearly a mile to the 'alum house', a complex of buildings where evaporation, addition of ammonia or potash, and final crystallization was carried out. Behind the alum house there is a shaft which goes down to shore level, with a short tunnel to a loading harbour cut out of the rock reefs at its mouth.

Many small buildings have been uncovered around the leaching tanks, including an office, blacksmith's shop, and store rooms. The cliffs are subject to heavy erosion by the sea, so that now some of the leaching pits are partly cut off at the seaward end. Frequent and repeated landslipping has from time to time interfered with the conduits so that their remains frequently present a complex system of repairs and replacements. The work of the group is still going on and its completion promises to reveal all the details of a very large and complex industrial site of late seventeenth to early nineteenth century working date. The position of the works perched on an enormous quarried shelf nearly half way up the highest cliffs (600 ft) on the Yorkshire coast makes a visit to them both spectacular and thrilling. Some of the excavation and photography has been carried out in positions where a careless backward step could have sent one vertically down to the rocky shore more than two hundred feet below. This is a brilliant piece of true industrial archaeology which must be visited to be fully appreciated, and which has the merit of revealing something which can be left for visitors to see.

Glass

Glass-making had spread from the Weald to a few other areas, but in the seventeenth century the greatly increased activity in house building created a demand both for window glass and for domestic vessels which was met by the establishment of many new glass works. A nearly complete furnace of the second period, 1560-1615, was excavated in the Weald, at Vann (SU 984377), in the 1930s, but in 1968 a remarkably complete, almost identical one, was discovered in Rosedale, in the North Riding (SE 745932), by R. Hayle and excavated by A. Aberg of Leeds University and Dr D. W. Crossley of Sheffield University with members of industrial archaeology groups. The furnace lay at the centre of a rectangular area 36 ft by 42 ft, which had been defined by rough stone walls. It had a central mass 10 ft square with wings at each corner, set at an angle approximately along the diagonals. These wings were 5 ft wide at the inner end, splaying out to 7 or 8 ft at the outer end, and 8 ft long. The working part of the furnace or kiln is a central flue about 1 ft 6 in wide, flaring out at each end between the wings. On each side of this in the central part there is the siege or shelf on which parts of broken crucibles were still in place, with glass adhering to them, and also running over some of the adjacent stones. The stones of the flue were heavily burned, the working temperature required for the furnace being about 1,200 °C. The wings appear to have a small annealing or fritting oven in each arm, taking heat from the central flue. All this structure is matched in the Vann furnace and in others of similar date, but not in such complete condition. An additional feature at Rosedale is a structure at the north-east corner of the large enclosure, a mass of masonry 15 ft by about 7 ft, which is the remains of two small ovens, possibly for annealing.

The furnace site is on a remote moorland with no direct access, and so after excavation it was decided to remove it and re-erect it in the Ryedale Folk Museum, Hutton-le-Hole. This was accomplished after many serious problems of labelling and removing the stones one by one, and then transporting them across difficult and boggy moorland, had been solved. The curator of the Museum, Bertram Frank, with a fine group of volunteers, organized and carried out this task, which included, among other things, the building of a stone causeway across one boggy area.[1]

Transport

During the seventeenth century salt pans were constructed at Shields on the Tyne and at Blythe on the Wansbeck, while a few were set up on the Wear at Sunderland. Seaton Sluice and Cullercoats on the coast only persisted because they were directly linked with collieries and owned by large landowning families interested in coal. A contributory factor to the success of Seaton Sluice was its direct connection by wagonway with the Delaval colliery. The areas of Northumberland and Durham adjoining the Tyne valley were those in which wagonways had their maximum development, and, although the first to be recorded was at Wollaton, Nottingham, in 1597, by 1606 there was one in Northumberland. In 1605 Huntington Beaumont, who had been agent at Wollaton, took, along with five partners, the remainder of a Crown lease of collieries in Cowpen and Bebside near Blythe. Beaumont introduced the idea of having a wagonway and in 1606

[1] A preliminary note of this discovery was given in the *Annual News Sheet, 1968, of Group 4 of the Council for British Archaeology*, by Aberg and Crossley, and in the *Yorkshire Arch. Journ.* Yorkshire Archaeological Register, (1968), 243 and fig. 2. Full publication is pending. An account of the transfer of the kiln to the Ryedale Museum was published by the curator, B. Frank, in the *Dalesman*, 32, No. 2. (May 1970), pp. 131–5.

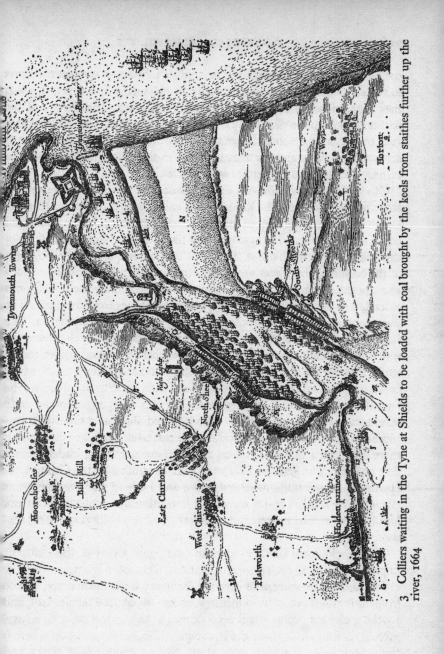

3 Colliers waiting in the Tyne at Shields to be loaded with coal brought by the keels from staithes further up the river, 1664

the partners built one, only five hundred yards long, to connect their pits to the salt pans. This was found to be an advantage and when, in 1614, they relinquished their pits and the salt pans, Peter Delaval, one of the partners, took up the wagonway and relaid it for use at his own colliery and salt pans at Seaton Sluice. In course of time this was relaid and extended, and with renewals and changes with the expanding industry served the colliery and the pans for nearly two centuries.

Other wagonways followed on Tyneside, the next one being on the south of the Tyne from the Ravensworth collieries to the river at Derwenthaugh, built probably along a line for which a wayleave for the carriage of coal had been obtained in 1530 – 1632 is the date assigned to the making of the wagonway along this line. The Civil War interrupted the development of the coalfield, and it was not until 1661 that the great era of the wagonways began. The Ravensworth way was restored, and about 1665 was extended to the pits at Marley Hill, about four miles from the Tyne. The wagonway ran to staithes on the river bank, called Team and Staithe. The staithes were built-up wharves along the river bank onto which the wagonway turned parallel to the river, and where coal was tipped and stored. It could then be shovelled down shutes into the keels – small boats which could pass the Old Bridge at Newcastle and carry the coal down-river to be loaded into the colliers waiting in the Shields anchorage. In the early seventeenth century as many as four hundred ships at a time were employed in carrying coal to London and the east coast ports, and on occasion there could be a hundred colliers in the anchorage being loaded from a fleet of keels. The keels and keelmen were controlled by the Company of Hostmen. As the trade increased, more and more of the river bank was taken up by staithes and a considerable boatbuilding industry grew up, building and repairing keels and eventually building colliers and other sea-going vessels.

The development of the wagonways was only a part of the transport improvement of the seventeenth century. Transport by water was the easiest and cheapest form of carriage for heavy loads in quantity, and so from early times goods from inland sources – wool, lead, stone, coal, and anything else for export – had been carried to the nearest point on a navigable river for carriage over the last stage of the journey to a port where it could be loaded on to sea-going ships. Shoals, acute bends, weirs, and other obstructions which had been negotiated by small boats when traffic was light became a serious matter when the bulk of transport was increasing rapidly. The seventeenth century was such a period and it was natural that attention and effort should be turned to the improvement of the river course and to the building of more efficient wharves and warehouses where the trans-shipment of goods could be accomplished with greater ease and safety.

The improvement started in the larger rivers and their estuaries by an attack on the shallows and mud banks which became more of a nuisance as boats became bigger and of greater draught. In the sixteenth century York Corporation encouraged schemes for dredging some of the shoals in the Ouse, but with little real success. The position of York as a port declined rapidly, not only because of the state of the river but also the rapid growth of Hull and its improved shipping facilities. The example of London and the Thames encouraged the York Corporation to think of an Act of Parliament to enable them to make cuts to get rid of some of the worst bends and to dredge and generally improve the river. There was a long struggle for the Act, which was eventually obtained in 1657, but it failed through lack of funds to be implemented properly.

In the second quarter of the century, Cornelius Vermuyden had drained the Hadfield Marshes, and by 1652 the Earl of Bedford had drained many thousand acres of the Fens around the Great Bedford Level. Some of the great drains were suitable for navigation and were soon used as waterways for short distances. This, with the example of the Thames embanking, encouraged work on the tasks of recovering flooded land and flooding rivers. Vermuyden had tried to control the Don by making a cut from the Don to the Aire between Snaith and Rawcliffe. This had caused extensive flooding round Snaith so a new and much longer cut was made direct to the Ouse at Goole, the canal-like so-called Dutch River. This cut out a very difficult part of the Ouse navigation and demonstrated on a big scale the value of cut-offs. This and many other of the seventeenth-century river improvements are still in use and a few of the works associated with them – wharves, banking, and so on – can still be examined.

An example of an industrial river port is Morwellham on the river Tamar in Devon. This was near the tidal head of the river and from the twelfth century had served as the port for Tavistock only four miles away. In the twelfth century also, Dartmoor was a busy tin-mining area with a coinage in Tavistock from which the tin was exported to Europe by way of Morwellham and down the river to Portsmouth. The completion of a canal from Tavistock to the hillside above Morwellham, opened in 1817, introduced a period of maximum extension, and the little port of Morwell-ham, which had kept steadily busy all through the intervening centuries, suddenly expanded into one of the busiest on the whole Devon coast. The local mines of copper and manganese were greatly extended and in 1844 the opening of the Devon Great Consols mine, which in the next half-century shipped nearly 750,000 tons of copper ore and 72,000 tons of arsenic, led to the making of a new dock in 1859. There was an import trade of timber from the Baltic and from Canada as well as a considerable general trade. The building of a railway link between Tavistock and Ply-mouth, however, robbed Morwellham of the Tavistock part of its trade and by 1890 the end of the Devon Great Consols mine marked the end of the little port. The docks were deserted and overgrown and the town shrank rapidly. Much remains of the port and its industrial buildings, with traces of the inclines from the canal to the river, and remains of many mines, and a scheme to make a museum area of part of the docks will certainly bring back much interest to the town (Plate 25).

Most shipping in the seventeenth century used the tidal estuaries for loading and unloading cargo and for shelter. Attempts to improve the estuaries and to make harbours of them were made by building a pier, to protect the entry to the river mouth from the most prevalent gales. A pier at Lyme Regis, built in the mid sixteenth century, had proved of sufficient advantage for others to be made at Dover and Hastings. Whitby also had benefited by a protective pier. The principal work, however, was still that of draining and land recovery and of the improvement of tidal rivers by embanking and confining the current by controlling banks. The construc-tion of true harbours was largely the work of the eighteenth and nineteenth centuries, while the river improvements of the eighteenth century were mostly linked with the development of canals and with light railways.

CHAPTER 13

The Industrial Revolution – the Eighteenth Century

The seventeenth century had been a time of experiment, during which many individuals were searching for new and more efficient methods for nearly all processes then in operation. The scientific revolution, typified by the foundation of the Royal Society, and the publication of their transactions with the accounts of many experimental observations, were turning attention from traditional and empirical methods to experiment. After the Navigation Act of 1651, there was a rapid expansion of international trade and a period of prosperity in this country in which the demand for all kinds of goods rapidly increased. This increase was beyond the power of the existing industries to supply. Larger and quicker outputs were required in all trades and only eventual mechanization could achieve this. The basic industries of mining and metallurgy were thrust into this expansive attitude. Mines had to be deepened, and this could only come about if haulage, ventilation, and drainage could be improved. Larger and more efficient furnaces must be developed if the output of iron and non-ferrous metals was to meet the new demands, and this meant that a substitute fuel must be found to take the place of the ever diminishing and more expensive charcoal. In all industries using heat, the substitution of coal for wood (charcoal) was the desired end of a multitude of experiments.

In spite of increasing demands the iron industry suffered a period of steady, slow decline which persisted from after the Civil War until the middle years of the eighteenth century. This was partly due to the increasing import of cheaper Swedish iron with some from Russia and America. After 1750, with the fairly wide adoption of coke smelting, and the better and larger design of furnaces, iron production began a rapid increase which led to a boom period in the nineteenth century.

During the seventeenth century many experiments were made to improve the smelting of lead and to clear the lead of the hard and brittle qualities which followed from direct contact with the impurities in coal in the ore hearth. A form of reverberatory furnace was in use on the Continent and in this country for glass-making. A furnace of this type was tried by Humphray Mackworth for smelting lead ore, but with little success. In 1678, George Grandison obtained a patent for a new way of smelting with coal, and this passed to Talbot Clerk whose father, Sir Clement Clerk, built a smelting works near Bristol which had been closed down in 1686, following a patent infringement ruling by the Privy Council. In 1692, Grandison's patent expired and a group of businessmen secured a charter as The Governor and Company for Smelting down Lead with Pit Coal and Sea Coal. They bought Talbot Clerk's works and started smelting lead ores bought from Sir Carberry Price's mines in Wales, but with no real success. After three years their smelt-mill was closed.

The charter lay almost dormant for another seven years. In the meantime Dr Edward Wright and a group of others (mainly Quakers) had secured the transfer of the charter of the Society of Mines Royal to themselves, and were working mines under the title of Royal Mines Copper of Wales. Another company in which Wright and many of his group were concerned was working mines in Alston Moor and smelting lead at their mill at Ryton on Tyne as the Ryton Company. Wright had perfected a true reverberatory furnace and with this was able to smelt and refine lead ores to produce lead and silver of high purity. In 1702, Wright managed the transfer of the Governor and Company charter, and, combining its privileges with the stock and works of the Royal Mines in North Wales and with the Ryton Company, founded the London Lead Company which worked officially under the old Governor and Company title.

This new Company had mines in North Wales and built a large smelt-mill and refinery at Gadlis near Flint, with five reverberatory furnaces – four for smelting and one for refining – a slag hearth, and roasting furnaces. The site can be seen close to the railway to the east of Bagilt station. They also had mines in Alston Moor with smelt-mills at Ryton and at Whitfield in Allendale, where the foundations of the mill can still be seen. They soon expanded and were working mines in Scotland and, after 1720, in Derbyshire. Near Wensley in Derbyshire, after opening mines and leasing old ones, they leased Bowers Smelt-Mill, Ashover, in 1734, took out the ore hearths and replaced them with reverberatory furnaces. Twenty years later they leased mines and a smelt-mill in Teesdale and built their Eggleston smelt-mills, again with reverberatories. They also in the same year, 1753, built their new mill at Nent Head in Alston Moor. For the rest of the century they continued experiments to improve the smelting, and brought it to a very high degree of efficiency. In 1778, Bishop Watson published his suggestion of flues between the furnace and a chimney to condense injurious lead fumes, and flues were soon added to all the Lead Company mills, and these remain some of the striking monuments of the eighteenth century. Remains of all the mills can still be seen, but they all have early-nineteenth-century additions, and to disentangle the whole history of the structure will need a good measure of patient investigation.

The mining in all fields in the seventeenth century had been badly hampered by water, and any expansion in the eighteenth depended upon securing the means of adequate drainage. These were provided in two ways: by the invention of the steam engine to operate more powerful pumps, and by the development of the use of drainage adits, which had been practised on a few mines in the preceding century. In the Cornwall–Devon mining field the use of adits to drain mines had been known for a few centuries, for at Bere Alston, Devon, in 1302, an adit was made for drainage, while a year or two later 'a certain trench underground to draw the water off from other trenches' was made in a mine at Baxenden in the Forest of Rossendale, Lancashire. These and later adits were very short, serving only a single small mine. In the eighteenth century adits were made on a new and vastly larger scale, and were driven, sometimes for a few miles, to unwater ground to new depths of forty, fifty, or even sixty fathoms. It had been common experience to be unable to sink much more than fifteen fathoms without being stopped by water. Pumps driven by the newly invented steam engine were working on individual mines, but by 1740 long adits were being planned to unwater a whole district (Plate 15).

An early example in Cornwall was the Pool Adit, started in 1740 near Tolvaddon. In its course it cut a splendid vein of copper ores which became the fabulously rich Trevenson mine. This encouraged the driving of many other adits in the area between Camborne and Chacewater. Between Camborne and Redruth several famous mines were made possible by the drainage adits, Dolcoath by the Dolcoath Deep adit, Cooks Kitchen, Tincroft, and Carn Brea by the Cherry Garden adit, and many others further west. The greatest venture was the Great County Adit started in 1748 from the Carnon valley from a point near Brissoe and driven to drain Poldice mine. Mine after mine was connected to this adit until by the end of the century its many ramifications totalled twenty miles, draining forty-six mines to a maximum depth of sixty fathoms. The driving of these adits and the discovery of new veins in their course was the cause, with the help of the steam engine, of the beginning of the great copper boom of the late eighteenth century. Output of ore in the five years 1745–50 had been 7,000 tons, whereas in 1795–1800 it was 49,900.

In Derbyshire many adits were driven in the same period. Mine historians in Derbyshire have for a long time been investigating the soughs – the Derbyshire name for adits – and it is estimated that at least 150 are known with certainty.[1] Hillcarr Sough was begun in 1766, near Youlgreave, from the Derwent valley and driven for two and a third miles. The entrance to the Hillcarr Sough is still open on the west bank of the Derwent at Darley Dale (SK 258637). Until 1787, it is said to have cost £32,000, but the profits from the new workings made possible are said to have repaid the cost in two years. A considerable portion of the Hillcarr Sough was driven level and kept with a depth of water sufficient to serve as a canal. The adit at the Speedwell Mine (SK 139827) was started in 1774 but intersected some stream caverns, so was flooded and used as a canal by which ore and waste rock was brought out. It is now a popular tourist attraction to visit the mine and be carried in a boat along the canal. Another unexpected find was made in the Hubbadale mine, where a sough started in 1768 struck a wonderfully rich vein of lead which made Hubbadale one of the richest mines in the county.

The prospect of driving through unknown country with the possibility, however remote, of cutting new, rich veins, was a great encouragement to mine investors. A famous adit is the Nent Force level, in Alston Moor. This was planned for the Greenwich Hospital Commissioners by Smeaton to drain the Nent Head mining field and to explore a length of ground for new veins. The mouth was beside the Nent Force on the river Nent, near Alston, where driving was started in 1776. It was designed to be a 9 ft square section but in some parts where there was loose rock it became 15 ft wide and 20 ft high. It was driven level and used as a canal. At Lovelady Shield, 13,325 ft from the mouth, there is a rise of 210 ft down which the

[1] The most energetic of the 'soughers' is Nellie Kirkham of Newcastle, Staffordshire, a member of the Peak District Mines Historical Society, in whose *Bulletin*, and in the *Derbyshire Miscellany*, and other journals, she has given us a wealth of accurate description and history of the soughs, many of which she herself has explored. These papers show the kind of records which may still be available, the methods of their assembly, and the analysis required to compile a satisfactory history.

water from the upper part plunges in a great fall. There are two shafts onto the level beyond this, one at Nentsberry, 4,800 ft beyond Lovelady Shield, and another at Gudhamgill vein in Wellgill, another 4,500 ft further along. The level terminates at the foot of the Brewery shaft, 4.94 miles from the mouth. For many years it was a regular attraction for visitors to be taken in boats as far as the Ladyshield falls. Recently a cliff fall has buried the mouth, but, like many other soughs, this adit remains a great monument to eighteenth-century mine engineering.

In each mining field there are scores of miles of these adits, as distinct from the mine workings, and a great part of them are still standing as the most extensive monument of the mining industry. Some can still be entered and examined, but none should be entered or explored except by experienced groups with proper knowledge and equipment for the job. The industrial archaeologist can make his contribution by seeking out the mouths of the adits and then supplying the necessary research among mine records to determine dates, mines served, and extent, and in some cases to prepare a map of the run of the adit from mine plans. This is more of a task than it sounds, but it can become a valuable piece of work.

Copper

In the eighteenth century, Cornwall for a time became a prime producer of copper. After the collapse of the Society of Mines Royal there was a period of stagnation in copper mining throughout the country. The Mines Royal Acts of 1689 and 1693 opened the way for mine developments, and in Cornwall copper deposits were explored along with tin. A revival of copper smelting had been marked by the establishment of the copper smelting houses of John Coster, 1680, and the English Copper Company, 1691, at Redbrook and Lower Redbrook on the river Wye below Monmouth. In 1717, the Swansea works were opened by the English Copper Company, and as the copper mines in Cornwall were opened out their ore was shipped at first to Bristol then later to Swansea, since it was a few miles nearer. The expense of shipping bulky ore to Wales induced some mine venturers in 1754 to form a Cornish Copper Company. The company moved from their original site at Camborne in 1758 and built their new mills on the Hayle estuary. They also built a harbour there to receive coal from Wales. Ten years later they improved their position by digging a canal from part of the river to their wharves, and making sluice-gates to impound the water to be used at low tide to sluice out the silt.

The discovery of the enormous deposits of copper ore, though only of low grade, at Parys Mountain, Anglesey, in 1768, with the facilities of a deep-water harbour at the nearby Amlwch, and short sea carriage to Liverpool and Lancashire coal for smelting, caused a rapid drop in the price of copper ore, from £7. 6s. 6d. per cwt to only £3. 13s. 0d. in 1780. This compelled the Cornish mines to seek ways of reducing costs. The only saving possible was in the costs of carrying ore to, and bringing coal from, South Wales. This was done by erecting roasting-mills to reduce the ore to a less bulk of regulus to go to the smelters in Wales, and by improving the performance of the steam engines used for pumping.

The opening of new copper deposits in Cornwall, such as the Trevenson mine discovery, and the deepening of mines with the help of the improved steam engines, enabled Cornwall to survive the competition of the Parys mine, which was coming to the end of its bonanza period by the end of the century. Apart from the sites of some of these early mines and their spoil heaps, the remains of the Copper Company's wharves and sluice-gates at Hayle are the most rewarding remains of this period. The greatest period of Cornish copper mining was between 1820 and 1870, and most of the visible remains belong to that time. In Anglesey, the most striking remains are those of the enormous open-cut working from which most of the ore was taken, and the remains of tanks and other works connected with ore dressing. Many of these may belong to the nineteenth-century workings.

There was some consumption of copper in brass-making in the seventeenth century, and in the eighteenth this was increased by the growth of the brass industry round Bristol. William Champion built his great works with associated housing at Warnley (ST 668728) about 1740. A little remains of these works – a factory or warehouse with a clock tower and a cottage with a tower, built of slag blocks. There is also a row of three-storey houses. There is the site of a mill pond on which is still to be seen the remains of a statue of Neptune made of slag blocks. Warnley House, which was built by Champion for his own occupation, overlooks the lake and ornamental walks. It is doubtful if many of the buildings date from 1740, but they all belong to an early period of the works.

Coal

The chief feature of the eighteenth-century coal industry was the increasing demand for coal in the smelting industries, for steam raising for the steam engines invented at the opening of the century, and in many other industries as substitution for charcoal. These demands were closely linked. Deeper mines both of metals and coal were dependent upon the new pumping power given by the steam engine. This in turn depended upon ample supplies of coal for steam raising. The increased products of the metalliferous mines demanded more coal for the smelt-mills, and the iron furnaces needed more coking coal to provide the iron of which the engines were made. With this intimate connection it becomes more and more difficult to keep the various industries separate and there must be ever-recurring overlaps in the various fields of investigation.

Little change was made in the actual ways of getting coal at the coal face. The chief change in the mines was that caused by sinking to get deeper seams, involving, as it did, new problems of winding, pumping, and ventilation. The winding and pumping was solved by Newcomen's invention of the reciprocating steam engine. The first one to be put at work was near Dudley Castle, erected in 1712. This was followed by others in Stafford, Warwick, Cornwall, Flint, and the north before 1716. The engines in Cornwall were on metalliferous mines, the others on coalmines. The first engine was put on a coalmine in the north at Tanfield Lea, Durham, by 1715, and was quickly followed at collieries on Tyneside, where at least 137 Newcomen engines were in use before the first Boulton and Watt engine was installed. The cylinders of the first Newcomen engines had been cast in brass and were very costly, up to £250 for one 29 in in diameter, the whole engine being about £1,000. In 1722, the Coalbrookdale Company began making cylinders in cast-iron and charging for them a fixed price of 32s. 6d. per cwt. This provision of cheaper cylinders was a direct result of Darby's success in smelting iron ores with coke as his furnace fuel.

The seventeenth century had seen many experiments to substitute coal for charcoal in the furnace, but none was really successful. Abraham Darby, with his knowledge of the properties of coke as used in malt kilns, was successful in 1709 in smelting iron with coke. This was achieved at Coalbrookdale in Shropshire, where he took over and adapted a furnace which had been built in 1638. In 1708, his accounts include items for making a new hearth, for 'charking coal' – that is, making coke – and repairing bellows, among many others, and in 1709 he made his first run of cast-iron. This iron was not very suitable for conversion into wrought iron, and the charcoal furnace remained the principal producer of iron until the middle of the eighteenth century. However, Darby was mainly interested in casting pots and household articles, by improved methods of casting, and his works became a foundry on a large scale. Some guns, grave slabs, and firebacks had previously been cast in the Weald, the first as early as 1543, but Darby really developed the idea of the foundry equipped to cast articles in great variety according to market demand.[1] In 1722 the Coalbrookdale foundry, besides casting domestic pots and pans, began casting engine cylinders, pump barrels, and pipe work, and so made the Newcomen steam engine an economic possibility.

The engine used large quantities of coal, and was the greatest success on the coalfields where low-grade coal was very cheap. In Cornwall, where all the coal had to be shipped from Wales, the steam engine was an expensive necessity. In the second half of the century, Smeaton made improvements in the Newcomen engine, and Cornish engineers, like the Hornblower family, Bull, and others, also made improved types of engine. Watt invented his separate condensing engine and with his partner, Boulton, was supplying his type of engine from 1777 to the mines in Cornwall. His patent prevented other types being used for many years. The tall engine house with its boiler house and chimney, required by these engines, became the almost universal mark of mines of both coal and other minerals, and many survive in Cornwall and a few in other places (Plates 17a and 26). Although most of the survivals are nineteenth-century structures, a few eighteenth-century ones are known and a few Boulton and Watt and other early engines are being preserved (Plate 16).

The foundry soon developed along two lines: casting pig-iron and large objects direct from the furnace, and making smaller objects from pig-iron remelted in a reverberatory or air furnace, or later in a special furnace called a 'cupola'. This separated furnace and foundry, as the foundry could now work anywhere where pig-iron and fuel could be brought together by the improving transport and supplies of moulding sand could also be had. The other important development in the iron industry was that of the forge which worked with wrought iron or steel. These may be made at the furnace, where the method of puddling iron had made large-scale production of wrought iron possible, and the use of rolls and slitting-mills could produce bar and rolled section in any variety.

The charcoal furnaces which continued in use until the mid century

[1] Darby was not the first to cast iron pots. His patent was for casting 'bellied pots' and other bellied ware in sand only. There was a foundry in London by 1700 casting pots and many other small articles.

were scattered about in relation to their wood and ore resources, and their pig-iron was sent out to forges, chiefly placed on sites selected for more water power, where bar and plate was made. In turn this went to a still wider scatter of small forges and wire-mills, making agricultural tools, spades, textile combs or other specialities. When the coke furnace, with its large output of four hundred tons or more pig-iron per blast, became common, the new type of ironworks came into being: usually more than one furnace, a bank of puddling furnaces, a rolling-mill, and possibly a foundry. The later eighteenth-century sites are thus more likely to be a big industrial complex, largely buried or lost among nineteenth-century improvements, replacements, and rebuildings.

Something of this was seen when it was decided to excavate the Darby furnace at Coalbrookdale. The site of the Old Furnace was accurately known – in fact an old pattern shop had been built against one side – but in the nineteenth century this was given up and the whole site and remains of the furnace had been buried under moulding floor refuse and building rubbish and levelled off with a pattern store built on top. This had collapsed and the whole area was invaded by shrubs and trees and temporary war building ruins. The removal of several thousands of tons of rubbish uncovered the whole Old Furnace. This was the one built, or more properly rebuilt, by Abraham Darby III in 1777 preparatory to casting the members for the Iron Bridge which he erected in 1779. This furnace was complete, only damaged in its upper few feet and with its lining all in place. The forehearth arch was supported by two cast-iron beams with ABRAHAM DARBY 1777 cast on them, and two others with BL 1638 BL on one of them. The tuyere arch also had cast-iron beams. When this furnace was completely uncovered, excavation was continued to see what its foundations were like, and on the side opposite the forehearth it was seen to be standing on the lower courses of an earlier slightly smaller furnace which at the back projected several feet from beneath the 1777 one. This was the original charcoal furnace which Darby had reconditioned for his 1709 experiments, and which had been reduced to about three feet and levelled with furnace stone work to be the foundation for the new one, to which he transferred the 1638 beams of forehearth and tuyere arch. Traces of the water wheel pit and tail race were also found, though these may have belonged to the later furnace.[1] In front of the Old Furnace there

[1] The later furnace is completely described in A. Raistrick, *Dynasty of Ironfounders. The Darbys and Coalbrookdale*, 1953, reprinted, David & Charles, 1970.

was the casting floor and beneath it a mass of 'bear' which may have belonged to the earlier one. Behind the furnace there were foundations of
other buildings and a large wheelpit which had served the grinding and
finishing shops. No doubt if the excavation area could have been extended,
more of the original works remains would have been found at this level,
about fifteen feet below the present surface. It is likely that other seven-
teenth- and eighteenth-century furnaces have suffered the same fate, and
their remains are now buried beneath the buildings or debris of later works.

Charcoal furnaces continued in use until after the mid eighteenth century, and many of them, away from the later areas of iron manufacture,
remain. Some have been excavated, like Charlcotte, which was in blast
from 1712 to 1792. This was discovered first in archives and then upon the
ground, where it was found to be filled with, and almost buried under, a
century and a half of rubbish, and overgrown by a thicket of trees. It was
recognized and with voluntary help has been cleared, and proves to be in
remarkably good condition.[1] These furnaces all follow a similar pattern,
the greatest differences being not in shape or size but in the lining, which
might be of brick or stone. They have a forehearth arch and a tuyere arch
separated by the pillar, the corner between them, which in some cases may
be strengthened. The watercourse and wheel are kept behind or to one side
of the furnace, as separate from the casting floor as is possible on the site.
Slag was run out in front of the furnace and its large accumulation may be
a very prominent feature, or may have given rise to a significant place
name, as at Charlcotte where the furnace is on Cinder Farm. The furnace
stack is commonly about twenty-five feet square at base, occasionally
stepped in in one or two stages, as at Coalbrookdale, or with a batter (a
slight inward slope to the top), as in the Morley Park furnaces, Derbyshire
(SK 380492), to a slightly smaller top. The hearth, boshes, and tunnel
lining are strengthened by a number of layers of brick or stone, and the
cavity between lining and shaft either filled up with rougher masonry or
with broken stone and brick rubble. The furnace is against a bank, with
the bridge leading to the top. There are a few free-standing furnaces, but
these are the exceptions.

As the application of steam engines developed, their use for blowing the
furnace with blowing cylinders or other means superseded the water wheel,

[1] This discovery and excavation was the work of N. Mutton and R. G. Morton of the Historical
Metallurgy Group in whose *Bulletin* some preliminary notices have appeared. The full account
of this furnace will be of the greatest importance.

and enabled stronger blasts and higher furnaces to be used and the blast to be kept up through the whole year. In the nineteenth century this led to radical changes in furnace design, to higher and differently shaped stacks, and to other new features, so that there is little difficulty in recognizing the remains of an eighteenth-century example. The improvement in the steam engine demanded more precision, and the development of machine tools followed, but the remains of these belong mainly to the nineteenth century.

The widely scattered furnaces and their charcoal-making sites presented an acute problem of transport. This can be seen in such a group as that of the South Yorkshire ironworks, which in much of the eighteenth century was a complex of furnaces, forges, mills, mines, and woods, connected through many partnerships in which the common factor was for a few generations members of the Spencer family. Some of the family had interests in the Rockley and Barnby furnaces and other furnaces and forges in the second half of the seventeenth century, but by the early eighteenth century their partnerships covered ten furnaces, eighteen forges, seventeen slitting-mills, and several wire-mills and smithies. To supply these they had leases of woodland in something like 175 places, with charcoal burners and woodmen at work, and iron ore mines at places along sixteen miles of outcrop. This large grouping, spread over about eight hundred square miles of country, created very large problems of carriage. There was the regular supply of charcoal to furnaces and forges, in many cases brought from woods ten or fifteen miles away. Practically the whole of the carrying was by pack-horse. The annual output of the group in the first half of the eighteenth century was over three thousand tons of pig iron. Add to this the fact that most of the area involved was also a part of the textile area and it becomes clear why this part of the Pennines more than any other has a close mesh of pack-horse tracks, causeways, fords, and bridges, almost unique in the country. Some of the tracks between furnaces and forges can be disentangled from the general mass, but to get the whole plan of tracks sorted out, with the many mines, charcoal pits, basket-making areas and other ancillary remains, will only be done, if ever, by piecing together the work of many industrial archaeologists and local historians.[1]

An outline account of this organization with some account of the technical side will be found in A. Raistrick, 'The South Yorkshire Iron Industry, 1698–1756', *Trans. Newcomen Soc.*, XIX 1939), pp. 51–86; and in A. Raistrick and E. Allen, 'The South Yorkshire Ironmasters 1690–1750)', *Econ. Hist. Review*, ix, 1939, pp. 168–85. The accounts and manuscript material relating to this group are in the Spencer MS, Sheffield City Library. To check scores of

Soon after 1750 most of the charcoal furnaces were blown out and the place of some of them was taken by coke furnaces with a much larger output and making large demands on the coalfields for their fuel. The coal was brought from much more localized areas than the wide scatter of charcoal sites, and the industry concentrated near the coal.

The most remarkable development of the coke blast furnace was in the ironworks founded in the northern edge of the South Wales coalfield, largely by men from Shropshire and other border counties. The ironworks, which include many famous names, have mostly ceased to work during this present century and have left large areas of ruins, among which there are several remains of early furnaces still to be seen. Although a great part of the remains belong to the nineteenth century, there are several structures of eighteenth-century date which can be recognized. This may be because many of the works had space which enabled them to add later furnaces on new sites alongside the old ones. The many works and their remains have now been fully documented by D. Morgan Rees for the National Museum of Wales, in a volume which is a model of industrial archaeological recording,[1] a model which one would like to see followed in other regional studies.

Steel

Steel assumed great importance in the eighteenth century by the further expansion of the use of cementation steel in the edge tool smithies and by Huntsman's discovery of cast steel. From 1709 steel was being made in Sheffield by this method. In the two decades between 1740 and 1760 Benjamin Huntsman was experimenting in methods which resulted in 1761 in his crucible process of making cast steel by remelting blister steel The cementation furnaces were housed in a tall brickwork cone, rather like a glass-house cone, and a few of these survive. One is in its original position in Sheffield, preserved by the Iron and Steel Research Association, and another, found many years ago at Derwentcote, near Rowland Gill, County Durham, is to be removed eventually to the Regional Open Air Museum at Beamish Hall, Durham (Plates 5a and 5b).

---

miles of these tracks, and to visit the remains of all the furnaces and forges, took more hours of walking and provided more happy hours and healthy exercise between 1922 and 1938, than one can enumerate, but such effort is indeed good training in industrial archaeology
[1] D. Morgan Rees, *Mines, Mills and Furnaces. An introduction to industrial archaeology in Wales* 1969, H.M.S.O. for the National Museum of Wales.

On the banks of the river Sheaf, three and a half miles south-west of Sheffield town centre, there is a group of workshops of the eighteenth century, now preserved as the Abbeydale Industrial Hamlet. In 1720, a scythe smithy was at work on the site. A lease of 1695 mentions a water wheel, and in the eighteenth century others were added so that four are preserved, two of 18 ft diameter and two smaller ones. There is a large grinding shop, and a tilt-hammer house with two hammers, a steel melting shop with five crucible furnaces, and six hand forges for individual workers. There are in addition a warehouse and office block and some workmen's cottages. All are ranged round a large courtyard, and the whole site covers half an acre. The site was bought in 1934, a few years after work ceased in it, and the purchaser, the Graves Trust, presented it to Sheffield Corporation who now maintain it. A public appeal in 1964 and the Council for the Conservation of Sheffield Antiquities raised sufficient money to enable the complete restoration of the buildings and their machinery, furnaces and water wheels, and the hamlet is now in working condition, open to the public (Plate 28).

Pottery
An industry which made radical changes in the eighteenth century was that of pottery. Most of the production in the early years of the century was still relatively coarse earthenware, but before the mid century new wares were being made. The Ellers brothers came to Stafford from Holland in 1692 and brought the knowledge of the salt glaze technique. In partnership with the older Wedgwood, new qualities of white glazed ware were made, using white clays and calcined flint to make the so-called stone ware. Josiah Wedgwood (1730–95), a potter like his father and brother, invented a finer cream ware which about 1750 became known as the famous Queens Ware. Some years later (1763) Wedgwood introduced the turning lathe for moulding some of his precision wares, and used transfer printing. The great difficulty of transport due to the geographical position of the Staffordshire potteries turned Wedgwood to taking an interest in promoting first turnpikes and then canals. His pottery was exported by Liverpool, Bristol, or Hull, and each of these demanded an overland carriage by pack-horse to some point on a river. It was eighteen miles carriage to Liverpool. For Bristol there was forty miles overland to Bewdley on the Severn, and the same to the Trent for Hull.

Wedgwood knew Brindley and the Bridgewater canal stimulated the idea of a Grand Trunk Canal to connect the Trent and Mersey via Stafford-shire, with a branch, the Wolverhampton Canal, to connect the Trent and the Severn. A Bill for the Grand Trunk Canal was obtained in 1766, and the greatest feat on its line, the Harecastle Tunnel, was at last opened in 1777. In anticipation of this, Wedgwood, between 1769 and 1771, built new works on an ambitious scale on an estate near the line of the canal, and there he built the workpeople's village, making the new industrial estate which he called Etruria. A short branch from the canal came to wharves and loading bays in the works. Much of the original layout and some buildings can still be seen.

The next great advance came when William Cookworthy of Plymouth, after much experiment with the petunz used in China in making their finest porcelain, recognized this as the mineral now named kaolin, the China clay of Cornwall. Cookworthy in 1768 patented its use for making true china and after a few years established china works in Bristol, along with Champion of the brass works. When Champion tried to renew the patent, Wedgwood and others managed to defeat him and took over the making of china, and this completed the establishment of the Staffordshire pottery industries. The remains of these eighteenth-century efforts are to be sought among the buildings of Etruria, in a few of the potteries, and most of all in the complex of the Grand Trunk Canal and its many associated branches.

Glass

In the eighteenth century, while the German type of glass furnace remained in general use, a new type of glass-house was being introduced in this country, the glass cone which enclosed reverberatory type furnaces. One, thought to be the oldest surviving example in Europe, was excavated in 1962. It is at Catcliffe, east of Sheffield, and above the river Rother. Since it ceased to be used about 1900 the internal structures had been removed and a concrete floor laid down. The brick cone is 68 ft high above the ashpit floor, and 40 ft 6 in inside diameter at the base. There are door and window and other openings at the base. An arched flue, 8 ft deep below the floor level, leads in and to the furnace firing hearth. The furnace had a bench 2 ft 3 in below the floor level on which the glass pots would stand (Plate 10b).

The glass cone was built in 1740 by William Fenny, who was previously the manager at Bolsterstone glass works which with others had been at work in South Yorkshire in the mid seventeenth century. The excavations were carried out by G. D. Lewis, Director of Sheffield City Museums, in September 1962 as a rescue operation, the cone being then marked for demolition. However, the significance of the cone revealed by Lewis's researches resulted in its being scheduled as an industrial monument and so saved, at least for the present.[1]

Corn-milling

The sixteenth- and seventeenth-century corn-mills were still essentially of medieval design, with the water wheel, shafting and gears made of wood, and the stones quarried from the nearest suitable grit and fettled by the miller. The eighteenth century did little to change the overall design and lay-out of the mills, but the second half was a period when there was a replacement of some of the machine parts by iron, an increase in the power of the wheel, and the expansion of many mills from two to four stones. A few of the earlier mills survive and a very few later ones are still working, but the post-war years have witnessed the end of many fine examples. The movement of corn-milling to the large mills at the ports has left the country mills to the smaller rural crafts or to the mercy of townsfolk seeking country houses. Each year one finds mills being stripped of their contents, given a new interior and being transformed into a modern resi-dence – 'The Old Mill', or, if it is big enough, 'Old Mill Cottage'. Fortu-nately, a few groups of people are doing valiant work in recording and preserving mills *in situ*, or as, at York, moving a mill bodily to be re-erected in working condition in a museum.

Examples of the parts and fittings of an early mill, with late-eighteenth- or early-nineteenth-century modifications which are not sufficient to change its essential character, have survived in many areas; disused as a mill, it may perhaps be being used as a convenient store for provender, a house for poultry, or some other kind of out-of-the-way dumping ground. The Low Mill, at Bainbridge, Yorkshire, affords excellent illustration of the machinery and arrangement of a mill which, although partly renewed in the early nineteenth century, is still essentially seventeenth-century in character and arrangement. The building is oblong, with its gable end to the river Bain and its length at right angles to this; it is of three storeys with

[1] The excavations have been recorded in G. D. Lewis, 'The Catcliffe Glassworks', *Industrial Archaeology*, I, No. 4 (1965), pp. 206–11; and *The South Yorkshire Glass Industry*, Sheffield City Museum, 1964.

a loft; the 'ground' floor is almost at stream level so is dug out of the river
bank and is for most of its area a cellar. The wheel is on the outside of the
gable but, in the nineteenth century, has been enclosed by adding a bay to
the older building, and getting an extra room over the wheel house. On
this basement floor, the pit wheel shaft and wallower,[1] and the stone
adjustment apparatus, take up part of the room, and part of the rest houses
the furnace of the drying kiln. The first floor, level with the outside ground,
now carries the four pairs of stones, and formerly housed the flour bolting
and other machines. The second floor has a further pair of stones for grinding oatmeal, and was mainly a grain store. In the loft there are two hoists,
one with an outside jib in the peak of the gable away from the river, the
other an internal sack hoist. There are the remains of a substantial stone
dam across the river a few score yards above the mill, with a penstock and
a covered leat to the wheel house delivering water at 5 ft 3 in above the
axle of the wheel, which rotated towards the upstream, anti-clockwise
looking from the stream (Diag. 10).

The wheel is 15 ft in diameter and 4 ft 5 in wide, with an octagonal axle
12 in across the flats, and a hub casting which is held in place by a mass of
wooden wedges so that it can be accurately centred and balanced. Wooden
spokes carry the iron rims, which are slotted for boards both for blades and
bucket floor. This is obviously a nineteenth-century replacement of the
older wooden wheel. The wheel shaft goes into the mill basement, and the
pit wheel there engages through a bevel gear wallower with the main vertical shaft, which carries a crown wheel 7 ft 10 in in diameter, being an iron
casting into which teeth of apple wood are fitted. The four stone nuts
engage with this, and a fifth one connects another vertical shaft to the
stones on the second floor. Other small spur wheels connect the crown
wheel with sack hoist, and other bevel wheels were for machinery now
removed.

The history of the mill has recently been documented and may prove to
be typical of many. It belonged to the Crown as owners of the Forest of
Bainbridge, but had been leased to a succession of millers. In 1797, the
old mill was taken down in June and 'the ground works was layd of the
mill by Thomas Metcalfe' of Gunnerside. The new mill 'was reared' in
September, and in October the 'cogg wheele & Axletree' were put in,

[1] The wallower is a wheel on the lower part of the main vertical shaft in a mill and has bevel
gears which engage with the pit wheel on the end of the water wheel shaft. It is the main driving
wheel of the mill. The origin of the name is doubtful.

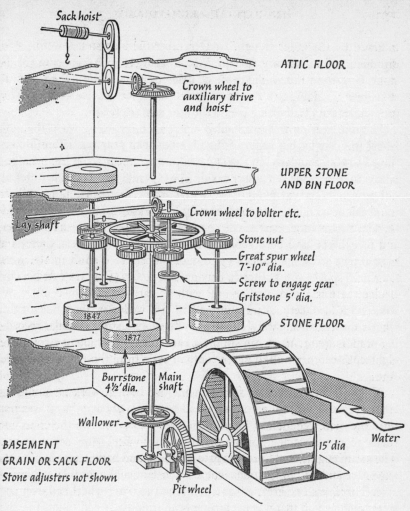

Sack hoist

ATTIC FLOOR

Crown wheel to
auxiliary drive
and hoist

UPPER STONE
AND BIN FLOOR

Lay shaft

Crown wheel to bolter etc.

Stone nut

Great spur wheel
7'-10" dia.

Screw to engage gear
Gritstone 5' dia.

STONE FLOOR

1847

1877

Burrstone
4½' dia.

Main
shaft

Wallower→

15' dia

Water

BASEMENT
GRAIN OR SACK FLOOR
Stone adjusters not shown

Pit wheel

10   Water corn-mill, Bainbridge, Yorkshire

followed by the water trough. In December the blue stones were set to grinding, and in January two grey stones came from Addingham (Millstone Grit from the Addingham quarries in Wharfedale). Both sets of stones were grinding on 5 February, and the cylinder was also working. The grey stones are 5 ft in diameter and the blue stones 4 ft 6 in.

The mill gearing was overhauled about 1860, probably when the new wheel was put in, but some of the older wooden gear was left and continued in use. Similarly, in the stone adjustment gear some has been replaced in iron but much is still wood. These partial replacements differ in different mills and examples of every part of an eighteenth-century mill in wood can be seen by going to three mills in Yorkshire, and the same could be done in any other part of the country. At Boston, where the wallower and pit wheels have been replaced by cast-iron bevel wheels, there is a magnificent 'great spur sheel' entirely of timber, 12 ft in diameter, with tangential spokes and 151 teeth, driving four stones (Diag. 11). At Newby Bridge there is a very similar mill with an early-eighteenth-century pit wheel with face teeth, gearing into a 'lantern' wallower, the whole of the wheels and axles being wood (Plate 23b). In every district a similar recording of measured remains can supply an accurate restoration of a complete eighteenth-century mill, different only in scale from those of the Middle Ages.

Although the Newcomen steam engine had been at work for pumping from 1712 and for mill work in a small way from about 1770, it was not until the more economical Boulton and Watt coupled with the crank for rotary motion became available that the water wheel had a serious rival. The steam engine could provide greater power and higher speeds but was expensive and tied to locations where a constant supply of fuel was available. There was one great advantage which the water wheel had over the steam engine, and that was in starting or in running at odd times. For the steam engine a boiler had to be lit and several hours spent in getting up a head of steam, and even then the boiler needed constant stoking and attention; and to economize fuel, the engine should run for long periods and the boiler be kept up to temperature with banked up fires overnight. With the wheel, a pull on the sluice rod or rope would set the wheel running in a matter of seconds; it could run for a few minutes for a small job and shut down just as quickly at any time.

Water wheels in sheer numbers and variety of uses remained the dominant power unit from about 1755 to 1830. The success of the wheel owed

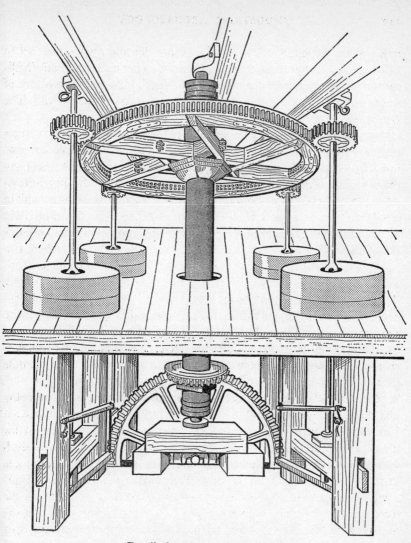

11 Details from Boston Mill, Yorkshire

much to the experimental work of Smeaton, who in 1752 worked with model wheels and got efficiencies of twenty-two per cent for an undershot and sixty-three per cent for an overshot wheel. The frequent failure of water-wheel shafts led Smeaton to make cast-iron shafts in 1769, and these were used, with wooden spokes, in many wheel replacements of the late eighteenth century. In the mining fields remote from coal supplies, large-diameter wheels remained in use until late in the nineteenth century, and many flax- and cotton-mills in the upland areas continued to use them into the twentieth century. A late-eighteenth-century wheel may have a cast-iron shaft and even a cast-iron rim into which wooden planks slot to make the buckets. The spokes also will be of wood. A wheel in which the buckets and spokes are of iron is likely to be from the nineteenth century (Diag. 12).

Textiles

The textile inventions were a product of the later decades of the eighteenth century, but their general adaptation to a power drive was bound up with the appearance of the mill or factory, at first water-powered. For several decades the machines were housed in small mills, some of them adapted corn-mills, on the many streams of the hill country, and it was not until the first quarter of the nineteenth century that the larger steam-driven mills appeared, closely linked in their location with canals for easy transport of goods and fuel. It is among these small abandoned rural mills that early mechanical remains will be looked for, but remarkably few survived, and almost everywhere there is a gap between the handloom cottage industry and the steam-power mill extending over forty or fifty years. A very concentrated search on this gap is needed (Plate 14a).

Transport

With the expansion of the iron, textile, and pottery industries, a mass of transport was created for which the parish roads and pack-horse ways were totally inadequate. Two sections of these new demands can be recognized: first, internal movement, such as that of fuel to the furnaces and iron from furnace to forge, the collected wool to the new textile centres, and other industrial raw materials or finished goods to works and to markets; and, secondly, the rapidly increasing amount of finished goods destined for export or for the London market. These led respectively to the improvement of the roads between towns and to the increasing use of

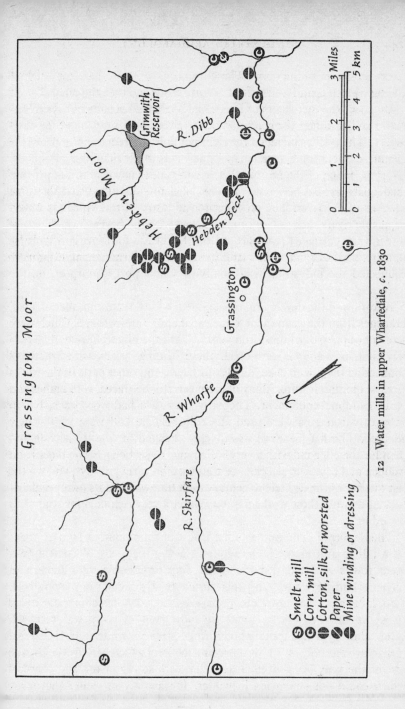

Grassington Moor

Grimwith Reservoir

R. Dibb

Hebden Moor

Hebden Beck

Grassington

R. Wharfe

R. Skirfare

N

3 Miles
5 km

Smelt mill
Corn mill
Cotton, silk or worsted
Paper
Mine winding or dressing

12 Water mills in upper Wharfedale, c. 1830

river navigation to the ports. These trends gave us, in the second half of the eighteenth century, first the Turnpike roads and then the canals.

By 1689, the merchants of Leeds and Wakefield sought powers to improve and maintain the condition of the rivers Aire and Calder for navigation. The powers included the right not only to dredge and improve the channels, but at some places to make new cuts to get rid of difficult bends. By 1774, much of the improved Aire and Calder navigation was proving inadequate and so new powers were taken to substitute canal for some sections of the river. The growing iron industry of the Midlands lacked navigable rivers such as Coalbrookdale had with the Severn, which gave it direct water carriage to the port of Bristol. The Staffordshire and Worcestershire canal of 1768, with a later junction from Birmingham, eventually connected the industrial Midlands with a new port, Stourport, on the Severn.

A feature of the developing canal system was the great number of small branches from the main canal to the canal basins and wharves which were soon a normal part of most iron works. Until the nineteenth-century railway system was well developed, these loading basins with tramways connecting them with coke hearths, furnaces, and other parts of the works were a common feature. Many of them can still be traced, with cranes and other handling equipment. The early tramways had wood rails, but in 1767 cast-iron rails were used at Coalbrookdale and were very widely adopted. The flat plate rail was quickly changed for the 'L' section and then for the edge rail with a very wide range of sections. Stone blocks and wooden and cast-iron sleepers were all used on early railways, and for the last quarter of the eighteenth century each tramway had its own peculiarities. As a group these works tramways offer a very rich field for study and recording.

The Report of a committee of the House of Commons, in January 1740, on a bill to amend the highways from Selby to Leeds, Wakefield, and other towns reported that the roads were impassable for wagons and carriages during winter, and this caused great difficulty in moving coal, corn, lime, and woollens. This emphasizes the worst defect of the existing transport – that to a large extent the movement of goods was seasonal, being almost, if not quite wholly, impossible in winter. The charcoal furnaces were only in blast approximately from October to March, the rest of the year being needed to accumulate stocks of ore and charcoal which could not be carried in winter. It was only in winter that some streams were full and regular enough to provide a sufficiently powerful blast for the furnace. Clearly an expanding industry could not be based upon a purely seasonal working, with only six months available for production. The steam engine promised a solution for the power requirements, while roads and canals could solve the transport problems.

Of the mass of turnpike roads few remains need any comment. The actual course of the roads is in large part absorbed into modern improvements. Some loops of the older course are left in a few places, and some of the toll houses but nothing of the toll gates can be recorded; a few watering troughs and milestones also remain to be found. The most permanent mark is seen in the widening of many bridges. Few new bridges were built but most of the old bridges to which the roads were brought were too narrow, and a new section was built alongside of, and joined to, the old bridge. The difference in structure can always be seen underneath the bridge and is worth recording.

The canals have had an abundant literature of their own in recent years, and not much beyond local details remains unrecorded. The relation of a canal to an individual works or industrial site has not been so fully recorded, and the means of handling, loading, unloading and storing different goods offer scope for far more study than they have yet received. The supply of water to the canals, reservoirs, stream catchments, and pumping stations, and the mechanics of conveyance, delivery, and control, can be very interesting.

As the canals came into use in the last quarter of the century, the advantage of the barge over the cart was soon appreciated. A horse could pull in a canal barge a load that would need many carts with several horses each to move it by road. For coal, iron, lime, and other materials of great weight and small bulk, the canals were ideal and there was an obvious advantage in having a canal alongside a works site where any of these goods were used or produced in large quantities. The new furnaces and integrated ironworks grew up with the canals and were either near them or connected to them by a tramway with a wharf, loading facilities, and storage accommodation at the canal side. Several examples of this kind of complex of canal and tramway are still to be seen. The Leeds and Liverpool Canal, among other traffic, carried limestone from Craven to the ironworks at Bradford and also to banks of limekilns built alongside it in its way through the Millstone Grit country where the demand for agricultural lime was high.

At Skipton, the Earl of Thanet secured an act for a short branch, the Springs Canal, which was made from a junction with the main canal, up the valley of the Ellerbeck, to a loading wharf at its head. The limestone quarries were one and a half miles away and a tramway brought the limestone to the lip of the deep valley in which the Springs Canal lay. Here a brake house operated a tramway incline down to the hoppers and shutes on the loading wharf. All these are to be seen, and were working within the last thirty years. The South Wales ironworks at Merthyr promoted the Glamorganshire Canal in 1790 to connect them with Pontypridd and so with the sea lock at Cardiff. The canal between Merthyr and Abercynon had a number of locks, and traffic along it became very congested. The canal is now mainly filled in, but its line can be followed, and some locks and wharves remain, as do some lengths of the Penydarren tramways. The Dowlais, Penydarren, and Plymouth ironworks joined to build a tramway to Abercynon to cut out the delays on the first part of the canal. It was on this tramway that Trevithick's locomotive was tried and run.

A revolution in transport with which the development of the canals was closely linked was that of the country's ports. The successful shipping of goods abroad or by coastal waters depended on harbours or anchorages where ships could shelter. This was often in river estuaries, as on the Tyne and Mersey, but, as ships became bigger, with more draft, artificial docks were made. There are references as early as 1495 to payment being made for 'mending the dokke for the King's ships . . . making of the gates and fortifying the head of the same dokke'. Later a dry dock was made big enough for a ship of 1,000 tons. Docks were built on the Thames at Blackwall in 1661, and others between 1703 and 1762. However, most docks at our various ports were begun in the later years of the eighteenth century or in the early decades of the nineteenth. Traces of eighteenth-century work should still be looked for, since not all of it has been swept away by later extension. Intimately connected with the shipping was the provision of lighthouses, the first on the Eddystone Rock built by Winstanley in 1696. The first of the modern type was Smeaton's in 1759, and part of this, replaced by a later one, is now erected on the Hard at Plymouth and should be examined for the splendid masonwork involved in its design.

CHAPTER 14

The Industrial Revolution – the Nineteenth Century

The features which most clearly differentiate the nineteenth from the eighteenth century are the vastly greater size and complexity of its industries and the application of steam power both to industry and to transport. The aggregation of an industry can be illustrated in the case of iron, in which the processes of manufacture were combined with the provision of all the requisite raw materials. A single company might own and operate coal and iron mines, coking plants, furnaces, foundries and forges, rolling-mills, and possibly even departments for turning their iron into merchants' goods. The cast-iron, wrought iron, and steel made in their works were further manufactured into stoves, pipes, tools, machinery, forgings, or other goods for the market. This had in a way been foreshadowed by the Coalbrookdale Company, which besides owning iron, coal, and fireclay mines was making domestic ware and stoves, as well as engine and structural components in the eighteenth century. In the nineteenth century it added locomotives, pumps, engines, structural and art castings, and a multitude of small goods. Not all ironworks were so fully integrated and some continued their modernization to concentrate on producing iron and steel and to sell that as their end product.

The integrated works, however, were very big and complex. An integrated ironworks of the first half of the eighteenth century, not to be regarded as a large one, would have two or three blast furnaces with their coking ovens, blowing engines and boilers, a foundry, a refinery and a forge, with hammers, perhaps up to twenty puddling furnaces, a rolling-mill for billets, other mills for bar, sheet, rod and section iron, a slitting-mill, and a vast agglomeration of stores, offices, repair and maintenance shops, tram or railway lines, hoists, cranes and other ancillaries – all this even if the ore and coal were bought from other people. A works like

Coalbrookdale in the early nineteenth century was employing about 3,000 people, while the Merthyr Ironworks were at one time in the nineteenth century employing 1,000.

A comparable integration was taking place a little later in some textile concerns, where wool or cotton was taken in the raw state and every process in preparation, cloth-making, dyeing, and finishing was carried through to the final warehouse where material was ready for sale. Some industries, however, offered no scope for such integration – potteries generally bought their clay and other raw materials from the quarrying industry in quantities and varieties from which they could make their own blends; tanners started at the purchase of raw hides, and the making up of leather goods, except perhaps for machinery belting, was a separate business. A factor which checked much complete integration until the later nineteenth century was the growing necessity to import raw materials which became the starting-point of manufactures.

The rise of these complex industrial groupings makes the work of the industrial archaeologist very difficult. The expansion of big works has overlapped and often buried the earlier stages of their growth, with old buildings and apparatuses often being removed to give space for new ones. One feature is the constant replacement of plant by more up-to-date forms. Machines take over more and more processes and the workpeople in manufactures segregate into two groups: those who make and maintain engines and machines, and those who operate them. The architects of this new phase were primarily the engineers, designers and makers of engines and machines, the men who could translate fuel and water into the energy of motion and then create machinery to use these motions to spin and weave, to plough, dig, lift, and propel loads, and to repeat all these things endlessly, tirelessly, and with accuracy.

In the sphere of the basic industries – mining, quarrying, and agriculture – mechanization had far less impact, and in the rural areas remote from coalfields water power continued to be very important even into the early twentieth century, and steam found little place until the last decades of the nineteenth.

Lead mining

There are many examples of partial mechanization in the lead mining industry, but one small and fairly self-contained mining field will serve as an example where the whole story has been recovered by intensive field work, and checked by the discovery of documentary material only many years later. Grassington Moor in Wharfedale (SE 030670 approx. centre) is an area of about six square miles, traversed by a large number of mineral veins, a high moorland between 1,000 and 1,600 ft OD, entirely the royalty of one owner, the Earl of Cumberland, and later the Dukes of Devonshire. It is almost devoid of streams, and is three miles away from the river. It was worked by shafts and presented the double problem of lack of water at the surface for ore-dressing and the difficulty of pumping and draining in depth. After a period of development from 1603 to 1790, the problem of bringing sufficient water for dressing a greatly increased output, and for water wheels for the mechanization of the ore dressing, was faced, and its solution brought a period of fifty years of great prosperity. Only scrappy records of output were available for the years before 1845,[1] and so the history of the working and mechanization was worked out on the ground by a long period of intensive large-scale mapping, checked where possible by excavation.

The first named working is Cockber vein on Yarnbury, which is a large quarry-like open cut, 250 yards long along the main vein, in parts about fifty feet deep. Below this depth, the vein has later been worked by shafts sunk on the edge, the spoil being tipped into the old working. To the west along the vein this open-cast passes into a chain of large bellpits with the remains of dressing floors, partly covered by the debris from newer shafts. The overlapping of debris from shafts of approximately known dating, and the way in which roads and watercourses cut through the spoil heaps of open cuts and bellpits, suggested that archaeological methods could be used in a survey of the area which mapped every detail. This task was spread over about four years, and proved far more profitable than had been expected.

It became apparent that the open cut work, much of it in the form of Cornish coffin work, was the earliest, with small bellpits on nearby or crossing veins frequently overlapping their debris into it. Larger bellpits followed veins in parts where there was no open cutting, and were found to be of later date. In mapping the many scores of bellpits, a few stones were found set in the ground not far away, like small head-stones, and carrying initials, sometimes with '& Co' and 'F' following obvious name initials, as 'FAW & Co. F'. These stones were added to the objects of the survey, and, assuming that many must have fallen, the turning of

The year for which Hunt's *Mineral Statistics* began to be published.

hundreds of fallen stones eventually brought the number with initials and occasional names to 157. The discovery of the Laws of 1737,[1] which said that the discoverer of a new vein should be given two meers (of 30 yds) along it, and other miners should then be allowed to take up further meers, brought to mind the similar custom in Derbyshire, where the 'takes' were to be clearly marked. It was assumed that these stones were markers, or 'meerstones'.[2] A search of parish registers showed names which fitted nearly all the initials which had been found, and these, and the full names carried by some stones – for example, GEO. FLETCHER & CO. FOUNDER – were shown in the registers to be names of miners, and their dates (marriages and christening of children were the most profitable sections of the register) lay between 1740 and 1790. The meerstones thus provided a tool for closely dating the discovery and development of veins.

Fragments of watercourses leading to dressing debris were abundant, and the mapping of these, often proved by trial excavation on suspicious-looking hollows, revealed a complex system with silted up or overgrown dams on the higher ground. The watercourses led either to dressing floors or to water wheel pits, several of which were partly excavated to find the proper dimensions and so deduce the size of the wheel. Areas of slag and cinders indicated respectively the site of a smelt-mill of 1611 and the location of half-a-dozen small blacksmith shops among the larger mine groups. The larger smelt-mill called Cupola, with its complex of ruins, its flue and chimney, was unravelled and stages in its growth correlated with the fragmentary records available. The first smelt-mill on the side of the river Wharfe, three miles away, built in 1603 was found with its remains of two ore hearths. Further details of this intensive survey[4] need not be given but a brief account of the conclusions derived from it might stand as a piece of industrial archaeology.

The first mine to be worked was the Cockber on Yarnbury, but by 161

[1] *Rara Avis in Terris or the Laws and Customs of the Lead Mines within the Mineral Liberty o Grassington cum Membris . . . 1737*, and an earlier MS, Yorke MSS, 192, 19 May 1642.
[2] The origin of meers is ascribed to a medieval custom on German mines where a man discovering a vein of ore stood to his waist in a pit and threw his hammer 'each way of the vein', thus marking his working length or meer. This length varies by a few yards in different mining fields, but i generally between 27 and 32 yards.
[3] Since this survey was completed and published a plan of a few veins on the Moor of about 1780 has been found which names the sections of the veins being worked and shows a meerstone at the end of each lease, thus confirming our assumptions. Oakes Deeds of Bagshawe Family Sheffield City Library, OD. 1241 and 1242.
[4] Carried out between 1945 and 1950 by the author and his friend, the late Arthur Waters.

mines had been opened on the High Moor and a smelt-mill built near them. The remaining recognizable early workings, partly open cut and partly the early bellpits, are mainly on the western edge of the Moor. Three areas and periods of working are to be recognized: from about 1630 to 1740, the rather primitive work now seen only in the western part of the Moor; the period of the 'free miners' who erected the meerstones, from about 1740 to 1790, with larger bellpits and small, deeper shafts in the central area; and the mechanization started in 1790 leading to the period of maximum activity from 1830 to 1870 in the eastern part. The second period was a time of great prospecting activity over most of the adjoining areas, and of the discovery of the eastern portion of the Grassington Moor field.

Turning to the second period, the remains still to be seen, additional to shafts, meerstones, and some underground workings, are a fairly large watercourse system connecting several dressing floors serving individual mines or small groups. The primitive buddles, a rare whim for winding, and the first phase of the 'Cupola' smelt-mill belong to this period.

Among the mine hillocks of the second phase, from about 1740 to 1790, amply dated by the meerstones and by a surprising number of court depositions relating to trespasses underground, there are many early buddles built in stone. The unit follows a general pattern. Barrow-ways lead from several bellpits to a cobbled or flagged area, the front edge of which is walled up two or at most three feet above another cobbled area, both being four or five feet square. The front edge of the first area is made with a few massive stones on which a boy, standing on the lower area, could crush the mine bouse with a bucker, and scrape the crushed mixture onto the second floor. Below this is the buddle, built at a slight slope, and fed with a stream of water. The first part is about 8 ft to 10 ft long and 3 ft or occasionally 4 ft wide, flagged with sides 1 ft or so high, and may be rectangular or oval. From its lowest part another channel only about 1 ft 6 in wide and about 10 ft long continues the slope. At the end of this there is the heap of fine stone debris, the ore having been caught in the buddle. After the buddle the ore was further dressed by sieving in a tub of water, and the finer slimes from this make a second very recognizable heap of debris (Diag. 13).

For winding, most of the mines used the jack-roller, but in 1755 the partnership working Coalgrovehead, a very rich mine, employed the engineer, William Brown, of Newcastle, to build a horse whim, probably

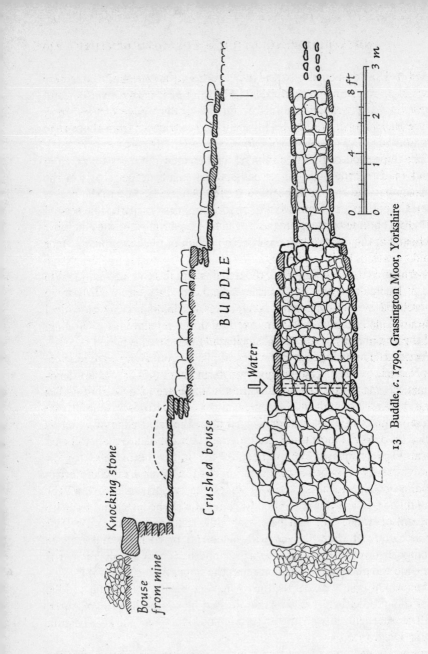

Knocking stone

Bouse from mine

Crushed bouse

BUDDLE

Water

0   2   4   6   8 ft

0   1   2   3 m

13 Buddle, c. 1790, Grassington Moor, Yorkshire

the first on the moor. This was soon copied, and after 1760 there were whims, remains of which are to be seen on all the newer shafts. The water for dressing proved inadequate as the mines extended, and so before 1780 an artificial Priest Tarn was made in a shallow col at 1,680 ft OD by embanking each end, and a watercourse brought the water to two dams on an edge above the mines, and from those to seven larger dressing floors each serving groups of mines. All this system is now dry, silted up, and overgrown, but some lengths were excavated, the penstocks in the dams uncovered, and all the dressing floors identified (Diag. 14).

In 1779 a new agent, Cornelius Flint, was sent from Derbyshire, and he encouraged the exploration of the eastern part of the Moor. With the work of him and his successor, John Taylor, the mines were replanned and a large-scale mechanization was carried through in the first half of the nineteenth century, the remains of which are now the prominent structures. A deep drainage adit, the Duke's Level, was driven under the Moor and completed in 1825; several new and larger shafts were sunk and crossconnected underground, and water wheels were introduced for the dressing floors, and for winding, with tramways to move bouse and ore about both underground and at the surface. A new water system with three large dams and about six miles of courses was built serving many water wheels, varying from 15 ft to over 50 ft in diameter. After 1840, the largest wheel had four wire ropes leading to the poppet heads of the principal mines, with a total length of 3,900 yards on the surface and 480 yards of shaft ropes. The wheelpit remains and the stumps of many of the pulley posts which carried the ropes are still to be seen. At least two of the larger mines were drained by using a remote water wheel and a great length of flat rods, leading to a bell crank lever chamber at the shaft head. The sites of these newer shafts and the large new High Grinding Mill and dressing floor have remains of Cornish stamps and roller crushers, circular buddles, stone-sleepered wagonways, and, at some of the newer shafts, larger whim circles, bobpits for pump rods and hoppers for bouse with floors for the first rough dressing (Diag. 15).

In 1756 the New Mill was completed on the Moor and soon replaced the two earlier smelt-mills. In 1792 the ore hearths were taken out and a reverberatory furnace took their place, with a short condensation flue laid up the Moor. The mill was soon afterwards enlarged and a second reverberatory, with slag hearth, roasting and refining furnaces, added. Much of the walling allows its plan and arrangement to be recovered, and almost a mile

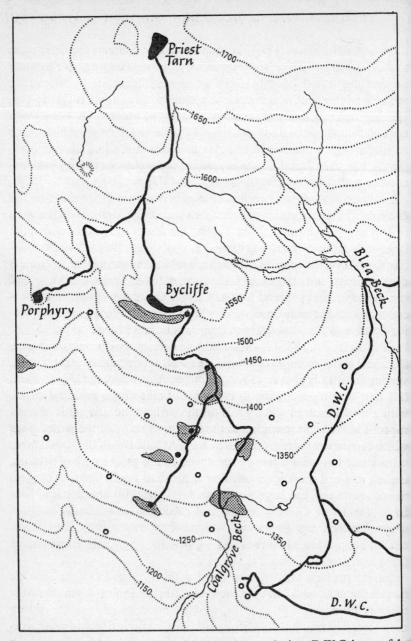

14 Priest Tarn Water Course with its dressing floors and mines. D.W.C. is part of the Duke's Water Course

of flues and the second higher chimney remain. The mining finished in the 1860s and smelting by 1880, but the history of 250 years of mining has been recovered in the first case by active field surveying and excavation. Only during the last two years, twenty years after the survey just described, have documents become available which have confirmed all the conclusions reached from the field work.[1]

In most of the north Pennine lead ore field the nineteenth-century expansion of lead mining relied on the use of water power. It was only in Derbyshire, near to the coalfields, that steam engines were used for pumping on a few of the larger and later mines.

The mining field of Cornwall and Devon, in spite of its distance from the coalfield of South Wales, was the area where the steam engine dominated the mines from the mid eighteenth to the twentieth century. Some of the finest beam engines in the country were built there and a race of engineers was trained which took the Cornish engine to the mining fields of America, Australia, and new fields all over the world. It is difficult to find a separating boundary between the industrial archaeology of the mines and the splendid history of their engines and engineers.[2]

While the steam engine made deeper mining possible, the principal changes during the first half of the nineteenth century were made in ore dressing, much of which was mechanized. The chief remains are those of crushing rollers and circular buddles, with their water wheels, slime settling pits, and buildings. The dressing was done more and more by machines, few of which have survived. A large wheel with crushers and associated buildings has been cleared and preserved at the Kilhope Mine in Weardale (NY 827429) and at Magpie Mine (SK 172682) in Derbyshire, and buildings, dressing floors, shaft head, and other equipment are being restored and preserved.

Coalmining

In coalmining, the first half of the nineteenth century was a time transitional to the modern methods. The beam engines of Boulton and Watt and

[1] Unfortunately a company re-working the mine hillocks in the last few years have destroyed the majority of these remains except the chimney, flues, and smelt mill. The photographs and detailed maps are now all the more valuable. The survey is described in A. Raistrick, 'The Mechanisation of the Grassington Moor Mines, Yorkshire', *Trans. Newcomen Soc.*, xxix (1955), pp. 179–93.
[2] The history of the engineering side has been adequately treated recently in D. B. Barton, *The Cornish Beam Engine*, 1965; E. Vale, *The Harveys of Hale*, 1966; T. R. Harris, *Arthur Woolf, the Cornish Engineer*, 1966; and A. C. Todd, *The Cornish Miner in America*, 1967. The preservation of a few of the best engines has been secured by the Cornish Engines Preservation Society.

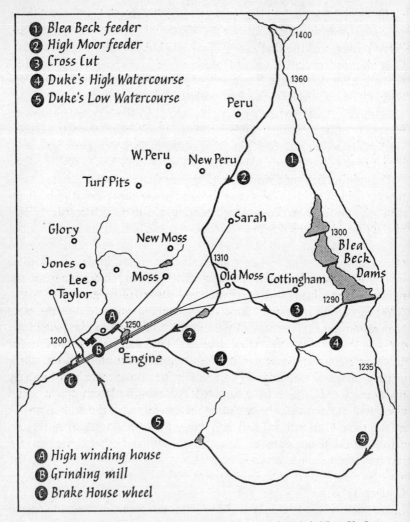

1 Blea Beck feeder
2 High Moor feeder
3 Cross Cut
4 Duke's High Watercourse
5 Duke's Low Watercourse

A High winding house
B Grinding mill
C Brake House wheel

15   Duke's Water Course, Grassington Moor, and Duke's New Shafts

of other makers continued to drain the collieries, some working even into the twentieth century, and are ideal for preservation, as at Elsecar, near Sheffield (SE 387001). Deeper mines were made possible by the introduction of better winding engines of the Trevithick high pressure type, better ventilation, and the invention of the safety lamp. After 1840, the wire rope for winding was a great advance. However, few of these have left remains for preservation except a few winding engines and numbers of safety lamps to be found in most coalfield museums. The great effort to 'tidy up' industrial dereliction is now destroying most hopes of surface remains in the coalfields unless one or two important examples can be selected for restoration and preservation. This makes recording all the more urgent.

It is to be hoped that while looking to the preservation of colliery remains, the coke ovens of all types and ages will not be overlooked. A bank of beehive ovens or of the oblong brick-built ovens sometimes found near smaller collieries would be a valuable monument. Every year sees more of the few remaining examples swept away in the non-selective clearance of derelict sites, and local groups of industrial archaeologists as well as individuals are doing good work when they survey these sites and press for some degree of preservation.

Iron

In the iron industry the advances in the period from 1790 to 1850 were the prelude to a vast expansion in which new furnaces of far greater capacity replaced old ones almost everywhere. In steel-making a completely new era started in 1863 with Bessemer's converter followed by the Siemens's open hearth furnaces. A great advance in blast furnace design was made in the 1830s when the output was raised from less than a hundred to more than two hundred tons of iron a week. The hot blast at greater pressures and furnaces up to sixty feet high accounted for much of this increase. The furnaces were being built circular with a brick-lined iron case. Waste gases and heat were drawn off near the top of the stack, and used for steam-raising. Mechanical hoists got ore and fuel to the charging platform and the charging bridge was no longer used. The blast air was heated in stoves which used some of the waste gas, and the furnace was now seen as part of a largely mechanized complex.

The larger and more powerful steam engines required for the rolls and slitting-mills, and also in factories of all kinds, were the product of a large number of engineering works. The key to these great engineering advances was the development of machine tools in a wide variety, led by the lathe with slide-rest and screw cutting gear. Maudsley (1771–1831) was the key figure in this development, introducing new machines which had an accuracy of performance to new standards, as set by his screw micrometer which could measure to an accuracy of 0·0001 in. No less important was the rigid training and fine craftsmanship enforced in his workshops which made such precision work possible. His workshop became the training school of engineers with a new dimension of accuracy and precision-working, who in turn established these methods in their own workshops. Such men as Bramah, Whitworth, Nasmyth, Clement, Roberts, and many others were concerned to use the new machine tools. One most valuable result was that machine and engine parts could now be made and finished in metal to a degree of accuracy which reduced friction and vibration to a minimum and secured complete interchangeability of similar parts, and, before long, the beginnings of mass production.

The remains of the work of Maudsley, and of this new race of mechanical engineers who, in fact, created this new profession, are mainly to be seen in early machine tools and their products, and these should be preserved in the museums of the engineering centres. They are well recorded in literature, in trade catalogues and in the technical press which was a necessary part of the engineers' professional organization. The recording and preservation of this aspect of industry is less the concern of the industrial archaeologist than of the librarian and museum curator, and the *Proceedings* of such institutions as the Mechanical Engineers and the Newcomen Society.

While the nineteenth century saw the growth of a great engineering industry bringing the steam engine towards its acme of development, there remained some pockets of industry still based, even in the twentieth century, on water power. These were in particular the making of gunpowder, snuff grinding, and bobbin turning, mainly in Westmorland and North Lancashire (Lancashire over the Sands, or Furness), and with a second area of gunpowder making at Faversham,[1] with textiles there and in Wales. Many small forges making tools, scythes, spades, hoes, and so on, also persisted on water power, more widely scattered over the country than the industries just mentioned.

The manufacture of gunpowder apart from that for military purposes was stimulated by the use of black blasting powder in mines and quarries. The London Lead Company were using blasting powder in their northern mines by 1740, and as slate quarrying expanded in the Lake District in the eighteenth century the powder-making industry became established on the rivers Kent, Leven, and Brathay, and a few other streams. Saltpetre

[1] A. Percival, 'Faversham Gunpowder Industry', *Indust. Archaeol.*, 5 (1968), pp. 1-42.

and sulphur were brought in via the small but busy ports at Greenod (Leven estuary) and Milnthorpe (Kent estuary), and charcoal was available from the whole area. Three works were established before 1800 – the first in 1764, and others by the middle decades of the nineteenth century. The last working mill closed only in 1937. There are many remains of some of these mills, with their widely separated and very numerous small buildings, which have provided ample material for the industrial archaeologists.[1]

Textiles, bobbin-making, snuff grinding, and paper manufacture, along with a few small forges which also used water power, make the country around Kendal and the southern and south-western fringes of the Lake District a rich area for the study of small water-mills of the nineteenth and early twentieth centuries. The pioneer work of Somervell[2] and the many papers of Paul Wilson, with the Lake Counties survey of Davies-Shiel and Marshall already quoted, make this one of the best recorded areas of Britain to be studied by all who are interested in water power.

Transport

The expanding industrialization of the early nineteenth century and the application of the many inventions of the mechanical engineers was only made practicable by the concurrent development of a sufficiently rapid and cheap transport system, based upon mechanical, not horse, traction. The canals had provided a cheap and efficient network by which heavy goods could be carried over the country, but only at the speed of a walking horse. The tractive power of a horse had been increased by amounts that must have seemed incredible for a time. An inquiry by engineers had shown that while a pack-horse could normally carry $\frac{1}{8}$ of a ton, a horse could pull in a wagon on a macadamized road 2 tons, and in a wagon on iron rails 10 tons, but could pull 50 tons in a barge on a canal.

Before 1830 the canal system was almost complete and in full operation. The canals had a major influence on the location of industry in what were rapidly expanding towns, in most of which factories and workshops of all kinds were being built along or near to the canal banks creating intensive

[1] Recent studies will be found in P. N. Wilson, 'The gunpowder mills of Westmorland and Furness', *Trans. Newcomen Soc.*, 36 (1964); and M. Davies-Shiel and J. D. Marshall, *Industrial Archaeology of the Lake Counties*, 1969, 75–88. These accounts are much more detailed than the survey and notes made by the author (1922–6), and should be consulted for description of the remains still to be seen.

[2] J. Somervell, *The Water Power Mills of South Westmorland*, 1930.

industrial zones (Plate 27). It is in these zones that many of the finest industrial buildings of the late eighteenth and early nineteenth centuries survive, with much of the industrial housing which filled in the space between the canal and the old town centre. In the textile areas in particular the pattern of industry is clear and distinct. The earlier mills using water power are strung out along the streams coming down from the hills, not directly related to the location of a village except perhaps in the case of the corn-mills. Transport of goods was by pack-horses or wagons and in many cases along tracks which kept out of the valleys and crossed the uplands. The use of steam engines and the consequent increase in size of the mills with the greatly larger amounts of coal and raw materials to be carried from the coalfields and to and from the ports made it essential to have a canal-side position. After 1830, however, the rapid development of the steam railways made a measure of dispersal of industrial sites possible, and new iron works, chemical works, collieries, and other industries were located in response to other geographic factors through the flexibility of railway routes compared with canals. A site for industry being chosen or imposed, a railway could be brought to it, even if in the very early years some of the steeper gradients were operated by inclines with stationary winding engines. A large number of the early railway tracks and inclines remain for investigation and recording. Many canals were reached from new industrial sites by short spur railways, and in a few cases canal and railway combined to make an important line of transport.

During the first half of the nineteenth century, while passenger carrying railways were building their complex systems, this different type of railway, more closely related to the colliery wagonways, was being built for many groups of mines and quarries, often linking not with another railway but with a canal. In 1789 a short canal with loading bays and locks had been built in Devon from the river Teign, near Newton Abbot, to Ventiford Brook, at a place to which china clay and granite were carried by a long and arduous pack-horse route. In 1820, a tramway was built between the canal terminus and the quarries on Haytor to do away with the pack-horses, which were by then quite inadequate for handling both the quantity and the size of some of the dimension stone then being produced. The tramway remained in use until the 1860s. Its outstanding feature is the use of large granite blocks, suitably carved, as rails. A long summit length of this line is now scheduled as an industrial monument.

In Cornwall, several railways were built to connect mines with the ports, the best known one being probably the Redruth and Chasewater line. A harbour, about 1800, had been cut out of the cliffs on the north coast at Portreath near Redruth, and a horse tramway was built from it to the rapidly developing copper mines around Scorrier. In 1819, Taylor had recovered the copper mines in Gwennap parish which became the Consols group, and by 1824 an Act was obtained for the making of a railway from Redruth to the Restonguet Creek on the river Fal, and so to the south coast, thus creating a rival route. This line was four foot gauge edge rails held in chairs on stone blocks, and most of its way from the Consolidated Mines Group at Gwennap, nearly to the wharves at Devoran, was a gentle incline – until 1854 a gravity-acting incline downhill and horse-drawn uphill. The port of Devoran grew to be one of the largest in Cornwall by about 1842. In 1854 the line was changed to locomotive traction, and though its importance declined it continued working until 1915. It is only one example of the large number of railways built to serve mines and quarries, some of them like this and the Portreath Tramway building their own ports.[1]

Some of these mineral lines were built in association with canals. The Cromford and High Peak railway in Derbyshire, at first carrying only lime, mineral, and goods traffic, is really an extension of the Cromford Canal which made a junction with the Erewash Canal and with two railways. It climbed onto the Derbyshire plateau by inclines and descended on the Lancashire side to the Peak Forest Canal near Whaley in Cheshire, thus connecting the Trent and the Mersey by means of two groups of canals and a railway. In 1887, the railway section was taken into the London and North Western system and passenger traffic was introduced. The line is now closed but its inclines, bridges, and viaducts with some of the track are important industrial monuments. To the industrial archaeologist, these numerous mineral lines offer a widespread field of study and a great variety of tracks and other structures.

By the mid nineteenth century Britain had become a truly industrialized nation, and showed the products of its industries in the Great Exhibition of 1851. This seemed to be the culmination of a period of rapid advance and invention but it could equally be regarded now as the marker between the age of the Industrial Revolution, with its exploitation of steam power

The line has been the subject of a very detailed study, D. B. Barton, *The Redruth and Chasewater Railway*, 1966 (2nd edn.).

with the maturing of the skill of the mechanical and civil engineers, and the new age of electricity, the internal combustion engine, chemical synthesis and, eventually, atomic physics. Soon after 1851, the Technological Revolution was under way and one of its important distinguishing marks was the rapid appearance of a purely technical press. The Encyclopaedias of Diderot and Rees which give such an extensive view of the industries as they were in the eighteenth and at the beginning of the nineteenth centuries were replaced by Ure's *Dictionary of Arts, Manufactures, and Mines*, 1845, expanded and brought up to date by Robert Hunt in three new editions between 1858 and 1875.

Smeaton had founded a society of engineers in 1818, which became the Institution of Civil Engineers; the Institution of Mechanical Engineers followed in 1847, and in 1852 the North of England Institution of Mining Engineers. In the *Transactions* of these societies technical advances were announced and discussed by the assembled professional members, and the findings of theoretical science were applied to the processes of industry and to engineering design. In 1856, however, a new type of journal appeared, the weekly *Engineer*, designed to record progress in all branches of engineering, and using abundant illustration of exceptional quality. Its lavish use of illustration along with the advent of photography began a new era of extensive pictorial and descriptive recording with a new standard of quality and accuracy. The remains of machines, engines, and buildings are becoming year by year more difficult to find and record, except among the larger civil engineering projects, but in the engineering and other kindred press there is a record far more complete than exists for any previous period.

Soon after the mid century, the new technology was being recognized as the application and union of science with industry, and the foundation of the Federal Institute of Technology in Zurich in 1855 and the Massachusetts Institute of Technology in 1865 followed by our own Imperial College in 1887, mark the opening decades of the Technological Revolution.[1] The second half of the nineteenth century was notable for new fuels and new forms of power as well as for the promise of completely new materials to come from the developments of chemical synthesis. The century from 1870 to 1970 was to see the steady displacement of coal by

---

[1] The first institution of the new type n this country was the Royal Polytechnic Institute London, 1838, for Arts and Science in Agriculture, Mining Machinery, Manufactures, and Industry.

oil, steam by gas and electricity, wool and cotton by artificial fibres, and the horse by the motor car. The twentieth century saw the coming of the aeroplane, radio-communication, atomic energy, and space travel, all beyond the normal scope of industrial *archaeology*. More and more work-people became machine-minders, and machinery grew more automatic in its operation. It is not possible to apply the terms and techniques of archaeology to these changes, whose pace is steadily increasing. It would seem sensible then to take some date in the nineteenth century as the effective limit of industrial archaeology and proceed from that with indus-trial recording, depending not so much on field investigations as upon the use of the very abundant, almost overwhelming material in the technical press and the archive collections. Recording of our fast-disappearing nine-teenth century towns can claim some priority with the photographers; a rapidly diminishing number of craft workers can be put on record before their skill and equipment is lost. The bulk of true industrial archaeology will have to concern itself essentially with the period before the Industrial Revolution and the Industrial Revolution itself, and with remains which will be recovered largely through the application of archaeological techniques.

The salvage work on industrial remains which is now being carried out by a rapidly increasing body of enthusiasts is raising considerable problems of preservation and display. The questions of restoration *in situ* or removal to a museum involve large financial considerations, and the efforts being made to answer these and other questions are still so new and experi-mental that little more can be done than to give a brief statement of some of the questions in a concluding chapter.

The kind of investigation which has been described in this volume as falling within the true definition of industrial archaeology will, of necessity, be carried out by small groups working under expert direction using skilled techniques of excavation and recording and with their findings calling for specialist interpretation. In a large proportion of their work the discovery of the site to be excavated will have entailed research and field work of high quality, or will be revealed by the accident of road or other construction calling for an emergency excavation. In practically all cases the remains will be at most only fragmentary foundations or partly or wholly collapsed structures, buried for years or even centuries beyond the memory of any living person. No old man can be brought in to tell what work was done there or how the work was done and only rarely will a document be found to do this. The purpose and functioning of the excavated structures are to be arrived at by deduction from the recovered evidence, by reference to such knowledge of processes and materials as the expert has. A great amount of research may be involved before a useable report can be produced.

Contrast this with the recording of a nineteenth-century mill just due for demolition. It is a complete structure which can be photographed, measured, examined in every part. People will be found who worked there and can speak of the workday activities. Directories, advertisements, trade catalogues, sale bills, and valuations often exist which detail the products it made. Machine makers' and engineers' catalogues can probably supply illustration or detail of the mill machinery and equipment – with research, a surprisingly full documentation can often be found for a factory of the second half of the nineteenth and early twentieth centuries. Company documents are now more and more being preserved, so that the working aspects of the concern can be accurately recorded.

Such a building, which is to be found now in most towns where the replanning involves large areas of demolition and site clearance, offers scope for a large and varied group to work at a full recording. The photographer, amateur or professional, can give us a permanent and full record, not just of the architectural features, but of a mass of details of internal structure – floor and roof supports and so on. Apply this to warehouses, workshops, housing, and other buildings, and there appears enough recording to be done to occupy persons of every kind of skill or interest who are now being attracted to the proliferating industrial archaeology groups.

Ought we to make a distinction between this later type of industrial recording, almost entirely concerned with still existing but threatened structures – salvage recording, in fact – and the earlier site work which involves possible excavation, and a large degree of technical interpretation of fragmentary evidence? There can be no attempt to evaluate one against the other, for they are equally essential and equally to be encouraged, but they are not equally entitled to be called archaeology, unless we are to add new meanings to a discipline already accepted throughout the academic world as a well-defined subject. Might it not improve the status of industrial archaeology if much of the recent work, particularly that concerned with twentieth-century industry and housing, were thought of as a supplement or appendix to industrial archaeology in the strict sense, or as a parallel subject equal and complementary to the older section?

In both sections alike the question of the preservation of some sites and objects, the nature and methods of permanent recording, and the real purpose and value of all this freshly oriented study must be examined. *Industrial Archaeology and Recording* would appear to be a title for what I am trying to say, but I hope something less clumsy will be found and adopted before long.

PART THREE

The Place of Museums in Industrial Archaeology

CHAPTER 15

Museums and Industrial Archaeology

If industrial archaeology is to become a subject of permanent educational value it must provide for the preservation, display, and publication of the results of its work. While it is an occupation for individuals or small groups, for whom it provides the thrill of exploration and discovery, the material with which it works is part of our national heritage which in the absence of proper recording and/or preservation can be irrecoverably lost The material evidence of the past occupations of man, of his living and working places, and of the things he made and used, is complementary to the documents from which the historian deciphers and writes his history. The discoveries of the industrial archaeologist, like those of the archaeologist and the archivist, are a national possession, part of our cultural background, the evidence of our progress in invention and industry. The results and records of our work must therefore as a normal and essential part of our efforts be made available to others, along with full provision for their preservation. Publication is not easy; it is generally expensive and must be selective of only the more important excavations or sites.[1] The volume of photographs, drawings, and notes which are required to form an adequate recording, even of a single building, is too great for publication in any journal, and too expensive to duplicate.

There must be a number of repositories where the fullest possible records as well as material artifacts can be held in safe keeping, being at the same time available for public inspection and for the use of the student and serious investigator. We have in this country already a splendid system of public museums and libraries which between them can offer this service. Concerning museums, however, many questions arise, to which a variety

---

[1] A valuable supplement to full publication can be a careful summary in the increasingly numerous group of *Newsletters* or *Bulletins*. These need as much care in their preparation as do the full publication, and good plans are essential.

of answers might be given. The larger museums are provided by the nation or by the local authority, but there are also an increasing number of company museums, made and maintained by business concerns to illustrate their own story. Private museums are increasing in number, created by individuals through their own interest, or, in a few cases, as a business. Railway and canal enthusiasts, groups with an interest in mill or pumping engines, in tramcars or in other special objects, are making collections. Never have there been so many collections in such variety available for public inspection.

The private collections, however, raise a very special question. Most of the material in museums belongs to the past, to the obsolete. An object lost cannot be replaced; each object is in a sense unique, and saved from oblivion. What is to happen to the private collection when its owner tires of it, or dies? It is the recurrent experience of all concerned with museums to see material which should be preserved for the public passing from these private collections, through the sale room or the broker, at best, into other collections, at worst scattered and completely lost. In a few cases the private collection has been safeguarded by will to the local museum, by gift or purchase. What happens to the company museum if the company goes out of business or is taken over by another concern with no particular interest in its history? The material may be dispersed through the sale room and some may find its way to other museums, but much of its value is lost when it is removed from its own locality or region or when the collection is dispersed. Every museum can show what Bronze Age implements are like by specimens which cannot be given a locality more precise than say, 'Ireland', but a single, even inferior specimen, precisely located as found in the museum's own region, is an important piece of evidence contributing to the area's history.

These doubts raise the whole question of trusteeship. Some private collections are now controlled by a body of trustees, but no such body should assume that its museum will continue for the whole foreseeable future. The safeguarding of the contents of such a collection in the event of closure should be properly considered and defined in the trust conditions.

A case in point of the fate of the company museum, though one with a fairly happy ending, concerns Tasker's Waterloo Ironworks, near Andover. This firm was established in 1813, and among other things had produced traction engines and many varieties of farm machinery. In the post-war years the company had got together a splendid collection of their products and formed a fine museum. The exhibits included twenty-seven steam traction engines, probably the finest collection in the country. When the company changed hands recently the collection was to be broken up and sold. Among others, collectors from America were interested and there seemed a likelihood that these fine English products would be lost to the country. Public interest was roused and the Hampshire County Council joined the effort to save at least some of the more important items. The funds raised enabled £13,000 to be used, with which eleven of the twenty-seven traction engines and about a hundred small lots were saved.

The County Council are making this splendid local material an important feature in their new Hampshire Rural Life Museum, being built at Chilcombe House near Winchester. Even with this great effort at preservation, more than half of the splendid collection was lost and has gone to the private collector. Only the vigilance of the local people, the generous response to appeals for money, and the very enlightened policy and assistance of the County Council has saved a proportion of the collection which was a visible record of the labour and skill of local people of a century and a half. It is urgently necessary that the possible dispersal of company and private museum collections should be studied and some provision for action in such event be made so that material of great local or national significance is not robbed of most of its value by removal into private ownership and away from local connections.

There are now so many museums becoming interested in the material of industrial archaeology, and this is being collected at such a rate, that the means and methods of its preservation and display are becoming an urgent and heavy responsibility laid upon the whole museum fraternity and indeed upon the nation. The problems have more than a single aspect. Besides the physical problem of providing room in which storage can be combined with an adequate measure of display, and of accessibility, there are many technical problems of preservation and maintenance. The cleaning and preservation of materials is adequately dealt with in the laboratories and workshops of the larger museums but new problems are introduced when such industrial exhibits as a mill engine, or a water wheel with part-wooden machinery, is to be preserved. The change in conditions from those of regular working under minute by minute care and maintenance to long periods of standing, in different conditions of temperature and humidity, with maintenance to be done in the absence of a skilled engineer or wheelwright with the peculiar and intense affection which the engine tenter developed for his charge, creates a serious problem.

Such problems as these are coming upon the museum curator in increasing numbers but their solutions can be confidently expected if the resources of technical institutions and the personal interest of technicians and engineers can be closely associated with the museums. All this is a problem for the museum profession, which is giving it very serious thought and study. A consideration more directly the concern of the industrial archaeologist is perhaps that of the type of museum in which his material will eventually be housed. This raises the whole question of the conservation and location of rescued material, because a large part of the industrial archaeologist's work is in the nature of rescue from complete destruction, particularly of the material of the last two centuries.[1]

As these new demands arise there is an increasing necessity to think in terms of differing kinds of museums and differing ways of conserving a sufficient number of artifacts and industrial sites. We might, for reasons of economy, space, or familiarity, decide to preserve only a few items in a limited number of locations to which the interested person can travel. A case in point is the large number of steam engines of the beam type that have become available in recent years. They are very large and expensive to house and preserve, and most types are well represented in the Science Museum and a few other places. How are we to decide what is a reasonable number to preserve; what criteria do we apply in making a selection? Is the preservation to be limited to rare types, or to the local accident of suitable accommodation? A century ago the beam engine was a normal and commonplace part of the environment of all industrial and of most mining areas. Do we treat it as a part of an environment we are trying to preserve or reconstruct in our museums, or are we to be interested only in the unusual type and allow the common type to disappear? There are many other examples which pose the same problem of selection, but all are dominated, unfortunately, by the problem of finance and maintenance This kind of problem is presenting the museums with a new dilemma, in the solution of which the industrial archaeologist has a vital interest. New kinds of museum and museum departments are being demanded by the abundance and nature of the materials provided from industry which need conservation.

[1] This will be given more consideration in the next chapter.

The industrial archaeologist cannot stand aloof from the museums; his work cannot be done except in the closest co-operation with them at every stage from the initial planning to the final recording and preservation of his results. The Museums Association is aware of this, and efforts are being made with some success to bring the groups into closer contact, but there is still room for the active industrial archaeology groups to achieve a closer integration with their local museum, and to give more serious thought to the problems of final conservation which at present tend to be overlooked in the thrill of a dig or of a recording project.

The normal local authority museum is primarily concerned with the display of objects of small size, not generally larger than can be accommodated in cases. A recent development, however, has introduced the reconstructed street of shop fronts as the medium for the display of the materials of trade as sold in the small shops of the eighteenth and early nineteenth centuries. Many museums can add to this the small craftsman's workshop of the period and can display the occupations of essentially domestic industries. Cobblers', saddlers', handloom weavers', woolcombers' workshops are sufficiently numerous and suitable in size to be found in many museums. The accident of preservation or the local incidence of a trade may add to these such workshops as those of the candlemaker, nail-maker, watch-maker, cabinet-maker, or country carpenter and others. These can display a wealth of tools and products in their proper environment of use and manufacture. There is obviously a limit of size, and an absence of any but the simplest machinery in these displays, but they represent an important step towards the display of industrial history and industrial archaeology. The museum that can bring its collection of the tools of a trade into such a method of display, particularly if the actual workshop or parts of it or its original furnishing can be used, is fortunate.[1]

When we consider an industry which has advanced beyond the craft stage, the whole problem changes. A factory, with its repetitive numbers of machines of each type and its large and often extremely massive power source and its transmission gear, be it steam engine or water wheel, must be broken down to those few and carefully selected items for which the museum can find room. Records of all kinds, photographs, drawings, raw materials and part-processed material to end product can often be dealt with. There is, however, a growing case for the use of models if these can

[1] The James Watt workshop removed with every detail and reconstructed in the Science Museum is perhaps the type example of this kind of preservation.

be obtained. This is a large problem, though both young and old engineers have provided a reasonable number of steam engine and railway models. For other machines of most industries, model-makers are sorely needed, and it would appear that professionals will have to be used.

The Science Museum

The National Science Museum, of course, houses the ideal collections of engines, machinery, and apparatus, scientific and mechanical, of every kind. These can display the history of technology through the important individual specimens of engines, machines, apparatus, etc. related to the circumstances and history of their invention and usages; and these range over the whole period of time, as in the engines from the Savery and Newcomens to the latest jet engine, from the most primitive water wheel to the high-powered water turbine. For machines as such, in their own right, and not necessarily visually linked with the industry they served, the Science Museum must be the prime reference source for the student of technology. Such a museum cannot be duplicated or maintained except on a national scale.

Industrial museums

The industrial museum is now being developed in several areas and has much promise for the preservation of the material particularly of the Industrial Revolution. While a case can be made out for the purpose-built new premises for such a museum, an equally strong case could be presented for the preservation of some industrial premises for this purpose. A museum in which the more abundant objects are to be those of the textile industry could preserve much of the use-environment if the premises used were in fact a mill. Bradford, in planning an industrial museum, has purchased a large textile-mill of substantial structure which in itself is an industrial monument in every respect worthy of preservation. Its several storeys have a structure and floors designed to carry heavy machinery, and they will form halls of great extent which can never be made to look insignificant or anything but naturally suitable for large machinery displays. A mill engine could never be better displayed than in a mill engine room, and other machinery, even if not of textile usage, will gain by the industrial nature of its surroundings. Something of this advantage was gained in the Museum of Science and Industry at Birmingham, though no old industrial premises can be adequate for the great variety of industry and transport with which they now have to cope, and the time has come when great alteration and improvement must be planned.

However, the use of some industrial premises for industrial museums might serve the double purpose of the preservation of an important building and the provision of something of the environment in which the museum exhibits had functioned. This, of course, raises the question of possible regional museums for special industries. It would obviously be easy, given the finance, to create a splendid museum of the textile industries in either the West Riding textile area or in East Lancashire. The important railway junction of York has now been decided upon as the location for the National Railway Museum, while such centres as Swindon seem suited for the display of more local material. A national or regional museum of malting and brewing might gravitate towards Burton-on-Trent, steel-making to Sheffield, small arms and the small metal industries to Birmingham. In some industries this is taking place naturally and must be welcomed; but does it imply that the fairly unique or particularly fine specimen in the non-specialist local museum should be transferred to the regional museum, and the local people be asked to give up what might be their prize exhibit? This is a matter for the Museums Association to discuss, but the industrial archaeology groups working in the areas in cooperation with their local museum must have a part in such decisions.

This matter of the location of collections within their regional environment is becoming more important as the uncovering of early sites and the preservation of industrial monuments proceeds. It should be possible, say in a textile museum of regional importance, to combine it with the field evidence (outdoor and *in situ*) related to its displays. Something of this is being done in an experimental way at Cusworth Museum near Doncaster, where the collections of industrial material are heavily weighted at present on the side of archival material. This, however, is supplemented by an excellent published and annotated list of the industrial monuments, sites, and remains which can be visited in a wide region around the museum. This close link between museum collections and three-dimensional outdoor material is essential where a museum claims a regional status. The value of such a list would be increased by exhibiting in the museum a series of adequate location and distribution maps from which visits could be planned. The compilation of the raw material of such maps and lists would be an excellent exercise for the local industrial archaeologists and could indeed be applied to almost any museum and not be restricted just to the regional and specialist ones.

It is inevitable that in an area which has maintained a particular industry for a long period, the remains and tools of that industry will form an important section of the local museum's collections. The Craven Museum, Skipton, can illustrate this point. It is within the fringes of the large mid-Pennine lead mining field, and has the only railway station and the largest bus centre giving access to the lead mining areas of Airedale and Wharfedale. It is the centre for several societies interested and working in lead mining history. It has large collections of lead mining tools and material, a very extensive mineral collection related to the Pennine mining fields, and a useful collection of documents concerned with the industry. Any student of lead mining history can study the material in the museum, and it is there within a thirty-minute bus journey of one of the larger of the fields where the remains of nearly three centuries of mining are easily accessible. In such a situation the closest possible links between the museum collections and the areas from which they have come should be maintained and exhibited. The production of a leaflet guide to the field remains would be of real service to students.

Many good gazetteers of industrial remains have appeared for areas varying from a whole county (at present the commonest form) to smaller districts, but many of these are either expensive or selective of larger monuments. The leaflet for a smaller area easily accessible from the museum, with a more summarized and selective text, which could be purchased at a very modest price in the museum, which would relate the museum to its surroundings, could be of great value to the visitor.[1]

Rural Museums

The rural museums, based to some extent on Scandinavian examples, are making for themselves a special and important place in the work of preserving the remains of the past. The concern with agriculture and domestic buildings, though by no means exclusive, is generally the dominant theme of the collections. The tools of agriculture gain in significance by being displayed in a rural setting, and many would be very difficult to accommodate properly even in a very large town museum. Many crafts and skills are rightly associated with a rural museum, but perhaps its distinctive

[1] This should be supplemented in the museum archives and where possible in display by detailed maps of the position of the listed sites in the area.

feature will be the preservation, by removal and re-erection, of early buildings which can contain the exhibits of contemporary furnishings, utensils, and tools in their actual environment. The possibilities are very wide and range from the rare medieval house and crucked building, through the timber-framed house and farm buildings, to such farm machinery as the horse-mill, threshing-mills, the steam traction engine, and even the modern tractor.

In preserving the domestic scene the rural museum will quite properly be concerned with such domestic detail as clothing and furnishing, food and cooking utensils. These, like many crafts – dairying, home-brewing, spinning, blacksmithing, saddling, and harness-making, with others – were part of the great occupation or industry in which the majority of the population was employed for many centuries. Agriculture is a vital section of industrial archaeology but its full museum display cannot properly be divorced from the land and from the everyday life of its workers. The rural museum offers the true solution to many difficulties and it must be thought of as being as much a part of the industrial archaeological world as any museum which is more mechanically orientated perhaps towards the engineering or textile industries.

The rural museum will by its nature approach something of a regional organization, and the natural differences of the major regions in the country will justify several such museums. The Museum of English Rural Life, in connection with Reading University, can well be regarded as an English national museum, but its collections will be dominantly southern. Others for the Midlands and the North would serve to emphasize the differences of soil, climate, and history that make these major regions distinct in their own right. The folk museum of the National Museum of Wales, and corresponding museums for Scotland and Northern Ireland, are essential if the rural material is to be preserved where the local population can see it.[1]

A new rural museum on a regional scale is the Weald and Downland Open Air Museum now being prepared at West Dean near Chichester. The site is a large and attractive area on the bank of the river Lavant. Buildings will be the larger objects, forming, as it were, a museum landscape. A fifteenth-century yeoman's house and a Tudor farm house have

[1] Welsh Folk Museum, St Fagans, Cardiff, a museum of Welsh life, crafts, industries, and culture. Ulster Folk Museum, Holywood, Co. Down. A growing section of the National Museum of Scotland.

been moved to the site and are being re-erected, and at least a dozen other early buildings await re-erection. The buildings cover the whole period of history: two eighteenth-century granaries and a nineteenth-century toll house represent the more recent past, while the fairly distant past has its reminder in a medieval shop. A reconstruction of a weaver's hut of Saxon date is only one of several reconstructions based upon the results of archaeological excavations (Plate 32).

Crafts, industry, and agriculture will be displayed through collections of tools, machinery, and products. The provision of power is well illustrated by horse-mill, donkey wheel, and water turbine, and the addition of a water-mill and steam traction engines will make this a complete and satisfactory section. A complete cooper's workshop, the tools of a wheelwright, and exhibits relating to the Wealden glass, pottery, and brick industries, form the nucleus of another section. These details have been mentioned as indicating, along with the display of domestic materials and utensils of all kinds, something of the great variety and potential possessed by the rural museum. It will be instructive to watch and assist the development of such a museum. Another, only in its initial stages as yet, is the Museum of Lakeland Life and Industry being formed by the Lake District Museum Trust as part of the Abbot Hall Museum and Art Gallery, Kendal. No doubt others are being planned in several regions and all offer great scope for the interest and co-operation of the industrial archaeologist, and for the preservation particularly of agricultural and domestic material. It may be argued that such early objects as a windmill or water corn-mill could quite rightly be removed to, and reconstructed on, such a museum area if they could not be preserved *in situ*. Such removal and re-erection cannot be carried out by the museum staff alone, and it is in such a scheme that an active industrial archaeology group could find an exacting and worthwhile project.

Several smaller, private and semi-private museums are being created on the 'folk' model, the distinguishing feature of which appears to be the preservation by removal and re-erection of early buildings, domestic and agricultural, possibly with a water corn-mill. The buildings allow the realistic display of 'bygones' in their furnishings. The reconstruction of such buildings can only be undertaken where land is available and the buildings can be reasonably spaced in a park-like 'open air' setting. A recently developed small museum of this kind is the Ryedale Museum at Hutton-le-Hole, using as a nucleus collections of folk material made during a long life by a local antiquary and historian.[1] This nucleus has had considerable additions under the present ownership and has now been to some extent safeguarded by trustees.

Company Museums

The post-war years have seen the creation or extension of a number of company museums, and it seems likely that more will be formed, though the cost of establishment and maintenance will tend to limit their number. Companies generally are developing an interest in their history and that of their trade, and are also realizing the advantage of showing their products to the public in the special way which the museum can offer. The more important of these company museums approach a national status when their collections illustrate the history of a whole industry and not just the products of a single firm. The Pilkington Glass Museum at St Helens is not only a most attractive display for the general public, enjoying great popularity, but it is a collection concerned with the whole history of glass-making to which the student and research worker would naturally turn. Attached to this museum there is a library for students, a lecture room where films on glass technology are shown, and an archives section. The descriptive catalogue of the collections is printed in three languages. W. & T. Avery Ltd have built up at the historic Soho Foundry, Birmingham, a fine museum of weighing machines and apparatus of all kinds; Kodak Ltd, at Harrow, have their museum of photography, and there are comparable museums of paper-making (British Paper and Board Makers' Association, at St Mary Cray, Kent), mining tools (Holman Bros. Ltd, Camborne), early textile machinery (T. M. M. Research Ltd, Helmshore, Lancashire), and other industries.

These are admirable if adequate archivist and curator assistance is available and if the collections can be made available at some times outside factory working hours. The most vital point of such a collection is that the company should make adequate provision against its dispersal if new ownership was not interested in it. Such collections are not made without considerable capital expenditure, only a fraction of which could be recovered by a break-up sale, at which the major value of the material as a single collection would not appear. Close consultation and contact with the professional bodies representing the public museums and with local government bodies might prevent or at least minimize the loss if such a

[1] Wilfred Crossland.

dispersal became necessary. The most encouraging development is in the adoption of such specialized museums by the trade organizations, as in the case of the museum of the paper industry, run by the British Paper and Board Makers' Association, a continuing corporate body.

One obvious advantage which the company museum has, particularly when it represents a whole trade, is that its collection can attain a degree of completeness almost impossible in a museum which has to display other subjects as well. A trade association has, through its members, the whole trade as a collecting ground. The whole technical skill and knowledge of the industry is available to ensure proper display and full explanations and could produce a model guide-catalogue if public interest justified it. An adequate library, records, and facilities for study would make such a museum the central reference point for all serious work on the history of the industry, at least for the period of the Industrial Revolution onwards. Again, the relation of such museums to the national and local authority museums is a matter for consultation and discussion within the museums' professional bodies.

Industrial Museums

There are two museums at present being formed which aim to be of a new type, something akin to a rural museum but with a dominantly industrial background. Both have originated in the last few years, and now that their organization and administration has been established each is busy with the serious practical problems of assembly and display of their material. Both in their literature include 'living' as an operative word, one as 'living history' and the other as a 'living museum'; each claims a large area of the life of which it hopes to represent. *The North of England Open Air Museum* takes the North-East – 'Teesdale, Weardale, Durham, Northumberland, North Yorkshire, etc.' – as its area. *The Ironbridge Gorge Museum Trust* takes the new town of Telford, Shropshire, as its location, and uses Coalbrookdale, about two miles of the Severn Gorge at Ironbridge, and Blists Hill, a part of the Coalport Beck valley, as its museum. Its interests spread over this and adjacent areas, which have sometimes been called the 'cradle of the Industrial Revolution'. Within its area each has large heavy industries established for a few centuries, set within the frame of countryside which is still rural. The industrial masses of Tyneside, Teesside, the Durham Coalfield and South Northumberland, have within easy reach the Durham Dales, the Yorkshire Dales, North York Moors and Northumberland National Parks, and seventy miles of fine coastline. The Ironbridge Gorge Museum has Coalbrookdale, the Wellington and Oakengates (now Telford) iron and engineering centres, and the derelict mining field around Dawley, Lawley, and Madeley, but is in reach of the Wrekin, Wanlock Edge, and the Welsh Mountains, and has the lovely river Severn running through it.

During the last ten years the staff of the Bowes Museum, Barnard Castle, County Durham, under Frank Atkinson, has been collecting material for an industrial section. From the richness and nature of the material becoming available the idea has evolved of an open-air site large enough for its proper display, and having a potential which no museum building could offer. Eventually Beamish Hall and a park of over two hundred acres became available when Durham County Council purchased it from the National Coal Board. This site is in the north part of the County, one and a half miles out of Stanley (NZ 212549), barely four miles from the A1. The preparation of the grounds has begun, about 10,000 objects (including all the very small ones) have now been collected, and some of the larger buildings, etc. are being erected in the Park. There seems to be no practical limit to what can be accepted beyond the state of the material and the availability of skill and labour to effect removal, transport, and re-erection in the grounds of the Museum. It is intended that every exhibit reasonably possible shall be out of doors and working. The four main sections will be buildings, houses, shops, craft workshops, and so on, in which goods and articles will be displayed as in the rural museums, and where craftsmen will be at work. Industrial objects will include the largest exhibits – a colliery winding house, engine and head-gear, coal 'drops', a wagonway with wagons, the equipment belonging to the glass-making industry, quarrying, electrical, and other north-east industries. A water-mill, at work grinding corn, will be part of the agricultural section, and tools, machinery, carts, wagons and the like will find a home in their appropriate buildings. The plan is on a large and generous scale, bold and exciting, and is being implemented with the help of a Friends of the Museum Association, a growing body of enthusiasts who provide voluntary labour and skills without which the project could not be carried through.

The Ironbridge Gorge Museum Trust originated from the consideration of the future of the Coalbrookdale Museum when the Dawley New Town area was designated. This covers much of the former industrial area

of the East Shropshire coalfield, and includes the whole of the Coalbrookdale in which the Darby works of 1709 are situated. The industry associated
with iron had spread during two and a half centuries down the gorge of the
Severn from Ironbridge to Coalport, and the fields of Lawley, Dawley,
Madeley, Broseley, and adjoining areas were the site of extensive iron,
coal, and clay mining, and the site of many famous iron and engineering
works. At Coalbrookdale the Old Furnace site, dating from 1638, rebuilt
and used by Abraham Darby for the first smelting of iron ores with coal,
had been excavated and preserved by the Coalbrookdale Company, and
with a museum of ironfounding was opened to the public in 1959 to
celebrate the 250th year of the company.[1] The wide interest in this
museum aroused a corresponding interest in other monuments in the area
around it, and by 1966 surveys had been made and the idea of a museum for
the region was being studied. A working party started in 1967 and reported
on the financial and physical tasks which would be involved in the formation of a trust to form such a museum. In 1968 the Dawley New Town was
designated as Telford New Town and the newly formed trust could
announce that 'now a living museum is being formed around the relics of
one man's momentous achievement. . . . The project is being undertaken
by men who believe that an industrial civilization, whose prosperity is still
based largely on the metal extracted from iron ore, cannot allow its most
precious monuments to fall into dereliction.'

The purpose of the trust is to preserve the Coalbrookdale and Ironbridge portion of the Severn Gorge, in its 'living' state, with houses,
cottages, works, wharves, and other features, and entire 'living' complex.
Blists Hill will form another part of the museum area – it is the site of early
blast furnaces, clay and tile works, and coalmines, and has part of the
Shropshire Canal and the Coalport Incline in its bounds. The Coalport
China Works, Bedlam Furnaces, and Maw's Tile works are all within the
area of the new museum. Monuments of national stature are also to be
seen, for the Iron Bridge, 1779, the Coalport Bridge, 1818, and the Albert
Edward Bridge, 1862, are all specimens of the Company's work.

[1] The excavation of the furnace was carried out by the Coalbrookdale Company and the
museum built largely by their own workpeople. G. F. Williams, Managing Director of the Midland and Northern areas of Allied Ironfounders of which the Coalbrookdale Co. was a part, and
one of many generations who worked in the Dale, took the oversight of all this work. The
general design of the museum and its construction was made jointly by Mr Williams and the
author with the help of many of the staff and workpeople of the Company, and the financial help
of Allied Ironfounders.

The general plan of the museum is to use Blists Hill as a working site on which the engine houses and at least one furnace will be restored; the great blowing engines of the Lilleshall Company have been removed there; colliery head gears and winders, horse, steam, and electric, are being erected over some of the colliery shafts on the site, and along with a drift mine will illustrate much of coalmining history. The canal is to be extended to include some different types of locks; there will be a re-erected charcoal furnace, some rolls as part of a forge and many smaller workshops, pottery and clay pipe-making. Many of these objects and much of the material is already collected and work on the ground is well advanced. Work is being done to restore the Coalport China works, and various buildings, houses, workers' cottages, and others are being restored. This will be a new type of museum, an effort to restore a complete working community with its monuments of an industry formerly of national importance and for a time of world-wide fame. The connection of Coalbrookdale with the first locomotives, with iron rails, with bridges, iron-framed buildings, and with structural and ornamental cast-iron, will be only a part of the interests to be displayed. It is an ambitious scheme, but the interest and support it is arousing ensure its success.[1]

[1] The Trust is under the experienced chairmanship of Bruce Ball, former Managing Director of the Lilleshall Company, with a number of persons prominent in the iron and kindred professions. Michael Darby, direct descendant of Abraham Darby, and the present writer are the Vice-Presidents under the Presidency of Lord Bridgeman, Lord Lieutenant of the County of Shropshire. The County Council is closely associated with the work.

CHAPTER 16

Preservation, Restoration, and Recording

This book has tried to bring into relief the over-emphasis on the remains of the nineteenth and twentieth centuries in recording industrial work and the constant recurrence in definitions of industrial archaeology of the phrase 'especially of the Industrial Revolution'. The rate at which industrial technology is changing today makes machinery, fuel and power sources, and even industrial buildings of the first decades of the present century, obsolete. The structures and machinery which supplied our needs even in the pre-war years are being demolished at an alarming rate. It is no wonder that the first popular response to the new subject has been dominated by the desire to record what we see today, which tomorrow may only be a heap of rubble or scrap metal. There has never been a time of such urgency as now, when demolition has become a matter of hours instead of weeks, when more and more powerful machinery for the job becomes available almost daily. It would be impossible, where any interest in the past exists or has been aroused, to resist this almost desperate urgency. Yet all this does not invalidate the claim that industrial archaeology as a disciplined subject must not be limited to recent time or take a restricted view of industry which minimizes its importance through prehistoric and historic time.

In the presence of this widespread demolition there is the urge to save something. Ancient Monuments and Historic Buildings can claim a small amount of protection by scheduling, and though this does not give a complete protection it does provide for investigation and deliberation before any change can be made. So far the scheduling of industrial monuments has proceeded with excessive caution and is only achieved with difficulty. It becomes clear that for the present the bulk of preservation in this field will depend upon individual and local efforts initiated by those who believe a site or object to be of a value worthy of preservation. The involvement of local authorities, voluntary bodies, and the general public with the raising of considerable finance will depend upon a very strong argument and a convincing demonstration of the merit of the object chosen for preservation.

The replanning of city centres, the removal of slum areas and the creation of more open space in towns and cities, along with rapidly increasing site values will make impossible the preservation of many old sites of industrial historic importance. Further, in such a replanned area it would be extremely difficult to retain an old factory in any environment which could make it acceptable. The only alternatives to complete loss are either removal to another site – which is rarely possible, except for small buildings and workshops of craftsman size – or a complete recording with perhaps the salvage of some small pieces of equipment of particular interest. A commercial building of architectural merit such as a Corn Exchange has a slightly better chance of survival and a better potential for possible usage.

On the outskirts of most industrial towns there are factories and workshops built during the boom years of the nineteenth century or even in the early years of the twentieth century when city sites for expansion were no longer possible. These substantial buildings, particularly the mills of the textile areas, often stand among fields or other open situations, away from any immediate threat of redevelopment. A few of the finest of these have a possible use as industrial museums, museum storage, and workshop centres, or even some use not connected with museums. One early flax-mill (Foster Beck, Pateley Bridge) with a splendid water wheel and large two-storey premises has been made into a high-grade restaurant, dance hall, and catering centre for large and small party occasions. In the well-known beautiful valley of Nidderdale and, by motoring standards, within easy reach of Leeds, Bradford, Harrogate, and other towns, it is becoming a popular place for tourists and townsfolk alike. The $36\frac{1}{2}$ ft water wheel and the building structure are preserved, and internal structural alteration has been kept to the minimum. In an area of a former very important flax industry, this is a valuable industrial monument, preserved by finding a completely new use for it, which nonetheless profits by the interest aroused by the character of the building.[1] Less than a mile away an old

---

[1] One regrettable feature associated with this mill is that when it was sold a few years ago the machinery still standing in it was broken up and sold for scrap, there being no local organization with the means to save any of it

smelt-mill has been preserved by its adaptation as offices and central service building of a large caravan site.[1]

By far the most numerous rural industrial units to survive are the water
corn-mills. At one time almost every manor in the country had one, and
even when the large steam-driven flour-mills were built at the ports to
deal with imported grain, many of the small country mills continued to
grind 'proven', oats, barley, and poultry and cattle foods. Other mills were
easily converted to saw-mills, or estate mills, or to house a local craft. It
would be impossible to preserve all of them but a case can be made for
keeping many of the best, not necessarily the largest. The removal of these
mills is not a formidable task, so most Rural and Folk Museums have
secured and re-erected one which they have working, and even a city
museum like the Castle Museum, York, has its working corn-mill as a very
popular item of display. Perhaps one of the most impressive of such small
mill removals is not a corn-mill but one where woollens were manufactured. This is the Esgair Moel Woollen Mill from near Llanwrtyd, Breck-
nockshire, built about 1760. This mill houses all the processes of woollen
manufacture from raw wool to finished products and was working until
1947. In 1950 it was given to the Welsh Folk Museum and was removed to
St Fagans, and re-erected there, where it is again in full work, still making
its old range of shawls and suitings from the wool of Welsh sheep. This is
a most impressive piece of preservation.

The village mill has been given a very sentimental position – 'the old
mill by the stream' and so on – in Victorian and Edwardian song and
literature, so that to many tourists it holds a position with the church and
the manor house as an essential mark of genuine village tradition.

There are practical reasons why many of these mills could be preserved.
People are flocking more and more to the countryside for recreation. More
interest is being generated in country houses and other objects of country
life, both past and present, and a working mill, open to visitors, will be a
sure attraction. It could become the seed from which, if properly nurtured,
an interest in industrial history can be started. Simple but skilled explanatory literature could move the mill out of the category of a mere curiosity
and could bring the interest and importance of our mechanical heritage
to the notice of a large number of people who have not yet been tempted to
enter an industrial museum. Most people find an interest in seeing some-

[1] Heathfield smelt-mill, which served part of the Greenhow Hill mines. The present building
was put up in 1855 to replace a very old one which stood on the same site.

thing working and in seeing how someone else works. It would appear that by their abundance, which would allow of considerable selection, and by their location in areas to which increasing numbers of visitors are going, the conditions for the preservation of the best of our water-mills are very favourable.

There is a more strictly educational aspect, which will apply not only to water-mills but to some other industrial sites. Schools are more and more including field days and other visits in their normal work, and these include museum visits. Those with experience know the difficulty in a large museum of getting the concentration of a class focused on one or two special objects among the distracting abundance of a whole museum. There is much to be said for the occasional visit to a single object, free from other distraction, where methods of observation and recording, sketching and description, can be practised and the working environment seen. There are sufficient remaining mills to provide one within reasonable reach of most large towns. The local authority might acquire one as the West Riding County Council have done in South Yorkshire. This mill, still working and now in their ownership, freed from the constraints of commercial competitive running, can be started or stopped at any time as school visits might require for detailed study. It will be included within a projected country park so will have a very large public to enjoy it at the weekends. The premises are large enough to house a small teaching museum to supplement the mill, and the adjoining mill house is already occupied by the miller, an ideal working caretaker-demonstrator. A two-hour visit to such a mill with its adjuncts of stream, dam, mill roads, and rural environment, has a great educational potential.[1]

The windmills which are numerous in the east and south-east of the country are equally suitable for this kind of preservation and much is now being done in this field. It may be that this preservation within its original environment is the answer to many of the problems of industrial preservation. The purist could argue with considerable justification that the removal of an industrial object should not be undertaken if this means the substitution of an artificial for a natural and little-changed original environment. The deciding factors of course will include the possible threat to survival if left in the original position and the advantages of supervision,

[1] In the preservation of this mill the Education, Architect's, County Planning and Finance departments of the County Council are all sharing, so that any restoration necessary will be carried out with professional skill.

care, and maintenance in a large collection to which generally the public will have easier access.

A case in point is perhaps the Longden-on-Tern canal aqueduct, the first in the world to be constructed of cast-iron. The canal it carried is now abandoned and dry; its structure is deteriorating rapidly, and it is on private land. Its only present use is its convenience as a cattle drivingway between the two sides of the small valley it spans. Its survival life is certainly short. It is now proposed to remove it to a new site within the Blists Hill area of the Ironbridge Gorge Museum Trust, at Telford, already described, where a short section of the canal is being restored, in association with which its siting will be considered and its reconditioning and maintenance assured.

The last few years have seen a remarkable growth in the idea of preservation, and societies devoted to the preservation of particular groups of industrial remains, and trusts for the saving and restoration of particular sites, are operative all over the country. The embarrassment of a steady flow of appeals for funds and participation in a multitude of schemes of amazing variety is more than compensated by the evidence of the growing public interest and the educative effect their literature must be having. It would be too big a task to list these societies, trusts, and appeals, but a selection can illustrate something of the variety of problems of preservation and restoration which are aroused when such an attempt is started.

An early group to become active in this field was the *Society for the Protection of Ancient Buildings*, which, particularly through its wind- and water-mill section, is producing a splendid series of handbooks on mills and their history and is also active in preserving many fine specimens. The Ministry of Public Buildings and Works have taken care of many monastic mills, though they are concerned only with the structure, and the National Trust own and preserve a few mills.

A fine group of water-powered mills was employed in the gunpowder industry, centred around Faversham, Kent. This industry started in the mid sixteenth century and two centuries later became the Royal Powder Mills. The Chart Mills, part of this complex, were rebuilt about 1815, retaining some of the original machinery. With some changes they remained in use until 1934. The threat of complete destruction came in recent years with the expansion of the town and the decision to clear the mill area for redevelopment. The local Faversham Society, however, decided if possible to preserve them. The developers generously co-operated by giving the site of one pair of mills to the Borough Council and selling to them a second site. The Faversham Society began to raise money for restoration and half of the needed £2,500 was promised by the Borough Council and the Government, the society raising the other half. Gunpowder works, for safety, were housed in scattered units sited among fairly heavy timber for screening, so the mills being preserved will stand on the edge of half a mile of wooded riverside which will provide a 'riverside walk', and, so far as visitors will see, a great deal of the working environment will be there. When completed, these mills with their water wheels and machinery will be a splendid example of *in situ* preservation carried out by the co-operation of a local society, the local government authority, the general public, and the site owners.

The iron industry offers many examples of the preservation *in situ* of forges preserved by a similar cooperation and by private societies. The early forges were situated on streams out in the country, and their locations are still of great attraction. There are two sites in and near Sheffield which will serve as examples of an increasingly widespread group of preservation schemes. The Abbeydale Industrial Hamlet is on the bank of the river Sheaf three and a half miles from the city centre in what is now a thriving suburb. This has destroyed some of the rural environment but the presence of the river and an adjacent woodland across the river, along with the self-enclosed nature of the site, minimize the intrusion of the neighbouring housing estates. The site has a row of workmen's cottages, warehouses, steel-making furnaces, grinding shop, a tilt-hammer forge, all ranged round an enclosed yard approximately 220 ft by 70 ft, between the river and the dam. The buildings are of the eighteenth century, and the forge which was making scythes and other edge tools continued in work until the 1920s (Plate 28).

In 1934 a Society for the Preservation of Old Sheffield Tools (now renamed the Sheffield Trades Historical Society) was formed and made its first large project to use this site as an industrial museum. The Graves Trust bought the site and gave it to the Sheffield Corporation. An attempt to preserve and restore the site in 1939 was frustrated by the onset of war, but in 1964 the Council for the Conservation of Sheffield Antiquities, with the encouragement of the Ministry of Public Buildings and Works, leased the site for seven years and began the restoration of buildings and machinery. In two years £42,000 was raised by public appeal and the restoration was assured. The two water wheels are now in working condition and the works and its machinery is now maintained as a part of the Sheffield City Museums, the site being open to the public. One of the cottages, modernized, houses a custodian.

The special interest of this site is its compact summary of Sheffield's major industry in its eighteenth-century form. Here a small community lived and worked on the site; they made their steel in a furnace with a bank of crucibles just as Huntsman made his. Cutting tools were made by forging the main body from wrought iron and then welding in a strip of steel for the cutting edge. Tool handles were made and fitted and the tools were ground. Every process from raw iron to merchants' product can be seen, and there is even a small steam engine used to supplement the flow of water when drought made the water wheels insufficient.

A second important site is the Wortley Top Forge (SK 294998), eight miles north of Sheffield. It is one of Yorkshire's very old sites, well documented from 1621, and a part of the Wortley Forge complex, Low and High Forge, of which the Low Forge certainly was a monastic forge between 1160 and 1200. The preservation, now in progress, of the Top Forge offers an example of a different method of organization. The Top Forge documents still extant begin with a lease in 1621 of 'Iron Smithies . . . and Delfs of Mine of Ironstone' along with woods for charcoal, and an iron bloomery. Three years later a wire-mill was added nearby. In 1658 the forge was taken into the Spencer partnerships and then had fineries, a chafery, and a tilt-hammer. In 1783 John Cockshutt leased the two forges and soon afterwards introduced puddling furnaces and grooved rolls. The Top Forge ceased to work in 1912 and the Low Forge in 1929, and here therefore is a site which, very much in its present form, had been active for three centuries.

In the years following the closure, the buildings deteriorated and much of the machinery and equipment disappeared. The Top Forge was eventually purchased by the Sheffield Trades Historical Society and the buildings were scheduled as an Ancient Monument by the Ministry of Works. The Sheffield Trades Historical Society includes in its membership a large number of Sheffield industrialists and their generous help made this purchase of buildings and land possible. One of the larger steel works gave considerable time and help in urgent preservation and protection. Preservation, reconstruction, and reconditioning of the machinery is not yet complete but will continue as quickly as the finances and labour of the members of the society admit.

This site is important not only for its content and long history but for its unspoiled environment. It is still sited in relatively open country which has changed little through the centuries except by the reduction of woodland and the enclosure of farm land, and which still gives a good impression of what these country forges were like in their earlier years. The buildings form a closed yard set within a bend of the river Don, and containing three water wheels with goits from the river and from a dam. Two wheels, 12 ft by 20 in and $13\frac{1}{2}$ ft by 45 in, powered helve hammers, and a third wheel, 9 ft by 44 in, worked blowers for two reheating furnaces and some other machinery. The hammers are complete and served by cranes to swing iron from the furnaces to the forge anvils. A set of rolls, the first to be used in Yorkshire, have been brought up from the Low Forge and set up here for their preservation. The iron from this forge has been held in the very highest esteem, throughout the nineteenth century, for railway axles, of which it is claimed that, in the tens of thousands, none from Wortley ever broke. The output of the two forges in the eighteenth century was between three hundred and four hundred tons a year.

Other forges are being preserved and restored *in situ* in other parts of the country, as at Sticklepath, Okehampton, in Devon. This foundry and forge, from 1814 to 1960, made agricultural tools in a great variety, well known and esteemed throughout the south-west. Much of the machinery is still in place, with three water wheels to drive hammers, blowers, and a grinding shop. To preserve and restore this forge, so recently working as to have suffered little depredation from the scrap merchants, the Finch Foundry Trust was formed and registered, which has undertaken the restoration of the site as the nucleus of the Sticklepath Museum of Rural Industry. The support of many responsible bodies, including Devon County Council, the Duchy of Cornwall, the Newcomen Society, the Ministry of Public Buildings and Works, the Pilgrim Trust, and the Worshipful Company of Blacksmiths, with a large number of the general public, including several from the engineering and allied professions, give confidence in the quality of the restorations and the future of the museum, which is now open to the public.

Other examples could be quoted of how many invaluable industrial sites can be restored in their proper location, by the work of trusts and organizations which are formed with the cooperation, in different degrees, of voluntary workers, industry, local authority and government bodies, and professional societies. In all these schemes there is great scope for the work of volunteers, both those with professional skills and those prepared to offer their strength for more humble labour.

There are two areas of industrial archaeology – transport and steam engines – where public interest, perhaps largely nostalgic, but having a tremendous potential for preservation work, has grown amazingly during these last two decades. The number of the associations for the preservation of railways and canals and for engines of many kinds is too great to list, but one or two must be given as examples of what might well be regarded as out-of-door, and possibly poor, relations of the more orthodox museum.

In the more orthodox museums interest has been taken in transport, and the Science Museum houses a magnificent display from one of the earliest Trevithick locomotives to present-day jet aeroplanes. The Museum of Transport at Glasgow and the Transport Museum in Belfast are of national standard and will remain the permanent record and reference collections for their respective countries. Many local authority museums have a growing transport section, some of them for all forms of transport, and others of one or two special sections according to local industries and circumstances. Ranking with the national collections there are the fine railway museums at Clapham and York,[1] and the British Waterways collections at Stoke Bruerne, Northamptonshire, on the Grand Union Canal.

Transport, however, has been the area where private museums and preservation societies have flourished and have demonstrated the possibilities of the working exhibit. The railway enthusiasts have taken the lead by forming groups and societies to lease or acquire small branch railway lines, both standard and narrow gauge, at their closure, and by voluntary labour of their membership have maintained the track and kept some trains running. These ventures have proved to be very popular and some, with the support of the visiting public, can pay their way. This seems to be the only means by which the public can still enjoy the sight of a steam train, and take a ride, however short, in one. These ventures have to be run on a commercial basis, and it is time that their position in relation to the museum world was seriously studied. They are surely something more than just a public entertainment and they should have a legitimate place in the world of the working industrial museums. This consideration may be fairly urgent. Many of the railways are being run by groups which include retired railway workers, drivers, guards, signalmen, and other staff

[1] The collections at Clapham are to be transferred to York, to make a single national museum.

who have had a lifelong interest and training in the working of a railway. With their skilled guidance and practical help, these small railways are efficiently and correctly run, but as this generation of railwaymen dies out the maintenance and running will depend more and more on amateur voluntary workers. The problem of giving this new group something equivalent to the old apprenticeship training will have to be solved.[1]

The Tramway Museum at Crich, Derbyshire (SK 345548), occupies the extensive Crich Quarries, from which an incline was built by Stephenson to carry limestone to the large bank of lime kilns at Ambergate. The quarry houses a fine collection of tramcars, with a track on which electric trams run and carry visitors. Other private museums house collections of transport vehicles, such as the Beaulieu and the Cheddar Motor Museums, the Aysgarth Carriage Museum and many others, the future continuance of which is not very clear. No doubt these private museums are preserving many vehicles which otherwise would have been lost, and if adequate provision is made for them when for any reason the private ownership ceases, a public service will have been done. Most of these private museums could not properly come within the sphere of industrial archaeology as set out in this book, but they are making a solid contribution to social, industrial, and technological history.

Preservation and Restoration

Two activities which in part share some of these questions, being mainly concerned at present with buildings and objects of late-nineteenth-century origin, but which have actually a greater application to the earlier material of industrial archaeology, are the methods of preservation and possible restoration of early structures and material. There is a growing interest, for example, in the magnificent steam engines built for the large mills and factories which have gone out of use only during the last decade or two, the typical 'mill engine' such as was the pride of many a mill in the textile areas. A second group of engines is those connected with mining, the giants of the south-western metalliferous mining fields, and the smaller but no less fine colliery winding engines. With these two groups will go the smaller group of pumping engines associated with water supplies and drainage, and with such large enterprises as some of the canals and the

---

[1] Information about the ever increasing railway museums has been gathered together in the *Railway Enthusiast's Handbook* (David & Charles), 1967.

Severn Tunnel. Some of the iron industry's blowing engines belong with this group. Some of these engines go back to the middle decades of the last century but most of them are more recent, while a few of earlier date are also known. Nonetheless they are magnificent and attractive monuments of a great profession, of the skilled engineers who designed and built them, and some at least of them demand preservation. No archaeological techniques of any kind are needed for their discovery, and a full photographic, measured and documented record usually only takes some patient and informed work to obtain. Most of the engines are dismantled at least for scrap, and so the purchase need not raise insuperable problems. The real problems and expense come in the cost of careful dismantling, transport and re-erection in a suitable site, the provision of which is often the greatest difficulty of all.

In the mining areas of Cornwall and Devon the voluntary Cornish Engine Preservation Society has preserved five of the best and most important of the surviving pumping engines, four of them in the engine house in which they worked, and one in the Camborne Museum established by the Holman Brothers. Supported mainly by public subscription and the urban and county councils, the society has now received splendid help from the National Trust, which has taken over the engine houses and engines.[1] In the North, originating in Lancashire but working also in Yorkshire, there is an active voluntary association, the Northern Mill Engine Society, which is concerned to preserve a selection of the finest remaining engines. It is difficult, for the present, to see such a collection being brought into one place, and it may be that, like the Cornish mine engines, most of the mill engines will have to remain dispersed in their own engine rooms. This problem, however, can be solved in time if the preservation of the engines is assured. In fact much of the work of the selection and preparation of a permanent resting place for many of the larger industrial remains will have to wait until financial and other factors make the best sites available. Many of these large exhibits may have to be in store or occupying some temporary site for some years yet and the main

[1] The five engines preserved by the society are: at Robinson's shaft, South Crofty Tin mine, Pool, Redruth, an 80-in cylinder built by Sandys, Vivian & Co. of Copperhouse, Hayle, 1854; a 90-in at Taylor's shaft, East Pool & Agar mine, Redruth, Harveys of Hayle, 1892; a 30-in rotative winding beam engine, East Pool mine, Redruth, Holman Bros. of Camborne, 1887; a 22-in rotative beam engine, Rostowrack Clay works, St Austell, now in Holman Museum, 1851; a 24-in rotative beam engine at Levant mine, 6 miles from Lands End, Harvey & Co. of Hayle, 1840.

anxiety will be to secure their proper maintenance through this intermediate period.

Some large engines can be preserved, as at Leicester, as the nucleus of
an industrial museum. There the pumping station at Abbey Lane has
become redundant, and the building which contains four beam engines
built in 1891 will be retained with the engines as the centre piece of a
seven-acre site to be used as a museum of working exhibits. This museum
is being made jointly by the city corporation and the local industries.
Another group of engines in working condition is that at Crofton, Great
Bedwyn, where the pumping station for the Kennett and Avon Canal contains two beam engines of exceptional interest, which have worked for
150 years and possibly more, having stopped only recently. One was built
by Boulton and Watt in 1808, but altered from its original design, though
it still has some original parts in it; the second also was made in 1808,
probably by Harvey & Co. of Hayle, Cornwall. It is said that the Harveys
overhauled both engines about 1840, and they were again reconditioned in
the early part of this century. Because of the tremendous interest and
unique character of these engines, a Crofton Restoration Committee was
formed, and the Ministry of Public Buildings and Works scheduled the
engine house buildings and gave a substantial grant, supplemented by one
from the Wiltshire County Council, for their restoration.

It would take a volume to describe all the preservation groups which are
now at work in the country, but a little thought must be given to preservation and its relation to restoration. Preservation may range from saving a
monument, structure, engine, piece of machinery, and the like, from destruction, which may involve actual work on the object to arrest decay or
deterioration, legal and financial effort to pay for some form of care and
maintenance, or the removal of an object to some museum where it can
be displayed in a simulated environment or as an isolated museum piece.
The repair of smaller buildings and structures with the consent or co-
operation of the landowner in many cases lies within the capacity of a
small group, and can save a structure from further destruction or deterioration, in some cases allowing time for a fuller preservation scheme to be
worked out.

An example of such a small voluntary group is the Earby Mine Research
Group with its valuable work. This title was given to a small voluntary
group to enable easier correspondence and reference through a secretary
and officers. The group has eighteen members, two of them with training

and experience in mining engineering, most of the others being engaged in building or contracting work, with skilled masons and builders and a scaffold hand. All have a keen interest in lead mining history and it is this common interest and the excursions taken in searching out the visible remains of mines and mining structures in the mid-Pennine mining fields that has drawn the group together in a strong desire to preserve some of the best of the few monuments which remain. Efforts have been concentrated on the smelt-mill chimneys, which from their position, usually on a prominent hill brow, are well-known landmarks (Plate 29). The few chimneys still standing have suffered a variety of damage – one has been attacked in an attempt to fell it for building stone and a large section of the base removed; in one a tree had rooted in a crack and after thirty years was splitting and forcing out masonry near the top; another was struck by lightning and badly damaged, while vandals for no understandable reason had begun to destroy another. A plan for proper repair was drawn up and in the course of a few years all have been soundly restored and repointed.

The working method is first to secure a complete photographic survey from which the damage can be estimated. A 'whip round' among the group members raises the price of cement, sand, and possible hire of scaffolding and ladders, though frequently these have been loaned by a friendly contractor. Some members of other societies to which some of the Earby group belong are drawn in as labourers and transport helpers and a series of weekends is planned for the work. Occasionally some of the members go to the site on Friday evening and camp there till Sunday, meeting the transport, getting scaffolding ready, and preparing for the Saturday working party. A few wives come and help with meals. In this way the group have now saved four of the best-known and most prominent chimneys in the area of the Yorkshire Dales mining fields, along with other structures, buddles, water wheel sites, and (still in progress) our only Cornish-type engine house. Photographs of this in 1922 when the roof was still on are guiding the rebuilding of much of the upper part of the house which has since fallen and the material of which is still lying about. The adjoining chimney has also been repaired and fully pointed and these and the other chimneys have been made safe for many years to come.[1]

[1] The Earby Mine Research Group, in its practical work, has already repaired the chimneys of the following mines or smelt-mills: Malham Moor, Cononley Gibside, Cononley mine, Grassington Moor; and Merryfield (Greenhow) and Cononley engine houses. Buddles and dressing

This example has been given at length to suggest that much can be done by small groups working with minimum finance to preserve industrial monuments on a small but valuable scale, provided that they work under the direction of some members with professional knowledge and skills. Another example of such work are the very successful reconstructions being carried out by members of the Peak District Mines Historical Society on a site within the Crich Tramway Museum. To this site mining remains which could not be preserved *in situ* have been brought, the main one being a crushing circle with edge roller. A 'coe' has been constructed, and a buddle, while two shallow shafts have been sunk – one to take jack roller winding and the other a climbing shaft – and there is a short length of rails from a level. Mine hillock material has been brought to complete the picture. This, though not an actual mine restoration, is an excellent contribution to an open air museum and does preserve some mining material. The repair of the buildings at Magpie Mine by the same society, to serve as a field centre for their recording of the Derbyshire mining field, is only the first phase of an extensive programme.

Restoration as distinct from repair and preservation may imply a certain amount of addition of new material to take the place of some which has altogether disappeared. It is probably the most difficult and arguable part of all to define and limit. In the case of pottery sherds the museum technician will commonly put together the many fragments of a broken pot which clearly fit and belong to the same vessel, and which are sufficient to define every part of the vessel's shape. Missing sherds can then be made up with new paste, and a completed vessel in which the restored parts are clearly visible can be exhibited. Sherds are usually so numerous, and so many pots to an identical pattern were made, that every part of a pot is represented by some fragment or other and the completed restoration of the individual vessel which had the most remaining sherds can be accepted as completely reliable. In structures it is not often possible to do this, but in a case like the Roman pottery at Cantley, Doncaster, where more than forty kilns in various conditions of preservation have now been excavated, sufficient is known about them for complete and reliable models to be made of all but their temporary timber and clay domes, which in use had

---

floors, horse gin race, shaft top and pump rod chambers have also been repaired at various mines, and several old mines have been located and entry made for their exploration and recording.

no permanence, though fragments of the baked clay from them are numerous enough to indicate the probable form of this covering.

Most very old stone-built structures have at some time or other been
robbed of much of their bulk as an easy source of material for re-use. The
industrial archaeologist has the problem of interpreting foundations or the
occasional two or three courses of a structure, the upper part of which has

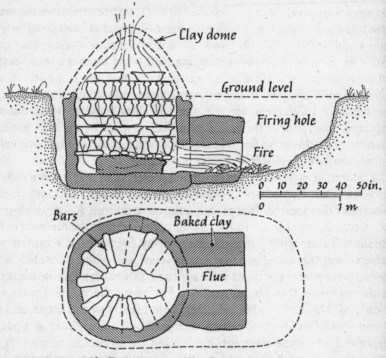

16 Roman pottery kiln, Cantley, Doncaster

left no remains whatever. In such a case, unless there is some definite
knowledge gleaned from the rare documentary source or from the accumulated hints gained from the excavation of a number of comparable sites,
any reconstruction can only be speculative and might well differ in the
judgement of different people. In such cases the only acceptable reconstruction would appear to be a model – perhaps even a full-scale one –
made in similar materials, with the original structure left as exposed by the
excavation, to be seen and pondered by others. A more certain idea of the

original structure will be gained as other comparable sites are discovered and studied.

A recent excavation of extremely high quality and with excellent recording which will stand as an example of how all such work should be done, is that of the glass-house at Rosedale, North Yorkshire. This glass kiln has already been mentioned and its plan discussed.[1] The kiln was found to be in a surprisingly complete condition so far as the foundations over most of the structure were concerned, and around the central furnace area several courses of masonry remained and this part was nearly complete. The kiln lay at the centre of a large rectangular area defined by a boulder wall, within which were at least two other structures, possibly annealing furnaces. The location was in one of the smaller dales of the North York Moors, near the edge of the cultivated land and no great distance from the valley bottom. Traces of other possible kilns have been found in the area.

Soon after the excavation, the remains, being on land owned by people interested in their preservation, were removed to a rural museum. This was accomplished for the central kiln but the associated structures were left. Excellent care was taken in the difficult removal and transport, and it was possible to re-erect the structure almost exactly as it had been found. However, in order to present a clearer picture for the visiting public, the kiln was then 'restored' by the addition of completing masonry to bring it to what was thought might have been its original size and condition. This work has been done with care and skill on top of the original remains and the kiln is now probably a reasonably good representation of what it was originally like. It is housed in a timber building which allows sufficient room for visitors to circulate, and there is provision for the display of plans and graphical illustration.

Some experimental part-domes of clay are erected over the siege and one wing of the kiln but these are, like the added upper parts of the kiln but with less evidence, purely conjectural, in fact nothing but intelligent guesswork. This kiln was the first of its kind to be found in the north of England and was in far better condition than all the examples previously known from other areas. It was the ideal site for preservation for further study at some future date when far more might be known about such kilns. For its conservation it could have been recovered *in situ* after such preservation of the stone work as the Ministry of Works use for medieval stone structures. It would have remained in its proper environment with its associated structures. As it is we have now only a probable but uncertain restoration as an isolated item in a museum with no trace of its original environmental location and the original remaining material now covered by the reconstructed upper parts. Here private enthusiasm seems to have outrun discretion and the obligation to preserve a rare site for future study with fuller knowledge available has been overlooked. The kiln has now no future other than that of a single unrelated object in a museum. All that this restoration has achieved could have been done with less cost and labour by a carefully built replica, possibly full-scale, of the conjectural completed kiln. Such removals and restorations should surely not be attempted unless urgent salvage must be made, or the object is one of a numerous group, and even then a model or full-scale replica would serve the same purpose.

Recording

The techniques of archaeological recording are now part of a well estab-lished discipline which must be studied and applied to all the earlier remnant structures and sites investigated by the industrial archaeologist. Survey and photography are taken for granted and where any question arises it is principally that of the quality to be demanded and the storing and availability of the records. As the records are intended to be a perma-nent reference source for something that is usually about to disappear and will not be available again for study, their quality must be the highest attainable and should be on the best materials. The popularity in the last twenty years or so of colour photography and the revival of the 'magic lantern' for the display of photographs has flooded homes and lecture rooms alike with coloured pictures, in the majority of which the colour is over-emphasized or is dominated by a pale green or blue wash.[1] In most recording of structures and structural detail the colour is irrelevant and a fine-quality black and white print which will be permanent is far more appropriate. A negative of quarter plate ($4\frac{1}{4} \times 3\frac{1}{4}$ in) or larger on glass will afford prints for filing and enlargements for display which more than compensate for the weight and bulk in storage and in the field (Plates 30a and 30b). This generation of recorders is not less strong than those who, fifty

[1] Some excellent work is being done in colour where sufficient skill in exposure and lighting is employed. The chief disadvantage of the colour transparency is the difficulty and expense of getting large black and white enlargements of museum display size from them.

years ago, carried their half- or even occasionally whole-plate cameras around the country to secure the photographs which are now among our choicest records. The colour film may be making quantity and pleasant appearance the substitutes for high quality and more selective work. This, however, is a matter for the photographer to argue out when the industrial archaeologist or recorder has decided what and how much he wants to record.

Photography is an aid to recording but is not sufficient by itself. It can never record more than can be seen from a single viewpoint and it is difficult even with a large number of prints looked at in succession to get an overall picture of anything at all complicated. The architects' and engineers' drawings are necessary for this and some training and experience in using them will be necessary before their full value is appreciated (Plates 31a and 31b). The usual orthographic projection of plan and two or more elevations, given the necessary skill, can be read in three dimensions, but a series of carefully constructed perspective drawings (on one of several modes) can be useful for display and for the less mechanically minded viewer. Two examples of this kind of perspective diagram are given in Diagrams 10 and 11. These are made from engineering measurement at the mills, measurement of their detail, and sketches of the most useful viewpoints. They supplement full engineering drawings in order to give an overall explanatory picture of arrangement which could illustrate a popular pamphlet guide or be used in conjunction with a display of detailed photographs. The one of Bainbridge Low Mill is in outline and is a preliminary sketch for a finished drawing. The Bolton Mill drawing is rather more finished and gives a connected view of an essential gear arrangement which in the actual building is separated into two sections by an intervening floor, and so could never appear in one photograph. These are examples taken from a collection of scores of such recordings being made by an enthusiastic engineer, and being constructed on a true perspective with the accompanying drawings could be used for making an accurate display model. One of the mills was demolished within days of the drawings being completed, and so these are an irreplaceable record. As good records are studied it becomes clear that recording is a skilled supplement to industrial archaeology which demands a degree of training, and every industrial archaeology group ought to include someone with the necessary skills or someone willing to give time and effort to learn them.

Most of the nineteenth- and twentieth-century industries are too complex for any but the highest professional and technical recording and cannot really find a natural place in industrial archaeology. The illustrations of blast furnace,[1] oil refinery, or chemical plant exhibit a world which is beyond the capacity of the amateur or of any but its own trained technicians to record. It is because of such amazing technical developments that it is suggested that industrial archaeology should have a terminal date not far from the middle decades of the nineteenth century, where it merges more and more into documented industrial history.

This problem of recording was studied by the steering committee of the Council for British Archaeology with the Ministry of Works, and a National Survey of Industrial Monuments was planned for which a standard index card was designed. The card, 6 in by 4 in, has spaces for recording the nature of the site and full references for accurate location, for the industry, and for the date. Space for an outline description, for machinery and other objects, for printed or documentary references and for the address of the recorder or society complete one side. The other side can be used to extend the description or for photographs or drawings. The cards are copied into the National Index and the originals are returned to the recorders. These can never be more than an index to monuments and their value will be enhanced only if they are also an index to fuller recordings. It is obvious that a site can only be indexed in the briefest outline and that the card should lead one not only to the site location but to the repository of the fuller reports and records. A full copy of the relevant part of the National Index ought to be available at a convenient place in every region. The great majority of the people now becoming active in industrial archaeology cannot afford time or money to make frequent trips to London to consult the national repositories, and a worker will in many cases need local records where they can be consulted on many unforeseen occasions. Even a journey to a county records office may be difficult in the larger counties (for example, in the West Riding of Yorkshire, where County Hall, Wakefield, is some seventy miles as the crow flies from Sedbergh in the north-west of the county, and far more by road, and Sedbergh is more than ten miles from a railway). More numerous and more local repositories are needed. In the case of the dales around Sedbergh, for instance, Kendal in Westmorland is nearer than any town in the West Riding.

All this may sound like a return to a narrow parochialism, but there is justification for it in the nature of what is being studied. The raw material

[1] Plates 2a and 2b.

of industrial archaeology is in buildings, structures, and material remains rooted in the locality, and which, except in the rarest circumstances, will never be removed from that location. Relevant records in the fullest detail should be available to the local workers at the nearest reasonable repository, library, or museum, at least near enough to be visited in an afternoon, or even in an evening for an urgent reference. This probably calls for some duplication of records or for a remarkably quick and efficient exchange between libraries and archives offices, the practical answer to which may lie in microfilm copying and the provision of large microfilm readers which can deal reasonably with plans as well as text. These problems will no doubt be solved by the archivists, the museums and libraries associations and the local authority finance committees.

It must be kept in mind that the world of industrial archaeology is not that of the professional scholar familiar with the national resources to be found in London, but of the ordinary person fully occupied during the day in the business of earning a living and limited to what time can be given from his leisure. It has been said in the first chapter that the subject should have an academic discipline, but this should never imply that its exercise is only for students and academic staff. It is a subject in which most of its workers will remain amateur, working with the help and direction of a few more experienced leaders, and who in time will have a status similar to that of the army of amateur naturalists and field workers who are the indispensable backbone of naturalists' recording. Their library and record work will be done locally and provision for this is one of the essentials which library and museums alone can provide.

The surest aspect of industrial archaeology is that it is still a new and experimental subject, and its general pattern has still to emerge, to be checked and developed by trial and error. Its relation to museums and records will be essential parts of its development, and this relationship must be part of the general experience of the subject from its earliest stages. This means that there must be a great degree of flexibility in all schemes which are now in progress, and schemes put forward as in this book can only be probings and suggestions to be tried out in practice, with no expectation that they are in any way final.

The rapidly acquired popularity of industrial archaeology appears to be stabilizing itself through excellent progress in work planned by an increasing number of local groups. At present, most attention is focused on the

Industrial Revolution and on the remains of fairly recent date which are threatened by destruction in the replanning of our towns. As techniques develop and outlook broadens no doubt the interest of these groups will extend into the many pre-Industrial Revolution centuries which cover much of the evolution of industry. This should lead to better definitions, and sharpen the awareness of industrial archaeology's great potential in bringing together the humanities of the social and economic historian and the special skills and knowledge of the technician. If this development comes about, the clumsy hybrid name may be forgiven and a dignified substitute found which will soon pass into our everyday language.

Bibliography

The selection of a bibliography for this subject is a task presenting many difficulties and there is no likelihood that an acceptable formal list of any completeness could do more than reflect the author's own limited choice of reading. Because of this only a few general observations are offered here which may serve as an introduction to the local reference library, which should be the industrial archaeologists' second workshop (the outdoors being the first).

The subject is new enough to have acquired only a relatively small literature under its own title. There is a steadily increasing series of area *Industrial Archaeologies* (David & Charles), and of gazetteers of monuments prepared by local groups. There are a few indispensable introductory books such as K. Hudson's *Industrial Archaeology: an introduction*, London 1963; J. P. M. Pannell, *The Techniques of Industrial Archaeology*, Newton Abbott, 1966; and a few pamphlets and magazine articles which discuss the purpose of industrial archaeology. The subject has its own journal, *Industrial Archaeology*, published quarterly, which provides a means of publication for short articles and current notes.

Two other groups of publications merit the attention of workers, though they do not carry the industrial archaeology imprint. The first group is that of professional and technical journals, in which are to be found many papers from the mid nineteenth century to the present, which today would have been claimed as industrial archaeology. The outstanding publication in this class is of course the *Transactions of the Newcomen Society for the Study of the History of Engineering and Technology*, starting in 1920, and which contains papers on a great variety of subjects which range in time from prehistoric to the nineteenth century. The professional *Journals* are rapidly increasing in numbers, but the older ones carry very important papers on work in the history of their subject. Among the most useful are the *Journals* of the Institutes of Civil, Mechanical and Mining Engineers and of the Iron and Steel Institute. Almost all technical subjects are now covered by comparable journals – for example shipbuilding, chemical engineering – and time spent in a library getting to know these and the kind of material they contain will be well spent. There are a few less professional but valuable periodicals by some of the local societies such as the *Transactions of the Cumberland and Westmorland Antiquary and Archaeological Society* which contain many important papers, and other similar ones, such as the *Sussex Archaeological Collections*, which are far too numerous to list. A recent periodical which is proving to be of the greatest value is the *Bulletin of the Historical Metallurgy Group*, in which detail is given of work on many furnace and iron-making sites throughout the country and of all periods from pre-Roman. The *Bulletin of the Peak District Mines Historical Society*, starting in 1959, is devoted to the investigation of mines, chiefly in the north of England, and its companion, the *Memoirs of the Northern Cavern and Mines Research Society*, starting in 1960 under the name of *Transactions*, ranges a little wider. Much information on local groups which publish news sheets or letters can be had from *The Industrial Archaeologist's Guide*, ed. N. Cossons & K. Hudson. Three more frequent publications which are particularly valuable in their earlier numbers are *The Engineer*, starting in 1856, and *Engineering* starting in 1866, with the *Mining Journal* starting as early as 1835.

The second group of reading is more concerned with giving a necessary background for successful work in industrial archaeology. As all industry is based on technologies, however simple or complex they may be, it is essential to have sufficient background of technology to recognize the probable nature of structures or remains being examined. It is always essential to know at least enough to realize that one needs the help of an expert, and to recognize the kind of expert to seek. An essential work of reference is of course the *History of Technology* in 5 volumes, Oxford, 1954–8, and the *Short History of Technology*, edited by T. K. Derry and T. I. Williams, Oxford, 1960. For special subjects, some excellent introductions are to be found in J. P. M. Pannell, *An illustrated history of Civil Engineering*, London, 1964; A. F. Burstall, *A History of Mechanical Engineering*, London, 1963; H. R. Schubert, *History of the British Iron and Steel Industry from c. 450 BC to AD 1775*, London, 1957; R. F. Tylecote, *Metallurgy in Archaeology*, London, 1962; and A. Raistrick and B. Jennings, *A History of Lead Mining in the Pennines*, London, 1965 (this gives an account of the development of mining methods and technology from pre-Roman times). There are a few other books which one cannot afford to neglect as sources, and among these are G. Agricola, *De Re Metallica* (1556), translated by H. C. and L. H. Hoover, reprinted by Dover, New York, 1950; L. Salzman, *English Industries in the Middle Ages*, Oxford, 1923; A. Wolf, *A History of Science, Technology and Philosophy in the XVIth and XVIIth centuries*, 1950. For illustrations of most industrial processes one must of course be familiar with the *Dictionary* of Denis Diderot with its 2,900 plates published between 1751 and 1765. Of these plates, 485 relating to industries have been reprinted with comment by C. C. Gillispie, in two volumes, by Dover, New York, 1959. A more recent work of standard reference is *Dr Ure's Dictionary of Arts, Manufactures, and Mines*, edited by R. Hunt, London, 1878, and extended from Ure's first edition in 1858.

Index

Abbeydale Industrial Hamlet, 233, 287
acid chambers, 82, 83
aggregate, 56, 59
agriculture, 88
Aire and Calder Navigation, 242
alabaster, 60, 70
Albert Mill, Liverpool, 91
Albion Mill, London, 91
Aldersley Edge, Cheshire, 24
alkali, 83, 84
alloy steels, 50
Alston Moor, 156, 222, 224, 225
alum, 62, 63, 64, 214, 215
Amlwch harbour, Anglesey, 226
Ancient Monuments Inspectorate, 2
ancony, 45
Anglesey, 24, 55, 225, 226
anhydrite, 65
aniline dyes, 68
aqueduct, 157, 286
Ariconum, 171
Arkwright, Richard, 105, 149, 150, 151
arsenic, 64
atmospheric engine, 118
Avery Museum, Birmingham, 277
Aysgarth Carriage Museum, Yorkshire, 291

badgers, 128
Bage's Mill, Shrewsbury, 150
Bainbridge Low Mill, Yorkshire, 235, 236, 238, 299
ball mill, 79
Bank Furnaces, 210
banker hand, 58
bar iron, 45
Bardon, Sussex, 170
barley, 91
Barlow Ironworks, Derbyshire, 67
Barnby Furnace, Yorkshire, 210, 231
Barton Aqueduct, 157

Baxenden, Rossendale, Lancashire, 223
beam engine, 118, 119, 167
Beaulieu Motor Museum, 291
Beaumont, Huntington, 216
bell casting, 40, 58
bell metal, 40
bell pits, 21, 51, 52, 247, 249
Belper North Mill, Derbyshire, 250
Bere Alston, Devon, 223
Bessemer converter, 49, 255
Bewdley, 154
bing stead, 24
black ash, 83
Blaencaraid furnace, Glamorgan, 206, 207
blast furnace, 31, 33, 47, 85, 206-9, 229, 230, 231, 232, 255
bleaching powder, 84
blister steel, 48, 211
Blists Hill, Telford, Salop, 278, 281, 286
bloom, 43, 45
bloom hearth, 207
bloom smithy, 29, 207, 209
bloomery, 25, 179, 180, 195, 200, 201, 207, 208, 209, 210
blowing cylinders, 230
blowing houses, 28
Blunden's Wood, Surrey, 196, 197
boat building, 137, 218
bobbin mills, 256, 257
bole hill, 25, 26
bord and pillar working, 52
boshes, 31, 205, 206
Boston Spa Mill, Yorkshire, 238, 299
Boulby, Yorkshire, 214, 215
Boulton and Watt engine, 227, 228, 238, 253, 254
bouse, 23
Bowers Smelt Mill, Derbyshire, 222
bowl furnace, 85
Bradford Industrial Museum, 272
Bradley Grange, Yorkshire, 180

Bramah, Joseph, 118, 256
Bramah press, 118
Bramhope quarry, Yorkshire, 187
brass, 33, 38, 42, 226
brewery, 92
bricks, 73, 74, 75
bridges, 133, 141, 142, 143, 157, 158, 186, 229, 243, 281
Brindley, James, 233, 234
British Paper and Board Makers Association Museum, 277
British Waterways Museum, Stoke Bruerne, Northants, 290
broggers, 97, 128
bronze, 39, 40
Bronze Age, 39, 167
Bronze Age cloth, 95
Brown, William, 249
Brunton calciner, 64
bucker, 23, 249
buddle, 23, 249
building, 144 ff
building stone, 56, 69, 186–92
Bulmer bevis, 45
Byrkeknott, County Durham, 182, 183, 184

canal inclines, 244
canals, 135, 136, 137, 144, 154, 157, 234, 242, 243, 244, 254, 257, 258, 259, 288, 290
canals, underground, 137
candles, 102
Cantley kilns, Doncaster, Yorkshire, 172, 173, 295
cast-iron, 31, 45, 47, 227, 228
cast-iron cylinders, 227, 228
cast steel, 49, 232
Castor, Peterborough, 175
Catchett's Mill, Derby, 149
Catcliffe glass cone, Sheffield, Yorkshire, 234, 235
Catterick Bridge, Yorkshire, 186
cattle, 99
Causey (Tanfield) Arch, Co. Durham, 138
Cawood, Yorkshire, 187, 188, 189
Celtic lynchets, 175, 178
cementation, 48, 232
ceruse, 37
chafery, 31, 32, 45
Champion, William, 33, 226
Chapman, Kenneth, 214
Chappell furnace, Yorkshire, 210

charcoal, 29, 31, 48, 121, 179, 209, 210, 211, 227–32, 242
charcoal furnace, 9, 29, 31, 48, 209, 210, 211, 227–32, 242
Charlcotte furnace, 230
Charterhouse Roman mines, 168, 169
Cheddar Motor Museum, 291
cheese, 103
Cherry Garden Adit, Cornwall, 223
Chiddingford glass works, Surrey, 80
Childe, V. Gordon, 5
china, 234
china clay, 59, 234
Churchill Forge, Worcestershire, 33
clamp kiln, 73
clapper bridges, 141–3
clay pits, 61
Clement, Joseph, 256
Cleveland, Yorkshire, 62, 63
coal, 51, 52, 124, 211, 212, 226, 289
coal ataithes, 218
coal gas, 68
Coal Measures, 54
coal tar, 68
Coalbrookdale, 3, 4, 54, 119, 138, 140, 227, 228, 242, 245, 280
coastal shipping, 212
Coed Ithal furnace, Monmouthshire, 205, 206
coffen work, 21, 32
coffin levels, 22
coinage, 39, 42
coke, 67, 124, 255
coke furnace, 227, 229, 232
coke ovens, 67, 255
Colnbridge Forge, Yorkshire, 210
Company of Hostmen, 218
Company of Mineral and Battery Works, 28, 201, 202, 203
Company of Mines Royal, 28, 201–3, 222
Company Museums, 268, 277
concentrates, 24
condenser flues, 223, 248
Coniston mines, Lancashire, 202
Cookworthy, William, 234
copper mining, 24, 38, 201, 202, 225, 226
copper smelting, 27, 202, 225
copperas, 64
corn-milling, 88, 89, 235
Cornish Copper Company, 225
Cornish engine houses, 228
Cornish Engine Preservation Society, 292
cotton, 104

counching house, 92
Council for British Archaeology, 2, 13
County Record Office, 300
Cowpen and Blythe wagonway, 216
craft workshops, 276
Cranbeck, Yorkshire, 174
cranes, 152, 153
Craven Museum, Skipton, Yorkshire, 274
Crofton Restoration Committee, 293
Cromford Canal, Derbyshire, 259
Cromford and High Peak Railway, 259
Cromford Mill, 150
Cromford Sough, 203
crosses (road-side), 128
Crossley, David W., 162, 208, 209, 215
Crowley, Ambrose, 211
cruck houses, 87, 145
crushing rollers, 23
Cullercoats, 212, 213
cupellation, 27
cupola, 47, 228
currier, 100
Cusworth Museum, Doncaster, 273
Cwmsynlog lead mine, Cardigan, 203

Darby, Abraham, 227, 228
Darby family, 2, 4, 47
Darby furnace, Coalbrookdale, 227, 228, 229, 230
Delaval family, 212, 213
Derwentcote cementation furnace, Co. Durham, 232
Devon Great Consols mine, 220
distilling, 93
docks, 244
Dolaucothi mine, Carmarthen, 33
Dolcoath Deep Adit, Cornwall, 223
Dove Gang mine, Derbyshire, 203
down-draught kiln, 74
drainage adits, 223, 224, 225, 251
drawings, 299
drift mine, 52
drove roads, 99, 130
drying kiln, 177
dyehouse, 107
dyeing and finishing, 149
Duke's level, Grassington Moor, Yorkshire, 251
Dutch River (Don), Yorkshire, 219

Earby Mines Research Group, 293, 294
edge mill, 112
Eggleston Smelt mill, Co. Durham, 223

elaterite, 69
elling hearth, 122
Elsecar engine, Sheffield, 254
Embsay Moor, Yorkshire, 191
Engineer, The, 260
engineers, 246, 253, 256
English Copper Company, 225
Erewash canal, 259
Esgair Moel woollen mill, 284
Etruria works, 234
exchanges, 155
extra-mural classes, 4

factories, 145, 148, 149
Farey, John, 6
Faversham Mill, Kent, 256, 286, 287
Faversham Society, 286, 287
Federal Institute of Technology, 260
Finch Foundry Trust, 289
finery, 31, 32, 45
flax, 103
flint mill (coal mines), 55
flying shuttle, 98
Forest of Dean, 200
Forestry Commission, 88
forge, 32, 33, 43, 44, 45, 46, 48, 49, 180-5, 207, 229
Folk Museum, National Museum of Wales, 275
Foster Beck Mill, Nidderdale, Yorkshire, 283
founder, 32
foundry, 47, 48, 228
fulling mill, 96, 98
fulling stocks, 96

Gadlis smelt mill, Flint, 222
galvanised iron, 42
ganister, 55
gas coke, 68
gas engine, 120
gig mill, 96
Glamorganshire Canal, 244
glass, 80, 81, 196, 214, 215, 216, 234, 235
glass furnaces, 80, 81, 196, 215, 216
glaze, 78
Gloucester, 136
gold, 33
Goole, 136, 209, 289
Gossage tower, 84
Governor and Company for Smelting down Lead with Pit Coal and Sea Coal, 222

Grand Trunk Canal, 234
Granite Railway, Devon, 258
Grassington Moor, Yorkshire, 247, 248, 249, 251
Great County Adit, 223, 224
Great Exhibition, 259
Great Langdale, Westmorland, 163, 165, 166
Green, E. R. R., 5
Greenhow Hill, Yorkshire, 25
Greenod, Lancashire, 257
Greenwich Hospital Commissioners, 224, 164
Grimes Graves flint mines, Norfolk, 163, 164
grindstones, 56, 57
guide-catalogue, 278
gunpowder, 256, 257, 286, 287
Gwennap to Devoran Railway, 259
gypsum, 60

hammer ponds, 32
Hampshire Rural Life Museum, 269
harbours, 213, 214, 220, 225, 226
Hartley, Northumberland, 212, 213
Hayle Harbour, 225, 226
Helmshore Museum, Lancashire, 277
hemp, 103, 104
Hetton railroad, Co. Durham, 141
high pressure engine, 119
Hillcarr Sough, Derbyshire, 224
Holman Brothers, Camborne, Cornwall, 277
Holme-on-Spalding, Yorkshire, 175
Holt, Denbighshire, 175
horse mill, 111, 202
horse power, 93
horse whim, 22, 52, 112, 249
Hoskins, William G., 8
hot blast, 255
hotching tub, 23
Huddleston Delf, Yorkshire, 187, 189
Hudson, Kenneth, 1, 4, 5
Huntsman, Benjamin, 49, 232
hushes, 20, 21
hydraulic engine, 117
hydrochloric acid, 84

igneous rocks, 60
Imperial Chemical Industries, 84, 195
Imperial College, 260
impulse wheel, 114
inclined planes, canal, 136, 244

indigo, 107
Industrial Archaeology, definitions, 2–14, 261, 262, 263
industrial building, 258
industrial housing, 156, 157
industrial monument, 2
Industrial Recording, 13, 36, 261, 262, 298, 299, 300, 301
Industrial Revolution, 2–7, 9, 12, 13, 14
Institution of Civil Engineers, 260
Institution of Mechanical Engineers, 260
Iron Age, 167, 226, 227
Iron Bridge, Salop, 143, 229, 281
Ironbridge Gorge Museum Trust Ltd, Telford, Salop, 278, 279, 280, 281, 286
iron industry, 9
iron-making, 29, 169
iron ores, 29, 54
iron rails, 53
iron works, 50

Jack of Newbury, 146
jack-roller, 21, 249, 251
Jew's Houses, 28
jute, 104

keels, 218
Kendal, Westmorland, 257
Keswick, Cumberland, 28, 202
kilns, grain, 90
kilns, pottery, 193
Kimberworth furnace, Yorkshire, 209
Kirkstall Forge, 210
Knowe Fell settlement, Malham, Yorkshire, 177, 178,
Kodak Museum, Harrow, 277

lead, 36, 132
lead mining, 20–7, 168, 247
lead pigs, Roman, 168, 169
Lead Road, 132
lead shot, 37
lead smelting, 25, 26, 27, 222
leather, 99
Leblanc alkali process, 83
Leeds and Liverpool Canal, 71, 157, 243
Leicester Industrial Museum, 293
level, 21, 22
lighthouses, 244
Lilleshall blowing engines, 281
lime, 69, 71
lime kilns, 70, 71, 72, 243
limestone, 59, 70, 71, 243, 244

linen, 103, 104
linoleum, 104
local crafts, 271
local records, 301
locomotives, 119, 140, 141
logwood mill, 107
London bricks, 75
London Lead Company, 156, 204, 222
London and Westminster Chartered Gaslight and Coke Company, 67
Longdon on Tern aqueduct, 157, 286
Longhead mine, Derbyshire, 203
Longstone Edge, Derbyshire, 21
loops, 46

machines, 35
machine tools, 255
Mackworth, Humphray, 222
madder, 106
Magpie mine, Derbyshire, 295
malt, 91
malthouse, 91
Manchester and Liverpool Railway, 141
marble, 59, 69
Massachusetts, Institute of Technology, 260
Maudsley, Henry, 255
mechanisms, 11, 111
mere stones, 247, 248
mild steel, 49
milestones, 133
milk, 105
mills, 111, 105, 150, 151, 258
mill cottages, 151
mill engines, 291, 292
millstones, 56, 192
Milnthorpe, Lancashire, 257
Minchinton, Professor, 10
mine drainage, 53, 223, 224, 225, 251
Mines Royal Act, 1689 and 1693, 275
mining sites, 20
mispickle, 64
model makers, 272
monastic forges, 179, 180
monastic roads, 129, 130
Morley Park furnaces, Derbyshire, 231
Morwellham, Devonshire, 219
Museum of English Rural Life, Reading, 275
Museum of Lakeland Life and Industry, Kendal, 276
Museum of Science and Industry, Birmingham, 272

Museum of Transport, Glasgow, 290
museum trusteeship, 268
Museums Association, 271
Muntz's metal, 42
Murdoch, Richard, 68
Myddleton, Hugh, 203

nailer, 46, 148, 149
nailers' row, 149
Nasmyth, James, 256
National Survey of Industrial Monuments, 300
natural gas, 66, 68
navigable rivers, 134, 135, 218, 219, 220, 242
Navigation Act 1651, 221
Nent Force level, 225
Nent Head, Cumberland, 156
Neolithic Revolution, 5
New Lanark, 151
Newcomen engine, 53, 227, 238
Newcomen Society, 8
Newlands mines, Cumberland, 202
newsprint, 88
North of England Institution of Mining Engineers, 260
North of England Open-air Museum, Beamish, Co. Durham, 278, 279
Northern Mill Engine Society, 292

oasthouse, 91
oil, 125
oil engines, 120
oilcloth, 105
oil shale, 69
oils, fats and waxes, 108
open cast mining, 21, 24
open hearth furnace, 49, 255
Osmond iron, 203
ore dressing, 23, 253
ore hearth, 26, 251
Ouse Navigation, 219

pack horses, 127, 128, 132, 231
Panningridge furnace, Sussex, 162
paper, 88, 108, 277
Parys mine, Anglesey, 24, 226
Parys Mountain, Anglesey, 55, 226
Peak District Mines Historical Society, 295
peat, 122
Penydarren tramway, 244
Petunz, 79

pewter, 39, 40
phosphoric acid, 84
phosphorus, 84
photography, 298, 299
piers, 220
pig and sow iron, 31
Pilkington Glass Museum, St Helens, Lancashire, 277
pillar and stall working, 52
plaster of Paris, 60, 72, 103
plug and feathers, 24
Pontecysyllte aqueduct, Llangollen, 157
Pool Adit, Cornwall, 223
porcelain, 79
Portland cement, 72
Portreath harbour, 259
Portreath railway, 259
pottery, 76–9, 167, 172, 173, 174, 175, 192, 193, 194, 233, 234
power, 11, 110–20
power loom, 105, 150
preservation, 269, 282, 291
private museums, 268, 276
publication, 267
puddling furnace, 46
pye kiln, 70
pyrites, 65

quarries, 55–60, 69, 70, 99, 136, 249, 250, 251
quarry inclines, 138, 244
quarry tools, 188
querns, 89, 177

railway inclines, 141
Railway Museum, York, 173, 290
railway societies, 291
railway stations, 158
railway viaducts, 158
railways, 140, 141, 158, 244, 259, 290, 291
Rastrick, John Urpeth, 141
Ravensworth wagonway, 218
recording, 298
records, 267
red lead, 37
Redbrook, Bristol, 28, 225
Redruth and Chasewater Railway, 259
refractories, 49
regional museums, 273
reservoirs, 136, 243
restoration, 286
retorts, 84
retting trough, 104

reverberatory furnace, 27, 78, 222, 251
Rievaulx Abbey blast furnace, 185
Rievaulx forge, 185
river improvement, 219
river ports, 219, 256
Rix, Michael, 2, 6
roads, 129, 130, 132, 133, 231, 233
roasting furnace, 226
Roberts, Richard, 256
rock salt, 62
Rockley Furnace, Yorkshire, 209, 210, 231
Rockley Smithy, Yorkshire, 208, 209
rod iron, 45
roller mill, flour, 91
rolling mill, 49
Roman bricks, 72
Roman industries, 167 ff, 175
Roman kilns, 77, 172, 173, 174
Roman roads, 129
rope, 104
Rosedale, Yorkshire, 215, 216, 297
Rosedale glass house, 297
royal mine, 204
Royal Polytechnic Institute, 260
running kiln, 71
rural crafts, 275
rural museums, 274, 275
Ryedale Folk Museum, Yorkshire, 276
Ryton Company, Durham, 222

safety lamp, 55
salt 61, 62, 83, 197, 199, 212, 213, 214
salt glaze, 233
salt names, 62, 199
salt pans, 61, 197, 212, 213, 216, 218
salt ways, 61, 62, 198, 199, 263
Saltaire, 155
scale, 43
scheduled monuments, 282
scheme of Industrial Archaeology, 14–1
Science Museum, 270, 272
Scotch kiln, 74
scribbling mill, 98
scutching mill, 104
Seaton Sluice, 213, 214, 216
Seven Arches, Bingley, Yorkshire, 157
shaft furnace, 26, 27, 85
shaft kilns, 77
shafts, 21, 22
shear steel, 49
sheep, 94

Sheffield Trades Historical Society, 287, 288
shipbuilding, 137, 218
Siemens brothers, 49
silver, 27, 204, 222
Skipton Castle quarries, 189, 191
slag, 30, 43, 45
slag hearth, 25, 27
slate, 59
slimes, 24
slitting mill, 45
Smeaton, James, 228, 260
smelt mill, 23, 25, 26, 27, 28, 29, 202, 222, 223, 225, 248, 251
smelting, 25, 26
smithies, 46, 207, 208, 209, 210, 231
snuff mills, 256, 257
soap, 109
Society for the Protection of Ancient Buildings, 286
soda, 83, 84
Solvay alkali process, 84
Somervell, Thomas, 257
sough, 203
South Shields anchorage, 218
South Wales, 28
South Wales coalfield, 232
South Wales ironworks, 232
South Yorkshire ironworks, 231
Speedwell mine, Derbyshire, 224
Spencer partners, 210, 231
spinning jenny, 105, 149
Springs Canal, Skipton, Yorkshire, 244
Staffordshire and Worcestershire Canal, 242, 254
Stainborough smithy, 210
staiths, 53, 138, 211, 218
stamps, 23
Stapleton Quarry, Pontefract, Yorkshire, 188, 189
steam boilers, 119, 120
steam engine preservation, 270
steam engine pumping, 253
steam engines, 98, 118, 119, 120
steam locomotive, 119, 140, 141
steam turbine, 120
steel, 49, 211, 232, 255
stemples, 22
Stephenson, George, 55, 141
Sticklepath Forge, Devonshire, 289
stocking frame, 147
stocking knitting, 147
Stockton and Darlington Railway, 141

stone axes, 163, 165, 166
stone ware, 79
Stourbridge, Worcestershire, 211
Stourport, Worcestershire, 136, 154, 242
string hearth, 207, 209
Strutt's mill, Derby, 150
sulphur, 65, 66
sulphuric acid, 65, 82, 83
sumpter pot, 26
Swindon, 155-6

tallow, 102
tan pits, 100
tannery, 100
tar, natural, 69
Tar Tunnel, Salop, 69
Tasker's Waterloo Ironworks, 268, 269
Tavistock, Devonshire, 219, 220
Taylor, John, 251, 259
teams 23
tentering, 97
textile museum, 273, 277
textiles, 95, 240
Thievesdale Quarry, Tadcaster, Yorkshire, 187, 188
through-draught kiln, 78
Thundersbarrow, Brighton, Sussex, 176, 177
tile drains, 75
tiles, 75
tilt hammer, 33, 38, 44, 233
timber, 86, 87
tin, 39
tin ores, 28
tin plate, 41
tin smelting, 28, 29
Tintern Abbey iron works, 202, 203
tramways, 137, 138, 242, 243, 244
Tramway Museum, Crich, Derbyshire, 291
Transport Museum, Belfast, 290
Trevithick, Richard, 119, 140
tunnel kiln, 79
tunnels, 135
Turnpike Trusts, 132, 133, 233
tuyere, 30, 206
Tylecote, Dr, 182
Tyne coalfield, 211

updraught kiln, 74
Upper Heaton, Huddersfield, Yorkshire, 193, 194
Upper Weardale, 25

Vale Royal glass works, Cheshire, 80
Vermuyden, Cornelius, 203, 219

Wadsley Bridge furnace, 209
wagonways, 52, 53, 137, 138, 216, 218
warehouse, 152
Warmley Brass Works, 226
waste gas, 255
water corn-mill, 89, 90, 235, 236, 238, 284, 285, 299
water courses, 90, 249, 251
water frame, 105, 201
water mills, 98
water turbine, 117
water wheel, 22, 28, 115, 116, 238, 240, 251, 256, 289
Watson, Bishop R., 223
Weald and Downland Open Air Museum, 275, 276
weaver's cottage, 147
weaving shed, 151
weaving windows, 97
Wedgwood, Josiah, 233, 234
weld, dye, 107
went, dye, 107
whims, 22, 52, 112, 248
white coal, 122

white lead, 37
white phosphorus, 84
Whitworth, Joseph, 256
Wilderspool, Lancashire, 172
Wilson, Paul, 257
windmill, 113, 285
wire, 38, 203
woad, 106
Wollaton, Nottinghamshire, 137, 216
woodland crafts, 87
wool cards, 46, 97
wool combs, 46, 97
wool trade, 95, 96, 97
wool weights, 97
woollen cloth, 95
Workers Educational Association, 4
workshop, 147
Worsborough Corn Mill, Yorkshire, 285
Wortley Top Forge, Yorkshire, 49, 288
Wright, Dr Edward, 222

York Castle Museum, 284
York Minster stone, 186, 187, 188

zinc, 41
zinc ores, 33